From Paris to Peoria

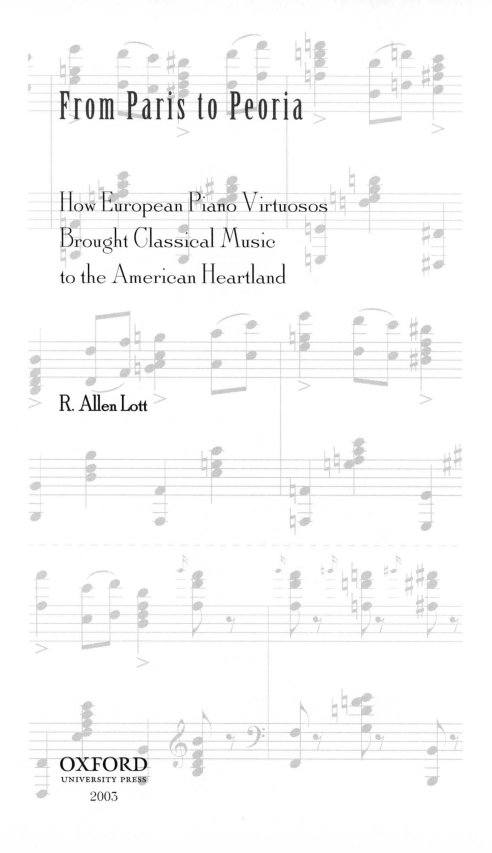

From Paris to Peoria

How European Piano Virtuosos
Brought Classical Music
to the American Heartland

R. Allen Lott

OXFORD
UNIVERSITY PRESS
2003

OXFORD
UNIVERSITY PRESS

Oxford   New York
Auckland   Bangkok   Buenos Aires   Cape Town   Chennai
Dar es Salaam   Delhi   Hong Kong   Istanbul   Karachi   Kolkata
Kuala Lumpur   Madrid   Melbourne   Mexico City   Mumbai   Nairobi
São Paulo   Shanghai   Taipei   Tokyo   Toronto

Copyright © 2003 by Oxford University Press

Published by Oxford University Press, Inc.
198 Madison Avenue, New York, New York 10016

www.oup.com

Oxford is a registered trademark of Oxford University Press

Library of Congress Cataloging-in-Publication Data

Lott, R. Allen, 1956-
From Paris to Peoria : How European piano virtuosos brought classical music to the
American heartland / R. Allen Lott.
p.   cm.
Includes bibliographical references and index.
Contents: Leopold de Meyer (1845–47)—Henri Herz (1846–50)
—Sigismund Thalberg (1856–58)—Anton Rubinstein (1872–73)
—Hans von Bülow (1875–76).
ISBN 0-19-514883-5
1. Pianists—Travel—United States. 2. Meyer, Leopold von, 1816–1883—Journeys—
United States. 3. Herz, Henri, 1803–1888— Journeys—United States. 4. Thalberg,
Sigismond, 1812–1871—Journeys—United States. 5. Rubinstein, Anton, 1829–1894—
Journeys—United States. 6. Bülow, Hans von, 1830–1894—Journeys—United States.
7. United States—Description and travel, I. Title.

ML397.L78 2002
786.2'092'2—dc21   2001052391
[B]

Publication of this book was supported by a grant from the
H. Earle Johnson Fund of the Society for American Music.

Illustration credits for part-title pages are as follows:
Part One: Music Division, The New York Public Library, Astor, Lenox and Tilden Foundations.
Part Two: Music Division, The New York Public Library, Astor, Lenox and Tilden Foundations.
Part Three: Bibliothèque nationale de France, Paris.
Part Four: The Harvard Theatre Collection, The Houghton Library.
Part Five: Author's collection.

1   3   5   7   9   8   6   4   2

Printed in the United States of America
on acid-free paper

To my parents

and

in memory of Carolyn

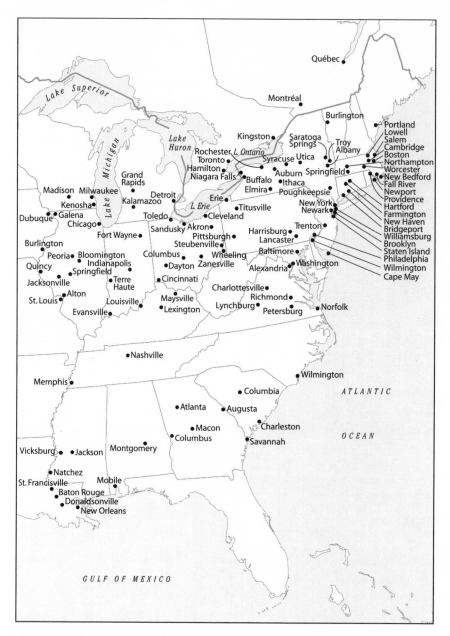

Map 1. Cities that received at least one performance by either Leopold de Meyer, Henri Herz, Sigismund Thalberg, Anton Rubinstein, or Hans von Bülow (excluding San Francisco, Sacramento, and Benicia, California).

PREFACE

It is not easy to imagine Franz Liszt performing in Kenosha, Wisconsin; Macon, Georgia; Peoria, Illinois; or Zanesville, Ohio. But his foremost rival, Sigismund Thalberg, did just that. In fact, during the mid-nineteenth century, citizens in more than one hundred American cities from Portland, Maine, to Charleston, South Carolina, and from New Orleans, Louisiana, to Dubuque, Iowa, had the opportunity to hear one or more of the world's most celebrated pianists, including—in addition to Thalberg—Leopold de Meyer, Henri Herz, Anton Rubinstein, and Hans von Bülow. Although some of their names have faded into obscurity, each of these virtuosos had already won acclaim in major European musical centers before embarking on an American tour. In the New World as in the Old, they captivated audiences through their unsurpassed technical skills, interpretive gifts, and colorful personalities.

The American visits of these five pianists that I examine in these pages took place between 1845 and 1876, a period of expansion and transformation in American musical life. Totaling nearly one thousand concerts (listed in appendix A), their tours are representative of the rapid spread throughout the country of European concert music by foreign virtuosos of the highest order, who began to flock to the United States in the 1840s. As a result of their extensive appearances, many Americans were introduced to the glories of the concert hall by some of the finest performers the world had to offer.

A chronicle of these tours contains a wealth of stories that will appeal to pianists, music historians, and general readers alike. The piano was reaching its apex as the central instrument of music making, artists were seeking fortune and adventure, entrepreneurs were inventing the profession of musical impresario, a still-adolescent country was striving to prove to itself and the world its appreciation of the art of music, and performers and audiences were establishing concert traditions that have yet to be superseded. As we explore these tours, I will document America's fascination with foreign virtuosos, examine the varied composition of audiences and their behavior, and chart the establishment of a canon of masterworks for the piano and the evolution of concert-giving into a highly organized commercial enterprise. In addition, tales will be told of humbug, romance, nervous breakdowns, physical exhaustion, and, most important, sublime musical experiences.

It is those experiences, shared by thousands of listeners in large cities and small towns across the country, that have come to intrigue me most. Trying to determine the influence or long-term effect of these virtuosos—positive, negative, or indifferent—is the most typical aim of a study such as this. Yet that goal misses the significance the audiences placed on these concerts. To understand what these musical experiences meant to nineteenth-century American listeners, we cannot afford to snicker at our predecessors or at the focus of their attention. The earliest of these pianists and their contemporaries have often been portrayed as first-rate performers but second-rate musicians, who flooded the New World with their misguided virtuosity, wowed musically uneducated Americans with technical displays of music of dubious value, and thereby delayed America's musical maturity by several decades. For many people, however, these performers offered thrilling, memorable, and sometimes intensely emotional experiences. I encourage you to attune yourself to the perspective of these audiences and to postpone worrying about whether their perception was true or not. It was true as far as they were concerned.

To this end, I have let the participants and observers speak for themselves as much as possible. We hear not only from the revered critic John Sullivan Dwight in Boston and the outspoken composer William Henry Fry in New York but also from unnamed reviewers in Baton Rouge, Louisiana; Janesville, Wisconsin; and other small cities, who reflect the opinions of a wide range of concertgoers. Some audience members understood little that they heard, preferring folk tunes or sentimental ballads; others appreciated the music or at least attempted to do so; and still others, though possessing little musical knowledge, were moved to tears and could express their feelings beautifully and powerfully.

I have, however, relied heavily on Dwight for several reasons. He is one of the few people who heard and wrote extensively about each of the pianists highlighted here, and thus his comments provide a consistent viewpoint. He was among the most

knowledgeable and articulate of the critics, and his conservative tastes—though these are frequently exaggerated—make him a perfect foil to these pianists. He was neither oblivious to nor silent about the negative aspects of the early virtuosos, who were often willing to subordinate musical concerns to the display of technical skills. Nevertheless, he found something to relish in what each of these pianists had to offer.

The nineteenth-century observer was more aware of the pros and cons of the traveling virtuoso than most modern writers will admit. There are enough caricatures and parodies, visual as well as literary, to make this clear, and they will be served up here on a regular basis. It is true that Barnum made some far-fetched claims about Jenny Lind, to take the most famous (and extreme) example, but most people knew it. Still, the chance to hear a legendary singer when she came to one's own small town drew audiences regardless of absurd advertising stunts. The distance between auctioning off tickets to Lind's concerts and the modern-day phenomenon of "The Three Tenors" is not so large. Of course, today we have more choices. If "The Three Tenors" arena performance is too vulgar and overtly commercial, we can still hear these great voices in more artistic venues. It is fine to laugh *with* our nineteenth-century counterparts, but there is no reason for us to feel smug when the problems and paradoxes created by the intersection of commerce and art are still with us today.

Although the reasons for concertgoing, ranging from curiosity and fashion to instruction and edification, have changed little in the past century and a half, concert etiquette was strikingly different in the 1840s. The transformation of audience behavior is an important thread in this study and one that has lately received scholarly attention. Early in the century, music was considered as much entertainment as art, and the audiences of De Meyer and Herz, for example, were often disorderly and raucous. Gradually, music came to be valued for its edifying qualities and was approached more reverently by audiences and performers, including Rubinstein and Bülow. This process, now commonly referred to by scholars as sacralization and brought to public attention by Lawrence Levine in *Highbrow/Lowbrow* (1988), was a complex one in which social and musical issues intertwined. Some scholars have suggested that the social elite attempted to restrict the access of the lower classes to cultural activities such as operas and symphony concerts by imposing restrictions on concert decorum. This tactic was irrelevant to the concerts of the visiting pianists, which survived on their own in the marketplace. In their concerts, sacralization occurred as the role of pianists changed and their repertoire shifted from the bravura works popular in the 1840s and 1850s, mostly fantasias based on operatic arias that were written by the pianists themselves, to the more serious works of Bach, Beethoven, Chopin, and Schumann. While interpreting the works of other composers, the performers demanded respect for the music so that listeners might have a profound aesthetic experience.

THE FIVE

Although many pianists toured the United States during the mid-nineteenth century, I have focused on only five of them; a few of the other pianists who toured during this period, lesser known though perhaps as talented, will be mentioned briefly. In my opinion, a thorough study of a selected number of performers based on extensive primary research will further our knowledge and understanding more than a survey of a larger number of pianists that relies too heavily on secondary sources.

In choosing my subjects, I looked for pianists who made the most dramatic impact on American audiences because of their well-established European reputation and their extensive travels throughout the United States. The earlier years of touring virtuosos, from the 1840s through the 1870s, were more uncharted and therefore seemed the best place to begin. Straddling the Civil War, the chronological period covered here was lengthy enough to trace the dramatic changes in concert life in the United States. By the 1880s and 1890s, the touring pianist was a well-established presence, and the proliferation of famous virtuosos impractical to document as thoroughly. Although the American pianist Louis Moreau Gottschalk met my criteria, I excluded him as a principal subject because his career has already received considerable documentation, most importantly through his own diary, *Notes of a Pianist* (1964), and a recent biography, *Bamboula!* by S. Frederick Starr (1995).

It is merely one of the felicities of history that my chosen subjects represent a variety of personalities (in order of appearance: a publicity hound, an adventurous raconteur, a refined gentleman, a passionate but aloof genius, and a neurotic intellectual) and are nicely spaced chronologically (two were here in the 1840s, one in the 1850s, and two in the 1870s). These pianists shared some traits, but no two were identical; each had a unique combination of personality, performance style, and repertoire, and each played a slightly different role in American musical life. Leopold de Meyer (U.S. tour 1845–47), the most flamboyant and least established of the five, was the first visiting pianist to create a sensation in America soon after first-rank European musicians began to brave the Atlantic. He relied as much on outlandish publicity as on his genuine pianistic ability to attract American audiences. Henri Herz (1846–50), a household name in America because of his many pieces for amateur pianists, followed closely behind De Meyer. More restrained than his predecessor, Herz nevertheless enticed American audiences with his extravaganzas for multiple pianos and was the first notable musician to perform in gold-rush California (1850). Appearing the following decade was Sigismund Thalberg (1856–58), at one time considered the only challenger to Liszt, one of the few top-ranked nineteenth-century pianists to forgo an American tour. Widely viewed as a significant innovator in piano composition and as a consummate performer, Thalberg was almost unani-

mously admired and of the five pianists gave the most concerts in the United States—more than three hundred in two seasons.

A drought in touring virtuosos during the 1860s, due partly to the hazards posed by the Civil War, was compensated by the appearances during the 1870s of Anton Rubinstein (1872–73) and Hans von Bülow (1875–76). Rubinstein was hailed for his charismatic interpretations of works by master composers during his now fabled tour, and Bülow, a prize pupil of Liszt, was praised for his scholarly and accurate performances that, however, failed to generate as much excitement as Rubinstein's. From the advent of De Meyer's tour to the close of Bülow's, audiences, repertoire, and traditions were transformed and were to change little thereafter: boisterous audiences were gradually replaced by more quiet, respectful ones; virtuoso show-pieces were supplanted by Beethoven sonatas and Chopin ballades; and the piano recital as it is known today was very much in place. That fascinating process is the subject of this chronicle.

❦

Additional information on the American tours of these five pianists is available on-line at www.rallenlott.info, including more details on each pianist's appearances and repertoire, biographical material on managers and performing associates, transcriptions of selected primary sources, complete pieces of music, and audio musical examples.

Acknowledgments

Youthful optimism and pure ignorance of the size of the task ahead of me made embarking on this study easy, but only family, friends, and colleagues have made it possible to complete. It is a pleasure to acknowledge their important role over the many years that have intervened since I first launched my work.

I am especially indebted to H. Wiley Hitchcock, who first enthusiastically encouraged me to pursue this topic and has steadfastly served as teacher, mentor, editor, and friend. I am grateful to Siegmund Levarie, another mentor and friend, who gladly provided expert help with the translations of Bülow's letters. I appreciate those who have read all or parts of the manuscript in its various stages and made suggestions for improvements, including Richard Crawford, John Graziano, L. Michael Griffel, H. Wiley Hitchcock, D. Kern Holoman, Siegmund Levarie, Ralph P. Locke, Tina Murdock, Carol J. Oja, Ruth A. Solie, Nicholas Temperley, and Sherman Van Solkema.

Several friends have been exceptionally influential in their encouragement over the years, including Sylvia Eversole, Tina Murdock, Carol Oja, and Katherine Preston. Other friends and colleagues have freely shared their expertise and the fruits of their own research, sent me leads to follow, and provided connections, motivation, shelter, and whatever else that was needed: C. L. Bass, Gerald Benjamin, Adrienne Fried Block, Nathan Bowers, Will Brown, Alan Buechner, Charles Calkins,

Martha Novak Clinkscale, H. Robert Cohen, Nym Cooke, Mary Jane Corry, Penny Crawford, Esther Rothenbusch Crookshank, Marcy Davis, Mark Dye, Susan Feder, Ed Ferlazzo, Edwin M. Good, Emily Good, Gary Gray, Betty Lou and Bill Hilles, Cynthia Adams Hoover, Daniel L. Hitchcock, H. Earle Johnson, John Koegel, Elise K. Kirk, Steven and Mary Lee Ledbetter, Laurence M. Lerner, Claudia Macdonald, Katherine Mahan, William J. Mahar, Michael and Eva Meckna, Andrew Mihalso, Nancy Newman, Vivian Perlis, Daniel Preston, Mike Pullin, Albert R. Rice, Deane L. Root, Ora Frishberg Saloman, A. H. Saxon, Krystine E. Scherr, Mary S. Schriber, Leslie Sheppard, Marilynn J. Smiley, Marc Southard, Henry Z. Steinway, Jonathan Suh, Charles Syrett, Mark Tucker, Marianne Wurlitzer, and Edward Yadzinsky.

The most important sources for my research were newspapers from the more than one hundred cities in which these pianists appeared. I searched many of them during several sojourns at the Library of Congress, one supported by a National Endowment for the Humanities Travel-to-Collections Grant and another as part of a sabbatic leave, and I worked in a couple of dozen major libraries, primarily in the Northeast and Midwest. Still, the geographical vastness of the study and the unavailability of some newspapers through interlibrary loan required that searches of some of the smaller cities be carried out with the help of library staffs. I gratefully recognize those libraries I was able to visit and the librarians who assisted me and graciously provided information through correspondence. I must first thank the staff of the Music Division of the New York Public Library, who often went beyond the call of duty to assist me, especially Jean Bowen, George Boziwick, Tema Hecht, Richard Jackson, John Shepard, and Susan T. Sommer. My appreciation also goes to Martha J. Rogers, Allen County Public Library, Fort Wayne, Indiana; Georgia B. Barnhill, American Antiquarian Society, Worcester, Massachusetts; William Cooper, Archives of Ontario, Toronto; Beinecke Library, Yale University; Amy J. Jeffrey, Benson Memorial Library, Titusville, Pennsylvania; Bibliothèque nationale de France; Bernard Huys, Bibliothèque Royale Albert 1er, Brussels; Frances E. Roehn, Bloomington (Illinois) Public Library; Boston Public Library; Robert B. Factor, Bridgeport (Connecticut) Public Library; Brooklyn Public Library; Norma Jean Lamb and Raya Then, Buffalo and Erie County Public Library; Lois J. Soltis, Burlington (Iowa) Public Library; Kirby Dilworth, The Carnegie Library of Pittsburgh; Chicago Historical Society; Chicago Public Library; Frances Forman, The Cincinnati Historical Society; Mary R. Naish, The Public Library of Cincinnati and Hamilton County; Jean Ashton, Columbia University; The Detroit Public Library; District of Columbia Public Library; Sister Mary Sheila Driscoll and R. Patricia Smith, D'Youville College, Buffalo; Cindy Kerchoff, Erie County Library System, Erie, Pennsylvania; William T. La Moy, Essex Institute, Salem, Massachusetts; Ann J. Arcari, The Farmington (Connecticut) Library; Michèle M. Gendron, The Free Library of Philadelphia; Susan L. Conklin, Department of History, County of Genesee, Batavia, New York;

Otto Biba, Gesellschaft der Musikfreunde in Wien; Richard H. Harms, Grand Rapids Public Library; Betty Fudge, Hamilton (Ontario) Public Library; Natalie Palme, The Harvard Musical Association; Julia Collins and Robert A. Wright, The Harvard Theatre Collection; Alfred Lemmon, The Historic New Orleans Collection; The Historical Society of Pennsylvania, Philadelphia; Donald Manildi, International Piano Archives, University of Maryland, College Park; Sharon K. Johnson, Iowa State Historical Department, Des Moines; B. F. Pine, Jacksonville (Illinois) Public Library; Phillip W. Rhodes, Jones Memorial Library, Lynchburg, Virginia; Susan Brower, Kalamazoo Public Library; Michael Dicketts, Kingston (Ontario) Public Library; Carol J. Nicholas and Robin Rader, Lexington (Kentucky) Public Library; Valerie Miller, The Library Company of Philadelphia; Music Division and Newspaper Division, Library of Congress; Rose Lambert, Louisiana Historical Center of the Louisiana State Museum, New Orleans; Memphis/Shelby County Public Library and Information Center; Gloria Gavert, Miss Porter's School, Farmington, Connecticut; Mississippi Department of Archives and History, Jackson; The Morgan Library, New York; Lisa Onofri, Museum of the City of New York; Cathy Carlson, The Museum of the Confederacy, Richmond; Nashville Public Library; New Bedford (Massachusetts) Free Public Library; Arthur D. Reinhart, New Haven Free Public Library; New Orleans Public Library; The New-York Historical Society; New York State Library, Albany; Diana Haskell and Cynthia Wall, The Newberry Library, Chicago; Rosemary Moravec, Osterreichische Nationalbibliothek, Vienna; Diane Mathews, The Oneida Historical Society, Utica, New York; Onondaga County Public Library, Syracuse, New York; Lynn T. Legate, Ottawa Public Library; Michael C. Walker, Petersburg (Virginia) Public Library; Myra Morales, The Greater Poughkeepsie Library District; Alma Lois Tyer, Quincy (Illinois) Public Library; Jan Stokes, Rockford (Illinois) Public Library; Sächsische Landesbibliothek, Dresden; Eleanor M. Richardson, South Caroliniana Library, University of South Carolina; Susan W. Price, E. S. Bird Library, Syracuse University; Tennessee State Library and Archives, Nashville; James C. Marshall, Toledo-Lucas County Public Library; Rosalie L. Wilcox, Tompkins County Public Library, Ithaca, New York; Robert B. Hudson, Troy (New York) Public Library; Elizabeth Pattengill, Utica (New York) Public Library; The Western Reserve Historical Society, Cleveland; and Franz Patzer, Wiener Stadt- und Landesbibliothek.

I am grateful for the support of my own institution, Southwestern Baptist Theological Seminary, especially through its sabbatic leave program that made much of the research and writing possible. The two deans I have served under, James McKinney and Benjamin Harlan, have consistently supported my work. Robert Phillips and the staff of Roberts Library graciously secured many items on interlibrary loan, and music librarian Fang-Lan Hsieh and the staff of the Kathryn Sullivan Bowld Music Library have invariably humored an obsessive researcher. Vickie Allen and Tina Murdock

played a crucial role in bringing organization to a mass of data, and my graduate assistants, including Tony Cunha, Barbara Davis, Catherine Knight Duncan, Ron Hall, John Jordan, Jason Runnels, and Anke Seay, helped with bibliographical research and translations and read portions of the manuscript.

I am pleased to acknowledge permission to use material from previously published articles of mine from the American Musical Instrument Society, the University of California Press, and the University of Michigan Press. For permission to quote extensively from the translation of Henri Herz's *Mes voyages en Amérique* by Henry Bertram Hill, I thank The State Historical Society of Wisconsin, which owns the copyright.

At Oxford University Press, I am indebted to Maribeth Anderson Payne as acquisitions editor and Niko Pfund as academic publisher for their interest in and support of the project. Ellen Welch, Robin H. Miura, and Kimberly Robinson carefully shepherded the book through a challenging production process. The H. Earle Johnson Fund of the Society for American Music provided a generous subvention to help defray production costs.

On a more personal level, I must thank three families in Fort Worth—the Houstons, Mehargs, and Shamblins—who faithfully stood by mine in the darkest hours. To family members Velma Little, John, Beverly, and Lauren Lott, and Jo Armstrong, I am grateful for their help in many and various ways. I dedicate this book to my parents, John and Katie Lott, whose love and support know no bounds. Among other things, they cheerfully joined me on several occasions to pore over nineteenth-century American newspapers and made a few unsupervised jaunts on my behalf. I remember with amusement the staff of one august historical institution who quizzed us dubiously at encountering a young scholar with parents in tow. All scholars should be so fortunate. The book is also dedicated to my late wife, Carolyn. A wonderful musician, she was fascinated with musicology, though we both laughed that she had graduated from a prestigious music school without reading Grout. She made my life complete, and I miss her. Finally, to my son, Andy, who during the last stages of book preparation unfailingly returned my paternal neglect with hugs, kisses, and encouragement, I promise a lot more pillow fights.

Soli Deo Gloria!

Contents

From Paris to Peoria

PRELUDE

The New World Beckons

A host of European performers found it profitable and invigorating to tour America in the nineteenth century. Joining pianists were opera singers and opera troupes; violinists, cellists, and harpists; singing families and handbell ringers offering folk and popular music; and dancers, acrobats, magicians, and lecturers. Visiting and immigrant performers on the concert stage and in the opera house were nothing new to America. Indeed, for some time concert life in America had essentially replicated the European experience, allowing foreign musicians to enjoy a monopoly in the concert hall.[1] Yet several developments coalesced in the mid-1840s that encouraged a new influx of performers, usually of a higher rank than those previously heard, to visit America. These factors included the healthy economy of the United States, the abundance of virtuosos in Europe, and vast improvements in transportation.

By the early 1840s America had recovered from the Panic of 1837, and an image of the United States as a profligate nation willing to fling riches at European artists became widespread. When the New York correspondent to *La France musicale* gave advice in 1845 to musicians considering an American tour, he began by relating one of several exaggerated views of the New World: "The European artist imagines that America is a country of gold, where he will acquire a fortune in two or three months,

where the president of the union will have him honored by congress; where the inhabitants of each city will give him serenades and carry him in triumph, for the greatest satisfaction of his enormous self-esteem." The following year the same journal announced that America had replaced Russia, specifically St. Petersburg, as the ultimate destination for the most talented performers, for the United States offered a "hundred cities where a lucrative success awaits the eminent artist, for it can not be forgotten that the *Yankee* is a good appreciator." It likened such performers as the violinists Alexandre Artôt, Ole Bull, and Henry Vieuxtemps, all of whom visited the United States in 1843, to "new Christopher Columbuses," who opened a route to a new El Dorado.[2]

The notion of America as an appreciative and wealthy consumer of music grew as the European music press assiduously reported the bountiful reception of most visiting artists in the United States, even though many Europeans had serious doubts about the artistic sensibility of Americans. Their skepticism was fueled by the biting observations in such firsthand accounts as Frances Trollope's *Domestic Manners of the Americans* (1832) and Charles Dickens's *American Notes* (1842) and *The Life and Adventures of Martin Chuzzlewit* (1844), both based on his first visit to the United States in 1841. The musical taste of Americans was more specifically condemned by the Hungarian composer and conductor Joseph Gungl, among others, during his orchestra's tour of this country in 1848–49: "Madame Musica . . . lies still in the cradle here. . . . It is a matter of course, that only the so-called anti-classical music can in any degree suit the taste of an American public; such as Waltzes, Gallops, Quadrilles, above all Polkas."[3]

Similar opinions were held by those without personal experience, such as the director of the Paris Opera, who remarked to the American composer William Henry Fry that Europeans considered America an "industrial country—excellent for electric telegraphs and railroads but not for art." Fry retorted that "although we had excelled in making electric telegraphs to carry ideas without persons, it was not a necessary consequence that we built railroads to carry persons without ideas." The American pianist Louis Moreau Gottschalk tells of being refused an audition with another Parisian, Pierre Zimmermann, the director of piano classes at the Conservatoire, because "America was only a country of steam engines"[4] (figure 1). Despite the misgivings some European artists had about America, many were willing to ignore them when faced with the prospect of glory and riches. Others, including such high-minded composers as Berlioz, Schumann, and Wagner, did not make the journey, although they seriously contemplated America as a solution to their financial and artistic woes.

A surfeit of virtuosos in Europe also encouraged performers to turn to the United States, where competition would be less fierce. Previously, as Henry Raynor ob-

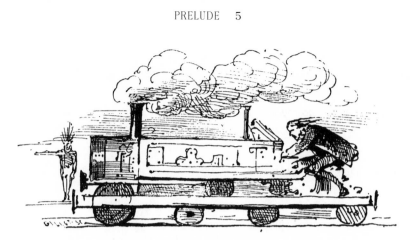

Nouveau piano à vapeur américaine.

Pour refouler au loin, par l'effroi, les peuplades hostiles.

Figure 1. *"Nouveau piano à vapeur américaine."* This "new American steam piano," supposedly designed to "drive back the hostile tribes, terrified, a long way," was imagined by a French artist who reinforced the perception of America as a nation filled with primitive people whose artistic ideas were subordinate to, or inevitably coupled with, industrial achievements. (*L'illustration* 50 [13 July 1867]: 25) (LITERATURE DEPARTMENT, THE FREE LIBRARY OF PHILADELPHIA)

served, eighteenth-century virtuosos toured primarily to establish their reputations, and "after that, further travelling seemed pointless," particularly when travel conditions were abominable. As transportation improved in Europe, however, more performers chose touring as a full-time career. At first, the best performers still in their prime did not need to consider an American tour. As the American musician Thomas Hastings wrote in the mid-1820s, "foreign executants seldom visit us till they get out of favour in their own country."[5]

The risks of an American tour were considerable, and the fear of the treacherous ocean voyage was infinitely more intimidating than concern about America's lack of culture.[6] Many artists feared for their lives, and eventually the requirements for snaring a distinguished performer for an American tour included a life insurance policy payable to the artist's family. Even if one's life was spared, the conditions on board were cramped and unpleasant. The commencement of travel by steamship in the early 1840s made the voyage, if not safer or more agreeable, at least quicker. A westward Atlantic crossing by sail could last from three to six weeks; eastward passage was usually a few days shorter. Steamers made the crossing in about two weeks with consistency, rarely if ever taking more than three. The sudden increase of visiting musicians of a top rank can be directly connected with the beginning of steam travel across the Atlantic.

Two Views of America

In 1855 the conductor and opera impresario Max Maretzek, who had immigrated to the United States in 1848, summarized the two widely disparate opinions of America circulating abroad among performers:

Some believe it to be a literal *El Dorado,* the Land of Musical Promise running with rivers of milk and honey. . . . These plant the land of their imagination with cities . . . filled with gold, and silver, and ivory. Their inhabitants are wealthy, confiding and generous, in the extreme. . . . In fact, the wealth, opulence, and prodigality of republican America has become proverbial. . . .

Others . . . regard America in a very different light. These believe it to be inhabited by a set of savages, barbarians, and Red Republicans. In their opinion, it contains a race of people who eat raw meat and devour uncooked vegetables, who chew tobacco, and void their rheum upon ladies' dresses and Turkey carpets, who drink unheard of quantities of brandy, schnapps, ale and Monongahela whiskey, while, instead of having been provided with a delicately palpitating heart like other races of mankind, Nature has in its place inserted simply a silver dollar, coined in their own mint.[1]

1. Max Maretzek, *Crotchets and Quavers: or, Revelations of an Opera Manager in America* (New York: S. French, 1855; reprint, New York: Da Capo Press, 1966, and New York: Dover Publications, 1968), 65–66.

In 1843, then, a consistent flow of first-rate musicians began with the appearance of a trio of outstanding violinists: Alexandre Artôt, Ole Bull, and Henry Vieuxtemps. Other celebrated performers followed quickly, including the violinist Camillo Sivori (1846) and the singers Laure Cinti-Damoreau (1843), Jenny Lind (1850), Marietta Alboni (1852), Henriette Sontag (1852), Giulia Grisi (1854), and Giovanni Mario (1854).[7]

The Piano and Pianists in Nineteenth-Century America

When De Meyer and Herz appeared in the United States in the mid-1840s, the piano had only recently been accepted as a solo instrument outside the chamber. In Europe around 1800, the piano was considered appropriate for the aristocratic salon or as the featured instrument in concertos. Within a few decades, improvements in piano construction and the development of the virtuosic school of piano playing gave the instrument a firm footing in the concert hall as a solo instrument. In a review of De Meyer's first appearance in the United States, the *New York Herald* proclaimed that the pianist had "clearly proved that the pianoforte is the instrument, *par excellence,* for a concert room."[8] Through its versatility as a solo and accompanying

instrument, its newfound recognition in the concert room, its suitability in the home, where a rising number of musical amateurs made music for their own enjoyment and that of their friends, and its usefulness as a tool in music education, the piano played a vital role in many aspects of music making. By mid-century, it had become by far the most important instrument in America.

The rise of the piano's popularity in the United States can be traced through the increased production of the instrument by American manufacturers. At the beginning of the century most pianos were imported; between 1800 and 1820 there were only about a dozen piano manufacturers active in New York, Philadelphia, and Boston. In 1829 American firms manufactured an estimated 2,500 pianos (equivalent to one instrument for every 4,800 inhabitants). By 1852 the number had risen to 9,000 (one for every 2,777 persons), and by 1860 21,000 pianos were produced in one year (one for every 1,500 persons). As early as 1830 one writer could declare: "We traverse the streets of our own city and the wires of the piano are thrummed in our ears from every considerable house. In cities and villages, from one extremity of the union to the other, wherever there is a good house, and the doors and windows betoken the presence of the mild months, the ringing of the piano wires is almost as universal a sound as the domestic hum of life within." An English writer, after living in the United States from 1821 to 1861, was positive that there were "ten pianofortes in every American town or village to one in England."[9]

Many of these pianos were purchased for the use of young women, who were expected to learn at least the fundamentals of piano playing as one of the "accomplishments" (like dancing, drawing, and needlework), and the study of piano and other instruments was consistently offered in female seminaries and finishing schools.[10] Although musical education for women was widespread, it was primarily designed to prepare them for domestic music making so they could attract suitors and be good wives and hostesses. It was generally thought improper for a woman to become skilled enough to pursue a concert career. Because music was often considered "merely an *accomplishment*," a piano method of 1834 complained about the resulting view that music could "be taken hold of in the most superficial manner." In the 1860s a Philadelphia correspondent to *Dwight's* voiced a similar concern that good pianists in his city were lacking despite the abundance of pianos and piano teachers, which he attributed to the notion that music was "cultivated as an accomplishment (using the word in its modern, society sense) as part of the outward gilding or lacquer necessary to shine in the world of fashion." Another criticism was that young girls were forced to study piano even when they possessed no musical talent or interest. One writer as early as 1840 took this position and ranted: "They might as well make all our men painters, though they were without eyes. Millions are annually wasted upon music—for those of whom *not one in a thousand* can ever hope to attain any tolerable proficiency, and in which mediocrity is detestable."[11]

These circumstances and the objections to them would continue to almost the end of the century. Nevertheless, this musical education, however cursory or unsuccessful, at least awakened an interest in musical activities, and women were important supporters of the concerts of these pianists.

The rudimentary level of much piano playing in mid-nineteenth-century America was attested to by the songwriter George F. Root. In 1891, he recalled his early years of piano study in the late 1830s, when "piano playing was not then what it is now, by a difference that it would be hard to describe. . . . A person even in Boston who could play as well as hundreds of young people all over the country now play, would have attracted universal attention."[12] Several fine pianists, however, had been active in America during the 1830s, including Henry Christian Timm, Daniel Schlesinger, and William Scharfenberg in New York.

Only a few pianists had ventured into touring. Louis (or Ludwig) Rakemann, a friend of Schumann—known as Walt in the Davidsbündler—was based in New York between 1839 and about 1843, but appeared as far west as St. Louis. According to the critic John Sullivan Dwight, Rakemann "was the first to introduce us to the New School piano compositions—to Thalberg, Liszt, Henselt, Doehler, Chopin." The violinist and pianist William Vincent Wallace also had performed in a number of cities from New Orleans to Boston in his American sojourn of 1842–44 and returned in 1850–54. Root believed Rakemann and Jane Sloman, a child prodigy who came to the United States with her actor parents in 1839 and made her debut two years later, "much excelled the best we had heard." Yet from the vantage point of fifty years later, Root held that their playing "now would be considered only mediocre," and that "every large city in the country has better players."[13] Thus, much of the country was still unexposed to exceptional piano playing when two traveling pianists—Leopold de Meyer and Henri Herz—came to the doorstep of thousands of Americans.

PART ONE

Leopold de Meyer

1845–47

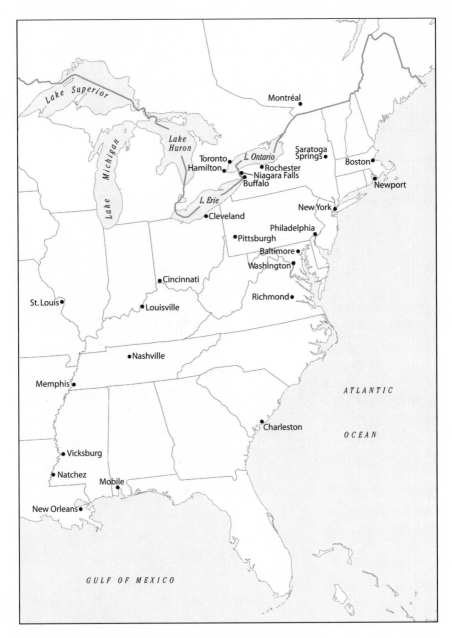

Map 2. Cities in which Leopold de Meyer performed.

The Lion Stalks America

America's first encounter with a bona fide piano virtuoso was provided by the colorful Austrian pianist Leopold de Meyer (1816–1883). During his two-season tour of the United States from 1845 to 1847, his forceful technique and imaginative compositions created a sensation throughout the country, and to many listeners his playing was a revelation. For a time De Meyer captured the attention of the entire western musical world. From St. Petersburg to St. Louis, he was hailed as one of the greatest pianists of the day, and his compositions were enthusiastically received—two of them were even orchestrated by Berlioz. Yet, like many pianist-composers of his era, his almost instant fame was almost as instantly lost. Today he is long forgotten.

FROM EAST TO WEST

Born Leopold von Meyer in Baden near Vienna, he demonstrated a talent for the keyboard at an early age and performed frequently in the aristocratic salons of Vienna. He pursued a law degree, however, following the desires of his father, a state counselor at the Austrian court. After his father's death, he was able to fulfill his own wish and aspire to a musical career. At seventeen he began studying with Carl Czerny and François Schubert, the latter a professor at the Vienna Conservatory. After two years of intensive study he embarked on a performing career, generally using the name Leopold de Meyer.[1]

De Meyer's career is a perfect illustration of how the routes traveled by virtuosos were shifting. Beginning in 1835, he spent most of the first eight years of his career performing in Russia and eastern Europe before moving across western Europe and eventually making his way to America. After leaving Russia, he made a brief visit to Constantinople, returned triumphantly to Vienna in 1843, and then proceeded to conquer audiences and musicians in the West. The following year in London he performed with such distinguished virtuosos as Julius Benedict, Charles-Auguste de Bériot, Ignaz Moscheles, Camillo Sivori, and Henry Vieuxtemps. The *Musical World* of London declared that he was "assuredly one of the most original and remarkable pianists of the age." In Frankfurt one writer claimed that "excepting Liszt, no pianist has met at this theatre a reception so enthusiastic as M. de Meyer," and in Brussels *L'Observateur* stated confidently that "nothing can be more brilliant, more finished, more powerful, more feeling, than the playing of this incomparable pianist."[2]

It was no small achievement that De Meyer attained what was probably his greatest success in Paris, then the undisputed capital of piano virtuosos. Within a few weeks in 1845 he was touted as "the principal ornament of all our great salons. . . . It is difficult to imagine the immense effect that he produces everywhere." In less than three months, he made almost thirty appearances in private soirées and concerts, including two solo recitals and a guest appearance at a concert organized by Berlioz.[3]

De Meyer was at the height of his European celebrity when he decided to visit the United States. His swift rise to fame in western Europe meant that his name was hardly known in America. To prepare his way in the New World, a pamphlet entitled *The Biography of Leopold de Meyer* magically appeared, purportedly the creation of friends and admirers. Such literary tributes with brief biographies and reprints of fulsome reviews were already common devices to herald performers. These publications were symptomatic of the European perception of American audiences as unsophisticated and uninformed, whose patronage could only be acquired through sensational publicity.

De Meyer's "biography" recounts his triumphs and adventures as "The Lion Pianist," as he liked to be called. Although its facts were mostly correct, its effusiveness suggested widespread exaggeration, and its caricatures—one depicted the pianist pounding the keyboard with his hands, elbows, and a knee—raised doubts about the performer's respectability. After praising a performance by De Meyer, Dwight denounced the pamphlet, "copies of which are strewed so copiously before his path wherever he travels," and the state of musical affairs that made it necessary:

> Persuaded as we are of the genuineness of him and of his art, we regard the book as of the worst species of *humbug,* since it represents him as a charlatan. . . . We know there is this excuse for it, that every thing now-a-days is done by management and pretension, that the world has got so schooled to humbug, that the genuine as well as

the false have to make use of it as an introduction, and that no man, in any department, be he ever so great, can get along in the world unless he will consent to do as the humbugs do.[4]

As Dwight makes clear, the art of humbug was already rampant in America. The word had been around for almost a century, but the method had lately entered a flourishing period in America. Dwight was mostly accurate in blaming management rather than artists for the widespread use of it, but he was too kind in De Meyer's case, for his only manager was G. C. Reitheimer, his brother-in-law.

DEBUT AT THE PARK THEATRE

De Meyer was in London when he was engaged for six appearances at New York's Park Theatre, the most fashionable playhouse in New York.[5] Crossing the Atlantic for only six performances may not seem worth the effort, but instrumentalists at this time rarely had a contract in advance for an American tour. They usually brought their own manager with them, if they had one, to arrange concerts once they arrived here. De Meyer sailed from Liverpool on 27 September 1845 on board the steamship *Great Britain,* arriving with little fanfare in New York on 15 October.

Like many newly arrived performers, De Meyer gave a private soirée in his rooms for a group of prominent musicians, painters, writers, professionals, and, most important, the journalists he hoped would arouse some excitement about his playing. According to the *Tribune,* the enthusiasm of the gathering, which included many of the leading pianists of the city, was "intense and the applause electric and unbounded" for the performer that "seemed a Musical Centaur, half man and half piano." Shouts and cheers were in order, and William Scharfenberg, a respected local pianist, toasted the new arrival: "Welcome to our shores, and success to the greatest pianist of this or any age—the incomparable Leopold de Meyer."[6]

Even though De Meyer had given a number of solo recitals in Brussels and Paris, his American debut on 20 October 1845 took place in much humbler circumstances as an intermission feature at the Park. For two weeks he appeared on alternate nights playing one piece (with an occasional encore) during each of two intermissions between such lightweight comedies as *Petticoat Government* and *The Dumb Belle.* He was billed as the "Imperial and Royal Pianist, by Diploma, to the Emperors of Austria and Russia" (titles which he consistently used and to which he had some claim) and more dubiously as the "Paganini of the Piano" and the "Greatest Pianist of Modern Times."

At his debut De Meyer performed his *Introduction and Variations on the Drinking Song from Lucrezia Borgia,* his *Marche marocaine,* which won him three recalls, and as an encore his *Airs russes.* The *Sun* thought it was the "most triumphant *debut* we ever entertained," and the *Herald* described the furor created by his playing:

It is difficult to afford an adequate idea of the unparalleled enthusiasm—it might be called a frenzy—with which [De Meyer] was received. The applause was so tremendous and withal so protracted, that we really began thinking that the audience were under the influence of some species of Tarantella; and everybody looked so excited, that a stranger, who would have entered the theatre after the *Marche Marocaine*, could have fancied himself in a lunatic asylum, with De Meyer—the only one who looked reasonable—as the keeper. Never did [an] artist make such an impression on his first appearance.

At his fourth appearance, De Meyer's performances proved to be so exciting that the critic for the *Broadway Journal* confessed it was only with great effort that he restrained himself from "running on the stage and embracing the artist."[7]

THE MUSIC OF DE MEYER

De Meyer appeared six times at the Park to crowded houses and introduced the core works of his repertoire. Like many pianists of his day, De Meyer performed mostly his own compositions,[8] and like much of the literature written by virtuosos, they were strongly indebted to Italian opera. Among his own works he performed in the United States were fantasias on Bellini's *Norma* and *I Puritani*; Donizetti's *L'Elisir d'amore, Lucia di Lammermoor,* and *Lucrezia Borgia*; and Rossini's *La donna del lago* and *Semiramide*. Such fantasias had become mainstays for the virtuoso pianist because they provided vehicles for the display of technical skills on themes familiar to audiences. Opera troupes were traveling all across the country, and best-selling sheet music editions of the arias — both in the original language and in English translation— attest to the popularity and acceptance of the music.

De Meyer's opera fantasias were received well enough, but his most interesting works—and those that generated the most enthusiastic responses—are undoubtedly several novel pieces evocative of the music heard in his travels. Some are inspired by folk material and range from straightforward keyboard transcriptions, as in the *Chant bohémien,* to more elaborate interpretations, as in the second set of Russian airs. In the *Airs russes,* Op. 43 (example 1.1), an artistic cousin to the *Hungarian Rhapsodies* of Liszt, an andante folklike theme is gradually transformed into a brilliant showpiece with rapid chordal leaps and octave runs. Other works, if not folk-based, are at least suggestive of a distant locale, such as *La danse du sérail,* Op. 51. Subtitled a "grande fantaisie orientale," it is a programmatic work inspired by the pianist's experience in Constantinople, where he supposedly played before the sultan. Its final section, the "Danse des odalisques" (Dance of the Concubines; example 1.2), may not seem all that striking today, but its provocative title, frequent chromaticism, and seductive figuration resonated among audiences who were just then enchanted with the exotic.

Example 1.1. Leopold de Meyer, *Airs russes,* Op. 43, (a) mm. 1–8; (b) mm. 109–20.

Example 1.2. Leopold de Meyer, *La danse du sérail,* Op. 51, mm. 234–40.

De Meyer's most popular work by far was the *Marche marocaine*. It also was inspired by his stay in Constantinople—despite its title—and the piece was originally published as *Machmudier: air guerrier des Turques*. De Meyer's outstanding success in Paris can be directly linked to this work, considered by a critic there as "one of the most original, the most eccentric pieces of piano music that exists."[9] When De Meyer performed the work at a concert organized by Berlioz, the French composer-critic marveled that it "electrified and transported" an immense audience, and he attested to the work's "most extraordinarily powerful impact."[10] The work was similarly received in America and quickly became the pianist's trademark. Dwight believed it was "one of his most original compositions," and although it was "simple and plain in its construction," it possessed a "breadth and fire entirely irresistible." The New York critic Richard Grant White explained some of its secrets:

His own *Marche Marocaine* is after all his most pleasing and astonishing effort. Its abrupt, gigantic theme, and its overwhelming power—its passages of wild sweetness—

its startling harmonies, and certain passages of full chords, which sweep from one end of the instrument to the other with the full force of his powerful arm, and the full capacity of his comprehensive grasp, combine to make it the most remarkable piano forte composition of the day.[11]

The *Marche marocaine*'s dense chordal writing and bravura octaves coupled with its insistent rhythmic momentum distinguished the work from the lyrical opera fantasias and the variations that emphasized delicate filigree, which were more typical of the period (example 1.3). The *Marche triomphale d'Isly,* a sequel to the *Marche marocaine,* was another stirring march with a full chordal texture. With its relentless rhythmic drive, the work was mesmerizing at the hands of the composer and "made the blood tingle through the veins," according to the *New York Evening Post.* The thick texture of his music was partly responsible for De Meyer's large sound, probably the most noted feature of his playing. The *New-York Daily Tribune* joked that the pianist "delights in masses of sounds and his compositions are to other musical works what the Niagara at the Falls is to other rivers."[12]

De Meyer was by no means a master composer, but he was adventurous, and his music possesses considerable charm, color, and excitement. Many of his pieces are remarkably original in an era of widespread conformity to opera-based variations. Dwight, who is today often characterized as prejudiced against all music except that of the highest order, had a balanced view of De Meyer's compositions. While he was intrigued with the "gusto" of the *Marche marocaine,* "with its wild, reeling, swaggering, yet powerful onsweep," he admitted that "if we could get no other music, this would grow intolerable; as it is, we admire and feel refreshed by its smart shock. . . . Because he is not a Beethoven, nor a Schubert, nor a Chopin, we shall not the less enjoy him for what he is—a genial, lifesome creature, whom music has chosen to be her best expression of the nervous energy and the champagne sparkle of life."[13]

GRAND CONCERTS IN NEW YORK

By the time De Meyer finished his six appearances at the Park Theatre, he had established his reputation and was ready to venture out on his own. He soon announced that his "first grand concert" would take place on 7 November in the Tabernacle. Originally built as a church, the Tabernacle was an amphitheater of almost three thousand seats on Broadway that did double duty as New York's principal concert hall. Philip Hone dubbed it the "omnium gatherum and holdall of the city," and the *Morning Telegraph* called it the "celebrated musical wash-tub." For De Meyer's concert the vast hall was "completely crammed," and the "applause was enthusiastic in the extreme." After De Meyer performed his *Marche marocaine,* the ovation was so vehement, one critic wondered that the "house did not break down under the thunder of applause."[14]

(a)

(b)

Example 1.3. Leopold de Meyer, *Marche marocaine,* Op. 22 (a) mm. 11–19; (b) mm. 58–66; (c) mm. 101–8.

Solo recitals were almost unheard of in America, and indeed they were still a rarity in Europe. Liszt had only introduced them in London in 1840, and it would be some time before they were common on either side of the Atlantic. An evening of nothing but one performer and one instrument was deemed lethally monotonous, so De Meyer followed the custom of engaging assisting artists to "fill up the chinks," as one newspaper put it. The program for his first concert was typical: four piano pieces alternated with as many vocal selections. The number of works actually performed, however, was usually higher and could almost be doubled because of the audience's persistent demand for encores. The satirical magazine *Yankee Doodle* facetiously defined the word *encore:* "A French word, which being translated into American, means, 'We intend to get the worth of our money.' Consequently, when it is used, the performer does not repeat the piece just given—as the word seems to indicate—but plays another. Authorities, Ole Bull, Sivori, Herz, De Meyer, &c."[15]

Now a celebrity, De Meyer appeared a few days later (10 November) as a guest artist in Ureli Corelli Hill's Festival Concert. Hill was a leading member of the New York musical establishment and had been in 1842 the "chief begetter of the New York

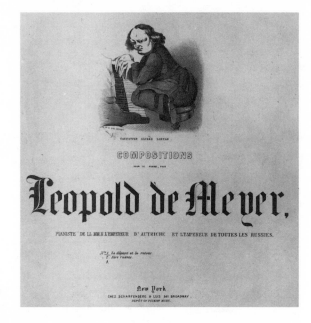

Figure 1.1. Sheet music cover for Leopold de Meyer's *Le départ et le retour.* (MUSIC DIVISION, THE NEW YORK PUBLIC LIBRARY, ASTOR, LENOX AND TILDEN FOUNDATIONS)

Philharmonic." De Meyer performed his *Marche marocaine* on the piano and also led the almost one-hundred-piece orchestra in the same work "as Instrumented by the great Berlioz . . . and executed in Paris under his direction with astonishing effect." Prior to leaving for Boston, De Meyer gave another concert in New York the following week (14 November), offering his *La danse du sérail,* which received a "thundering *encore,*" and *The Battle of New Orleans,* a march "expressly composed" for the concert.[16] His success in New York would not prepare him for his lukewarm reception in Boston.

MAESTRO OR MOUNTEBANK?

If De Meyer is remembered at all today, it is through the caricatures of him that seem to depict a ludicrous entertainer—a "faker," suspects Harold Schonberg—not a sincere artist (figures 1.1, 1.2). Such fanciful caricatures were widespread, however, and one can no more conclude from them that De Meyer used his shins to play tone clusters than one can that Thalberg had eight hands (figure 7.2). Written descriptions may at first appear to confirm the iconographical evidence, but many of these are literary burlesques in the same vein. There is no doubt, however, that De Meyer had eccentric mannerisms at the piano. One quirk was his habit of gazing at the audience while performing. The *Brooklyn Star* described how he occasionally "glare[d] upon his auditors with a kind of insane stare." Richard Hoffman, an admirer of the pianist who studied briefly with him in London, claimed he was a "per-

Figure 1.2. Sheet music cover for Leopold de Meyer's *Meyer-Polka.* (MUSIC DIVISION, THE NEW YORK PUBLIC LIBRARY, ASTOR, LENOX AND TILDEN FOUNDATIONS)

fect mountebank on the stage," and a New Orleans critic confirmed that his manner at the piano was "too ferocious, too theatrical." A. N. Johnson, an associate of Lowell Mason and editor of the Boston *Musical Gazette,* acknowledged that De Meyer was "really a great performer," but was outraged at his stage deportment: "It seemed to us that if, immediately after striking the last chord of the piece, he had turned a summerset over the piano, it would have been in perfect keeping with the performance."[17]

A few writers, however, entirely refuted the pianist's platform antics. A Rochester critic "saw nothing very remarkable" about De Meyer's "position at the piano. . . . He sits erect, producing the most astounding effect with the least apparent effort." A New York critic was also perplexed by the wild accounts, finding that all the "soul-throwing, instrument-crushing, shrieking, torturing and expiring . . . utterly escaped [his] observation."[18]

The conflicting evidence suggests that De Meyer was a dynamic performer, who flamboyantly demonstrated—and probably exaggerated—the difficulty of his playing at a time when most pianists were striving to make their performances appear as effortless as possible. One critic suggested that the pianist deliberately acquired extravagant stage mannerisms for American audiences; he recalled hearing De Meyer

previously in Europe, where he "did not . . . mingle much tom-foolery with his performance."[19]

His idiosyncrasies aside, De Meyer excited wonder in his audiences through his facility and, above all, his power. They had never before heard such playing. "He overwhelms the sense and makes the brain ache and throb with the bewilderment of his tempest-like accords," moaned one writer. A critic for the *New York Sun* was taken by the "rare delicacy" of the pianist's touch and was also startled at the "headlong vehemence with which he bounds along the whole range" of the piano, "literally flagellating the instrument." Richard Hoffman remembered his touch as the "most wonderful combination of superb power and exquisite delicacy."[20]

De Meyer's "superb power" was due in large part to the full chordal texture of his compositions, but it must also be attributed to his revolutionary use of arm weight. This technique intrigued the young pianist William Mason, who later became one of America's leading piano pedagogues:

> It was from a careful study of the manner of his playing that I first acquired the habit of fully devitalized upper-arm muscles in pianoforte-playing. The loveliness and charming musical beauty of his tones, the product of these conditions, greatly excited my admiration and fascinated me. I never missed an opportunity of hearing him play, and closely watched his movements, and particularly the motions of hand, arm, and shoulder. I was incessantly at the pianoforte trying to produce the same delightful tone quality by imitating his manner and style.

Dwight reported that De Meyer credited his power not just to his *arm* weight:

> He congratulates himself on his advantage in being the only one of the great pianists who is fat; this enables him to bear the immense amount of physical exertion and nervous excitement, which is the greatest wonder about his playing. Indeed his physique is extraordinary; he is himself a Grand Piano, and can stand any amount of violent vibration without any symptom of exhaustion.[21]

Despite his shenanigans on stage, De Meyer was still almost unanimously declared a great pianist and the best to appear in America. Dwight believed that it was "true and undeniable" that his "music is a genuine thing, and that his skill quite distances all that we have heard." In a review of the pianists who had performed in New York, one critic claimed that De Meyer came as an "undisputed wonder, for we have had no one in this country who can be classed in any way with him." A Charleston critic had "no hesitation in ranking him far above any piano forte player whom it has been our lot to hear," and in New Orleans another believed it was a "conceded point" that "De Meyer is, by many furlongs, in advance of any pianist who has ever visited America."[22] These

assertions, combined with the knowledge of De Meyer's successes in Europe, where audiences had heard Liszt, Thalberg, and others, make it clear that he was a technically superior pianist, whose exhilarating performances astonished his listeners.[23]

BOSTON REVOLTS AGAINST DOLLAR CONCERTS

At his only Boston appearance that season (21 November 1845), De Meyer was received with the "highest degree of enthusiasm," but the audience was classified as "select" and "intelligent"—frequent euphemisms for "small" and "elitist." He postponed a second concert because of a "slight indisposition," later minutely specified as an injury to the "muscle of the fourth finger of the right hand," although one rumor claimed the pianist had been thrown from a horse and had dislocated his right arm. De Meyer finally left Boston almost six weeks later without giving a second concert, still "entirely disabled from performing anything which requires power." The *American Journal of Music* believed De Meyer's mysteriously fragile condition was not due to any accident. It held that the "unfortunately sprained one" left "enraged and disappointed, because he could not draw dollar houses. . . . As the M.D.'s of Boston had not the essential salve (the Melodeon crowded at one dollar per ticket) to cure the gentleman, he has gone south to better his 'finger,'—and pocket."[24]

Like most visiting musicians for the past several years, De Meyer had charged a dollar admission to his concerts in both New York and Boston. Apparently many Bostonians stubbornly refused to attend concerts with such a price tag when admission to programs of local performers was still only fifty cents. A dollar was, in fact, a substantial amount: most unskilled and factory laborers had to work an entire day to earn it. With justification, then, the *American Journal of Music* argued that "people cannot—and more—*will not,* pay the extravagant sum of one dollar to attend a single concert." The journal chided De Meyer and other musicians for charging such an unreasonable amount, and—recalling the almost empty houses that Ole Bull had suffered—warned them that past failures should teach musicians "the utter fallacy of appealing to the monied few."

Injured or not, De Meyer did not give his final two concerts of the season in New York until early February. New York was still infatuated with De Meyer: the huge Tabernacle was packed for both concerts (5 and 12 February 1846), and the audiences vociferous in their appreciation. The pianist "was repeatedly encored and covered with wreaths thrown by his admirers"; one paper, in fact, marveled that it had never seen "bouquets and garlands bestowed so freely upon a man."[25] The musical highlight of both concerts was De Meyer's two-piano paraphrase of Félicien David's *Le Désert,* which introduced Americans to the programmatic work. Based on Arab themes, David's piece had received its premiere in Paris in December 1844 and had had an extraordinary success. De Meyer arrived in Paris during the height of the

Figure 1.3. Program for Leopold de Meyer's concert in New York, 5 February 1846. (MUSIC DIVISION, LIBRARY OF CONGRESS).

work's popularity and appeared in several of David's concerts. He performed his version of the work first with Charles Perabeau (figure 1.3) and a week later with George Loder. One of the conductors of the New York Philharmonic, Loder was to lead the first American orchestral performance of *Le Désert* on 2 April 1846.

De Meyer's financial success was very much on his mind when he wrote to his friend Joseph Fischhof, professor of piano at the Vienna Conservatory, after his New York concert of 5 February 1846: "Yesterday I gave my twelfth [*recte* tenth] concert here in New York and again caught 3000 people—flowers, wreaths, etc., but mainly dollars. . . . I am glad that I am the first to risk this dangerous trip, because only the first can make money here—because the people are still quite new to music. However, the second and even . . . Thalberg will not make a penny here."[26] Obviously, De Meyer's gift of prophecy did not equal his piano skills.

THE BOISTEROUS CONCERTGOER

Four concerts in Philadelphia (one as a guest artist with the Musical Fund Society), three in Baltimore, and two in Washington, D.C., followed quickly during the next month and were well attended.[27] In Philadelphia, De Meyer began inviting "Ladies and Gentlemen who have a desire to become acquainted with his touch of the Piano, to take their seats on the Platform near the instruments," an invitation that

would be frequently repeated and accepted. His audiences in Washington, which greeted him "with long-continued shouts of applause," included a distinguished array of foreign ministers, congressmen, and officers of the army and navy, as well as former President John Quincy Adams and the uncle and nephew of President James K. Polk.[28]

Perhaps the most notable aspect of De Meyer's concerts in Philadelphia and Baltimore was the reaction of the audiences to his variations on "Hail, Columbia" and "Yankee Doodle," later published as *Airs nationaux américains.* Almost every visiting artist felt obliged to compose a musical homage to his host country based on patriotic or popular tunes. Critics usually groaned at yet another hastily composed set of formulaic variations on tunes seemingly incompatible with what they saw as the high calling of music.[29] Nevertheless, audiences greeted them with gusto, and they demonstrated that the line between popular and art music had yet to be drawn decisively. In Philadelphia the variations "took the audience by storm, and caused such a *furor*" that one critic "had serious apprehensions for the safety of the hall." In Baltimore the audience was positively rowdy: "We never saw a more thoroughly delighted and excited audience—so much so, that while his thunders lasted, they could not keep their seats, and what is worse, their tongues. . . . Mr. De Meyer did not bargain for any accompaniment of sticks and umbrellas, to the performance of our national airs, and according to our opinion, such things had better be reserved for the pit of a showbooth."[30]

Such raucousness was not unusual for theater audiences of the time, who were notorious for their participatory zeal, believing it was their right to express approval through frequent applause or disapproval through hissing, stomping feet, or tossing vegetables. The concerts of visiting virtuosos were usually more sedate because the high single-admission price of a dollar—eight times the cheapest gallery seat in a theater—effectively kept out the lowest economic classes. Little wonder that such events were soon dubbed the "fashionable concerts" when only the well-to-do could easily attend; high ticket prices would be a chronic complaint for decades.

Still, nineteenth-century concert audiences were far from models of modern concert decorum, particularly in their timing of applause. Although they rarely showed disapproval, they were more than willing to demonstrate their admiration for a performer by applauding not only after a work was completed but *during* the performance itself in response to a splashy bit of fingerwork or an especially pleasing section. Theater audiences did this all the time, and, in fact, were encouraged to do so because it inspired the actors. At his first appearance at the Park Theatre, for instance, De Meyer's performance "was interrupted by the most frantic applause whenever a pause afforded opportunity," and later in New Orleans there were "frequent outbursts of admiration."[31]

Spontaneous Applause

Spontaneous applause during a performance was not a custom unique to America. Mozart, for instance, was pleased that he had so perceptively judged Parisian taste that during the first performance of his "Paris" Symphony there was a "tremendous burst of applause" in the middle of the first movement, and another round of applause interrupted the opening measures of the finale. A century later, Bülow boasted in a master class in the mid-1880s that he always received applause after the opening cadenza of the Beethoven "Emperor" Concerto. Such a practice seems strange today, after audiences have been cowered into stifling their involuntary outbursts by imperious conductors and pious performers so that they do not dare to applaud even between movements of a symphony or sonata, much less in the middle of one.

Herz, Thalberg, and even much later, Rubinstein on occasion, were all subjected to such a continuous barometer of the effectiveness of their playing. In a New York concert, for instance, Herz performed his Fantasia on *Lucia di Lammermoor*, "at every pause in which there was a loud burst of applause." In San Francisco "so frequent and long were the applaudings of the audience" that it was "sometimes with difficulty, that [Herz] could get through his pieces." The appreciation of Thalberg's troupe in Charleston "again and again manifested itself in spontaneous bursts of applause." During a performance by Rubinstein of his Fourth Piano Concerto in Philadelphia, "every passage was warmly applauded," and in Boston, the enthusiasm of the audience "manifested itself in vigorous but well-timed applause."

While such applause was surely as distracting to the performers as it was encouraging, it made the listener an active participant in the proceedings, requiring knowledge and attentiveness. Not much intelligence or musical sensitivity is required to applaud when the music stops, but to know when to applaud during a piece—that takes musical judgment. In an article on "Annoyances in the Concert Room," the *New York Herald* complained about the "misplacement of applause." For those audience members who wished to applaud but were "not perfectly *au fait* to time and place," it suggested they "watch some spectator upon whose judgment you can rely, and take your cue from him." The comic magazine *Judy* believed that the fashionable opera goers also were likely to "expose themselves many times during an evening by making some *faux pas* or other in the way of applause." It humorously, and prophetically, suggested to the management that a "telegraphic contrivance" controlled by the prompter could signal to the audience when to applaud, smile, laugh, or cry bravo.[1]

1. Mozart, Letter to his father, 3 July 1778, in Emily Anderson, *The Letters of Mozart and His Family*, 3d ed. (London: Macmillan, 1985), 558; Theodor Pfeiffer, *Studien bei Hans von Bülow* (Berlin: Luckhardt, 1894), trans. in Richard Louis Zimdars, *The Piano Master Classes of Hans von Bülow: Two Participants' Accounts* (Bloomington: Indiana University Press, 1993), 44; *New York Herald*, 6 November 1846; San Francisco concert in *Sacramento Transcript*, 16 April 1850; *Charleston Mercury*, 2 February 1858; *Philadelphia Evening Bulletin*, 29 October 1872, 2:1; *Boston Daily Advertiser*, 22 May 1873, 10:1; *New York Herald*, 13 November 1846; *Judy* 1 (16 January 1847): 88.

There were times, however, when the pyrotechnics of a virtuoso induced a hush of amazement. When De Meyer appeared in Saratoga Springs, "so astonishing" was his performance that "during his most rapid and powerful execution, most of the audience involuntarily arose, and gazed upon the performer with countenances beaming with admiration." When he gave a concert in a church in Pittsburgh, "at one moment, men, women and children, would be standing up in the pews, or leaning forward with breathless attention, to catch each succeeding note—and then, falling back as if in utter exhaustion from the intensity of feeling, excited by the performance, [would] listen with silent astonishment! They were literally music mad."[32]

CHAPTER 2

De Meyer in the South and Midwest ◖◐

After risking their lives crossing the Atlantic, most touring performers were determined to gather as many American dollars as possible. Therefore, they rarely limited their appearances to the Northeast but tried to visit a substantial number of major cities in the thriving New World. In addition, their itineraries often included smaller cities because of their location and accessibility rather than their population. In the South and Midwest, where transportation still relied heavily on boats, smaller river towns (like Natchez and Vicksburg) were frequented by traveling performers because they were conveniently situated between larger cities on an important waterway. Most tours began on the eastern seaboard, with Charleston a principal stop, continued by ship to New Orleans, and then headed up the Mississippi and Ohio rivers. They might extend into Canada and conclude during the summer at resort areas (or "watering places" as they were frequently called) such as Niagara Falls, Saratoga Springs, and Newport, where a fashionable clientele would be in residence.

ON THE ROAD WITH PIANOS

Beginning in late March 1846, De Meyer followed this already established route on his first inland tour. Accompanying him were several grand pianos "manufactured purposely for himself" by Erard, the leading Parisian piano manufacturer. He had

already become so closely identified with that make in Europe that writers had concocted such giddy epithets to describe him as "the hundred-fingered demi-god of Erard's thunder-proof horizontal seven-octaves." In the United States, De Meyer performed on two Erards, most likely alternating between two pianos placed back to back. This would have allowed both sides of the audience to receive an unobstructed view of the keyboard. Just before he left New York in February 1846, De Meyer received yet "another magnificent piano . . . manufactured expressly" for him by Erard, and he performed on all three grands at his first Philadelphia concert.[1]

Traveling with his own pianos assured De Meyer of quality instruments at a time when no American piano had yet achieved an international reputation. More to the point, American grands were still rarities, although by the 1840s square pianos were plentiful throughout the United States.[2] The splendid Erard grands became an important attraction in their own right and were praised as much for their luscious tone as for their endurance under the onslaughts of the pianist. Recognizing their promotional value, De Meyer spotlighted them in his advertisements, occasionally reaching implausible heights. In Pittsburgh he scheduled his first concert for the theater, as "the only apartment in the city large enough for his monster instruments." A Rochester advertisement boasted that he would use "one of his four magnificent Monster Pianos." Once, in St. Louis, the "monster piano" ploy backfired when De Meyer applied for a license to give his concerts, a requirement in many cities. According to one perhaps apocryphal story, the city authorities wanted to charge De Meyer $75, several times more than the average fee. "'Mein Gott!' cried the musician, 'shust for play mein piano two-tree night?' 'Why, yes,' said the functionary applied to, 'I know it's more than usual, but then, Mr. De Meyer, your piano is *such a large one!*'"[3]

Although transporting the pianos must have been a nuisance, only once did they impede the tour's progress. Upon arriving in New Orleans by steamer from Charleston, De Meyer could not announce his concerts because his pianos were still in transit, and "it was impossible to produce a piano in New Orleans which could withstand the electrical shock of his embodied thunder." The instruments used in Charleston were on their way by ground via Montgomery, and as a precaution pianos had also been dispatched by ship directly to New Orleans from Baltimore. De Meyer was in New Orleans a full week before the pianos finally appeared and he was able to schedule his first concert. After that ordeal, he reduced the number of pianos—now claimed to be four—he had in his caravan and advertised an "entirely new" Erard for sale "on account of the great inconvenience and expense of travelling with so many Pianos."[4]

The frequent moving and climatic changes must have taken a toll on the instruments. At the time, a European piano was acknowledged to have a better tone than

an American one, but it was more susceptible to severe shifts in temperature and humidity than its American counterpart, which usually had an iron frame. De Meyer's Erards were at least transported in special containers to protect them. When the pianos arrived in St. Louis ahead of the performer, they aroused the public's curiosity during the early days of the War with Mexico:

> De Meyer's *monstre* music box—his piano shell—stands outside of the Planters' House, and attracts very general attention. Some wag in New Orleans, while the strange looking affair stood outside of the St. Charles Hotel, wrote upon it in huge letters: "THIS BOX CONTAINS THE BODIES OF SIX MEXICAN OFFICERS"— an announcement which added considerably to the interest of the exhibition.

In addition, the pianos were probably tuned regularly. In Cincinnati they were "tuned, and the complicated mechanism kept in order, by the able Accordist, Mr. Klepfer." In St. Louis the "accordist" Mr. Groteguth was commended because his tuning was "able to withstand a two nights' battering . . . under De Meyer's *assaults.*"[5]

MANAGEMENT

Presumably Reitheimer, De Meyer's brother-in-law, assumed most of the managerial duties of the tour, although his name rarely appears in advertisements or public communications. Impresarios were not yet appropriating top billing and "presenting" artists, although they would soon want to share the limelight. De Meyer and Reitheimer traveled at a leisurely pace, arriving in new cities with no specific engagement and with little advance publicity. In Mobile, for example, the first announcement for the pianist's opening concert appeared just two days before the occasion, and even then the "particulars and place [were] not yet arranged."[6]

Reitheimer's first of several tasks in each city was to secure a location for the concert. Most cities had suitable buildings, ranging from concert halls and theaters to the meeting rooms of various societies and fraternal organizations. Occasionally hotel ballrooms and dining rooms, as well as churches, were commandeered for concerts, although not always successfully. When De Meyer appeared at the Planters' House, a hotel in St. Louis, one writer objected to the cramped quarters and poor sight lines because the pianist's "singular power requires corresponding space" and, with the performer hidden from some of the audience, "his characteristic energy loses one-half of its effect."[7]

After securing a hall, arrangements were made for the sale of tickets at music stores, bookstores, and hotels, as well as at the door. Tickets were for general admission with no reserved seats, a service that would not be common for another decade. Consequently, a local newspaper in New Orleans warned that "ladies should be early in their attendance if they would find choice seats unoccupied."[8]

Tickets were still one dollar, but their price might be reduced for additional concerts in the same city, and, for appearances in a theater, gallery seats might be as cheap as twenty-five cents.

The next stop for the manager was the newspaper office, where an advertisement was placed and perhaps an agreement made—accompanied by an exchange of money—for the publishing of an editorial calling attention to the forthcoming concert and the reprinting of reviews from other cities to stimulate public interest.

Although concert announcements do not always list them, local performers—most often vocalists—usually assisted De Meyer. A visit to a music store probably yielded him the names of resident professional musicians and even proficient amateurs who occasionally shared their talents with the public. The nonprofessional status of the latter was always emphasized and their identity safely guarded. It would have been too indelicate for a lady amateur in particular to have her name printed in the newspaper as if she were a common professional musician.

An occasional tactless encounter with these local performers was De Meyer's chief problem on tour. The first estrangement occurred in St. Louis, where De Meyer was assisted by members of the Polyhymnia Society, a recently organized orchestra. William Robyn, the society's musical director, "was appointed as a committee of one to visit all great artists and offer the service of the Polyhymnia to assist in their concerts." After performing the overtures to *Norma* and *The Barber of Seville* at De Meyer's second concert without remuneration, the society expected a favor in return, according to Robyn:

> I told [De Meyer] that our society was going to give a concert and we would be very much obliged to him if he would play one piece at our concert to help our society along. He said yes he would play one piece if we would pay him one hundred dollars. I told him it would be no more than right after assisting him in three concerts that he should play one piece for us. He burst out laughing, and said: "I did not ask you to assist me, you offered your services." With that I left and thought it a good lesson.

In Cincinnati, De Meyer antagonized another local performer, Joseph Tosso, the violinist famous for popularizing "The Arkansas Traveler." De Meyer "grossly insulted" him by "offering him a small sum for playing at his first concert."[9]

De Meyer was occasionally successful in developing friendships and denying his own self-interests for a noble cause. In New Orleans, he gave a benefit concert just two weeks after hostilities broke out with Mexico to provide the Louisiana Volunteers with "a fine Band of Musicians to accompany them to Mexico." In Cincinnati, he found an amiable partner in the cellist George Knoop, who assisted in two concerts there. Knoop, described as "ever ready with his violoncello—a cheerful volunteer on public occasions, and for the benefit of others, in a genuine spirit of good-nature and self-sacrifice," may have been a good influence on the pianist.[10]

De Meyer's final concert in Cincinnati was a benefit for Knoop and his singer-guitarist wife, and in a departure from his custom of using local artists, the pianist engaged Knoop to perform at his two Pittsburgh concerts.

CARICATURES CENSURED

While on the road De Meyer did not forget to inundate the press with his *Biography* and his prized caricatures that adorned his stationery and concert programs. Although most people blithely accepted their inherent silliness, a Cincinnati newspaper took exception to them and to De Meyer's method of distribution:

> We do not wish to detract from the just worth of this far famed pianist. We believe he is the "Lion Pianist" of the world. But what of that? There are, doubtless, thousands—yea, thousands in the world *almost* as big a lion as he, and not half as big an a—! We didn't say what. . . . He has insulted good taste by parading over the city, at the bookstores, and other places, caricatures of himself! Who ever heard of such an act by any well bred gentleman? A modest man, truly, thus to represent himself—to cause the stare and wonder of the multitude. The aristocracy of Europe are caricatured—he must be; the former by the mass, the latter by himself! We notice by one of his caricatures that to *his* head is attached a monkey, playing a piano with his tail! Admirable. Another has the head of the *Lion* Pianist and the body of a donkey! Most admirable.

In New Orleans a critic was "prepared for a clever display of talent, embroidered and bedizened with any amount of humbug," and the playbill adorned with a caricature confirmed his expectation:

> In looking over his programme . . . the first thing that arrested our attention was a cut exhibiting him in a most grotesque and equivocal attitude. It was not till after a second inspection of the pictorial illustration of the "bill of fare" that we ascertained that he was represented as sitting at the piano. . . . At a glance he might have been thought to be sitting on a rail as well, or perhaps undergoing the manipulation of a toothpuller. This woodcut, we suppose, he takes with him wherever he goes, to give a tragic aspect to his small bills, and to impregnate his audience with wonder as to what is in store for them.

Despite his initial skepticism, the critic was eventually won over by De Meyer's performance, and the "suspicion of humbuggery" gave way to the "acknowledged splendor of his acquirements."[11]

Certainly to De Meyer's delight, his concerts in New Orleans inspired another caricature, this time by the local artist Arthur Andrieu (figure 2.1). Above the opening bars of the *Marche marocaine,* De Meyer carries two of his Erard pianos slung over his shoulders, with Orlando Guilmette, the singer who appeared in the New

Figure 2.1. Caricature of Leopold de Meyer by Arthur Andrieu with the caption: "Drawn from Life by Andrieu, after the Lion gave his eighth Concert with extraordinary success at the St. Charles Theatre, New Orleans, April 1846." (MUSIC DIVISION, THE NEW YORK PUBLIC LIBRARY, ASTOR, LENOX AND TILDEN FOUNDATIONS)

Orleans concerts, perched on one of them. One of the pianist's hands is in a pocket of his trademark plaid pants; the other holds a moneybag inscribed with the names of recently fleeced cities—New York, Boston, Philadelphia, and New Orleans.

The Curious Concertgoer

The substantial press coverage De Meyer received—whether flattering or derogatory—sparked an interest in the public to attend his concerts. A Nashville paper speculated that even "those who cannot appreciate the 'concord of sweet sounds' will wish to see *the man* whose praises have so long filled the air." A New Orleans critic reported that "public curiosity has been powerfully stimulated to hear him, such marvels have been related of his performances." In Montréal, the newspaper believed that those citizens who did not attend his concerts would "betray a sad lack of taste and an inconceivable want of curiosity."[12]

People have always attended concerts for a variety of reasons. A critic for the *American Review,* writing about the influence of De Meyer, Bull, and Vieuxtemps, remarked that "too many of those who crowd the concert-room are probably attracted thither by motives somewhat foreign to music and the love of it." Dwight once observed that "concert-going has as many motives as church-going," and a Cincinnati writer, while describing the audience at a Thalberg concert, listed some

of them: "curiosity, vanity, art, fondness, or desire to be in the mode." Perhaps through their ability to attract concertgoers who attended for other than musical reasons celebrated artists like De Meyer and Thalberg had a significant effect on the general American public. Gottschalk believed the foreign celebrities appealed to an audience that, "through curiosity and fashion rather than from taste, made it a duty to go and see the lion."[13]

Much of this era's publicity, including De Meyer's, was specifically designed to attract the inquisitive. Undoubtedly the most famous publicist of the time was Barnum, whose strategy for promoting Jenny Lind relied on similar principles. The impresario Max Maretzek contended that Barnum did not care "whether she produced any enthusiasm as a songstress, provided she excited curiosity, as angel, woman, or demon." Maretzek believed that "public curiosity had been so industriously stirred up by [Barnum], that out of every five persons one would have been glad to hear, but four were restlessly desirous to see her." Furthermore, once a celebrity was able to attract large crowds, others began to wonder why so many were attending the concerts. A Buffalo newspaper held that "thousands listened to Jenny because other thousands did the same."[14]

Of course, the advertising schemes of De Meyer, Barnum, and others were frequently denounced as antithetical to the high artistic aims of music. A writer in 1854, criticizing the current method of concert-giving, believed one of the faults of the extravagant concerts then popular was that "mere curiosity and love of wonder among the people are appealed to, and not a legitimate desire for musical gratification. . . . Mere curiosity is easily cloyed, and those who go from this motive are soon satisfied. The desire for musical gratification, on the other hand, increases with indulgence, and thus is a permanent source upon which to draw." While curiosity may not have been the purest reason for attending a concert, it did encourage some people to be introduced to a new world of music. Several writers disagreed with the cynical judgment of curiosity expressed above. While De Meyer was in New Orleans, the *Daily Picayune* maintained that "the first curiosity which was felt to listen to the great musical prodigy, has given place to a profound admiration of his science and skill."[15]

Reception

Whether as a result of curiosity or purely musical interest, large audiences routinely gathered to hear De Meyer in the nineteen cities he visited on his tour. Attendance reports of "immense throngs" and halls "crowded to suffocation" were consistently favorable if annoyingly vague and perhaps exaggerated.[16] Roughly half the cities visited by De Meyer enjoyed more than a single concert, one indication of success for a performer. He gave two concerts in five of the nineteen cities, three concerts in Mobile, St. Louis, and Cincinnati, and five in New Orleans.

As a city with a rich musical tradition, New Orleans was the site of one of De Meyer's biggest triumphs in the United States. The local musicians serenaded him—a genuine sign of respect, since professional musicians do not give away their services to just anybody—and his concerts were packed. At his first concert (16 April 1846), the fifteen-hundred-seat hall was "completely filled—every passage being entirely blocked up by persons unable to find seats" and many people "went away not being able to obtain even standing room." The second concert was "crowded to overflowing," and at his fourth, the "stage was filled with ladies and gentlemen," who had accepted his offer to become acquainted with his touch.[17]

De Meyer was eagerly received by critics and audiences alike with few exceptions. One New Orleans critic was "lost in unqualified astonishment and admiration" during the concert and while writing a review had "scarcely yet recovered calmness and *sangfroid* enough to analyze the merits of this extraordinary pianist. . . . The extravagance of the New York press which declared that the piano seemed actually to wail, sob, shriek or groan beneath his touch, ceased to strike us as absurd or hyperbolical." In Toronto, he "was greeted with a perfect storm of applause . . . at the close of each of his pieces." One critic there had "never before . . . witnessed such enthusiastic demonstrations of feeling on the part of any audience." William Cullen Bryant recorded an unusually spirited reception in Buffalo in one of his occasional letters to the *New York Evening Post* as its editor. Although Bryant did not attend the concert, it was an item of conversation on the steamer from Buffalo to Chicago the next day:

> I saw no occasion to be surprised at what I heard of the concert of Leopold de Meyer, at Buffalo, the night before. The concert room was crowded with people clinging to each other like bees when they swarm, and the whole affair seemed an outbreak of popular enthusiasm. A veteran teacher of music in Buffalo, famous for being hard to be pleased by any public musical entertainment, found himself unable to sit still during the first piece played by de Meyer but rose, in the fullness of his delight, and continued standing. When the music ceased, he ran to him and shook both of his hands, again and again, with the most uncomfortable energy. At the end of the next performance he sprang again on the platform and hugged the artist so rapturously that the room rang with laughter.[18]

Amid the endless accolades regarding De Meyer's unsurpassed technical skill lurked an intermittent dissatisfaction with his repertoire. While a few eastern critics might have preferred less bombast and more Beethoven, the general public often found De Meyer's music too complex and desired more familiar tunes clad in a simpler style. A Cincinnati critic believed that it required a "musical taste, educated far beyond the ordinary standard, to appreciate the skillful and scientific combinations of de Meyer." Predictably, the people voiced a preference for his versions of

"Hail, Columbia" and "Yankee Doodle" (and, in Canada, "God Save the Queen"). In Louisville his variations on American tunes "seemed to create quite a sensation, showing that it suited the taste of the audience much better than the tunes and airs which he brings from his native country."[19]

A consternation with the repertoire of these traveling pianists would be a recurrent theme during much of the century. Although it is fashionable today to deride the compositions of De Meyer and other virtuosos, their music was often beyond the comprehension of the many Americans who had had little opportunity to hear cultivated music.

CHAPTER 3

The Lion Tamed

D̶e Meyer had enjoyed a prosperous debut season in America. He had traveled to at least twenty-four cities and given more than sixty-five concerts, most of them well attended. There was no reason to doubt that another year could be almost as successful. During his first season, however, he had been a novelty and had had little competition from other virtuosos. In the fall of 1846, the unexpected arrival of the famed pianist Henri Herz sent De Meyer scurrying to the South in advance of his potent new rival. Even before that threat, his new season had begun ominously with allegations of his scandalous publicity maneuvers and malicious acts toward his fellow musicians.

PUBLICITY TACTICS UNVEILED

On the day of De Meyer's first New York concert of the 1846–47 season, a lengthy newspaper article exposed the crafty manner in which the pianist had arranged publicity for his American tour. Further indictments concerning his manipulation of the American press were soon forthcoming. If the reports came as a shock to the general public, they were no surprise to the musical community. By the time the pianist arrived in the United States, the publicity machinery for such an artist was already in place and well oiled. The daily newspapers, in particular, were considered the key to success and their support—in the form of rave reviews and lavish editorials

The Publicity Game

A "musical connoisseur" furnished the following detailed report of the preparations De Meyer had supposedly made before his arrival in America:

He begins the game at least two years before we have the felicity of seeing him on our shores. No expense is spared in puffing. The London press, which is just as venal as any other London commodity, is glutted with "puffs." These "puffs" are carefully "cut out" and reprinted (in most cases without consideration) by American newspapers precisely in the same manner as a quack doctor puffs himself in the *advertising* columns of one paper, cuts out the paragraph, publishes it in another, giving credit to the first, as if the article had been *editorial* opinion. The artist, moreover, publishes extensive biographies of himself, adventures with kings, emperors, sultans and women, illustrated with engravings, in some of which he is the fine and accomplished gentleman, as well as artist, while in others he is made to figure in rather a ludicrous light; by this means removing from the minds of the envious all ideas of his personal vanity.

In short, biographies and pictures, paragraphs to suit all palates, both grave and gay, do the work.—Who is there among us that can tell fine music from very fine? Not one in a thousand; and should this one lift his warning voice who would attend to it? When all was "fixed" for his advent the man himself comes over—opens his huge Paris piano—closes one eye in a knowing wink, and leeches us to perfection. Well, we are willing to bleed once for the curiosity of the thing, but we don't want to be bled dry.

New York Evening Post (2 October 1846)

("puffs")—had to be bought. A New York correspondent to the *Musical World* in London held that Ole Bull's outstanding success a few seasons earlier was due to the "skillful manner in which he made the American press serve his purpose," which "must have cost him a mint of money." In contrast, Vieuxtemps, who was in America at the same time as Bull, "did comparatively nothing in the United States" because he failed to pay for publicity. The correspondent then remarked on De Meyer's status:

The art of puffing was never so transcendently developed as by Leopold De Meyer. . . . You would imagine that a man of De Meyer's unquestionable talent stood in no need of such charlatanic aid; but I can assure you it is absolutely necessary in America. Without it, nothing can be done; the finest talent, for want of it, will be neglected. Nothing, indeed, can surpass the despicable corruptibility of the American press. For one line of truth there are a dozen lines of falsehood, in almost every paper.

The *Musical Gazette* of Boston confirmed the assertions of the preceding report:

> The corruption of the city daily press is almost past belief. With regard to musical matters, not the slightest confidence can be placed in the statements of any of the prominent papers in the great Atlantic cities. They are entirely bought up by interested persons, and no falsehood is too great for them to publish, provided they are well paid for the service. The statements in the correspondence are true to the letter, as every one versed in city musical operations well knows.

A Philadelphia newspaper also agreed: it was wary of the seemingly inflated reports of De Meyer's abilities because the "praise bestowed in the newspapers of New York is always received with caution, for it is well known how they make reputations, and what is the consideration." The widespread, unscrupulous practice was not soon eradicated, either. When Rubinstein toured the United States in the 1870s, a music journal maintained that "even he is overpraised by the men who style themselves critics, but are in reality 'puffers,' at so much per puff. They abound in New York."[1]

At least one episode in New York revealed De Meyer's collusion in the puffing assembly line. One writer, Charles Burkhardt, took De Meyer to court for not paying him for a series of articles he had translated to be used as puffs. Burkhardt sued only for the payment of one fee among many—the sole transaction with witnesses—and won in a jury trial.[2] The performers were not solely responsible for the appalling circumstances: the press had to share the blame for its version of journalistic blackmail. The *New York Herald,* an unfailing supporter of De Meyer, was often criticized for its alleged policy of demanding a fee before giving its backing to artists. The *Morning Courier and New-York Enquirer,* for example, decried the "ridiculous and fulsome puffs of [De Meyer] which have appeared continually in the *Herald,*" and condemned the "shameless venality of this notorious sheet." The rival paper held that it was "well understood to be *prima facie* evidence that an artist is a humbug if he be puffed by the *Herald.*"[3] De Meyer appears to have had an exceptional relationship with the *Herald,* with its publisher James Gordon Bennett, and, more important, with Bennett's wife, the paper's occasional music and drama critic. The pianist dedicated his *Airs nationaux américains* to her in the fall of 1846, and the *New York Evening Mirror* provocatively accused Mrs. Bennett of accepting from De Meyer a diamond bracelet, a valuable watch, and "other small favors, 'secret, sweet, and precious.'"[4]

Henri Herz, who was in New York sporadically from 1846 to 1849, ascribed the attacks on the *Herald*—the paper "most vigorously accused of blackmail"—to the jealousy of the less successful papers, and he believed the accusations against the American press in general were greatly exaggerated: "I can declare that as far as I was concerned I was never the victim of blackmail, even in the slightest degree. On

the contrary, the American journalists I saw were completely independent." The *Evening Mirror* also doubted that very many musicians could bribe the press because "few artists can afford it."[5] In any event, the periodic discussions of De Meyer's questionable relations with the press supplied journalists with a juicy topic but did little to tarnish the pianist's reputation with the music-loving public.

De Meyer and Reitheimer also mastered other means than the newspapers to produce successful concerts, or at least those that appeared so. The pianist became notorious for the bouquets of flowers he received at his concerts, and it was generally understood that he orchestrated their presentation, despite his feigned astonishment at receiving them. Once when "his female admirers, as usual, showered bouquets upon him," he created "not a little amusement on his encore, by raising one to his lips when his right hand had half a bar rest." The *Morning Telegraph* wondered sarcastically, "What in the world was the audience tittering and chaffing about, when he received those bouquets? Surely a man has a right to receive his own bouquets, if he is fond of flowers."[6]

One method to ensure a frenzied response by an audience was to hire a claque, although its purchased enthusiasm was often all too obvious. For one of De Meyer's concerts, a critic believed that a "great number of free tickets [were] given to *claqueurs*," and the *Evening Post* complained about the pianist's "friends," "the club of Germans in the gallery" who "did not applaud in the proper places, and consequently spoiled all the music, and made themselves supremely ridiculous."[7]

DEADHEADS

One of the worst forms of publicity for a performer was a newspaper report of a poorly attended concert. Many people were reluctant to venture to hear an artist unfashionable with the public, but as William Mason explained when describing De Meyer's concerts, "the piano-lovers were not so numerous then as they are now, and it was difficult to fill the hall, even with the help of deadheads."[8] "Deadhead" was the distinctive American colloquialism coined just a few years before De Meyer's arrival in the United States to refer to anyone who was admitted free of charge to theaters and concerts as well as railroads and other modes of travel.[9] To ensure full houses, free tickets were often given to friends and even total strangers in addition to critics and members of the press. Supposedly the news of a crowded hall would encourage people to investigate—with the help of cold cash—the subsequent concerts of such an apparently popular performer.

As early as 1838, an article titled "The Way to Give Concerts in America" satirized the "easy practicability of making *charlatanism* succeed where genuine talent is neglected," and gave advice on how to fill a concert hall with deadheads, although they had yet to be christened with their name:

When you announce your concerts, send at least one hundred and fifty tickets to the press—dine with the editors—call upon all lovers of music who don't know you. . . . While you are introducing yourself among the people to secure a good attendance at your concerts, give to a friend who has a wife and daughters *one* ticket, and he will be under the necessity of buying several more; be sure to give away enough to fill the concert-room, if you feel doubtful of your hold upon the public favor. This will cause a jam, and give you an opportunity to repeat your concert, and to announce that "those who purchased tickets for your first concert and were unable to get admission, will be admitted with the same at the second;" (this will be all *hum[bug]* of course.).[10]

While he managed Thalberg and the Academy of Music in 1857, Bernard Ullman employed three men to select names from the city directory and mail "free tickets to doctors, clergymen, politicians, and journalists, etc., in order to give the house an appearance of increasing popularity and a thriving business." The "financial prosperity" of Thalberg's first concerts in Boston was attributed to the "very liberal distributions of free tickets to persons not likely to feel able to go at their own charges. It is said that [Ullman] gave away a thousand the first night, and five hundred the second, and that after that the hall filled itself with good paying people."[11]

The use of deadheads endured for decades, and is still with us, though now known as "papering the house." *Dwight's* New York correspondent writing in 1862 believed the "dead head system is carried to such an extent in this city, that when I meet a person at a place of amusement, I decide, until I have absolute proof to the contrary, that he belongs to the noble army of D. H.s." In 1873, William Steinway complained that he was "overrun with applications for deadhead tickets" and for the opening concert of the New York Philharmonic that year, the president of the society, George Templeton Strong, confessed to his diary that "it would be indiscreet to enquire what was the percentage of deadheads."[12]

Although sometimes effective, the scheme had its drawbacks. "Deadheads are the most severe critics," Maretzek explained. "Any person who once goes to the theatre on a free ticket will sooner agree to pay for a $10 supper at Delmonico's after the opera than ever again give the entrance fee of $1."[13]

Uncooperative Artist

More damaging accusations than manipulating the press or staging ovations were made against De Meyer during his second season. The truth is difficult to ascertain with reports varying from newspaper to newspaper—the *Herald* steadfastly backing De Meyer, the *Morning Telegraph* lecturing him on his moral shortcomings, and others wavering between the two positions. The *Morning Telegraph,* his harshest critic, published a series of articles summarizing his devious activities and dubbed him the

Figure 3.1. "The Celebrated Racer, De Meyer, *(The property of G. C. Reitheimer, Esq.)* Winning the Great Fall Sweepstakes of 1846." This caricature of Leopold de Meyer (part man, part lion, part piano with the pianist's signature plaid pants) depicts him beating the violinist Camillo Sivori in a race for the concert public's patronage. (*Yankee Doodle* 1 [17 October 1846]: 18) (LITERATURE DEPARTMENT, THE FREE LIBRARY OF PHILADELPHIA)

"Lyin' Pianist." The most serious charge was that he attempted to sabotage the concerts of Charles Perabeau and Camillo Sivori. Perabeau, a New York–based pianist, had earlier served as piano accompanist for two of De Meyer's concerts and had performed *Le Désert* with him. More significantly, Perabeau had written a laudatory article about De Meyer soon after his arrival in the United States. The two pianists had had a falling out, probably when De Meyer replaced Perabeau with George Loder for a second performance of *Le Désert*. Ultimately Perabeau testified against De Meyer in the "puff trial," for it was an article on *Le Désert* by Perabeau that the plaintiff had translated. The web of deceit was by now quite tangled. Perabeau himself had already admitted plagiarizing an article from the respected *Blackwood's Edinburgh Magazine* as a puff for De Meyer that was published in the *Herald*.[14]

Sivori, the other performer whose concerts De Meyer was said to have undermined, was an Italian virtuoso violinist who had arrived in New York in late September and had the potential to usurp De Meyer's position as the leading musical celebrity (figure 3.1). The *Daily Globe* thought an "attack on Sivori began before he ever arrived in our country, and Leopold de Meyer was the originator and first cause of these attacks, and jealousy and narrow-mindedness prompted the Pianist." The *Musical World's* correspondent explained how the press dealt with the competition that the violinist posed for De Meyer:

The arrival of Sivori has been the cause of much disquietude in certain quarters. The "lion" loves to roar in solitude, and cannot abide even a growl from a brother lion. Accordingly certain of the venal press in his lionship's interest have commenced a regular warfare against the late comer. Sivori, however, is not without advisers, and De Meyer, owing to some personal peculiarities, has a considerable number of enemies. The consequence has been a counter attack upon De Meyer from that portion of the press that has not benefitted by his *largesses,* or at least not enough to satisfy them. Doubtless they expect to be most liberally rewarded by Sivori, who on the other hand, is shut out from the giant journals which have been bought wholesale by De Meyer at extravagant terms. Only when De Meyer has gone will these journals be open to a treaty with Sivori. . . . In the meanwhile, the American public believe the criticisms of these men, and is influenced by them!!!¹⁵

De Meyer billed his three New York concerts of the season (2 and 8 October and 3 November) as "Grand Musical Festivals," and in addition to the usual array of vocal soloists, he was assisted in each of them by George Loder and his orchestra of forty-two members. With no concerted works to De Meyer's credit, the orchestra offered his *Marche marocaine* and *Marche d'Isly,* both as orchestrated by Berlioz, the latter in its world premiere.

If some of the press now scorned De Meyer, the audiences still flocked to his concerts. Either the public did not know which scandalous reports to believe, or it did not care about such matters. If nothing else, the pianist received more attention than he ever had before. At the first concert, the *Courier and Enquirer* claimed that the "Tabernacle has rarely seen a larger, and never a more brilliant audience. . . . We heard it generally remarked among the musicians and amateurs, that great as he always is, on this night he was greater than ever." For his second concert, one journal believed "there could not have been less than three thousand present."¹⁶

When De Meyer returned to New York after two moderately successful concerts in Boston in mid-October, he began to cooperate openly with his fellow musicians, and the *Morning Telegraph* took some of the credit: "The effect of our moral lessons to the 'Lyin' Pianist' is beginning to be plainly perceptible. . . . We have already heard of his anxiety to wash his character clean." De Meyer lent one of his Erards for Sivori's performance of Beethoven's "Kreutzer" Sonata with Julian Fontana, a friend of Chopin temporarily in the New World, and the *Evening Gazette* was pleased to report that De Meyer showed "his kindness by introducing his brother and rival pianist, M. Herz, to all his influential friends with hearty commendation and requests for their good offices for him."¹⁷ In addition, his final concert in New York was a benefit for the German Society of New York. De Meyer continued his benevolence in Philadelphia, where he "kindly volunteered his services" for a Philharmonic Society concert, in which he conducted the orchestra in Berlioz's arrangement of the *Marche d'Isly* (figure 3.2).

Figure 3.2. Program for Leopold de Meyer's appearance with the Philharmonic Society of Philadelphia, 10 November 1846, which lists a performance of De Meyer's *Marche d'Isly* as orchestrated by Berlioz and includes the pianist's endorsement of pianos by E. N. Scherr. (THE LIBRARY COMPANY OF PHILADELPHIA)

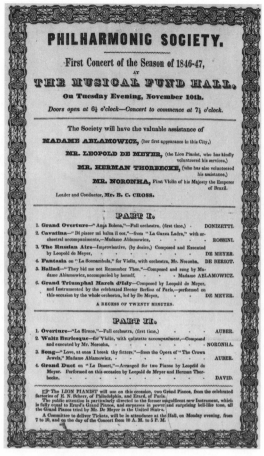

AMERICAN PIANO MAKERS COURT DE MEYER

If De Meyer had been tamed by the New York press, he immediately became involved in another controversy in Philadelphia. His endorsement there of pianos made by Emilius N. Scherr provoked the jealousy of two other local piano makers. In the advertisement and program for the Philharmonic Society concert, De Meyer declared that Scherr's piano on which he performed was "fully equal to Erard's Grand Pianos, and surpasses in power and surprising bell-like tone, all the Grand Pianos tried by Mr. De Meyer in the United States."[18] Scherr's ability to secure such an endorsement was a significant prize for an American instrument and symbolized the rapidly increasing craftsmanship of American piano manufacturers. There was a dispute, however, over what prompted De Meyer's judgment.

Although De Meyer had consistently performed on Erard pianos throughout his tour, American instruments had been used a few times in his concerts.[19] Most of those pianos, however, were squares relegated to accompanying singers. One maker who had furnished such instruments was Conrad Meyer of Philadelphia, who was incensed at De Meyer for championing Scherr's pianos and submitted a letter to the press. He whined that De Meyer had "never called at my store to try my fine pianos, and when repeatedly requested to call, ha[d] refused." He urged the public not to trust the pianist, for his endorsement of Erards was the result of a "large compensation," and similar testimonies—like the one for Scherr—were doubtless obtained

the same way. He recounted how De Meyer had already given a certificate to a Charleston dealer, for which the pianist admitted he was paid. In addition, De Meyer had spoken highly of Meyer's pianos in New Orleans, but Meyer had not paid for a written certificate because he "disdain[ed] such methods of obtaining a reputation" for his pianos.[20]

De Meyer's rebuttal discloses Conrad Meyer's desperate but futile attempts to obtain the pianist's endorsement. He claimed that Meyer and his friends had been "imploring and begging" him for a certificate ever since his arrival in America, but he had "invariably evaded the request." Moreover, when asked for a favorable opinion of his pianos by an agent, De Meyer had responded:

> I said that his Pianos were good enough as accompaniments to songs, &c., and appeared very well—alluding more to the cabinet work, than to their power and strength of tone. This verbal opinion was given frankly; and yet, to my infinite amazement, I found that Mr. Conrad Meyer had published circulars at the National Fair, in Washington, in which he claimed to have had an opinion from me, placing his instruments beyond and above all others. When I reached Philadelphia, he called upon me, conscious of the injustice he had done to me, and hoped I was not offended at what he had published, and that I would not expose him. . . .

De Meyer then reprinted a letter he had received from Meyer, in which his "sycophancy and flattery . . . contrast strangely with his present abuse and ill humor." Conrad Meyer verified De Meyer's statements but still accused him of fickleness in his choice of pianos.[21] De Meyer appears to have been sincere in his support of Scherr, for his pianos were the only American grands he used for solo pieces at more than one concert and in more than one city. Several more rejoinders appeared between Meyer and the pianist before the dispute—carried out in full view of the public—subsided.

This episode demonstrates that American manufacturers were sometimes relentless in their attempt to acquire the blessing of a celebrated pianist. Conrad Meyer was perhaps singularly frantic in his obsession for De Meyer to test his pianos, but other manufacturers probably besieged De Meyer and the pianists who followed him with such pleas, if perhaps more politely. John H. Schomacker, another Philadelphia piano maker who entered the debate, agreed with his fellow tradesman that the judgment of pianos should be made by such scientific organizations as the Franklin Institute of Philadelphia and not by biased performers compensated for their opinions. But Schomacker scolded Scherr, not De Meyer: "We feel sorry that Mr. Scherr should so far forget himself as to accept or court a certificate for publishing to an American public, which is full of arrogance and self-assuming authority."[22] Such courting would soon become standard practice for American piano manufacturers.

JOSEPH BURKE

While in Philadelphia, De Meyer forged a successful partnership with the Irish-born violinist Joseph Burke (1817–1902). They had both performed in a Philadel-phia Musical Fund Society concert the previous spring and had already appeared on each other's concerts in New York. The pairing of the artists must have proved con-genial, for Burke appeared in all of De Meyer's remaining concerts in the United States. This "apt and brilliant combination," as one critic described them,[23] became the first of several notable pianist-violinist teams to tour America: Herz and Sivori, Thalberg and Vieuxtemps, and Rubinstein and Wieniawski.

Burke had already had a sensational career principally as a child actor but also as a violinist and singer. After a decade of touring the United States, he had abandoned the stage to study and practice law in Albany. In 1844, however, he went to Europe to study the violin with the renowned Bériot and returned to America in the fall of 1845 as a polished violinist. He would later give the American premiere of Men-delssohn's Violin Concerto with the New York Philharmonic Society in 1849 and ap-pear with Jenny Lind during her 1850–52 tour of the United States.

Ignoring Burke's Irish birth, advertisements occasionally billed him as "the great American Violinist" or the "American Paganini." An American heritage might make the public take pride in his playing, but it would not necessarily draw more people to hear him, since audiences were more interested in foreign-born artists than in home-grown talent. A New Orleans critic boasted with patriotic fervor that, after lis-tening to Artôt, Bull, and Vieuxtemps among others, he could declare Burke the greatest violinist he had heard. Yet he was concerned that the violinist's modesty would be detrimental to his career: "A little more assurance, or impudence, to call it by its true name, would be more apt to catch the vulgar gaze, and consequently stretch the purse a little longer. Ole Bull knew this well, and indeed, the 'Lion' is no novice in the art."[24]

Burke was an ideal complement to De Meyer not only in his unostentatious plat-form manner but also in the "spirituality and sweetness" of his playing that was quite unlike the startling power of De Meyer, according to a St. Louis writer. A Cincinnati critic contended that Burke played "rapturously . . . not with his fingers and arm alone . . . but with heart and soul."[25]

This admiration for Burke's playing was directly related to his repertoire. He performed some of the standard bravura works by such virtuosos as Artôt, Bériot, Ernst, and Vieuxtemps, but he also played simple ballads dear to the American heart, like "Home, Sweet Home" and "The Last Rose of Summer." His own *Le retour en Amérique* contained "several of the sweetest American melodies, with variations, in imitation of the Flageolet, Guitar, Flute, &c."[26] This was music read-ily understood and enjoyed by audiences. For many, it was a welcome relief from the elaborate virtuosic literature of De Meyer.

FLIGHT FROM COMPETITION

After appearances in Philadelphia and Baltimore in November 1846, De Meyer and Burke abruptly ended their season in the East, which ordinarily would have lasted several more months. Their sudden departure for the South was no doubt prompted by the competition presented by the newly arrived Henri Herz. That De Meyer was agitated by Herz's surprise appearance in late October was suggested by De Meyer's antagonist, the *Morning Telegraph,* which hinted that Herz's presence at a concert had caused the pianist to play "worse than we have ever heard him play before." De Meyer had had no strong contender the previous year for the public's attention, and during the new season he had given two successful concerts in both New York and Boston before Herz appeared. The large attendance at his New York concerts, which had been "filled to overflowing" and "crowded to excess," had prompted the *Albion* to predict that De Meyer would "surely not be in haste to leave the United States while he continues to attract such audiences."[27]

Upon the arrival of the more famous Herz, however, De Meyer's prospects were no longer so promising. As a newcomer, Herz would have a decided advantage in attracting audiences. The New York correspondent to the *Musical World* in London reported on the threat Herz presented to De Meyer:

> Herz has already given a concert at the Tabernacle with great success, and the friends of De Meyer are in dismay. What is to be done? Herz is a novelty; De Meyer is no longer new. Herz has a name celebrated all over Europe; De Meyer is comparatively little known. All the amateurs play Herz's music; few professors, even, can play De Meyer's. Nothing is left, *on dit,* for De Meyer, but to pack up his portraits, his caricatures, his Erards, and his *chargé d'affaires,* and quit America ere the sun of his glory shall begin to set before the rising sun of his rival.[28]

De Meyer did not completely panic and retreat to Europe, but he tried to avoid any direct confrontation with his competitor by staying one step ahead of him. Only in Baltimore, where Herz suddenly appeared after postponing his Philadelphia concerts, did the two pianists engage in a conflict (over the storage of their pianos in the concert hall).[29] De Meyer wasted no time in giving himself a headstart in the rest of the country to prevent any further encounters with Herz: within a week of their Baltimore appearances, De Meyer and Burke left on their southern tour.

In his second tour of the interior, De Meyer concentrated his efforts on cities where he had been particularly successful the previous year, bypassed those which had warranted only a single concert, and appeared for the first time in Memphis and Nashville. His first stop after departing the East Coast in late November, however, was Cuba, which enjoyed a brisk musical life with a resident opera company and frequent visits from touring performers. He and Burke gave concerts in Havana and Matanzas, where "the success they obtained was colossal," before leaving for New Orleans.[30]

De Meyer's earlier popularity in New Orleans should have guaranteed the two performers large audiences, but foul weather thwarted their first two appearances. At the first, the cold weather was "severe enough to chill the most enthusiastic," and the expected crowd did not materialize. Perhaps because their first audience was so small, De Meyer and Burke opted to appear next at the St. Charles Theatre on a bill with two comedies. Such a combination of music and theater was not unusual, but De Meyer had not been forced to resort to such measures since his debut appearances at the Park Theatre. A heavy rain this time spoiled the attendance, and one newspaper reprimanded the local citizens for permitting the weather to keep them from a rare musical event: "We are aware that it is asking a good deal of our fair ladies to leave their comfortable firesides at night when the thermometer is at the freezing point, or to run the risk of wetting their dear little feet, in trudging through the rain. . . . But . . . they must consider that there is only one De Meyer in the world."[31] After another appearance on a bill with plays, the two musicians left New Orleans with less cash than they must have anticipated.

De Meyer and Burke's following concerts in Memphis and Nashville (where a "large part of the audience were forced to remain standing during the entire performance") were well attended, and their five appearances in St. Louis in March were the triumphs of their season. A reduction of ticket prices to seventy-five cents (with a lady and gentleman admitted together for only a dollar), a policy later followed in Cincinnati, was effective in drawing crowds. This markdown was not made quietly; on the contrary, the advertisements credited it to De Meyer's noble desire of "affording every facility to families, schools and students of the Piano-forte and violin."[32] The desire to fill up the house with paying customers was not mentioned.

The hall for De Meyer and Burke's first St. Louis concert was so crowded that a special announcement appeared for the next concert: "To prevent confusion and to avoid the possibility of a great number of ladies being unable to obtain seats, as was the case at the last Concert, they are respectfully requested to come early." For this second concert, the hall was "crowded to suffocation, and every piece was received with enthusiasm"; the third had an "overflowing assemblage." Such oversold houses were the occasional result of selling unreserved tickets at more than one location. For their fifth and final concert, they had to assure the public that the number of tickets would be "strictly limited to the capacity of the room."[33]

Amends were made between De Meyer and the Polyhymnia Society, which assisted him again at his first concert. De Meyer, now in a more cooperative mood, volunteered his services—perhaps at Burke's urging, given the cause—for a "Grand Concert for the Relief of Suffering Humanity in Ireland." The pianist continued his goodwill in Cincinnati, where he was once again assisted by George Knoop in two concerts, and he and Burke then volunteered their assistance for a concert given by Knoop.

DEPARTURE

De Meyer and Burke unaccountably cut short their season in Cincinnati in late April 1847, although De Meyer was in no hurry to leave the country. Burke returned to Albany, and in late May, De Meyer gave his final performance in the United States at a concert of the Philharmonic Society of Philadelphia. Within a few days De Meyer was in New York making arrangements for his departure and disposing of his pianos. He had already sold one, and he placed an advertisement for another Erard grand that had only been used in his New York concerts. The "magnificent instrument would cost $1200, imported," but it would be "sold at a comparatively low price" in consequence of De Meyer's "speedy departure."[34]

During his two-season tour of the United States and Canada, De Meyer had performed at least eighty-five concerts in twenty-six cities with considerable success. The New York correspondent to *La France musicale* claimed that "since Fanny Elssler and Ole Bull, no artist has gathered in a more glorious harvest in America than Leopold de Meyer."[35]

Although De Meyer frequently antagonized people—a few local musicians, several piano manufacturers, and some members of the press—he achieved a rapport with others. His alliance with Burke must have been harmonious, for the two performed together for six months. That neither musician continued to give concerts without the other suggests that they mutually agreed upon the dissolution of their partnership. In Philadelphia, De Meyer was particularly successful in finding acceptance. During his second season, he made two guest appearances with the Philharmonic Society, and at both he was honored by the musicians. At the first concert, the society gave him a "superbly wrought silver cup . . . ornamented with musical emblems and a design of a Lion playing on the Piano"; at the second he was presented with a crown.[36]

De Meyer's original compositions captivated the musical world surfeited with fashionable operatic fantasias. His flamboyant performance style excited a public with little experience in hearing exceptional piano playing. His outlandish publicity measures brought him much attention and undoubtedly created interest in his concerts among a wide range of people, although the publicity eventually lost him support in some quarters. Today, the caricatures of him and the accounts of his eccentric mannerisms have too often obscured the evidence that he was, above all, a virtuoso pianist.

When De Meyer left the United States from Philadelphia on 25 June 1847, he promised "his numerous admirers" to return in October 1868. He was to make good on that promise, returning exactly two decades later in 1867. By that time, however, the musical taste of many Americans had outgrown the Lion Pianist.[37]

PART TWO

Henri Herz

1846–50

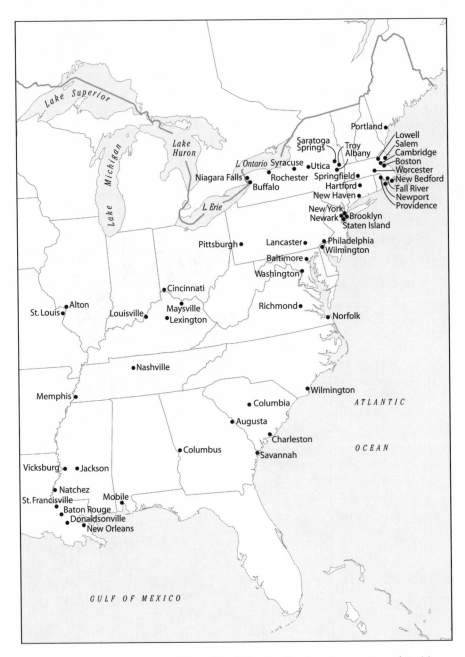

Map 3. Cities in which Henri Herz performed (excluding San Francisco, Sacramento, and Benicia, California).

Chapter 4

A Refined Parisian Pianist

Perhaps no pianist could have displayed a more noticeable contrast to De Meyer than Henri Herz (1803–1888). While De Meyer was an obscure newcomer, Herz, a decade older, had a well-established reputation as pianist, composer, teacher, and piano manufacturer. The former was flamboyant on stage; the latter was reserved. De Meyer was coarse and impetuous; Herz was the perfect embodiment of an elegant, self-composed, and refined gentleman. Herz quickly surpassed De Meyer in the American public's esteem during his sojourn in the United States, which included three seasons on the eastern seaboard and appearances in gold-rush California.

Herz had already achieved a fabulous success as a pianist in the Old World. Born Heinrich Herz in Vienna in 1803, he began studying piano at the age of four with his father and continued in Coblenz with Daniel Hünten, father of the pianist Franz Hünten. He entered the Paris Conservatoire as a child prodigy in 1816 and was later strongly influenced by the playing of Moscheles, who visited Paris in 1821. Herz emerged as one of the most celebrated pianists of the second quarter of the nineteenth century, and he was one of the reigning virtuoso pianists in Paris until Liszt and Thalberg partially eclipsed him in the mid-1830s. With the French capital as his base, he made numerous concert tours to Belgium, England, Germany, Spain, Poland, and Russia.

In addition to his career as a performer, Herz was a manufacturer of pianos, the builder and owner of an important concert hall in Paris, and an extremely popular teacher. He was professor of piano at the Conservatoire from 1842 to 1874, and also taught privately at a pace so strenuous that it became legendary. Charles Salaman, a former pupil, remembers having to squeeze his lesson into Herz's packed schedule at five o'clock in the morning. The magazine *Le Corsaire* quipped that Herz occasionally woke in the night and asked his *valet de chambre* if a pupil was waiting for him.[1]

Herz was even more famous as a composer than as a performer or teacher, and he was notoriously successful in the sales of his music. According to Loesser, Herz's compositions "sold more than those of any other composer whatsoever" during the late 1820s and early 1830s, and "publishers reputedly paid him four times as much per page as they did almost anyone else." Today, Herz's music is remembered primarily through the pungent invective of Robert Schumann. The overwhelming popularity of the virtuoso's works enraged the younger, idealistic composer and inspired him to help found in 1834 the *Neue Zeitschrift für Musik*. Writing twenty years later, Schumann remembered that "the state of music in Germany was at that time hardly gratifying. Rossini still ruled the stage; Herz and Hünten, almost by themselves, held the field in piano music."[2]

Schumann's contempt was driven by Herz's deliberate cultivation of the lucrative market created by the growing number of parlor pianists. Many of his compositions were simple pieces written specifically for the amateur performer: polkas, waltzes, rondos, and arrangements of popular tunes. By no means, however, did Herz's music appeal only to amateur pianists, nor were performances of it limited to the home. It was standard fare for many concert pianists during the 1830s and 1840s. Even Charles Hallé and Clara Schumann, two pianists noted for their crusades to program the most profound piano repertoire, included Herz's music in their early appearances, and Liszt still remembered a piece by Herz late in his life.[3]

Testimony abounds that Herz's music was widely disseminated throughout America before his arrival. A Philadelphia newspaper stated that "long has his music—from the instruction book to the concerto—been on every piano," and a Charleston paper asserted that there was "not a house, in which there are refined inmates, who play the Piano, in which *his music will not be heard!*"[4]

FIRST CONCERTS

As a household name, Herz could quietly ease into his American tour unconcerned about whetting people's desire to hear him perform. He arrived in Boston without advance notice on 21 October 1846 on board the steamship *Caledonia,* seventeen days after leaving Liverpool; his pianos arrived two days later on a ship from Le Havre.

Herz immediately observed the "national pride of the Yankee," when an American climbed aboard the ship and quizzed the pianist on how he liked America. "Isn't it a wonderful country?" the American asked. Herz could only reply with vexed amusement, "Wait at least until I get ashore." Despite the urging of Boston citizens to make his debut there, he continued immediately to New York, where his surprise appearance the following evening in the audience at a concert by Joseph Burke caused a "great sensation." Such an unobtrusive arrival immediately distinguished Herz from De Meyer and endeared him to many critics who had grown weary of the publicity tactics of the Lion Pianist and others. The *Tribune* was pleased that "Mr. Herz comes among us utterly unheralded, unpuffed, with no sounding of trumpets nor parade of great names."[5]

Herz claimed to have arrived in the United States without engagements or a manager, so he was quickly barraged with the "most enticing offers" from theater directors and concert managers. He rejected them all, wanting "to be free to follow [his] own fancy." Yet he wasted no time in scheduling his first concert, which took place in New York on 29 October 1846 at the Tabernacle, with three more following in quick succession in early November. George Templeton Strong recorded that the first concert was "not very crowded" since Herz had not been "preceded by the chorus of glorification, with jackass accompaniment obbligato" that had heralded other performers. Nevertheless, the pianist was enthusiastically welcomed by those in attendance. The *Albion* believed that "rarely has such continuous and universal applause been awarded to any Artist who has visited this country." The captivated audience repeatedly interrupted the rondo of his Second Concerto with bursts of applause and demanded—unsuccessfully—its repetition.[6]

During his second concert, the audience wielded canes, hats, and handkerchiefs to show their approval. At one point, when Herz was about to perform an encore, a gentleman, "whose patriotism and face were very much inflamed," was inspired to give a speech. He sprang up and

> waving his hand in the air cried, *"Honneur à ton beau talent! Honneur à ta——Honneur à ta——Ah sacre bleu, qu'est ce que c'est?"*—rapping at his forehead. . . . *"Bravo! bis! bis!"* cried a distinguished *savant*. . . . Thus encouraged, the gentleman in a state of French inflammation again rose and cried *"Honneur à ta modestie. Ah, c'est ça"*; and sat down evidently much relieved. . . . Herz then rose and said: "Gentlemen and Ladies: Since you have done me the honor to ask a second piece of me, I will play for you one which I wrote this morning—my first composition in America."[7]

Audiences responded so zealously to Herz's music not only because it was familiar but also because it was scintillating in its brilliance. Herz exploited the improvements in piano construction—in which he was involved himself—that facilitated

Herz's Story

Soon after his tour, Herz published a series of articles in *La France musicale* recounting his American experiences.[1] Written for a music journal, the articles concentrate on the state of music and musical institutions in the United States, and Herz occasionally manages to praise Americans in their musical interests and abilities. He was especially complimentary to the New York Italian Opera under Maretzek, the New York, Boston, and Philadelphia Philharmonic Societies, and the composer William Henry Fry.

When he revised the articles for a book aimed at a more general audience, Herz often glossed over musical issues to focus on the quirks and customs of Americans, with discourses on such topics as the American navy, the Quakers, slavery, and the unique custom of "shopping" without purchasing anything. His comments are telling in their often condescending attitude toward Americans and significant in how they reinforced stereotypes fostered by the spate of similar travelogues by European visitors. Although he commends the industriousness and hospitality of Americans, Herz refers to the American people as being "so naive at times, and so often infantile."[2]

The only claim Herz made for his book in its introduction was that the reader would find some "unerring glimpses of the art which I have studied all my life—that of the recreative anecdote." His reminiscences are indeed entertaining, primarily because he was more concerned with telling a good story than getting the facts straight. His version of the truth is often chronologically inaccurate, and some anecdotes are too ridiculous to believe. Too often taken as gospel today, his account was immediately recognized as partially apocryphal. One reviewer thought his stories would "gain him the reputation of 'drawing the long bow'"; Herz's characterization of the writing of other visitors to the United States—that they are "marked with a strong dose of exaggeration"—could easily be applied to his own statements.[3] A few of his tall tales will be recounted here from time to time, more for amusement than for information. Their credibility will be left to the discretion of the forewarned reader.

1. Herz, "Mes souvenirs de voyage en Amérique," *La France musicale* 15 (12 October 1851) – 16 (22 February 1852).
2. Herz, *Travels,* 38.
3. *Western Musical World* 4 (August 1867): 115; Herz, "Mes souvenirs," *La France musicale* 16 (4 January 1852): 413, free trans. in *The Musical Times* 4 (24 April 1852): 395.

rapid passagework. Notwithstanding its considerable technical challenges, Herz's music was never bombastic, but it was always delicate and elegant. Even more significantly, as one journal observed, his music was "not above the comprehension of common concert-goers."[8] Most of Herz's large-scale solo works were variations and fantasias on opera themes, another aspect that made them accessible. His *Variations brillantes di bravura sur le trio favori du Pré aux clercs*, Op. 76, typifies his style. Based

on a trio from Ferdinand Hérold's opera *Le pré aux clercs,* the work transcends its simple thematic foundation through a wide variety of figural variations, from nimble fingerwork in variation 1, to sudden shifts in range, articulation, and dynamics in variation 2, to interlocking chromatic chords and a cross-hand *tour de force* in variation 3 (example 4.1). Herz played the work frequently in the United States, occasionally with orchestral accompaniment, and it never failed to create a sensation. In San Francisco, the "spirited and brilliant manner" in which he performed it caused him to be "frequently . . . interrupted by a burst of applause," and certain portions of the audience were "unable to restrain themselves." The *New York Herald* thought it was "one of the sweetest gems" among Herz's works, and the piece inspired the *Courrier des Etats-Unis,* the French-language newspaper in New York, to pronounce Herz the "king of the variation." Dwight believed it was a "spirited and graceful composition, with more unity, more systematic and significant development than we sometimes find in his too ingenious and unnaturally elaborated strings of variations." Moreover, it "combined all his brilliancy, delicacy and variety," and allowed the audience to be dismissed "exquisitely satisfied, if not deeply moved."[9]

While in America Herz also performed his fantasias on Donizetti's *Lucrezia Borgia* and *Lucia di Lammermoor,* Bellini's *Norma* and *I Puritani,* Auber's *L'Ambassadrice,* and Méhul's *Joseph.* With guest artists he presented several of his own works for two pianos based on Rossini's *La donna del lago* and *William Tell,* Meyerbeer's *Il crociato in Egitto,* and Auber's *Le Philtre.* In addition, he composed works based on American patriotic songs and minstrel tunes. Despite his music's popularity with the public, the critics soon tired of its superficiality, though they acknowledged Herz's contribution to the expansion of piano technique and many had to admit his works possessed a certain amount of charm. Even Dwight conceded that Herz's music "may be useful in the way of pleasure, such as one can very properly afford himself sometimes in going to see fire-works."[10]

There was hardly a dissenting voice, however, when it came to appraising Herz's technique. Everything Americans had heard about him for the last two decades was amazingly true. His performances were not only immaculate but also graceful and effortless. Herz's strain-free presentations were worlds apart from the intense writhings of De Meyer. The performance styles of the two pianists were inextricably wedded to their own music: while De Meyer's *Marche marocaine* provoked strong visceral responses, Herz's delicate variations on tunes such as "The Last Rose of Summer" appealed to the sentimental emotions easily aroused in nineteenth-century audiences. Their different styles and effects on audiences were aptly summarized by a critic from Mobile: "De Meyer may break a piano, but Herz can break a heart."[11] The public who had been whipped into a frenzy by De Meyer's energetic performances now basked in the calm playing of Herz. Some perhaps were even a little embarrassed for having become so readily infatuated with the earlier pianist and now did

Example 4.1. Henri Herz, *Variations brillantes di bravura sur le trio favori du Pré aux clercs,* Op. 76, (a) Theme, mm. 1–8, (b) Variation 1, mm. 1–6; (c) Variation 2, mm. 1–6; (d) Variation 3, mm. 1–6.

not hesitate to criticize him in light of their new discovery. Nevertheless, as writers compared and contrasted Herz and De Meyer, most acknowledged their differences and only occasionally gave one priority over the other.

Herz's cool manner, however, was not to everyone's taste. The *Tribune,* after extravagantly praising his technique, demurred: "But we must confess that we were not excited by his playing; nor did it seem to be any part of the effect at which he aimed to rouse his hearers—rather to subdue, delight and soothe them." The *Albion* also had qualms, believing that, although his *"andantes* are given with much feeling

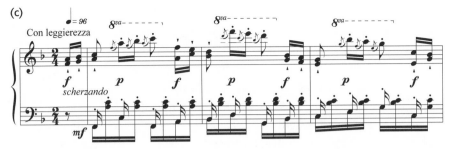

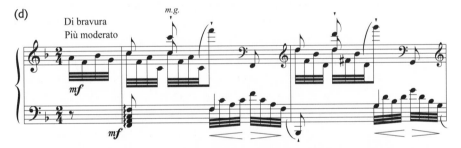

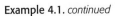

Example 4.1. *continued*

and expression, . . . deep and thrilling passion is by no means a characteristic of his performance—indeed it would not be in keeping with his compositions."[12] Herz's execution was so remarkable, however, especially when he was performing his own works, that few people were able to find fault.

In addition to his solo pieces and the usual array of assisting vocalists, Herz regularly showcased his concertos and other works for piano and orchestra in his appearances in the larger eastern cities. These were often greeted by the musically sophisticated with more favor than his formulaic variations. The *New York Evening Mirror* considered Herz's Second Concerto a "composition of rare merit," and Richard Grant White in the *Morning Courier and New-York Enquirer* praised its orchestral writing and its "beautifully chaste" style. It was not, he declared, "one of those flimsy combinations—called concertos by some modern performers—composed of rapid airs with humdrum accompaniments and unmeaning cadenzas, and which might as well be played commencing at the middle or the end, as at the beginning."[13] Herz also performed his relatively new Fourth Piano Concerto (he would write four more) and three of his other works for piano and orchestra, one based on the march from Rossini's *Otello*, another on the march from *William Tell*, and one on the trio from *Le pré aux clercs* already discussed.

The orchestras supporting Herz were of varying quality and size. For his debut the orchestra was billed as "select"—a typical phrase—and White thought "it was small enough to have been more select."[14] One of Herz's few run-ins with the local musical establishment was in choosing conductors for his orchestra in New York. Herz selected Michael Rapetti, the conductor at the Astor Place Opera House, for his first two concerts. In an apparent attempt to involve as many local performers as possible, Herz then engaged the pianist George Loder, who occasionally conducted the New York Philharmonic Society, as the conductor for his next two concerts, and consequently bruised the overly sensitive ego of Rapetti. In a paid advertisement in the newspapers, Rapetti accused Herz of choosing Loder because a powerful faction with press connections had threatened to sabotage his concerts if he did not do so. Rapetti also believed the reason Camillo Sivori was attacked by the press was because the violinist had steadfastly used him as his conductor and had not capitulated to the clique. Rapetti feared that the sudden change in conductors would imply Herz was dissatisfied with his work. He claimed that Herz admitted that influence "was brought to bear upon [him] with such force and power—with such threatenings of storms, tempests, and the exterminating wrath of the press," that he found it "impossible to resist." In a second public communication, he quoted Herz as telling him:

> I assure you that I have been actually forced to take Loder, by the importunities of his friends and that even this morning, Loder himself was here to torment me, until I yielded; nor can I repeat enough that my preference in all respects, is for yourself; in

proof of which I shall take you again for my fourth concert, which will do him more harm than good, by showing that I was dissatisfied with him. This, of course, must be a secret between us.[15]

Both Herz and Loder rebutted the charges, and the *Evening Mirror* among other newspapers answered on Herz's behalf. It praised him for not yielding to the "scandalous monopoly" held by some local musicians. It decried the "instances where popular artists in this city have refused to sing, because certain great performers refused to engage them for every concert they gave. In some cases they have gained what they demanded, through the means of powerful friends upon the press."[16] Herz escaped unscathed in the controversy, for the public was simply too enraptured with his playing to allow some petty squabble to interfere with their pleasure of hearing him perform. Rapetti fared reasonably well, too; he performed with the pianist again less than two months later.

WORKS FOR MULTIPLE PIANOS

Herz's first concert after dismissing Rapetti (10 November 1846) was perhaps his best attended one, no doubt as a result of his programming the Overture to Rossini's *Semiramide* arranged for sixteen pianists on eight pianos (figure 4.1).[17] Herz may have been more refined than De Meyer, but he was no stranger to musical sensationalism. Such works for multiple pianos had been extremely popular in Europe for a couple of decades, and it seems that everyone participated in them sooner or later, no matter how lofty his standards. Friedrich Kalkbrenner, Ferdinand Hiller, Ignaz Moscheles, Johann Pixis, Thalberg, Liszt, even Chopin and Clara Schumann, albeit in the early stages of their careers, were all guilty of succumbing to the thrill of performing en masse with their colleagues. The works were fun for audiences and for the performers, too, and no one pretended they were art. Although such arrangements were not totally unknown in the United States, Herz appears to have been the first to introduce them here to any great extent.

The concert was standing room only in the cavernous Tabernacle, and many people were turned away at the door. Several papers claimed it was one of the largest crowds ever assembled there, and the *Evening Mirror* estimated an audience of 2,600 to 2,800. George Templeton Strong found the crowd "insufferable," the heat "intolerable," and the air nearly asphyxiating. Despite the poor conditions for the audience, the performance "produced prodigious enthusiasm" and was "long and loudly applauded." Even such an exhibition, however, failed to suppress a frequent nuisance of concert life—the premature exodus. The *Herald* upbraided the more than one hundred people who had "no considerations of decency towards the performers, nor charity for the ears of the thousands present." Ironically, some of the early leavers, who saw just a few minutes of their time as invaluable, were the same ones who had claimed a prime seat an hour before the concert began.[18]

Figure 4.1. Excerpts from program for Henri Herz's concert in New York, 10 November 1846, which included a performance of Rossini's Overture to *Semiramide* arranged for eight pianos and sixteen pianists. (MUSIC DIVISION, LIBRARY OF CONGRESS).

If the keyboard extravaganza was generally popular with the audience, it did not find favor with the critics. The *Evening Mirror* pronounced it "entirely ineffective," for it was "only tolerably well performed," and besides, the eight pianos produced nothing but a "heavy monotony of sound." The *Morning Telegraph* believed the pianos were not well tuned with each other and hoped that a few of the performers would "mind the conductor's arm and baton a little better on the next occasion." Nevertheless, the work was repeated several days later. Richard Grant White, who thought the arrangement pointless, sarcastically described the second performance:

> Quite a long funereal procession ascended the platform, marching two and two. We observed that it consisted of fifteen of our most esteemed professors of the piano forte, and M. Herz, who, preceded by Mr. Loder as chief mourner [i.e., conductor], appeared to bury the poor *Semiramide* in eight of M. Herz's queerly shaped piano fortes, which were scattered over the stage, making it look like a coffin-maker's exhibition at a National fair.[19]

Ignoring the gibes from critics, Herz programmed such works wherever he could muster enough pianists, giving more than ten performances of them in six American cities.[20] Once introduced to America, multiple-piano works quickly established themselves in the repertoire, especially as a staple in concerts at female seminaries.[21]

Herz's success and the attendant financial windfall he experienced during his opening performances made the news back home. *La France musicale* reported that Herz's four concerts in New York had a net profit of "THIRTY-EIGHT THOUSAND FRANCS!" (more than $7,500) and stated that "a draft, on Rostchild, of 32,000 francs, which we have seen and touched, testifies better than a journal article of the triumphal reception that Henry Herz received in the capital [*sic*] of the United States." Herz disingenuously stated that his decision to visit America was "partly to obey my natural inclination to travel and partly in answer to the frequent pleas that I allow myself to be heard in the United States."[22] But everyone knew the most important reason was money.

Bernard Ullman

In his memoirs, Herz claims that it was the plan of his new manager, Bernard Ullman, to perform as often as possible multiple-piano works, which Ullman called "financial music" and which Herz admitted "had the gift of drawing crowds . . . everywhere in America."[23] Herz was surely not so innocent, for he had participated in such performances in Europe, and he doubtless brought with him to America the music of at least the *Semiramide* arrangement.

While giving his first series of concerts in New York, Herz was so besieged by "solicitations of all sorts" that he left his hotel for two days to hide from them.[24] Somehow, Ullman, a recent Hungarian immigrant who was just beginning his managerial career, was able to obtain an audience with the pianist and, as a result, would significantly alter the course and overall tone of the pianist's tour. Herz recounts the aggressive interview of Ullman, who was a "very young man who pursued wealth as everyone in America does." Though lacking in experience, Ullman persuaded Herz that he knew "how to get things done":

> Try me. I will take care of the concert posters, I will have your programs printed, I will see that everything is in order in the hall where you hold your concert, I will present you favorably to the newspaper editors. The newspaper is the key to artistic success, just as money is the key to success in war. If you wish it, I will give you my advice on whatever steps I think useful to take, for it does not always suffice to have only talent to succeed.

Taken aback by Ullman's "good sense" and "conviction," Herz agreed to a trial period. He soon praised Ullman's "ability, . . . lively imagination, and . . . tact," and acknowledged that Ullman was an expert in fixing "public attention on the artist." Ullman quickly established himself as an effective, if controversial, impresario; he

remained with Herz for almost three years, coordinating all the planning and pub-licity for the pianist's tours. Although Herz frequently portrayed Ullman unsympa-thetically in his memoirs (the primary source for the caricatured view of the impre-sario today), he seems to have routinely followed his advice. By the end of Herz's four New York concerts, Ullman had completely taken control of Herz's affairs, as the pianist relates:

> One day Ullman came to tell me that we were to leave for Philadelphia, where *we* were to give a concert the next day; that the hall was rented, that the posters were up, that all the seats were sold in advance, that our trunks were closed, that our railroad tickets were bought, and that a carriage awaited us at the door to take us to the sta-tion. I had made it my invariable rule to obey Ullman.[25]

CLASH WITH THE LION

Ullman was not so well organized for Philadelphia as Herz reports. He had been un-able to reserve a hall there, which forced Herz to appear first in Baltimore between two concerts of De Meyer, who had managed to stay one step ahead of his rival. There the first and only direct confrontation between the two pianists occurred, and not surprisingly, fireworks ensued. A dispute erupted because De Meyer's pianos had been left in the hall overnight and were in Herz's way. The two pianists engaged in a brief but intense quarrel in the newspapers, amusing the populace and deliber-ately gaining more attention for themselves. De Meyer volleyed first, addressing his communication "to the public." He claimed that at six o'clock on the evening of Herz's concert, just when the "rain was pouring down in torrents," he had received a note from Ullman, as Herz's "servant," demanding that he remove his pianos from the hall immediately. Reitheimer supposedly approached Herz asking him to recon-sider, but "Mr. Herz observed that he should not interfere in the matter, and that whatever had been done by his servant was by his approval." De Meyer further charged that Herz, "with a most strange and vague idea of the proprieties of life," had tried to appropriate one of his grand pianos for a New York performance involv-ing eight instruments. De Meyer had been warned by telegraph in time to stop him.[26]

While Herz carefully remained aloof, Ullman responded. He admitted writing the note, but said he had warned Joseph Burke early in the morning that the hall's platform was so small that one of De Meyer's two pianos had to be removed. His note became necessary when no attempt was made to move the piano. As for the inci-dent in New York, Ullman held that De Meyer had offered the use of his pianos to Herz in the presence of witnesses, and when one of his pianos had been moved to the Tabernacle, Reitheimer "ordered it away just previous to the concert." De Meyer supposedly apologized to Herz in person for Reitheimer's action. As a parting blow,

Ullman alluded to De Meyer's supposed difficulties with other performers, including Thalberg, Sivori, and, in fact, "with every other artist who appears . . . to stand in his way." His actions were only convincing the public, Ullman argued, that De Meyer was forced to rely upon "other means for giving himself consequence than professional science."[27]

This squabble was particularly acrimonious because Ullman and De Meyer had already had one dispute. The *New York Morning Telegraph* stated that the pianist had previously quarreled with Ullman, "who had also been his friend." With his journalistic experience and newspaper connections, Ullman had apparently helped the pianist with publicity. Indeed, in one of the Baltimore communications, Ullman suggested that some of De Meyer's "present insolence may be attributed to the indignation" with which he had refused from the pianist a "gold snuff box as the price of a desired puff."[28]

When De Meyer replied, he denied Ullman's claims and accused Herz of exhibiting a "discourtesy unworthy of a true artist" and of hiding behind his agent. Referring the readers to the controversy with Rapetti, De Meyer believed Herz's character traits were "calculated, unhappily, at once to excite pity and contempt." De Meyer was incensed at receiving a "menacing note" from Ullman, who, "with a degree of impudence and presumption, I scarcely know which most to admire, desires me to refrain from any notice of his publication, under peril of being assailed by him in the press of New York, Philadelphia and Havana. This very simple minded individual has yet to learn that he has entirely mistaken the character of the undersigned."[29] De Meyer may not have been as brave as he sounded. Ullman unquestionably had influence with the press, and the fear that he could use it viciously may have prompted De Meyer to leave the East early for Cuba and the South, which he did within the week.

In the meantime, Herz's three concerts in Baltimore alternated with five Philadelphia performances, the latter including a guest appearance at a Musical Fund Society concert. Each of the first two Philadelphia concerts only attracted about five hundred people. To increase attendance Ullman displayed his knack for hyperbole by advertising that the next concert would be "on even a more magnificent scale than that produced by [Herz] at the Tabernacle in New York, which has been unanimously pronounced to have been the GREATEST MUSICAL FESTIVAL that has ever been presented to the citizens of America."[30]

An often repeated, if improbable, tale by Herz concerns Ullman's plans for a "political concert" in Philadelphia that would include such original works as a cantata titled *Homage to Washington,* a *Concerto on the Constitution,* and a choral work, *The Capitol.* Huge performing forces would be assembled, including five orchestras, all the military bands from Philadelphia, eighteen hundred singers, and forty pianists.

Herz claimed that "the bizarre, impossible things which Ullman could dream up with the hope of exciting the interest of potential concert-goers, now a little tired of music, would provide, I swear, the necessary material for any number of fantastic tales. . . . I more than once greeted an accounting of his latest project with a burst of laughter." Ullman's schemes were, according to Herz, based on his definition of music: "Music is the art of attracting to a given auditorium, by secondary devices which often become the principal ones, the greatest possible number of curious people so that when expenses are tallied against receipts the latter exceed the former by the widest possible margin."[31]

Herz succeeded in convincing Ullman not to pursue the political festival, if he indeed did propose it in the first place. Herz's last two Philadelphia concerts of the season (4 and 9 December), if hardly more magnificent than any New York concert, were still lavish, and included concerted works by Herz accompanied by an orchestra and the Overture to *Semiramide* performed by sixteen pianists. These attractions combined with a reduction in ticket prices drew about four thousand people to the first of the two concerts, and some ticket holders could not obtain seats. Herz claimed that upon leaving a rehearsal at four in the afternoon, people were already waiting in line to buy tickets and to claim seats—all unreserved—when the doors opened at seven for the eight o'clock concert. The room was crowded in minutes after the doors were opened, and it took Herz a quarter of an hour to make his way through the crowd to the piano. For his last Philadelphia concert Herz reported that "there were so many people in the hall when I came in to play that it was literally necessary to carry me in."[32]

Boston and Dwight

Herz moved on to Boston, though he had to postpone his first concert there after cutting one of his hands while washing them in a china basin.[33] His two Boston concerts (17 and 19 December) included an orchestra but no multifinger extravaganza, probably a wise decision for the more staid Bostonians. Dwight praised the "exquisite finish" of Herz's playing and believed the "precision and delicacy of his touch surpassed every thing we have heard." He was still rhapsodic about Herz's performances the following season:

> It seems almost impossible to conceive of anything more perfect than Herz's mastery of his instrument. His touch so delicate, precise, and forcible, individualizing every note, and economizing to the best purpose the material of beauty commanded by each key; his running passages so smooth and even, that a gentle breeze playing over the bending surface of a field of grain could not announce its presence by a more sure and uniform and quiet display of power; his admirable graduation of force and accent through the whole; his power of imparting life and lustre to every form of melody, till

the whole thing gleamed like burnished steel as it passed by you; and the accomplishment of all this with less show of exertion than it costs an ordinary player to perform an easy piece:—all this made real the imagination we have always had of Herz.

Dwight's comments on Herz's Second Concerto, however, cut to the quick of Herz's desire to be popular. His chief merit as a composer, Dwight thought, was the

> power of graceful appropriation for whatsoever unique and happy thoughts and forms of music are already popular, and the power of working them up into a progressive beautiful whole. . . . It must be acknowledged that there is less of original material, less of the deep and permanent poetry and soul of music in Herz than in either Thalberg, Henselt, Chopin, Liszt, or even Leopold De Meyer. Nevertheless he is a master.[34]

Herz returned to Boston after the first of the year to appear with the Boston Philharmonic Society (2 January 1847), who had assisted at one of his concerts and had postponed their own so as not to interfere with his. The society was just a few years old, but in Dwight's estimation it had recently transformed itself from a wind band that "by turns brayed out noisy overtures, or murdered unmeaning solos" to a "veritable orchestra" that could provide a "rare pleasure in the orchestral performances." Herz was also quite complimentary of the society, praising their "irreproachable" execution and their "intelligent audiences," who "admire with discernment the great and sublime beauties of the music of Beethoven and Mozart." The hall was completely filled some time before the concert began, and many of the audience members were "obliged to 'stand it out,'" according to the *Transcript,* and others went "into the neighborhood to borrow chairs." With the orchestra's improved abilities Dwight could exclaim, "With such an accompaniment what a treat was it to hear Herz!" The pianist displayed his usual flawlessness at the keyboard, and Dwight was impressed with his "perfect mastery of orchestral effects."[35]

Audiences—Amateur Pianists and Music Lovers

In only a few months Herz had endeared himself to his newfound American public and was praised with few reservations. To many concertgoers, Herz was already an old friend because they had been familiar with his music for so long. De Meyer was a virtual unknown before his arrival and to attract audiences relied as much on publicity as his technical ability, but Herz's longstanding fame as pianist and composer was all he needed. Dwight, for instance, was not surprised that Herz had drawn "by far the largest audiences ever commanded [in Boston] by any artist in the same line" because of his reputation:

> He had only to appear; his name, his compositions, his position in the musical world, had prepared for him beforehand numerous admirers, to whom it was too good a

thing to find him suddenly amongst them. "Variations *à la* Herz" have been the staple of parlor, school and concert playing for these twelve years back among us; and whole armies of misses now and misses once were curious to see how easy and how grace-ful a thing the author makes of what to them has been matter of much patient labor and indifferent success. With such a guaranty of interest every where, he could jour-ney like an emperor among his subjects . . . whose compositions are more known in cultivated circles than those of any writer. . . .

The views were the same from Boston to San Francisco, where *Alta California* later corroborated Dwight's statement about Herz's celebrity:

There is scarcely an amateur musician who is not familiar with the name of the com-poser, and fond of the productions of his rare genius—scarcely a piano that has not given a feeble echo of his Heaven-inspired thoughts. To hear this musical celebrity, then, perform his own melodies and give them all their force and character of which his soul is capable, was a treat which but few could resist the temptation of enjoying.

The *New York Evening Mirror* went one step further in its claim for Herz. Not only was his name familiar throughout the "whole length and breadth of this vast conti-nent," but his "music has extended a love for the piano-forte into tens of thousands of places where, but for it, that love would never have reached." "No man," the newspaper declared, "has done so much for the piano as Henri Herz."[36]

Few amateur pianists who had struggled through Herz's music would have denied himself or, more likely, herself the revelation of hearing a favorite piece performed by its creator. For instance, when Herz performed *La Violette* in New York, one critic believed it was "enthusiastically received" since it was "familiar to every person pres-ent."[37] Herz or Ullman was more than aware of that fact as is clear from their ad-vertising the inclusion of that particular work in a number of concerts: "In selecting the latter piece, with which every pianist is familiar, Mr. Herz believes to anticipate the wishes of every student of this instrument." Ullman further appealed to pupils of the piano in the pricing of tickets. After a couple of concerts in a given city, ad-vertisements often magnanimously stated that since Herz was "anxious to afford every facility to families, schools and students of the piano forte" to attend his con-certs, groups could purchase family tickets at two dollars for three people or three dollars for five people instead of paying the usual one dollar per person.

Herz's audiences, then, were unusually rich in amateur pianists, most of whom were probably women, who came for instruction and inspiration in addition to pure aesthetic enjoyment or simple entertainment. Even one critic, who believed Herz's music had contributed very little to "foster a love for the truly poetic in music," thought there were no better pieces for "young ladies who only desire to play so as to shine in the *salon*."[38] The procession of "misses now," to borrow Dwight's phrase, with Herz's

Figure 4.2. "Going to Herz's Concert; or a growing taste for music in the rising generation." (*Yankee Doodle* 1 [19 December 1846]: 130) (LITERATURE DEPARTMENT, THE FREE LIBRARY OF PHILADELPHIA)

piano methods tucked under their arms on their way to a concert of his at the Tabernacle was seen as a positive event in the eyes of many commentators (figure 4.2).

Of course, even those with no practical knowledge of the piano found plenty to appreciate at Herz's concerts. A New Orleans critic believed that the "thorough bred musician and the untutored ear of the million, are alike gratified by his performances." The writer and abolitionist Lydia Maria Child, a self-proclaimed music lover who professed not to understand the technical aspects of music, was surprised, however, at her enjoyment of a performance by Herz:

> I was enchanted, perfectly enchanted, with Herz's playing; the more so, probably, because I did not expect to be excited. Of course, I could not be otherwise than familiar with his long established reputation as artist and composer; but I supposed that his merits were of a kind to be more readily appreciated by professional musicians than by a simple lover of music like myself. Moreover, I had often heard his music executed; and though it is not always true of criminals, it is of music, that it is dead when it is executed. But when I heard Herz play his own compositions, I was carried away with unqualified delight.[39]

By contrast, Child had been astonished by but not impressed with De Meyer, who she thought expressed no feeling in his music. She was "vexed" by De Meyer, who was not a genius but "such an admirable imitation of it, that it might at times 'deceive the very elect.'" She bemoaned the "tendencies of the age," which produced "great whirlpools of complication" rather than speaking more simply to the heart.[40]

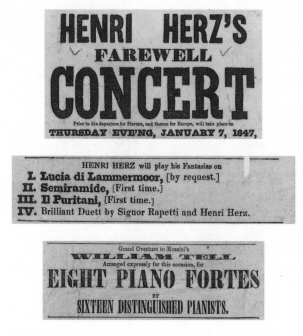

Figure 4.3. Excerpts from program for Henri Herz's concert in New York, 7 January 1847, which included a performance of Rossini's Overture to *William Tell* arranged for eight pianos and sixteen pianists. (MUSIC DIVISION, LIBRARY OF CONGRESS)

A FIRST FAREWELL

Although Herz remained in the Western Hemisphere for five years, he had received only a six-month leave of absence from his teaching post at the time of his arrival in the United States. After only three months in America, Herz was planning his farewell to New York because his request for an extended leave was not granted past April and he had plans to visit Cuba and the South.[41] If not for the denial of his request, he could easily have remained in the eastern cities giving concerts for several more months, especially with De Meyer's early departure from the scene in late November.

Herz's farewell New York concert on 7 January 1847 was a gala affair, with the Overture to *William Tell* for sixteen pianists, "The Prayer of Moses" performed by the Italian Opera Company in their first American appearance, and a profusion of candles in the Tabernacle in addition to the gas lights (figure 4.3). Herz recalls Ullman's reluctance to share with his client his idea for the candles, just one of his many promotional gimmicks. "You are the last person I would like to tell about it," Ullman admitted to Herz, "for I know from experience that you disagree with me on the proper ways to arouse public interest, and you can't be reasoned with too easily." Because the Tabernacle was so poorly lit, the candles were actually well received

instead of ridiculed. The *Gazette and Times* was thankful for the "judicious care in providing wax lights and suspending a large manifold lighter from the centre of the dome," which made "less than usual of the darkness visible, for which the Tabernacle is so disagreeably famous." Herz's version of the concert, in Philadelphia rather than New York, has a disgruntled audience member interrupting the performance because in counting the candles he had come up with eight short of a thousand. The Overture to *William Tell*, which was arranged for the concert by Hermann Saroni, received the brunt of the critics' complaints. The *Evening Post* thought it was "perhaps the least satisfactory of the performances," and the *Gazette and Times* found it "much better done than the former experiments with the *Semiramide* overture; it was, nevertheless, a failure."[42] As is often the case, critics rarely speak for the common person.

CHAPTER 5

With Sivori and Knoop ◟◉

H erz's projected three- or four-month tour of the South and Cuba before returning to Europe grew into a seven-month tour of the South and Midwest
ending in New York. In April 1847 Herz wrote from Natchez, Mississippi, to Hiram
Fuller, editor of the *New York Evening Mirror,* that the French government had
extended his leave of absence. Like De Meyer touring with Burke during the same
season, Herz also traveled with a violinist. He credits Ullman for the idea of "associating a magic bow"—that of Camillo Sivori—with his piano.[1] Sivori had performed with Herz in Europe and had made his American debut shortly before his
new partner.

CAMILLO SIVORI

Sivori (1815–1894) considered himself the successor to the spellbinding Paganini,
and, indeed, the early circumstances of his life seemed to anoint him for that role.
He was born in Genoa, the birthplace of Paganini, and the night of his birth, so the
now disproven legend went, his arrival was hastened by the thrill his mother experienced attending a Paganini concert. Sivori began playing the violin at an early age
and in 1822–23 studied briefly with the master himself. After his debut in 1827, he
made several short concert tours before his first major one in 1841—not coinci-

dentally the year *after* Paganini's death—that took him all across Europe and to Russia. He made his American debut five years later in the fall of 1846.[2]

The diminutive violinist (he was "scarcely five feet high") with large black eyes that were "lustrous and full of sentiment," according to the *Herald,* was eagerly greeted by Americans, despite their having already feasted a few years earlier on Artôt, Bull, and Vieuxtemps. The *Boston Transcript* called him "the little man with a great soul," and Dwight, who was scornful of mere pyrotechnics, declared "beyond a doubt" that Sivori was not merely a "wonderful performer," but a "great Artist."[3]

The almost unanimous praise lavished on Sivori was tempered by a brutal attack from Richard Grant White, the surly critic for the *Morning Courier and New-York Enquirer.* Besides finding numerous faults in Sivori's technique, White did not believe the violinist's claim that he was the "only pupil of Paganini," as he liked to bill himself, a declaration Paganini had substantiated in a private letter of 1828. Sivori documented his position by displaying lessons in Paganini's hand that the elder violinist had composed for him as his teacher. That was good enough evidence for most local musicians, and many eminent ones made protests on his behalf. White, however, classified the violinist as a "mere imitator" and did not believe that a "few lessons and MSS received in infancy" gave Sivori the right to "proclaim himself the pupil of Paganini." (Ironically, an acquaintance stated that Sivori later "admitted frankly that Paganini was probably the worst teacher of the violin who ever lived.") Two rumors attempted to explain the rationale for White's vindictiveness: either De Meyer had masterminded the attack on a newly arrived virtuoso invading his territory or White had not been sufficiently paid off by Sivori. As a lone voice, White had little impact on Sivori's reception, but the dispute preoccupied the press for weeks and smoldered into the next season.[4]

Sivori's appearances in cities other than New York (including Boston, Philadelphia, Baltimore, and Washington) had generally been successful. Nevertheless, he was probably relieved to join with Herz and place his immediate future in the hands of Ullman, who undoubtedly assured him that he would no longer need to fear the press.

Herz recounts Ullman's proposal for making their joint tour as profitable as possible using imagination and strategy, the latter as "indispensable to impresarios as to army generals":

> "Our great virtuoso Sivori will make his way through the West while our excellent master, Henri Herz, steers his course to the South, after which he will follow the western path of the former, who, in his turn, will gather laurels in the South."
>
> "Is it laurels you want me to gather?" Sivori asked.
>
> "Certainly," replied Ullman. "Laurels in the form of dollars, which are, without question, the best kind of laurels. When you have finished this harmonious and lu-

The Bleeding of Sivori

Some members of the press attributed the attack on Sivori by the critic Richard Grant White to the violinist's not having purchased good reviews. The *Boston Transcript* wondered, for instance, if Sivori had "bled as freely as his brother artists." The satirical *Yankee Doodle* also referred to the letting of blood in regard to Sivori. It published the imaginary correspondence between the hardly disguised names of Cammomile Silverbow (i.e., Camillo Sivori); a friend of his in New York, Signor de Buffo (the singer Giuseppe de Begnis); Silverbow's agent, Z. D. Fantocini (Zani de' Ferranti); and J. G. B., the editor of the *New York Puff* (James Gordon Bennett of the *New York Herald*). Signor de Buffo's letter to the *New York Puff* requesting the paper to "make some big blows" for his friend in introducing him to the public was responded to tersely: "Five hundred down, and a hundred per column." After J. G. B. heard Silverbow perform in London, he gave instructions to his editorial staff to support the violinist. "Let De Mud [De Meyer] and his Erard go down stream. He will bleed no more—at any rate not so well as Silverbow. It is astonishing how much blood there is in his little body." The correspondence gave a twist to White's vendetta against Sivori. Silverbow's agent suggests paying the *Morning Bluster* (*Morning Courier and New-York Enquirer*) to blast him. He explained that "if the *Bluster* should abuse you, every one else will praise you out of spite."[1]

1. *Boston Daily Evening Transcript,* 15 October 1846; *Yankee Doodle* 1 (7 November 1846): 58.

crative crisscross, everything is arranged, without the loss of a day, for the three of us to join up again in New Orleans. Then from there we will set out together to exploit jointly the cities that each of you exploited alone. What do you think of that, gentlemen, and do you consider it an example of strategy—strategy of the very best?"

"Ullman," said Sivori, "you are a powerful genius."

"Ullman," I added, "you are an incomparable man."

"I believe what you say, gentlemen," was the simple reply of my secretary, in a tone of profound conviction.[5]

This often-cited plan was never followed in full. The two performers, in fact, did not go opposite ways but traveled in the same direction, albeit sometimes on a staggered schedule. The most important aspect of Ullman's scheme, the performers appearing separately first then jointly, was occasionally observed.

Thus Herz and Sivori began their tour separately without even performing together in New York before their departure. Sivori left New York first with his own agent, Marco Aurelio Zani de' Ferranti, "who had detailed instructions from Ullman on the cities to visit and the number of concerts to give in each," according to Herz.

Known as the "guitarist to the king of the Belgians," Zani de' Ferranti had not performed publicly in the United States, serving only as his friend Sivori's agent. One journal credited Sivori's early problems to being "rather over-heralded" by his agent before his arrival in the country when the public was "just on the turn of a nausea with these overdone provocations to their appetites."[6]

Sivori's first stop was Richmond, where he gave two concerts alone. He and his agent parted ways there, with Zani de' Ferranti remaining in Richmond to give a concert before returning to New York and eventually Europe. Sivori caught up with Herz in Charleston after the pianist gave his "First and Only Concert" with the threat of leaving for Havana. Sivori followed suit with a "First and Only Concert." Then, in accordance with Ullman's plan, the two joined together for a concert, seemingly—at least to the public—due to the serendipity of their both being in the same place at the same time.

Since their joint concert in Charleston drew an overflow crowd, Herz and Sivori gave another concert there, and then together performed two concerts in Savannah and Columbus, Georgia, before departing for New Orleans. Although in Savannah "many persons [were] unable to find seats at their first Concert," only a meager crowd braved a severe storm for a concert in Columbus. Through their graciousness and "modest and gentlemanly deportment," the artists convinced the devoted few that, unlike Ullman, they were not solely concerned about their bank accounts:

> They came forward and played through the programme, with even more spirit and magnificence of execution than they did the night previous—and this although there were but fifty people in the house; and they did so, because, as they afterwards said, they knew that the persons who would come out on such a night, must be amateurs, and genuine lovers of the art.[7]

A FRENCHMAN AT HOME IN NEW ORLEANS

Although Herz and Sivori arrived in New Orleans together in early February, they first appeared separately following Ullman's scheme before combining for several more joint concerts. When a New Orleans newspaper boasted that "Herz has probably been more successful here than in any city of the Union," it was not exaggerating, for in his first season he gave more concerts there than in any other American city.[8] Herz's repertoire was perfectly suited to the longstanding operatic tradition of New Orleans, the first American city to have a permanent opera company. Yet what made Herz so popular there was the very strong French connections of both the city and the pianist. Although a Viennese by birth, he was a Frenchman at heart, as is clear from his first reaction to the city:

> I cannot tell you how happy I was when I arrived in New Orleans and heard French spoken, saw French faces frequently, and read signs in French. A person must have

traveled in distant countries to comprehend the sweet and lively emotion which is evoked by anything that recalls his native land or the land to which he has given his affection and considers his own.[9]

The local citizens responded to Herz as enthusiastically as he did to them. The *New-Orleans Bee* described the crowded scene at his first concert:

> From six o'clock in the evening a distinguished and brilliant crowd surrounded the entrance to the St. Louis Hotel in order to find a place in the too confined hall where Henry Herz gave his first concert. Twelve hundred chosen had the good fortune to clear the threshold, while four or five hundred persons were obliged to return home, disappointed in neither being able to be admitted nor in being expressly promised they would be more fortunate next time.

Herz recounted his successes in a letter to Frédéric Gaillardet, editor of the *Courrier des Etats-Unis* of New York: "I am at my fifth concert, and have had invariably crowded audiences. At the first concert there must have been five hundred persons turned back from the door. Last Friday I played at the French Theatre, and, *if my modesty did not stand in my way,* I should tell you that I produced an effect which fairly made enthusiasm *curl.*"[10]

Herz seems to have been active socially thanks to the combination of French and Southern hospitality. The pianist was welcomed into the home of Pierre and Armantine Soulé, "the meeting place of all the distinguished people in the region" according to Herz. Soulé was a U.S. Senator and his wife had a "skill at playing the piano" that Herz deemed "rare in an amateur." Herz dedicated his *La Pastorale* to her, and she was perhaps one of a "troop of lovely Creoles" that took lessons from the pianist, who found that the "Louisianian ladies are as musically organized as they are seductive." Mrs. Soulé also participated in two performances of the Overture to *William Tell* arranged for eight pianos. All but two or three of the fourteen local pianists (both "Ladies and Gentlemen") were amateur performers; Herz and Sivori brought the total to sixteen. Herz claimed that at one benefit performance for charity, when one of the pianists failed to appear, he attempted to enlist from the audience a young lady totally ignorant of music. She met his pleas with numerous objections.

> "If I only knew a little music. . . ."
> "Then you would be afraid."
> "But what would my friends say?"
> "They will say that you have a great interest in the poor and that you saved me from great embarrassment."
> "And if some time they ask me to play the piano?"
> "You will reply that you know nothing by heart."

"And if they get some music?"

"You will say that you play only pieces written for sixteen pianists, no more, no less."

In order to complete the symmetry on stage, she finally yielded and feigned playing without actually striking a note. This she accomplished with gusto, running her "hands over the keyboard with the rapidity of a swallow skimming the fields. But when a series of rests indicated that we all should stop for a moment, she continued to pretend to play alone, with a most laudable zeal."[11]

MUSIC FOR AMERICANS AND IMPROVISATION

From New Orleans, Herz and Sivori followed the now typical route up the Mississippi and Ohio rivers with a few side trips (to Jackson and Nashville). The two appearances of Herz and Sivori in Baton Rouge left one newspaper editor unaffected: "Their performances were no doubt, grand, and most difficult to acquire—but for real, down right heart touching music give us the 'Star-spangled banner,' played by a full regimental band, and in the way of sacred music, that venerable air of 'Old Hundred' sung by a full chorus of old men, women, boys and girls, with their voices in full blast." Such remarks expressing a desire for simpler music probably inspired Herz's bleak view on America's musical development: "Musical taste in America has improved in recent years, so I hear. At the time when I traveled in the United States, however, artistic appreciation in general, and that of music in particular, left much to be desired, in spite of several good philharmonic societies and the efforts of a number of good musicians to popularize the works of the masters."[12]

Herz did very little himself to "popularize the works of the masters," but he did provide music accessible to Americans, and a Richmond writer was gratified with his effort "to please the non-musician by humoring the popular taste." Herz had immediately gotten a pulse on American popular music and had delighted audiences by freely incorporating in his performances patriotic songs, minstrel tunes, and Irish ballads that were then the rage. They were usually reserved for encores, which might mix and match the popular tunes with the opera arias he had just performed. Dwight, for instance, was taken with an encore that included the "most exquisitely delicate rendering" of "The Last Rose of Summer," which returned "with a delicious shock" to the finale of Herz's variations on *Le pré aux clercs*. A New York audience was thrilled when he repeated his Fantasia on *Lucrezia Borgia* and included "Yankee Doodle" in a "very playful manner." Another New York encore comprised snatches from *I Tancredi*, *Der Freischütz*, "Lucy Neal," and "Dandy Jim," among others, making a "great hit."[13] Such a mélange of opera arias and popular songs may seem bizarre today, but it illustrates that such widely disparate types of music were well known to the public and were not so distantly related in the minds or ears of the performers or audiences.

In his memoir Herz complains he was "condemned . . . to improvising" because Ullman believed his audiences wanted it, and according to the pianist, it brought him "great prestige and notoriety with the American public." He claims that at one concert fifty or sixty themes were submitted on which he should improvise, ranging from well-known songs to tunes from the "discordant repertory" of native Americans. For those who could not notate the theme, Herz had them whistle it while he transcribed it. Then he invited the audience to help him select five or six themes that he would weave together in a fantasy. On only a few occasions, however, did he advertise that he would improvise on themes suggested by the audience, and no reviews refer to this practice. Instead, he generally limited his improvisation to encores and they could have easily been rehearsed, an idea that he had proposed to Ullman, who quickly rejected it.[14] By the 1840s improvisation, which earlier had been a favorite device for a performer to display command of not only the instrument but also the art and science of music, was a disappearing tradition, and Herz was one of the few pianists to continue it while in America. De Meyer seems only to have improvised transitions between excerpts from his own works while playing encores. A decade later, Thalberg would not improvise at all.

Beginning with his concerts in Mobile and New Orleans, Herz offered Americans a new piece, *Variations brillantes et grande fantaisie sur des airs nationaux américains,* the hodgepodge of patriotic tunes required of every visiting artist. Through this work Herz exploited the even greater than usual amount of American patriotism incited by the War with Mexico, which had been under way for almost a year. The successful American campaigns, especially the victories at Buena Vista (23 February 1847) and Vera Cruz (29 March), and the imminent conclusion of the war can be followed in concert advertisements of the work. Although it was variously titled and consistently offered as a "first performance," the piece was always characterized as a "national fantasia" or "fantasia on American airs." Herz announced the work's first performance at a concert in Mobile, for which it was "expressly composed and executed for the first time in America," on 5 April 1847, the same night as the city was celebrating the victory of Buena Vista:

> The whole city was in a tumult of joy and a blaze of light last evening in honor of the battle of Buena Vista. . . . Rockets were sent off, guns fired, crackers popped and rattled. . . . [At the] Mansion House . . . eight hundred lights, at the given signal, flashed, as by magic, in the darkness, and for the space of two hours, rockets and fire balls were streaming from its roof in every variety of pyrotechnic splendor. It was a night to be remembered.

Herz advertised the work a few days later for a New Orleans concert (9 April), also claiming it was a first performance. A month later in Vicksburg (4 May), almost certainly the same piece became the "Victory of Vera Cruz . . . expressly composed on

that occasion"; yet another month later in St. Louis (1 June), it was "The Battle of Buena Vista . . . expressly composed in honor of that event"; two weeks later in Nashville (15 June) it became "The Return of the Volunteers, A Heroic National Fantasia," which Herz was to "execute for the First Time In This Country."[15] If mostly formulaic, the work was effective as a *pièce d'occasion*. It is based on three American patriotic tunes: "Jackson's March," "Hail Columbia," and "Yankee Doodle." Each tune is varied individually before the three are united in a rousing finale.

A more enduring work proved to be Herz's *The Last Rose of Summer*, Op. 159, a set of variations on the most popular of the Thomas Moore settings of Irish melodies that had enjoyed phenomenal success in the United States. Herz offered this new piece, which was "alike grateful to the simplest ear, and the most highly cultivated," consistently on his tour through the Midwest.[16] Like many of Herz's variations, it begins with a dramatic and harmonically imaginative introduction based on the opening motive. A wispily ornamented statement of the theme suggestive of its folk origin follows with three variations (example 5.1). The first contains swift and light passagework for the right hand, which is typical of Herz's style, and the second is marchlike (though still in triple meter). The third variation employs a favorite device of Herz: the theme is presented in rapidly, but delicately, repeated notes with the barest of accompaniments. This repeated figuration, generally referred to as a tremolo effect, was possible only with the recent perfection of the double-escapement action, which Herz himself had helped refine. The work's brilliant but ethereal passagework combined with the familiarity of the tune made it Herz's most popular work written in America. The sheet music was available for decades, and one edition purported that 75,000 copies of the piece had been printed (figure 5.1).

In addition to these newly written American-oriented works, Herz performed a number of works with Sivori, including a piece by the violinist based on Donizetti's *Lucia di Lammermoor* and Herz and Charles Lafont's duos on Rossini's *Moses in Egypt* and on Auber's *Fra diavolo*. By far their most frequently programmed work—and the warhorse of most violin and piano teams of the time—was Osborne and Bériot's Duo on *William Tell*. Dwight thought the composition a "noble one, full of energy and a great meaning," in which the two performers "produced a power and breadth of tone almost orchestral. . . . It is an exercise worth remembering to have heard it interpreted by two such masters as Sivori and Herz."[17]

Sivori exploited his relation with Paganini to the fullest. Besides identifying himself as "the only pupil of Paganini," he advertised with some exaggeration that his violin was "the same upon which Paganini played at all his concerts."[18] His solo repertoire naturally focused on the works of the master, often with new material by himself. Such works as *Il Campanello, The Carnival of Venice,* and the Concerto in B Minor were frequently programmed. Sivori's main vehicle was Paganini's *The Prayer of Moses* (based on the Rossini opera *Moses in Egypt*), which was billed as "ex-

ecuted upon a single string." Sivori did not ignore the American penchant for hearing national tunes gussied up by foreign visitors. In his own variations on "Yankee Doodle," Sivori, according to Dwight, made his "fiddle whistle it, squeak it, buzz and grind it out, in the manner of a hurdy-gurdy, and thus with a graceful humor consigning that immortal melody to its true place."[19]

ULLMAN QUICKENS THE PACE

After New Orleans Herz and Sivori continued their association for the remainder of the 1847 season, and except for a few separate concerts in St. Louis, all further concerts were joint ones. Occasionally Ullman still tried to draw a larger crowd by announcing how fortunate the public was to have the opportunity of hearing both performers in the same concert. The most flagrant attempt, filled with outright deceit and sycophantic flattery of the local residents, appeared in a Vicksburg advertisement:

> Through some misunderstanding on the part of their respective agents Messrs. Herz and Sivori arrive in this city at the same time; and although they have reason to believe—from the well-known Musical taste of the citizens of Vicksburg—that they would have met even separately with a liberal share of public patronage, they prefer combining their efforts in offering to the public a pleasant evening, without a change in the price of admission, and trust that the arrangement will be appreciated by a music-loving community.[20]

Ullman's calculated press releases and a clearly defined strategy for Herz's tour distinguished it from that of De Meyer. His most significant innovation was advance preparation in many of the cities. After the New Orleans stint, Ullman generally traveled several days ahead of his clients to secure halls and assisting artists and to place newspaper advertisements. Thus, the performers were able to give a concert almost immediately upon arriving in a city, instead of waiting several days for an advertisement to attract a sizable audience. With this procedure, more concerts could be given, and, even better, more laurels (and money) reaped.

After their return to New York in late July, Ullman soon booked his artists on a busy tour of New England, with a couple of weeks having concerts scheduled almost every night. During the next two months, they performed without assisting artists in cities in New York, Connecticut, Massachusetts, and Rhode Island, as well as in such popular resorts as Niagara Falls, Newport, and Saratoga Springs (figure 5.2). A fashionable Saratoga audience, which included former President John Tyler and his wife, gave them a curiously silent reception according to one spectator, who observed that they had probably never given a "concert at which there was less applause. I believe it is not polite in fashionable life to clap hands in applause." Another but more widespread custom the performers encountered was the objection

(a) Andantino espressivo

(b) Un poco più mosso e brillante

Example 5.1. Henri Herz, *The Last Rose of Summer,* Op. 159, (a) Theme, mm. 1–8; (b) Variation 1, mm. 1–8; (c) Variation 2, mm. 1–8; (d) Variation 3, mm. 1–5.

(c)   Risoluto e ben marcato

(d)   Primo tempo

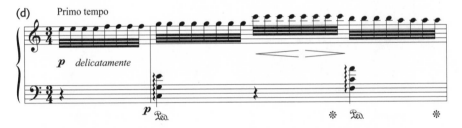

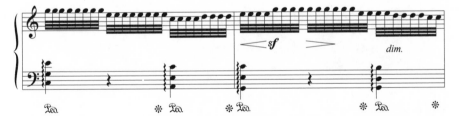

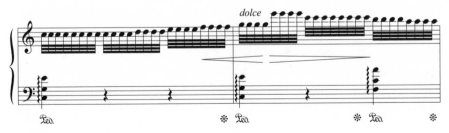

Example 5.1. *continued*

Figure 5.1. Sheet music cover for Henri Herz's *The Last Rose of Summer* identified as "75th Thousand." (AUTHOR'S COLLECTION)

to holding concerts on a Sunday, a day not considered appropriate for entertainment. To counter opposition, Sunday concerts were sometimes advertised as sacred concerts, but most people saw through the ruse, particularly when there was little or no change in repertoire. A Sunday concert given by Herz and Sivori in Fall River, Massachusetts, drew only about a hundred people despite its billing as a sacred concert and a reduction in ticket prices to fifty cents.

> Had it been given on some other evening, we doubt not it would have been much better attended, for we know many individuals who were absent because they considered it improper to be present at such an exhibition on the Sabbath. Whoever advised

Figure 5.2. Program for one of Herz and Sivori's joint concerts. With no date or city printed on it, the same program could be used for many different appearances. A date in pencil of "Oct 26/47" identifies this as the program used in Worcester on 26 October 1847. (COURTESY, AMERICAN ANTIQUARIAN SOCIETY)

the persons to give it on that evening, acted with very little wisdom or judgment, especially if their object was to insure a large attendance.

In his memoirs, Herz voices intolerance of the American reverence for the Sabbath, which banned most forms of entertainment and secular pastimes, and gladly but inaccurately reports that, years after his visit, the "absurd tyranny . . . has most happily disappeared."[21]

A New Season and George Knoop

Herz and Sivori continued their partnership with the opening of a new season in late September 1847 in New York. Since they had not performed together in the major

eastern cities the previous year, their combination provided a new element to keep their concerts fresh for their second American season. Attendance at their New York concerts was consistently high; "nearly four thousand persons" supposedly attended their first one.[22] Because of the overflowing houses, concertgoers were requested to purchase tickets in advance, and eventually ticket prices were lowered from one dollar to 75 cents for those purchased before six o'clock.

The numbing effect of giving so many concerts—almost one hundred during his first season—seemed to be taking its toll on Herz, or so the critic for the *American Review* thought. He found Herz "still a most delightful pianist" and his perform-ances with Sivori were "exquisite" and "always new and refreshing." Nevertheless, after enduring a "summer's campaign in our yet unmusical country," Herz did "not seem to take so much pains as formerly, and goes through most of his pieces . . . in a lifeless manner, that, with all his skill, makes them fall dead upon the hearer." More pointedly, he thought the public was beginning to tire of Herz's music, partic-ularly the airs with variations, a fact he thought the "lovers of really good music" would be glad to hear.[23]

One such music lover growing weary of the repetitive offerings was George Templeton Strong. After Herz and Sivori's second joint New York concert (6 October 1847), he complained that the evening consisted of "listening for three hours to the small talk of music," although performed with as much "refinement and gentility" as possible. Such "elegant nothings" would be "delightful for half an hour in a par-lor," he thought, but a "bore" when it was the "substance of a long concert." The critic Henry Watson in the *Albion* suggested that, instead of endlessly repeating the pieces that were already well known, Herz "should endeavor to produce novelty" and present the works of other composers, including Mozart, Beethoven, and Mendels-sohn. Watson believed that the "public would gain the highest intellectual enjoyment" and Herz could do so "without injuring in the slightest degree his well-earned reputation."[24] The suggestion fell on deaf ears. A pianist performing the works of other composers in public was a relatively new practice and not one Herz would follow in America in regard to his solo repertoire.

As usual, the undercurrents in the musical establishment and the press dis-tracted audiences from the art of music. The feud between Sivori and the critic Richard Grant White was rekindled in the fall of 1847, thanks in part to Ullman. Al-though the press almost unanimously supported the violinist, Ullman's refusal to allow White to attend Sivori's concert, even if he purchased his own ticket, was a breach deemed highly improper. A group of New York musicians, including William Scharfenberg, Henry C. Timm, Michael Rapetti, and Julian Fontana, condemned White for his attack on Sivori. White discounted their viewpoint because they were "foreigners, without an American name among them" and because they had joined together to "hold up to public odium and distrust, an American newspaper, because

that paper publishes honestly and independently." The *New York Evening Mirror* astutely observed that White's attempt to "excite the base passions of the mob against
these gentlemen on account of their non-citizenship, instead of standing upon its
right as an independent journal, was a tacit confession of conscious error."[25]

In concerts in Philadelphia, Brooklyn, Boston, Baltimore, and many of the New
England cities they had appeared in during August and September, Herz and Sivori
offered mostly their familiar warhorses. Beginning in early November, they aug-
mented their forces and repertoire by joining with the cellist George Knoop. Knoop,
who had been in the United States since the early 1840s and was then based in
Cincinnati, had performed there with De Meyer, as well as with Herz and Sivori.
Knoop's technique was exceptional, but he possessed something more than mere
virtuosity. In contrast to his opinions on Sivori, White considered Knoop "the greatest instrumental artist who has ever visited this country. . . . Not as to his command
of the difficulties of his most difficult instrument . . . but in elevation of sentiment,
directness, simplicity and purity of style and fervor of expression, we know not his
equal." Dwight was in complete accord with White. He held Knoop to be "perhaps
the truest artist who has been among us." He lamented that Knoop was returning
from apparent "obscurity and poverty" while "more superficial celebrities have kept
up a *furore* in our cities." His playing made Dwight feel as if he had been "admitted
into the very holy of holies of Art."[26]

The addition of Knoop made possible a greater variety of repertoire outside the
usual domain of the solo virtuoso. When the three performers first joined together
in Cincinnati, Herz and Sivori publicized their new repertoire in a way that ironically disparaged their usual offerings:

> Desirous of complying with the wishes of many lovers of Classical Music, H. Herz
> and C. Sivori beg to announce that they will give a Concert Spirituel, in which, be-
> sides a number of brilliant and pleasing pieces, principally calculated for the Concert
> Room, they will introduce several Classical and Standard compositions of the high-
> est order, which cannot fail to make a profound impression upon those who look upon
> Music as something loftier than a mere display of execution.

Sivori was no stranger to the classical tradition. Most notably, in London in 1845
he had been the first violinist in the first performances of a complete cycle of the
Beethoven string quartets.[27]

The three artists performed two trios by Beethoven, in C minor (Op. 1, No. 3)
and B♭ major (presumably Op. 11), and the second trio of Joseph Mayseder, their
most frequently programmed work. Dwight was ecstatic about their performance of
the Mayseder trio in Boston, extolling the presence of a "unity, a perfect co-operation,
a breadth, a finish in this performance, and an all-convincing energy and fullness of
expression, which no Trio, nor even Septette, ever carried with it before in Boston."

He had reservations about their performance of the Beethoven C minor, but thought the "opening Allegro, and still more the Rondo Finale were played with true fire, as well as firmness and precision." Although he believed "Herz's part was finely played, so far as execution went," he "could have desired more of the feeling of Beethoven, which would have subdued the part to true proportions; as it was, the piano forte was too loud. Yet we hesitate not to call it a sublime performance; it went deeper than anything yet given in theatre or concert room this winter." Herz observed that the works they performed by the "great masters of instrumental music" were listened to quietly and respectfully, but the more modern pieces based on operas they offered were received with unanimous applause and cries of "encore!"—"the most pleasing of words to the ear of an artist."[28]

The added attraction of Knoop and reductions in ticket prices (eventually to fifty cents) succeeded in drawing large audiences to their remaining concerts. In a few cities (Baltimore, Washington, and Richmond) Knoop did not appear at the first concert, but was held in reserve to induce the audience to attend yet another. Knoop stayed on in Richmond to give concerts on his own, while Herz and Sivori made their final joint appearances in the United States in Charleston in late December 1847 and early January 1848. From there they proceeded to Havana, with Sivori going on to Mexico and South America alone, and Herz, still managed by Ullman, eventually returning in the fall to New York for his final season in the eastern United States.

CHAPTER 6

French Pianos, Italian Opera, and California Gold

While audiences focused on Herz's immaculate performances and brilliant compositions, the businessman lurking inside the pianist was intent on promoting his own instruments. Herz's significant role as a piano manufacturer remains largely undocumented, and details of his firm's early years are sketchy. Some accounts of Herz's American tour suggest that it was undertaken to raise capital to build a piano factory or bolster one that was struggling. It seems unlikely that any concerned owner would have abandoned a failing business for five years as Herz did. Herz's enterprise may have needed an infusion of capital, but in many ways it was flourishing. In 1844, shortly before Herz left for America, his factory employed more than one hundred workmen, who produced four hundred pianos a year, and his instruments were awarded a gold medal at the industrial exposition in Paris.[1] In addition, he had already patented a simplification of Erard's double escapement action that is still the model for most grand pianos today. In the second half of the nineteenth century his pianos would be ranked with those of Erard and Pleyel.

In this country, Herz consistently performed on his own pianos that were prominently billed as instruments from "Mr. Henri Herz's own Factory in Paris" and their gold medal pedigree was touted. More important, as Herz traveled throughout the country he established a network of agents to distribute his pianos. In Pittsburgh, for example, he found two rival dealers to represent his firm. One of them, Henry

Kleber, proudly announced that he had personally selected pianos from Herz's "extensive stock in New York," that the instruments would be "sold lower than can be purchased East," and that "a good performer will be in constant attendance to exhibit the Pianos."[2]

The pianos that Herz marketed while in the United States ranged from a semigrand piano of 6¾ octaves to a small upright called a pianino. Upright pianos were the rage in Europe at this time but less common in America, where the square piano was still the principal style. Herz was especially proud of his pianino and introduced it in a New York concert in early November 1847. A review in the *New York Herald*, sounding more like a paid advertisement, praised the instrument for its sweet tone.[3]

Herz was becoming so ensconced in America giving concerts and marketing pianos that plans were under way for him to build in New York a music hall and piano factory modeled after his establishments in Paris. In the fall of 1847 the *New-York Daily Tribune* was able to describe the plans in considerable detail. Though neither hall nor factory was built, Herz did establish a sales room in New York, where pianos from his Paris factory were finished to withstand the varied and demanding climates of the United States. Buyers were to request a piano for a northern or a southern climate.[4]

THE CASE OF THE PIANO PANTALOONS: MYTH OR MISUNDERSTANDING?

Given his position as a piano manufacturer, Herz was not surprisingly critical of American instruments, remarking that in the United States "the making of pianos has for some time left much to be desired," though by the time he published his book in 1866 he could add kind words about the Chickering. Herz remembered the first time he saw an American square piano, which struck him as being "so square, so heavy, that from a distance I might have taken it for one of those antediluvian animals Cuvier has reconstructed."[5]

Two of Herz's more outlandish anecdotes concern Americans and pianos. In one, he witnesses a "new method of testing pianos," in which a woman enters a music store and selects a piano to purchase solely by poking the keys of several instruments with her parasol. Another story combines the subject of pianos with Herz's contempt for the conservative morality of Americans:

> I have known solemn puritans whose sense of decency reached out beyond the human species to include furniture. I am thinking especially of American pianos. One day I actually saw one of those pianos of which the legs, as thick as tree trunks, had been encased with slip covers made out of a bathing suit. Such an arrangement could hardly fail to attract my keenest attention.
>
> "Why, my dear lady," I asked the extremely modest owner of this piano disguised as a bather, "have you put your piano into a bathing suit?"

"I did it," replied the puritanical woman, shyly lowering her eyes, "because it is not proper, even for a piano, to display its nude limbs."[6]

Despite the common belief today that covering piano legs for this reason was a common nineteenth-century American custom, the evidence that survives to support its existence is so scanty that most piano specialists and cultural historians believe it was a figment of the overactive imagination of visiting Europeans intent on caricaturing Americans. The piano historian Cyril Ehrlich, for example, states that "years of diligent research have produced not a shred of evidence" for this "curiously persistent myth." Peter Gay, in his massive study of the nineteenth-century bourgeoisie, believes that "this peculiar bit of prudishness is either wholly fictitious, unique, or very rare." Patricia Anderson, who has written on Victorian mores, concurs that "reliably documented examples are rare and unrepresentative of conventional practice"; she speculates that it was simply one aspect of a "decorating fashion based on the principle of abundance," in which the Victorians "ruffled, fringed, and covered practically everything else."[7]

Probably the first reference to the legendary tradition was made by the writer and retired British naval officer Captain Frederick Marryat in his account of a visit to the United States in 1837–38. Marryat supposedly escorted a woman to a "seminary for young ladies," where the "mistress of the establishment" had dressed the four "limbs" of a square piano in "modest little trousers, with frills at the bottom of them!" This she had done so that the "ladies who visited their daughters, might feel in its full force [her] extreme delicacy . . . and her care to preserve in their utmost purity the ideas of the young ladies under her charge."[8] Although his novels had been popular in the United States for more than a decade, Marryat's "remarkable lack of political discernment," according to one scholar, caused so much ill will with the American public that before the end of his visit, he "had been threatened by a lynch mob, had watched his books burned in public bonfires, and on at least two occasions had seen himself hung in effigy by angry crowds." His diary of the trip met with similar disdain. One American review stated that "this very contemptible publication" was constituted of four simple elements—"pretension, ignorance, flippancy, and mendacity"—and complained of the "narrator's indifference to truth" and his "sneering ill-humor."[9]

Two decades later, the Frenchman Xavier Eyma, a visitor to the United States who wrote numerous volumes about his experiences, attributed the practice to the Quakers of Philadelphia, who covered their pianos' legs (a word they refrained from saying) with *pantalons* in the "interest of decency."[10] Interestingly, Herz's account, which appeared six years later, shares Eyma's setting of Philadelphia.[11]

It is perhaps tempting to dismiss these anecdotes, since they are isolated cases that do not describe a widespread practice and could easily be fabrications by con-

descending Europeans. Yet one contemporary American account, which attempts to set the record straight about the peculiar custom, acknowledges a grain of truth in these reports. Its author, Richard Grant White, was a notable but cantankerous music critic, the one who had vehemently attacked the violinist Sivori. His son, the architect Stanford White, is more famous today, but the father enjoyed a considerable reputation in his own time as a Shakespeare scholar and an expert on English language usage. He published widely in those fields and was a frequent contributor to such magazines as *The Atlantic Monthly, The Century, The Galaxy,* and *Harper's*.[12] His interpretation of the piano trousers appeared in an 1883 article titled "Some Alleged Americanisms" that dealt with language:

> One assertion has been made, and made so frequently, through so many years, that it may as well be disposed of now and here forever. It is that "the Americans" (the general term universally applied, as usual) are so exceedingly shamefaced that they put the very legs of their piano-fortes in trousers or pantalets. This ridiculous story was told long ago, in the Mrs. Trollope day; but I believe that it first appeared in Captain Basil Hall's book. Since that time it has pervaded British books and British newspapers. It has been one of the stock illustrations of "American" manners. I have seen it three or four times within the last few months. Now it is true that in Mrs. Trollope's and Captain Hall's day most "American" housewives who then had piano-fortes did cover the legs of them. And yet the story, as it was told and is told, is absurdly untruthful. About that time the legs of the piano-forte, which had previously been small, straight, square mahogany sticks, began to be highly ornamental, with fluting and carving. The instrument became the most elaborately made and highly prized piece of furniture in the drawing-room, or rather parlor; and in the careful housewifery of that day (which kept parlors dark, that the sun might not fade the carpet) it was protected, except on grand occasions—"a party," or the like—with a holland cover; and the legs, that they might not be defaced, were also covered with cylinders of holland. That is all. Tables and chairs and sideboards had legs also; but they were not covered, simply because they were not ornamental and easily injured. Moreover, at festive gatherings, when the room was filled with a mixed company, in which young women predominated, the trousers, the pantalets—oh, horror!—were deliberately taken off the "lower limbs" of the instrument, which were then shamelessly exposed to the naked eye. And this is the truth of that matter, which has been left to be told at this late day.[13]

White's explanation is supported by a brief reference in a source from the 1870s that casually lists common piano maintenance duties: "cover up the legs, dust it every morning, have it tuned every week." That protection was the main reason to conceal parts of a piano was confirmed a decade after White's article appeared, when scarves and draperies had become fashionable. One author stated: "It must be

always remembered that the object of having covering, scarf or mats upon a piano, is primarily to preserve the case from injury."[14]

With his reputation as a scholar and music critic, White theoretically should be a reliable witness, despite a possible hidden agenda to improve the reputation of his countrymen. His account offers the appealing compromise that the foreign observers were not totally fabricating stories but were only misinterpreting—intentionally or unintentionally—their significance. If truthful, White teaches us that myths are sometimes based on facts and that pantaloons on a piano are as American as plastic slipcovers on a sofa.

A Piano Academy and Minstrel Shows

In 1848 Herz's performing schedule was drastically reduced. After leaving Charleston in January with Sivori, he seems to have gone to Cuba first and then Jamaica, where "cruel trials awaited" him:

> Believing I had lost the use of my right hand, I endured crushing physical pain, accompanied by mental tortures a thousand times more disheartening. Only virtuosos, those who love their art and practice it with devotion, can comprehend all the poignant regrets which then tore at my heart. The loss of my sight would have meant less to me than the loss of my fingers. Fortunately, the malady was not without cure, and three months after my arrival in Jamaica I was able to continue my concert tour through the two Americas.[15]

It was probably from Jamaica, with Herz incapacitated, that Sivori went on his own to Mexico and South America. After recovering, Herz may have toured briefly in the Caribbean before returning to New York.

Once back in the East, Herz's schedule slowed to a standstill. Perhaps he spent his time overseeing the distribution of his pianos or teaching at the piano academy he had established in late summer 1848 "on the principles of the Paris *Conservatoire*."[16] He was certainly doing little performing. From November 1848 to March 1849 he gave only seven concerts and made three guest appearances, despite excellent attendance at his concerts. He was possibly tiring of his vagabond life, but he had a compelling reason to remain in the United States, at least for some time longer. Returning to Paris would have been an uncertain move because of the French revolution of June 1848, which had prompted many musicians to flee the city.

During his leisure time Herz wrote several new works in honor of his host country, including a group of *Three New American Polkas,* Op. 160, of moderate difficulty and a more challenging *Tribut à l'Amérique,* Op. 161, comprising a Chopinesque nocturne and a scintillating polka. Herz's fondness for the polka idiom—he would write yet another while in California, *La Californienne,* Op. 167—symbolizes his role as a composer of music designed to provide agreeable entertainment rather than

profound discourse. He also paid tribute to the minstrel show or, more likely, tried to capitalize on the spectacular success the genre was then enjoying. His *Impromptu burlesques sur des mélodies populaires des Christy's Ménestrels,* Op. 162, is based on Stephen Foster's "Oh! Susanna," on which he had frequently improvised, and Charles T. White's "Carry Me Back to Old Virginia." At its first performance in New York in late 1848, the work was met by "tremendous cheers."[17]

Herz had mixed reactions to the minstrel show itself. He was as shocked by the large crowds that assembled nightly to hear the "barbarous songs" of the minstrels as he was by the enormous sums that could be made by such "buffoonery." But he was taken by the songs that, instead of trying to make the audience laugh, possessed a "simplicity and charming naiveté," and admired the multitalented performers. He was also fascinated by the instruments: the guitars in a "bizarre shape" (i.e., banjos), the violins that were "almost in pieces," and the bones that were played with an "incredible dexterity."[18]

FRANS COENEN AND AN OPERA TROUPE

Herz made his final two New York concerts in late 1848 grand affairs; the first (30 November) was billed as a "Great Solemnité Musicale." His assisting artists included several recent immigrants, some of whom were fleeing the European revolutions of 1848. Max Maretzek, newly arrived as conductor of the Astor Place Opera House, led the soloists and orchestra of the Italian Opera Company at both concerts. Joseph Gungl also performed with his orchestra, one of three German orchestras that had recently arrived, and at the second concert (21 December), the Bohemian pianist Maurice Strakosch and the Dutch violinist Frans Coenen assisted. Strakosch (1825–1887), who was to become one of the most energetic impresarios in the New World, had made his American debut the previous June, and Herz had made a guest appearance at one of his concerts. Coenen (1826–1904), a pupil of Vieuxtemps, made his American debut at Herz's concert. The combination of a violin and piano once again proved congenial, and Coenen performed in the remainder of Herz's concerts in the United States and accompanied him to Mexico. Although these concerts were generally well received, Herz's performances of his own works and such grand musical festivals were no longer novelties. One writer could not understand Herz's failure to move beyond his past successes: "Why will Mr. Herz, with his music, remain behind the age? Have his own brilliant *tours de force* woven a net around him, which he cannot break through? Or does he delight, as he sits before the piano meditating on by-gone days of glory, [in] recalling to memory . . . those very pieces which, twenty years ago, were already the delight of the boarding-school misses?"[19]

After several appearances in New England cities in early 1849 with Coenen, Herz once again returned to New York. A full two months elapsed before he began

his final series of appearances on the East Coast, in conjunction with Coenen and three soloists from the Italian Opera Company at Astor Place: soprano Teresa Truffi, tenor Sesto Benedetti, and bass Settimo Rossi. The original goal of the troupe was to travel far beyond the East Coast: one article about the company carried the headline "Musical Expedition in Pursuit of the Gold of South America" and described the troupe as a "sort of gold-digging California association."[20] Beginning in April 1849, these musical forty-niners made appearances in cities along the East Coast, including Baltimore, Washington, Richmond, Norfolk, Charleston, Savannah, Augusta, and Columbia.

The singers offered condensed versions of operas stripped of expensive sets and tedious recitatives, accompanied by Herz and Coenen, who also performed solos and duos between the acts. In Baltimore, for example, they gave "Italian Opera Soirées" consisting of "all the Airs, Duets, Concerted Pieces" of operas "with Action and in Full Costume." Each performance was devoted to one or two operas in the standard Italian repertoire, including Donizetti's *Lucia di Lammermoor* and *Lucrezia Borgia*, Mercadante's *Il Giuramento,* and Verdi's *I Lombardi*.

Herz's attempt to form a new coalition was short-lived. After twenty-five performances the talented but temperamental singers turned back. The *New York Herald* reported that Herz and Benedetti "apparently quarreled about some important question—probably the difference between tweedle-dum and tweedle-dee."[21] Herz, Coenen, and Ullman pressed on without them toward California via Mexico. A year passed before Herz finally arrived on the West Coast, without either of his compatriots.

CALIFORNIA GOLD

In January 1848 gold was discovered in California, but it took until almost the end of the year before the seemingly outrageous reports of the gold and the ease in acquiring it reached the East Coast and were finally believed. By early 1849 thousands were headed to California for quick riches and high adventure. Forty thousand people arrived there in 1849 alone, bringing the population to one hundred thousand. Although concert music rarely made it to the frontier on the first wave of migration, it appeared in California unusually early since it was an extraordinarily rich territory.

Several routes were possible to California, and each of them had disadvantages. Crossing the western frontier brought risk of Indian attack, severe weather, and starvation; sailing around Cape Horn was safer but much too slow—more than three months. A more popular route involved going by ship to Panama, crossing the isthmus, where yellow fever posed a serious threat, and sailing from there to California. Herz chose a middle route through Mexico, a more civilized passage that offered several cities in which to perform along the way, but it, too, had its perils. A few years

later in 1854, for instance, the celebrated German singer Henriette Sontag died of cholera while in Mexico, and bandits were a frequent menace to traveling parties. Ullman depicted his travels with the pianist in Mexico as a "laborious affair, attended with all kinds of dangers" and deplored "the wretched conveyance by means of mules and the insecurity of the roads."[22]

The trip was worth the potential dangers, for Mexico's overwhelming response to Herz made his enthusiastic reception in the United States seem lukewarm by comparison. Upon his approach to Mexico City in July 1849, for example, about sixty leading citizens, musicians, and amateurs greeted him eight miles from the edge of town and escorted him into the city, where he was feted with a dinner and a serenade. He was similarly received in another Mexican city, where "twenty carriages, drawn by two horses, and five by four, were sent by the principal families to meet him on the outskirts of the town; a state carriage was placed at his disposal, and he was escorted by thirty artists on horseback and eight dragoons, and, on reaching his hotel, he was entertained with a magnificent dinner." His concerts were no less successful. One extravagant report, based on a letter from Herz to a friend in Boston, claimed that one of his concerts netted $12,000 and that "many of the bouquets with which he was almost smothered . . . contained diamonds."[23]

Herz had an amicable relationship with the Mexican government as well as the people. Soon after his arrival, he announced his intention to write a national hymn for the country. With the government's approval, a public contest was held for the text, and Herz set it to music.[24] When the pianist left the capital to visit other cities, the president ordered the governors to see that he was protected by guards against the bandits.[25]

From Mexico Herz followed the gold rush alone to California; Coenen went on to South America, and for reasons unknown Herz dismissed Ullman after three years of service.[26] Herz sailed from Mazatlán on Mexico's Pacific coast to San Francisco with 260 other passengers on board the *California.* In early March 1850 it had left about fifteen hundred people in Panama desiring passage and "hundreds at Mazatlán and other places on the coast offered $400 and $500 for tickets in the steerage to San Francisco."[27]

When Herz arrived in San Francisco on 26 March 1850, that city was not the most likely destination for a virtuoso pianist from Paris. The following day the leading newspaper, *Alta California,* stated that Herz's arrival would "cause considerable surprise to his friends and admirers in the United States and abroad." He was, in fact, the first notable musician to visit California, although many soon followed him, including the singer Catherine Hayes, the violinists Miska Hauser and Ole Bull, and the pianist Maurice Strakosch.[28]

In a letter to the editor of the *Courrier des Etats-Unis* in New York, Herz shared his initial impressions of the bustling international city:

On arriving at San Francisco, I found there so many friends, French, English and German, that I was immediately perfectly *at home.* However, most of these friends were completely metamorphosed. Those whom I had been accustomed to see pass their life in New York in the delights of a fashionable *far niente,* are here selling coats, shoes, hardware, &c. Others whom I had left trying to be lawyers, or parlor singers, have become auctioneers, and acquit themselves very well in their new business.

I have seen young Parisian lions selling the product of their sporting at exorbitant prices; and professional painters consecrating their pencils to sign making, at *an ounce of gold per letter.* I have met with perfect *gentlemen,* offering to transport my pianos, receiving therefor, in different sums, up to $300 for their services. In fine, I have seen so many extraordinary things that I dare not communicate them, for fear of being accused of exaggeration.[29]

Herz was not completely metamorphosed himself after passing through the Golden Gate, but he was conscious of the necessity of appealing to a public more concerned with panning for gold than with attending concerts. Although the programs differed very little from his eastern appearances, he did publicize their more sensational aspects. At his first San Francisco concert (2 April 1850), the finale was an extemporaneous performance of several American, French, Italian, and German popular songs. One of the American tunes was "Oh! Susanna," on which he had already published a set of variations and which now had virtually become the theme song of the forty-niners. Herz knew his public, for *Alta California* thought the "extempore medley was more universally pleasing than either of his other selections," although perhaps not as great an "exhibition of scientific skill" as the others.[30]

The finale of his second San Francisco concert was billed as a *Voyage musicale,* the principal addition to his California repertoire, in which Herz "introduced the National Airs of all the principal countries, including La Marseillaise and Yankee Doodle, an imitation of a Storm at Sea, and the California Polka," an extravaganza that was found to be "perfectly electrifying."[31] To top the *Voyage musicale* Herz advertised his third appearance as a "Monstre Concert," a phrase the press had already applied to many of his concerts but he used for the first time in an advertisement. It created some confusion, particularly when the finale was vaguely billed as "the Marche Nationale on four pianos." The names of two singers and a trumpet player but no other pianists were mentioned in the advertisement. Thus, many people were severely disappointed when Herz did not perform on all four pianos by himself but was assisted by three other pianists. *Alta California,* which had previously voiced its support of Herz, took him to task for his apparent cunning deception under the heading "Monstrosity":

We dislike the system of "gaggery" which professional people seem to think necessary to tincture all their public announcements with. We are willing to acknowledge that

the public are so good natured that they are frequently gulled to a very great extent, but it is really unkind to take advantage of their credulity and impose upon their good nature too much. . . . An artist with talent of acknowledged excellence, and a name familiar to all, needs no puffery to back him, and it is bad taste to use the article at all. We were not a little annoyed at the announcement of Mr. Herz's last concert being a "monster" concert. If he had been assisted by a few anthropopagi, gronies and other monstrosities, the name would have been applicable enough, but from the fact that he was assisted by two or three amateurs only, nothing monstrous could be discovered. The ingeniously worded programme relative to the *Marche Nationale,* upon four pianos, was a very gentle equivocal announcement approaching to a "sell." Many individuals went with the expectation of seeing Mr. Herz throw off his usual modest and quiet demeanor, and distribute himself among his four pianos, playing upon all of them at the same time. They did not exactly understand how he was going to do it, but probably imagined it was something similar to the performance on the bass drum, pandian pipes and cap of bells, by a well known character in this city. If he had have announced that he would preside at the grand piano, and be accompanied by a lady, Mr. Jenkins and Mr. Brown, each upon a piano, with a few notes from the cornet à piston of Mr. Villiers, some of his ardent admirers would have stayed away perhaps.[32]

Herz moved on to Sacramento at the invitation of several of its influential citizens and gave a similar series of three concerts in mid-April: the first included an improvisation on popular songs, the second featured his *Voyage musicale,* and the third was a "monster concert." This time Herz explicitly stated that he would perform his *Marche nationale* on three pianos with "several pianists" who had "kindly volunteered their assistance."[33]

In two of his Sacramento concerts, Herz was assisted by the singer Stephen Massett, whom he had previously met in New York and had run into again on the steamer from San Francisco to Sacramento. Massett had been the first musician to give concerts in California in June 1849, almost a year before Herz's arrival. At both events Massett performed "several Songs, Ballads and Comic Recitations, together with Imitations illustrative of the peculiarities of Yankee Character." The singer records in his amusing autobiography how two rats with very long tails appropriately scurried across the stage during his performance of a comic recitation of the "Frenchman and the Rats," which created a "roar of laughter" among the audience and "quite convulsed" Herz.[34]

Like most prices in inflation-ridden California, ticket prices were four to six times the rate in the East. For Herz's first San Francisco concerts, tickets were six dollars for reserved seats in the boxes or parquette and four dollars for seats in the pit. Californians had little trouble paying these prices, however, with their freshly mined gold dust. At one concert the money-taker supposedly had a pair of scales and

"fierce, ill-looking fellows, clad in the strangest of costumes . . . filed past him in order, and each in his turn placed in his hand a black leather purse. The official opened the purse, took from it a pinch of gold dust, weighed it, and then delivered the ticket." At the end of the concert Herz was taken aback when presented with a "large plate, filled with yellow powder," worth more than two thousand dollars.[35]

There was money to be made by Herz outside the concert hall as well. He claims to have been asked to play in a gambling saloon for $2,000 a month. Herz was told that "even cards and dice become at last monotonous; and nothing is more agreeable than to hear a pretty piece of music in the intervals of the games." When the pianist was offended at such a proposition, the Californian responded with equal indignation, "We have artists in California of the highest reputation who do not disdain to perform in the *cafés,* in the gambling houses—everywhere, in fact, where they are paid."[36]

Herz attracted an international audience, accurately reflecting the makeup of the émigrés to El Dorado. *Alta California* experienced a "little mortification" when "there was but one or two American ladies present and but very few gentlemen" among the large and mostly European gathering. Herz's audiences also comprised a wide range of social levels. One account complained of ruffians who were responsible for "uproar, and confusion, and disorderly and disgraceful behavior." Yet there were people of "beauty and fashion," terms that a San Francisco newspaper was pleased to inform its readers were "no longer allegorical" in California. Herz was astonished to find a "public so knowledgeable and enthusiastic about music." He could have believed he was in New York or New Orleans. The *Sacramento Transcript* explained that Californians "crave amusements of a higher order" because its citizens hailed "from the polite capitals of the world, and from the country towns, where the blaze of civilization, of enlightenment has had its effect." The *San Francisco Daily Pacific News* claimed that, to the citizens of San Francisco, Herz was "an artist whom most of them have so often listened to before."[37]

Californians were so eager to hear Herz perform that they overcame with alacrity all potential obstacles that were plentiful in a mining territory. In Sacramento, where there was no concert hall, one was made ready specifically for Herz's appearances according to his directions. In Benicia, the temporary lack of a piano did not deter them either, as Herz related:

On arriving I found the hall—it was the church of the place—densely packed; only one thing, and an essential one, was wanting—a piano. I asked if there was not one in town. "There is one," was the answer, "but we have not been able to find any one to transport it hither." The audience began to grow impatient. I mounted the platform and explained the mishap which had occurred. "Is that all!" they exclaimed, "let us go after it." And in a few minutes the piano arrived, borne by the dilettanti of the place.[38]

Outside the concert hall, Herz was cordially welcomed into the polite social circles of both San Francisco and Sacramento and claimed to "have found there the best of friends." After a concert in Sacramento he attended an impromptu party, where many audience members spent the rest of the evening in "dancing and social converse." The host, who had already amassed half a million dollars in California, presented the pianist with a "most magnificent and valuable watch chain composed entirely of [gold] specimens," and Herz was overheard as saying, "He couldn't have given me anything that would have pleased me more." Another reception and complimentary supper were given in his honor in San Francisco, where Americans, Englishmen, and Frenchmen were "all centered in a brotherhood of festivity."[39]

Herz's final concert in San Francisco was the first occasion on which he suffered a lapse into pure entertainment, when he was assisted by the newly arrived Signor Rossi, a magician and ventriloquist who, among other things, imitated animals and insects. When news of this program reached New York, Hermann Saroni, who had arranged the *William Tell* Overture for sixteen pianists for performance at Herz's concerts and now published a music journal, blasted Herz. Saroni must have had a severe falling out with the pianist judging from the severity of his sarcasm. He wondered how Herz would depict seasickness in his *Voyage musicale* and suggested that if the pianist had plans to visit the "polar ice-regions," he should take a display of animals to amuse the public:

> Oh! Mr. Herz, you have mistaken your vocation! In the musical world you are but an ordinary mortal. As showman in a menagerie, you would make yourself immortal. We can just imagine you with that bland smile which never deserts your countenance, as you point with a cane to a large bear, calling out: "Dish, Ladies and Gentleman, is de great California bear vot is so woracious as to heat hens and chickens alive; dhis is dhe Brazilian hape, vot makes a capital rope-dancer; dhis is an Orang-outang, vot axts occasionally as my substitute at the piano," &c.[40]

As Herz was about to give a farewell concert in San Francisco, a major fire broke out, destroying the concert hall and signaling to Herz it was time for his departure. During the fire, he was amazed at the coolness of the local citizens, who, instead of attempting to extinguish the fire, excitedly planned to rebuild the city once the fire had run its course. Herz's brief visit to California, which in just three more months would be admitted to the Union as a state, must have been arduous, but as an adventurer he relished it:

> I have no cause to regret the voyage, for I have visited the most curious country of the world. . . . I have given twelve concerts, the success of which has exceeded my hopes by far. Besides, I have had an opportunity of appreciating the incredible activity and spirit of enterprise of the Americans. No other nation in the world would have made of California what it has now become in their hands within fifteen months.[41]

After California, Herz toured for more than a year on the western coast of Latin America, before returning to Europe in the summer of 1851.[42]

Herz's tour of the United States exemplified the new businesslike approach to bringing music across the country. Recognizing the complexity of touring in a foreign land, Herz engaged a professional manager to assist him. Most later performers had managers, too, and soon impresarios would take the initiative in seeking artists to represent, rather than the reverse. As Herz's agent, Ullman was an imaginative publicist, and although his notices were cleverly designed to attract the public, he usually did not overwhelm the music he presented with humbug. More important, Ullman was organized, and his efficient execution of his well-planned tour for Herz became a model for others. Under Ullman's management, Herz visited a larger number of cities than De Meyer (fifty-eight instead of twenty-six) and gave more concerts—almost two hundred instead of eighty-five. Herz was here longer than De Meyer, but his activity in the United States was concentrated in two periods—from November 1846 to December 1847 and from December 1848 to June 1849—that were not much longer than De Meyer's tour.

Herz brought a refinement to the concert hall that De Meyer lacked. His simple but elegant stage manners and his graceful music charmed the American public. His repertoire may not have been profound, but it was well known to Americans, and they relished the opportunity to hear it performed by the composer. With the exception of the works for multiple pianos and a few selections in his California appearances, Herz emphasized in his concerts the music itself and returned a soberness to the concert room.

INTERLUDE I

⟪℮

With so many virtuosos touring the United States and commanding center stage in America's musical life, some writers took a cynical view of their influence. Schumann, the watchdog of misguided virtuosity, had sarcastically evaluated the trend from Europe as early as May 1843: "The public has lately begun to weary of virtuosos, and . . . we have too. The virtuosos themselves seem to feel this, if we may judge from a recently awakened fancy among them for emigrating to America; and many of their enemies secretly hope they will remain over there; for, taken all in all, modern virtuosity has benefited art very little." A failed virtuoso himself, Schumann did not disclose to his readers that he and his wife, Clara, had seriously contemplated an American tour of their own to accumulate enough wealth so they could pursue their higher artistic ideals. Robert's letters to Clara in March and April 1842 reveal his hesitant consideration of a visit to the New World, a step that both geographically and ideologically proved to be "too enormous." Yet, a year later and just two months before his public statement he confided in their joint marriage diary (14 March 1843): "I have America in mind. A horrible decision. But I firmly believe it would have its rewards."[1]

If Schumann and his ilk rejoiced at the widespread migration of purveyors of astounding technique but dubious musical values, only a few American critics spoke against the effect of the virtuosos. A St. Louis writer believed Americans lavished

too much money on "remarkable musical artists" and too little on "endowing academies of musical science." "The sums wasted upon musical prodigies," he observed,
"would be sufficient to establish permanent operas and academies of music, which
would do more to elevate the public taste, in one year, than those meteoric visita-
tions would in ten."[2]

Most Americans, however, focused on the benefits their musically adolescent
country received from the virtuosos' tours. Such pianists as De Meyer and Herz were
believed to be useful models for budding pianists. Though highly critical of De
Meyer's repertoire, the *Musical Gazette* of Boston nevertheless argued that students
should attend his performances:

> We wished that every scholar we had, or that intended to choose us as instructor,
> could have been present, to witness the perfect mechanism of his execution. We have
> to lecture not a little on the best way of striking with the fingers, with the wrist, with
> the arm. . . . It is replied, that nobody, or very few, play as we say, and we suffer a great
> deal for want of models. Now here is a living specimen.

Other writers believed the visiting virtuosos were responsible for awakening a general
interest in music and improving the public's discrimination. A different St. Louis
writer, for example, claimed of Herz that "everybody perceives that his influence will
be beneficial to mind and taste." In a review of a New York concert by De Meyer,
the critic George William Curtis, a close friend of Dwight, attributed an advancement in the musical understanding of Americans to that pianist and other visiting
artists:

> It is verily refreshing to feel that our great Gotham, in spite of its devotion to the
> twin idols of Mammon and Fashion, is beginning to give evidence of real progress in
> the appreciation of Musical Art. . . . The crowded audiences which have attended the
> more than usually numerous musical entertainments of the present season, attest
> the hold which Music is taking on the general heart.
>
> Foremost among the causes of this growing love of Music, are the visits with which
> we have been favored by distinguished artists of the old world, and which have al-
> ready exerted a great and beneficial influence upon the public taste; awakening a love
> of music where it had lain dormant, and giving, to those who were already alive to its
> pleasures, higher and wider views of the beauty, significance, and world-wide rela-
> tions of this divine art.
>
> To none among these welcome visitors has a more cordial reception been given
> than to Leopold de Meyer.[3]

In the fall of 1847, the music educator Elam Ives surveyed the state of music in
New York and concluded that, based on the patronage of concerts, the

public is becoming intelligent and discriminating in the higher points of the art, vocal as well as instrumental. That, which, two or three years ago would have excited admiration, is now flat and unsatisfying. The narrow distinction which exists between the *beautiful* and the *ridiculous* is getting to be more generally appreciated: clap-trap, and all sorts of trickery, meet with but a cold reception by an audience, and consequently are less resorted to by public performers.

Such dramatic changes do not occur overnight but require years of steady development with some backsliding every now and then. In early 1848, while Herz was completing his second American season, Dwight observed that the "taste for solo concerts seems to be on the wane with us" and complained that Bostonians were "capricious" in their patronage of music. "In spite of all the interest which has been manifested in concerts of the highest order now and then," he wrote, "we scarcely dare affirm the existence of any settled taste among them for the art." The public was not earnestly in love with music, he believed, it only wanted to be amused.[4]

While the positive and negative influences of the virtuosos on the state of music in the United States were variously dissected, a typically American response was to find humor in the latest fad. The pretensions of the fashionable audiences who fawned on the touring European artists and the critics who feigned intimate knowledge of music and its multilingual vocabulary received a series of spoofs in the *Knickerbocker*. Musical criticism, generally of foreign artists, was a feature in the fictitious newspaper the *Bunkum Flag-staff and Independent Echo* that appeared in numerous issues of the magazine during 1849–51. The articles critiqued the singing "Puffington Family" and the violinists "M. Screitch Oüel," who performed the "*caveat* to *Luscreechia*" (i.e., cavatina to *Lucrezia Borgia*), and "M. Fidel Stickh." The *Bunkum Flag-staff*'s most elaborate satire centered on the pianist "Herr Smash." He seems modeled primarily on De Meyer, who had already left the country two years before, but the caricature is probably a composite. A bushy-headed pianist with an "exentrik" appearance, Herr Smash played with such a powerful force that his body had to be secured with ropes and his coattails nailed to the piano bench.[5]

After Herz departed the East Coast in 1849, plenty of singers, violinists, and pianists made their way to the New World to entertain, instruct, and edify. Some made the usual quick trip for riches, but many desperate musicians arrived because of political and economic necessity as a result of the failed European revolutions of 1848. In late December 1848, the *New York Herald* could report that "during the last few weeks we have had nearly a hundred musicians, of all ranks, arrived from Europe." Perhaps the most significant musical outcome of those catastrophic events was the arrival of the Germania Musical Society, an orchestra of about twenty-five musicians that eventually introduced many Americans to the early romantic symphonic repertoire. The ensemble gave more than nine hundred concerts across the United States

before it disbanded in 1854. (One of its conductors, Carl Bergmann, will play a prominent role later in this study.) One immigrant musician, Thomas Ryan, remembered the success of the Germania as the "cause of much trumpeting all over Europe that America was a country which wanted music and would pay for it."[6]

The most astonishing musical event soon after Herz's departure was doubtless the American tour of Jenny Lind, the "Swedish Nightingale." Her wildly successful tour of 1850–52 was attributable to her sweet and pure voice, her angelic innocence and modest demeanor, and, as Austin Caswell has suggested, her embodiment of democratic musical ideals that appealed to middle-class Americans.[7] P. T. Barnum's sensationalized publicity, of course, helped to fuel the record ticket sales and widespread hysteria. Lind valiantly maintained her dignity in spite of Barnum's ballyhooing and eventually bought out her contract with him.

The details of Lind's tour have been well documented and need not detain us, but the effect of her extravagant monetary windfall was a catalyst for both European performers and American managers who hoped to emulate this new financial standard. Alexander W. Thayer, for example, quoted a "private letter from Europe" in his column for *Dwight's Journal of Music* that noted how Lind's success "excited all the dramatic and operatic artists" who wanted to "partake in the glorious American harvest."[8]

The dilemma was whether only a tour à la Barnum with humbug and hokum could duplicate the profits. Barnum's crass handling of Lind's tour only confirmed many misgivings about American taste and raised questions about what was required to be successful in the United States. Toward the end of Lind's American sojourn, Friedrich Wieck, the father of Clara Schumann and Marie Wieck (the latter also a talented pianist), wrote to a correspondent of *Dwight's Journal of Music* (identified by Dwight as "a German friend in Virginia") that he had been advised to tour America with his daughter Marie and the singer Louise Wölfel. But he wondered if America was "yet ripe for exhibitions of Art so fine and noble, and which evidently are not of the taking order?" The German friend offered his opinion to Dwight: "They are artists of the highest rank. . . . They never will employ a Barnum or somebody to sound the trumpet before them; they are too true Artists . . . and will never submit to posting up, paying trumpet-sounding agents, &c., &c."[9]

ALFRED JAËLL

Nevertheless, performers came, if not Marie Wieck. Several pianists were active on the American scene before the advent of Thalberg in 1856, the next world-famous pianist to visit America. The one who most fits our interest—a visiting European virtuoso—was Alfred Jaëll (1832–1882).[10] Probably as talented as De Meyer or Herz, he had neither the fame of Herz nor the spunk of De Meyer to succeed as a star performer. He was less inclined to seek the spotlight and was more than comfortable

serving as an assisting artist to greater celebrities. He made his American debut on 15 November 1851 in New York. After giving a number of concerts, he soon teamed up with the Germania Musical Society. After spending much of 1852 and 1853 touring with the Germania throughout the East and Midwest, he associated himself with Henriette Sontag, with whom he had appeared at her first New York concert in the fall of 1852. During the 1853–54 season he toured with Sontag and returned to Europe in May 1854 while Sontag went on to Mexico.

Jaëll offered the best of both worlds as a virtuoso. With the Germania, he often performed superbly the Mendelssohn piano concertos and the Weber *Konzertstück,* reflecting the orchestra's focus on the early romantic German repertoire. On the other hand, he was no stranger to the virtuoso showpieces of the day, programming numerous works by Thalberg and his own pyrotechnical fantasies and lighthearted galops. As Dwight observed, Jaëll was "master of most that has become classical" (including the music of Bach, Beethoven, Mendelssohn, and Chopin) and of "all the bewildering brilliancies" of such virtuosos as Liszt and Thalberg.[11]

Despite the high acclaim he received from critics, Jaëll was considered to be unusually modest and unpretentious for a virtuoso. In addition to his suffering from "very bad management," one music journal suggested that if he had "assumed a dashing and wild character" he might have been touted as a "piano wonder" and have had thousands of admirers.[12]

Two Americans: Gottschalk and Mason

Two other important pianists made American debuts of sorts before the arrival of Thalberg: the Americans Louis Moreau Gottschalk (1829–1869) and William Mason (1829–1908). Both were returning from abroad, where they had distinguished themselves as students and performers. Gottschalk had won the favor of Parisians in the capital of virtuosity, and Mason had been a prize student of none other than Franz Liszt. Americans were proud of their native sons, but they had curious ways of showing it at the box office. Although they might boast of American talent, they would only pay money to hear the more alluring Europeans.

Gottschalk, who had left New Orleans in the early 1840s, returned first after spending more than a decade in Europe. The considerable success he had achieved there was due partly to such exotic pieces of his as *Le Bananier* and *Bamboula.* He made his New York debut in early 1853. Instead of a hero's welcome after his European triumphs, he lost money in his first concerts in New York and Philadelphia. The *Musical World* chastised the public that could allow such an unpatriotic crime:

> Shame on the communities that have made foreign artists to stagger under the load of weighty favors imposed on them, to let an American artist, the executive rival of Thalberg and Liszt, to find the fruits of his honorable ambition turned to ashes!

Liszt and America

Rumors of an American tour by Liszt became frequent by the mid-1840s. In 1845, the *Boston Musical Review* had included a spoof that described an apocryphal voyage by Liszt to the New World. By 1855, Dwight referred to the "Liszt-coming-to-America" rumor as one that "re-appears annually." In the same year Liszt denied such a report to his friend Franz Brendel and admitted that "there are many people who would be glad to have me out of sight!" Like many famous performers, however, it was difficult for Liszt not to at least consider America, however remote the possibility. In 1849, when Liszt was contemplating one such visit, his friend Berlioz advised him: "Your project for a tour of the United States seems violent to me—to cross the Atlantic to make music for Yankees who just now are only thinking of California gold!"[1]

Music journals frequently reported Liszt's latest thoughts on America; two articles on the topic appeared in 1857 during Thalberg's first season in the United States. In one, Liszt, despite many urgings to visit America, seemed to "have the smallest possible respect for the musical intelligence of the Yankees, and refuses all offers of speculators." "He thinks something of gaining money," it was reported, "but not everything—and 'will not play,' as he says, 'where he may be stared at as a *rara avis,* but not understood or appreciated as an artist.'"[2] Another account, reported by the New York music publisher Charles Breusing who had visited Liszt, revealed the pianist's thoughts on America to be more charitable:

> Liszt told him that he had been often invited to visit our country, and that he feels greatly inclined to do so, not only on account of the prominent place it begins to occupy in the musical world, but also on account of the friendly, sympathetic calls he had so often had from here. Unfortunately, his time for the next three years was so much engaged by carrying out his plans with regard to his position as a composer in Germany, that he would not be able to respond to the multiplied invitations for a visit which he had received, unless some extraordinary circumstances should force him to give up his dearest wishes. But if he should come, it would be as a pianist and as a teacher, and with the intention not to leave this country any more. As he felt that he had some talent for teaching, his ambition would be to start here a conservatory of music, in the superintendence of which he would conclude his days. In the mean time, he authorized Mr. Breusing to give all rumors with regard to his coming over this season, or next season, under the management of this or that agent, a *flat* denial.[3]

1. *Boston Musical Review* 1 (1 September 1845): 19–20; *Dwight's Journal of Music* 7 (21 July 1855): 125; Franz Liszt, Letter to Franz Brendel, Weimar, June 1855, in *Letters of Franz Liszt,* ed. Marie Lipsius, trans. Constance Bache, 2 vols. (London: H. Grevel, 1894), 1:246; Hector Berlioz, Letter to Franz Liszt, *ca* 25 March 1849, in *Correspondance générale, III, 1842–1850,* ed. Pierre Citron (Paris: Flammarion, 1978), 614, trans. in *Hector Berlioz: A Selection from His Letters,* ed. and trans. Humphrey Searle (New York: Harcourt, Brace & World, 1966), 110.
2. *New York Musical World* 17 (7 March 1857): 150.
3. *New-York Musical Review and Gazette* 8 (22 August 1857): 257.

Shame on the communities that should allow the first great performing artist that our country has produced, find that the blood of his youth, the tears of his early enthusiasm, the religious devotion of his nights and his days, have been deprived of adequate recompense![13]

Mason returned the following year after five years of study. He had already performed quite a bit in the Boston area before his European sojourn and was not an unknown quantity. That his father was Lowell Mason, a respected church musician and pioneering music educator, gave him as much name recognition as an American musician could possibly have, and he was a student of Moscheles, Dreyschock, and Liszt to boot. Those credentials, however, were not enough for the American public. An ambitious but poorly attended concert tour throughout the country was canceled midway and never again attempted.[14] Mason firmly established himself as a leading piano pedagogue, an able chamber musician, and a reliable soloist. Yet Americans were unable to perceive him as a star virtuoso.

Mason's lack of success as a touring soloist could be attributed to his serious demeanor and repertoire and a lack of warmth or showmanship. Yet Gottschalk, who had been one of the first in line when charisma was handed out, fared little better. True, he eked out a living as a touring pianist, but not until the next decade did he come into his own. Gottschalk and Mason were both the victims of America's continuing discrimination against native-born talent, who could not hope to duplicate the undefinable mystique of European performers that proved irresistible to the American public. The favoritism shown to visiting musicians was not new, and it thrived for many more years, despite the increasing numbers of first-rate American musicians.

Hearing De Meyer and Herz only whetted the appetites of Americans to experience the two most famous pianists of the time: Liszt and Thalberg. Reports of proposed American tours by each of the artists abounded, but they were mostly wishful thinking. Thalberg would wait a full decade before venturing to America, and Liszt would never cross the ocean, primarily because he had withdrawn from active concertizing in 1847, just as America mania was sweeping the continent.

PART THREE

Sigismund Thalberg

1856-58

Map 4. Cities in which Sigismund Thalberg performed.

CHAPTER 7

A Rival of Liszt

By the time Sigismund Thalberg (1812–1871) crossed the Atlantic—first in 1855 to South America,[1] then to the United States the following year—two decades had passed since his rise to fame, and his technical superiority as a pianist was reportedly on the wane. One American music journal described him just before his arrival as "*once* the greatest living pianist."[2] However dusty Thalberg's reputation as a pianist was then, his former preeminence as a virtuoso was indisputable. He had been the only pianist to challenge Liszt's supremacy in the 1830s and had competed head to head and finger to finger with his rival. The spirited debate over who was the greater pianist culminated in a now legendary concert in 1837 in the Parisian salon of Princess Belgiojoso that was a combination duel and reconciliation. Many biographers of Liszt have perpetuated a myth that their subject was proclaimed the winner, but the duel, in fact, was considered a draw. The critic Jules Janin reported on the concert:

> Never was Liszt more controlled, more thoughtful, more energetic, more passionate; never has Thalberg played with greater verve and tenderness. Each of them prudently stayed within his harmonic domain, but each used every one of his resources. It was an admirable joust. The most profound silence fell over that noble arena. And finally Liszt and Thalberg were both proclaimed victors by this glittering and intelligent assembly. . . . Thus two victors and no vanquished.[3]

Liszt's withdrawal from performing in 1847 left Thalberg unchallenged as the reigning performing pianist.

Thalberg's career had begun in the late 1820s and had included the usual tours of a virtuoso. His early years, however, were anything but ordinary. The circumstances surrounding his birth are still unclear. Born in Pâquis, Switzerland, near Geneva, in 1812, he was considered during his lifetime to be the son of Prince Franz Joseph Dietrichstein and the Baroness Wetzlar. Yet the record of his birth states that his parents were Joseph Thalberg and Fortunée Stein of Frankfurt. Whether Joseph Thalberg was the natural father or simply assumed paternity on behalf of Dietrichstein remains a mystery.[4] At age ten, however, Thalberg went to live with Dietrichstein in Vienna, where in an abundantly rich social and musical milieu he prepared for a diplomatic career and gratified his love for music. He attended the premiere of Beethoven's Ninth Symphony when he was twelve and studied theory with Sechter and piano with the virtuosos Hummel, Kalkbrenner, Moscheles, and Pixis. After a few appearances in London in 1826, the pianist gave numerous performances in his adopted Vienna, embarked on his first international tour in 1830, and achieved his first success in Paris in 1836. Thalberg never denied his aristocratic birth, and the public's belief in his elite origins enhanced his romantic appeal as a virtuoso.[5]

Thalberg's triumphs as a performer as well as his virtuoso works for piano had long made him famous in the United States before his arrival. The *New-York Musical Review and Gazette,* for example, asserted that he had "been known in America by reputation for many years" and that the "piano-forte of every advanced amateur and pupil has borne upon its desk the *Lucia Fantasia,* or some other of his compositions." The *New-York Daily Times* likewise believed he was "an artist who is known in every clime, and whose compositions are the glorious effort of every beautiful and aspiring *pianiste.*"[6] Because of his exceptional prestige, Thalberg could be presented simply to the American public with only an occasional bit of nonsense.

ULLMAN AGAIN

Thalberg's remarkable American tour, during which he made more than three hundred appearances in two seasons, was the result of the initiative of Herz's manager, Bernard Ullman (figure 7.1). By the 1850s American impresarios were no longer content to wait passively at home for a visiting performer to approach them for assistance. Instead, they aggressively pursued artists they wished to represent and often made trips to Europe in search of new stars. For Ullman, managing Thalberg was an opportunity to validate his position as one of America's leading impresarios. After breaking with Herz in 1849, he had suffered a reversal in his managerial career, but soon regained his footing with the notable American tour of Henriette Sontag (1852–54).

THE IMPRESSARIO.—ULLMAN.

Figure 7.1. Caricature of Bernard Ullman by Thomas Nast. (THE HARVARD THEATRE COLLECTION, THE HOUGHTON LIBRARY)

Ullman mostly handled Thalberg's tour in a serious manner, focusing attention purely on his client's skills as pianist and composer. There were no scandals that had made the visits of De Meyer and Herz so extra-musically entertaining. Ullman's general lack of sensationalism, especially noticeable after Barnum's coarse handling of Jenny Lind's tour, was consistently praised, although Thalberg usually received the credit. The *New York Herald's* position was typical but ironic, considering it had been such an avid supporter of De Meyer: "The great success of M. Thalberg . . . is a real tribute to the merit of a great artist, unassisted by any of the dodges or humbugs that were resorted to by his predecessors. . . . There was no Barnum or Leopold de Meyer humbug—no serenades or rehearsals, or tickets sold at auction, or any of the other tricks that have disgusted everybody."[7]

To be sure, Ullman had no qualms about enticing audiences with cunning announcements that played on their sense of obligation to the performer's talent, the manager's labor, the progress of art, and the reputation of their country. What would Europeans think, he seemed to imply, if Americans did not adequately patronize Thalberg's concerts? Guilt was almost as effective as humbug in drawing a crowd in America. Ullman also increasingly assumed a more public role as an impresario by signing his name to press communications and basking in the glory of his famous clients.

Thalberg's arrival in New York on 3 October 1856 on the steamship *Africa* hardly created a ripple in the press. Over the past decade, New York had grown accustomed to visiting celebrities and was now rather aloof at their advent. Some time would have to pass before it let an artist induce hysteria as had Jenny Lind. Originally planned to begin on 20 October, Thalberg's concerts were postponed because of the intense excitement created by the presidential election, in which James Buchanan would defeat John Frémont. The pianist's American debut was rescheduled for 20 November and announced with a flourish customary of Ullman in its mock humility and pretentious stance. His "Card of the Management" tried to convince the public of Thalberg's self-sacrifice and his altruistic efforts on the behalf of art. Thalberg would be "content with the fame which appreciation can alone bestow." Instead of choosing the largest hall to accumulate as much money as quickly as possible as most visiting artists would, Thalberg "cheerfully relinquished" the financial advantages of a large hall and chose a smaller one, Niblo's Saloon, where the "*nuances,* the lights and shades, the delicate tints, and the broad contrasts which impart an individuality to piano-forte playing, may be gathered with the ease and comfort of a home circle." And to top it off, the admission prices would be moderate. "Too moderate," in fact, given the expenses, to afford Thalberg that "just emolument to which he is entitled."[8]

Once his concerts finally began, Thalberg performed at a furious pace. In a nonstop schedule masterminded by Ullman, Thalberg appeared almost every night of the week (with the usual exception of Sunday) for the next eight months. Occasionally he performed two or three times on the same day, giving concerts for schoolchildren in the morning and matinées in the afternoon in addition to evening performances. After two weeks of concerts in New York, he began appearing in rapid succession in other eastern cities. He often shuttled back and forth on alternate nights between two major cities like New York and Philadelphia or Baltimore and Washington, D.C. At other times he used a major city as a hub and alternated performances between it and smaller surrounding cities, as he did in Philadelphia and Boston. In just over five months he made almost 150 appearances in the eastern cities alone—more than De Meyer had made in his entire twenty months in North America and about three-quarters as many as Herz had in almost two years.

Such a dramatic increase in the number of concerts and the rapidity in which they were given was partly attributable to the rise of the impresario as a vital force in the musical life of the United States. The *New York Dispatch,* which considered Thalberg's career in this country to be "more brilliantly successful than that of any great artist that has preceded him, without any exception whatever," credited much of the achievement to the meticulous planning of his management. It believed the "quickness of his movements, the combinations of attraction, . . . [and] the economy of time . . . [were] more perfect, more closely calculated, and more energetically car-

ried out, than was ever any similar undertaking in this or any other country."[9] Ullman's stunning execution of Thalberg's tour was dependent on his decade of experience in honing his managerial skills. Orchestrating such a complex tour was possible only through Ullman's knowledge of advertising and journalism; his familiarity with cities, concert halls, and transportation; and his numerous contacts in the musical world. The innocent days of leisurely crossing the country without a manager were gone. The fledgling American profession of musical manager was now quite developed, and taking music to large sections of the nation was quickly becoming a lucrative, if occasionally uncertain, business.

The importance of Ullman's strategy was equaled by the vigorous growth of musical interest in the United States. The sophisticated planning of an impresario is worth little if the public has no desire to hear the artist. Only a few performers like Thalberg, however, could have fueled the public's enthusiasm during such an extended series of concerts. During his first season alone, he gave thirty-eight concerts in New York, twenty-two in Boston, thirteen in Philadelphia, seven in Baltimore, and five in Washington, D.C. The fervor induced by Thalberg and the public's faithfulness to him were considered to be second only to those associated with Jenny Lind. In each city, crowds flocked to his concerts without abatement. Dwight reported that for Thalberg's fifth Boston concert at the packed Music Hall, he finally "found a seat with hundreds on the stage." After sixteen concerts in New York, the *Times* declared that "the interest in this great and genial artist appears to be on the increase." Even after Thalberg had given twenty concerts in Boston, the *Post* believed that the "people do not tire of the distinguished pianist's entertainments, for, after they have long ceased to be novelties, they are attended by as large and brilliant audiences as at first."[10]

THALBERG AS PERFORMER AND COMPOSER

Thalberg's devoted audiences were continually enthralled by his flawless performances of his celebrated virtuoso showpieces. Whatever doubts Americans may have harbored about Thalberg's current status as a pianist immediately vanished upon witnessing that his formidable technique was still intact. The *New York Herald* believed it spoke the "unanimous sentiment of the art world" when claiming that "no such finished and artistic pianoforte playing has ever before been heard in America." "We unhesitatingly affirm," vowed a Chicago critic, "that [Thalberg] is the greatest pianist we have ever heard. De Meyer, Herz, Gottschalk, Mason, Strakosch, and the rest have all their merit, and great merit too; but none of them . . . have acquired that complete control of the instrument, that power to produce great effects by quiet means and ease of execution." Dwight was as entranced by Thalberg's playing as anyone else: "The execution was so perfect that the mind did not begin to analyze, or hardly ask itself what it was hearing; it might break the charm to ask a question.

There was a singular completeness about it. The execution was perfection, the like of which we had not heard before."[11]

Almost as extraordinary as Thalberg's accuracy was the seeming effortlessness with which he accomplished it. Dwight observed that the pianist performed with ease "what we have seen so many sweat and strain themselves to do but passably." American audiences were also enchanted by Thalberg's conspicuous lack of taste-less mannerisms typical of so many would-be virtuosos. The *New York Herald* be-lieved that "his quiet, modest, thoroughly gentlemanly manner at the piano makes him almost as many admirers as his splendid playing." A Boston critic was delighted that there was "no upturning of the eyes or pressing of the hand over the heart as if seized by a sudden cramp in that region, the said motions caused by a fit of thank-fulness." Another writer in Providence was glad that Thalberg resorted to "no tricks, no sentimentalities, no galvanic liftings and frenzied dashings down of the hands, no rapt listenings to his own sweet strains (though this might show its warrant), no flip-pancies directed at his audience, no civilities to any of them beyond his general and dignified bow."[12]

Although audiences unanimously admired Thalberg's unpretentious perform-ance style, there was disagreement over the effect of his relentless perfection, which some listeners found as maddening as it was amazing. A Richmond critic quipped that "it would be a sort of relief to hear a discordant note," and in New York Richard Grant White, who believed Thalberg's accuracy was "marvellous to the verge of the miraculous," retold the story of an Englishman, who having followed Thalberg "in vain for three years in the hope of hearing a false note, blew out his brains in de-spair." Others were exasperated by the invariability of his performances that seemed to be more machine-made than man-made. A Cincinnati correspondent to *Dwight's* wondered whether Thalberg played with a "great deal of expression, but rather little feeling." Reflecting on the pianist at the time of his death in 1871, one writer re-membered that Thalberg's "perfection" made his performances "dry and monoto-nous," and joked how the pianist "never became excited, aye, in the hottest days he could not even perspire." On the other hand, a Springfield critic believed "the grand secret of his playing, or rather of its effect upon the audience, is that his soul is in it."[13]

Thalberg's phenomenal success in the United States was due as much to his fame and popularity as a composer as to his astonishing technique. Amateur pianists were attracted to his concerts just as they had been to those of Herz. One newspaper reported that for his first Philadelphia concert

> every one with a piano talent or a piano ambition was there, from the miss who had labored over the simplest one of Thalberg's specimens of *"L'art du chant appliqué au piano,"* to the accomplished amateur or professor who, having mastered all the me-chanical difficulties of the "Moise" or the "Sonnambula" fantasies, was eager to see and to hear how the great master himself would perform them.[14]

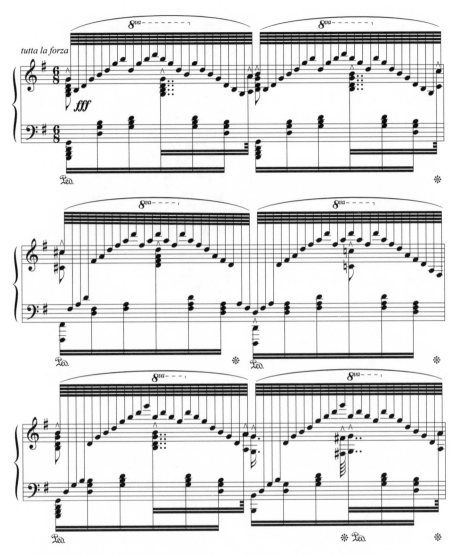

Example 7.1. Sigismund Thalberg, Fantasia on *Moses in Egypt*, Op. 33, mm. 297–99.

For many Americans, Thalberg's works were the culmination of what could be achieved by a lone performer on a single instrument. As a leader in implementing the new technological capabilities of the piano, Thalberg required of the performer an immense technical facility and exploited the full range of the instrument aided by the pedal. Dwight believed that it was Thalberg who "first undertook to overcome the short-comings of the piano-forte" and "first made the piano speak through the whole length of its keyboard like an orchestra."[15] Although Thalberg was capable of grand masses of sound rivaling the orchestra, he was noted for his emphasis on a

Figure 7.2. Caricature of Sigismund Thalberg. (BIBLIOTHÈQUE NATIONALE DE FRANCE, PARIS)

singing tone, no matter how virulent the accompaniment. The French critic Henri Blanchard claimed that "no one has ever sung at the piano like Thalberg."[16]

Undoubtedly, Thalberg's claim to posterity was his cultivation, if not the invention, of the texture in which a melody in the middle register of the piano is divided between the two hands, while both of them alternately swirl arpeggios, scale passages, and other figuration above and below the melody. He first introduced the technique in his Fantasia on Rossini's *Moses in Egypt* (example 7.1), the piece he performed in his concert with Liszt, and he used it frequently in later works. This technique amazed audiences, who supposedly stood up to see how it was accomplished, for it gave the impression that three hands were required. Referring to a popular caricature of Thalberg with eight hands (figure 7.2), the *New-York Daily Times* jested that it was "hard to believe that one man can do so much with the ordinary number of fingers, and one looks at his hands suspiciously, expecting to see them branching out with supplementary fingers."[17]

Thalberg's emphasis on a singing tone and brilliant virtuosic display coalesced in his opera fantasias, in which a lyrical melody from an operatic source is surrounded by the most severe technical demands. Instead of merely assembling a string of mechanical variations, Thalberg molded the work into a dramatic unity, gradually building toward a grand climax through various restatements of the unchanging theme while the accompaniment shifted kaleidoscopically. Mostly based on early nineteenth-century Italian operas, Thalberg's fantasias formed the core of his repertoire in the

Three Hands

Thalberg's signature three-handed texture was described by a correspondent from Spring-field, Massachusetts, to Dwight's Journal of Music, *whose affected homespun humor was completely accurate (and prophetic):*

By Jove! his thumbs are all fingers. Really, I thought Mason, Gottschalk, Strakosch and those tall players did the piano well, but I am just as much in the fog as to what piano perfection is, as when I first heard cousin Jane thump out "Home" as a waltz on our forty dollar concern. This man plays a few notes of the melody in the middle of the piano with his right hand; at the same time his left, full of "muttering wrath," crawls up and attacks the melody, and then the right steals way up to high C, sees what's to be seen, and then softly tumbles back just in time to carry on the melody, while the left hand leaves for the lower regions on an excursion for "di-minished sevenths," "flat ninths," "curious tenths," and all them sort of things, and gets back in the region of middle C in time to relieve the right hand of the melody, to cut up its pranks in the upper octaves. Really, I believe the next *great* player who comes here will play a part at each end of the instrument, while he plays an obbligato accompaniment inside on the wires!

Dwight's Journal of Music 10 (10 January 1857): 116

United States. The works he most consistently offered included fantasias on Mozart's *Don Giovanni;* Rossini's *Moses in Egypt* and *Semiramide;* Donizetti's *L'Elisir d'amore, Don Pasquale, La fille du régiment, Lucia di Lammermoor,* and *Lucrezia Borgia;* Bellini's *Norma* and *La Sonnambula;* Auber's *La muette de Portici (Masaniello);* and Meyerbeer's *Les Huguenots.*[18]

If Thalberg's music is remembered at all today, it is because of the reputation of the fantasias. Yet these works, so typical of the period, are perhaps the least likely to engage today's listener. Their grandiose effects and overtly emotional appeal are no longer fashionable, and their existence in limbo between arrangement and original composition make their artistic value suspect. The smaller, less pretentious works of Thalberg, in which technical demands are less stringent and more often subordi-nate to musical ideas, may be the best introduction to his music. Critics had consis-tent praise for Thalberg's caprices, etudes, nocturnes, romances, and waltzes. Dwight found "a certain grace and flavor . . . a certain poetry and delicacy of feeling, some-thing like original creation" in these works which placed Thalberg among the "minor poets of the piano."[19]

Among these smaller works that Thalberg performed in America is a dizzying *Tarantelle,* Op. 65, a not exceptionally difficult perpetual-motion study (example 7.2). The "delirious ecstacy" with which Thalberg performed it enchanted Dwight, who described it as the "exquisitely, feverishly, delicate, delicious *Tarantella.*" The

Example 7.2. Sigismund Thalberg, *Tarantelle,* Op. 65, (a) mm. 18–27; (b) mm. 50–59; (c) mm. 82–91.

more serious *Thème original et étude* in A Minor, Op. 45 (usually subtitled "Repeated Notes"), is unified by a single motive, first hinted at in the developmental introduction, prominent in the lyrical central section, and then transformed into a virtuosic challenge in the closing etude, in which the theme appears in rapidly repeated notes alternating between the hands. Dwight considered it one of the "most poetical and delicate of [Thalberg's] productions,"[20] and it was one of two works by Thalberg that Anton Rubinstein played on his American tour. Other nonoperatic

Example 7.2. *continued*

works Thalberg performed include an *Andante,* a *Barcarolle,* a *Marche funèbre,* and a collection of *Airs russes.* He often offered as an encore a charming set of concert waltzes, *Souvenir d'Amérique: Valses brillantes* (example 7.3). By turns graceful and brilliant, the waltz strains are a delightful cross between Chopin and Johann Strauss.

Like most visiting composers, Thalberg was compelled to write variations on tunes popular in America, including "Home, Sweet Home," "The Last Rose of Summer," and "Lilly Dale."[21] His setting of "Home, Sweet Home" was an exceptional success in both its popularity with audiences and its sales as sheet music (figure 7.3). Reports of his performances of the work are unashamedly sentimental. A writer in Auburn, New York, was moved to tears:

> But oh! wonderful power of Genius! Thalberg again got possession of me. As he played, all the beauties and enticements of a beautiful and enticing home crowded up before me—even down to the very poker and tongs—(fact; don't laugh!)—and—beautiful provision of Nature—the tears stood in my eyes till all of that audience were shut out; and there I sat in that lovely home—and Thalberg playing to me.

Such naive responses were typical of all audiences, not just those in smaller cities. The critic for the *New York Evening Post* described the work's effect on audience members, who "became fixed in their places, as if by a charm—not a muscle moving until the lips began to quiver, and the breast heave with stifled sobbing, and the tears stole in their eyes." During Thalberg's performance of the piece in Boston, "the most deathless silence prevailed" and the "remembrances that it carried to many hearts brought into requisition numerous handkerchiefs, and thoughts of the past

Example 7.3. Sigismund Thalberg, *Souvenir d'Amérique: Valses brillantes,* (a) Strain 3; (b) Strain 5.

came rushing to the memory over which the grass of forgetfulness [had] almost grown green." The work seduced even Richard Grant White, who believed the "purely vocal style in which [Thalberg] gave it, the tenderness which he threw into its unadorned phrases, and the manner in which he made the piano-forte sing it, made the performance of it a great piece of art."[22]

Although at first highly regarded as a composer, Thalberg dropped rather suddenly in the public estimation partly because his imaginative technical innovations were copied by so many composers that his own works were soon considered clichés. As early as 1841 he wrote to his friend Ferdinand Hiller about his improvements in

Example 7.3. *continued*

using the thumbs in the middle voice, claiming he was the "inventor and exploiter, but unfortunately not the monopoliser." And in 1852 Lenz could state that the current piano technique of the day consisted "only of Thalberg simple, Thalberg amended, and Thalberg exaggerated; scratch what is written for the piano, and you will find Thalberg."[23]

Because Thalberg as a composer ranks below his greater contemporaries, his music is undeservedly ignored today. A critic like Dwight, who acknowledged that profundities were not to be found in Thalberg's music, could understand, however, that its aim was to "illustrate the possibilities of the piano, in a way to strike and astonish, but above all to please the general ear of music lovers." Dwight was able to

Figure 7.3. Sheet music cover for Sigismund Thalberg's *Home! Sweet Home!* identified as "100th Edition." (AUTHOR'S COLLECTION)

enjoy the "all-pervading taste and sense of fitness everywhere, . . . the symmetry, the architectural balance and completeness of the whole work . . . without asking ourselves what it is not." He even had to admit that the fantasias, after having heard them played by Thalberg himself, seemed a "much more genuine thing than formerly; under his hands they justify themselves."[24]

GOTTSCHALK, MASON, AND OTHERS

Just as he carefully planned Thalberg's itinerary, Ullman cleverly rationed a continuously changing roster of assisting artists to help maintain interest in the pianist's almost endless string of appearances. After four months, the *Times* was impressed by the "prodigality" of Thalberg's concerts that "exceeds anything we have experienced in this country" and admired the pianist's modesty in surrounding himself with so many first-rate artists. Ullman's most unusual twist in programming, and indeed his masterstroke, was teaming Thalberg with America's two leading pianists, Louis Moreau Gottschalk and William Mason. Although still not as highly regarded as they deserved, the two performers were clearly Thalberg's chief rivals in the United States. Ironically, the *Times* believed that Mason and Gottschalk, by developing in the public a "genuine appreciation of piano-playing," had "contributed in an enormous degree to the success which attends and which awaits Mr. Thalberg." Even

more telling was the critic's confession that "we should have forgotten all about the twain, had we not seen their enthusiastic faces at these concerts, beaming genial reciprocity on the great artist whom they honor with true artist's pride," indicating just how undervalued the two performers were. Their ten respective joint appearances with Thalberg provided Americans with the prospect of a showdown à la Liszt-Thalberg and the opportunity to demonstrate their pride in American talent without sacrificing their desire to hear a celebrated European artist.[25]

Thalberg may have suggested joining forces with the two pianists, for he had known both of them in Europe, and he had renewed acquaintances with each of them soon after his arrival in the United States.[26] Early in the season, Gottschalk joined Thalberg for performances of the latter's two-piano fantasia on *Norma,* igniting a sensation. The most electrifying moment in the brief partnership occurred when Thalberg appeared at one of Gottschalk's farewell concerts in New York on 26 December 1856, for which Gottschalk composed a two-piano fantasia on *Il Trovatore,* now lost (figure 7.4). The pianist Richard Hoffman, who claimed the piece "created the most tremendous furore and excitement," remembered that a "remarkable double shake which Thalberg played in the middle of the piano, while Gottschalk was flying all over the keyboard in the 'Anvil Chorus,' produced the most prodigious volume of tone I ever heard from the piano." Another observer was concerned about the work's severe demands, especially the incessant crashing chords from one end of the piano to the other played by Gottschalk. The writer was distressed by "the extreme pallor of the composer as he rose from the instrument," and thought the audience's demand for an encore, with which the performers complied, was a "very cruel one." Gottschalk appeared "too slight for such great physical effort."[27] During the rest of his career, Gottschalk performed this fantasia, proudly indicating on programs the circumstances surrounding its premiere.

The public was especially fascinated by the obvious contrast between the players. One critic described the furious battle between the respective followers of Gottschalk and Thalberg, a feud he found more bitter than the recent election and one that divided families and broke engagements. Gottschalk, more admired by the young, was "impassioned, irregular, fitful," and "surprises, moves, entrances," while Thalberg, preferred by the "travelled people, the *blasé,* the critics," was "calm, unimpassioned" and "diffuses serene pleasure, and performs unheard-of feats with perfect ease."[28] If the adherents of the pianists were argumentative, the performers's apparent cordiality to each other on stage was a pleasant surprise.

Although Gottschalk gained prestige from his appearances with Thalberg, he must have rankled at the unqualified success enjoyed by his European counterpart. He had yet to receive similar acclaim at home and was surely jealous of the attention his countrymen paid to a foreigner. With Thalberg virtually monopolizing the market for piano concerts in the East, it was fortunate that Gottschalk had already

Figure 7.4. Program for Louis Moreau Gottschalk's concert with guest appearance by Sigismund Thalberg, New York, 26 December 1856. (DAVID STANFORD SCRAPBOOK OF MUSICAL PROGRAMS, RARE BOOK AND MANUSCRIPT LIBRARY, COLUMBIA UNIVERSITY)

made plans for his second trip to Cuba.[29] Perhaps it is no coincidence that he began his diary during his five-year sojourn in the Caribbean, which is curiously silent about Thalberg, in an effort to deal with his role as prophet in his own country.

Except for two New York concerts, Ullman scheduled all of Mason's appearances in his hometown of Boston and other New England cities, where the pianist had a solid reputation. (Ullman had just as wisely used Gottschalk outside of New England, where he was slower in gaining popularity.) Most critics were proud of Mason's ability to perform on a level with Thalberg in his *Norma* Fantasia, although some admitted he was not quite Thalberg's match. Dwight, for example, praised Mason but with reservations:

Wonderfully well was the whole thing executed, the younger pianist bearing his banner proudly side by side with the winner of a thousand battles. The difficulties were about equally shared between them, and the ensemble was quite perfect. Yet on Thalberg's side there was the still finer touch, and what was clear before, stood out all the clearer and the bolder when his fingers took their turn.[30]

Other performers who appeared with Thalberg included the violinist Joseph Burke, whose playing had become "disconsolately rusty since the days of Jenny

Lind," thought the *Times,* but who still played with a "tender sweetness"; the young Theodore Thomas as violinist, then under Ullman's management as concertmaster at the Academy of Music; and the cellist Carl Bergmann, the former conductor of the disbanded Germania Musical Society who also conducted most of Thalberg's concerto appearances. Thomas was to become one of America's great conductors and toured with Rubinstein during his American visit; Bergmann, who became an important conductor of the New York Philharmonic, played an important role in Bülow's tour. In March 1857 the two performed the "Archduke" Trio with Thalberg in several New England concerts. Supporting vocalists included the American-born Cora de Wilhorst, who was new to the concert stage, and two operatic veterans both making their American debut in the fall of 1856: Elena D'Angri and Bertha Johannsen. This "excess of accessory attractions," as Dwight called it, was an attempt to please a wide range of listeners. Such programs were still the custom of the time, but at least a few critics were beginning to object to these miscellaneous compilations that distracted from the main course. As they saw it, the same hackneyed arias were tediously repeated from concert to concert, and only delayed in hearing the principal attraction. Frequently, the repertoire was not deserving of the talented performers, the discriminating concertgoers, or the extravagant admission fees.[31]

BEETHOVEN CONCERTOS

Following Thalberg's initial concerts in New York, Philadelphia, and Boston, Ullman engaged an orchestra to preserve the excitement generated by the pianist's appearances. The nightly expenses would be doubled, Ullman apprised the public, but Thalberg had incurred an obligation to his audiences for their overwhelming support, he reasoned unctuously. The *Times* acknowledged Ullman's astuteness as a manager for adding new attractions in the "very hey-day of prosperity." Most managements, it speculated, would have "continued in the old course, and reaped the full harvest of success down to the very stubble."[32] Ignoring his own youthful piano concerto, Thalberg offered the first movements of Beethoven's Third and Fifth Piano Concertos, works he had performed in Vienna more than twenty years earlier.[33] Both concertos had already received complete performances in the United States—the Third as early as 1842, the Fifth not until 1854—but neither had been played frequently. Surprisingly, two of New York's most discerning critics were not especially thrilled to hear the works. Richard Grant White in the *Courier and Enquirer* did not believe the "union of the piano-forte with the orchestra a very congruous one," since the piano did not "seem to have sympathy" with any one or all of the tones of the orchestra. William Henry Fry of the *Tribune* argued that there was "no logic in an accompanied concerto now," given the recent developments in piano music, especially those cultivated by Thalberg. He saw no reason for an orchestra to "putty up the cracks of pianism, when the new lights have orchestrized the piano,

doubled its volume, its expression and its interest, and made it, according to its circle, perfect."[34]

Despite his reservations about the combination of piano and orchestra, White believed that Thalberg played the Third Concerto with "absolute precision and most delicate appreciation of its significance," and he was enraptured with Thalberg's elaborate cadenza—"itself a concerto"—that was "so consonant with the spirit" of the original work. The *Times,* the only newspaper that dared to question Thalberg's interpretations, considered his style too "chaste and exquisite" for Beethoven's music, which demanded "rough vigor and fire." Yet as America's most perceptive admirer of Beethoven, Dwight was the most enthusiastic about Thalberg's performances. He believed the pianist played the "Emperor" Concerto with "masterly power and beauty," and his rendering of the Third Concerto was a "miracle of perfection" and "witchingly beautiful":

> Thalberg played it not only with the utmost precision, force and clearness, but with the finest light and shade, bringing out with exquisite feeling and accent all those little melodic phrases which in Beethoven's music melt out of the tone mass. . . . But what held the audience in breathless delight for some minutes was the long and elaborate cadence introduced by Thalberg at the orchestral pause near the end. It was marvellously ingenious and beautiful, an abstract, in fact, of the entire movement, as if it had caught its own image in miniature in a distant mirror. . . . Certainly it was clearly settled that evening that Thalberg can appreciate and can play Beethoven.[35]

These performances by Thalberg—his most significant venture outside the repertoire of his own works—verified beyond any doubt his preeminence as a pianist and musician. The *Boston Evening Transcript,* for example, believed his "claims to be recognized as something more than a mere virtuoso performer on his instrument can scarcely be questioned." Dwight's only regret was that Thalberg did not subordinate himself more often in a "higher and more glorious calling" by programming more of the "beauties of inspired works like those of Beethoven." Judging by a private letter to *Dwight's* New York correspondent, Dwight's view was a minority opinion. Observing the reaction to the concertos, the writer was disheartened because audiences seemed indifferent to the better quality of music. "Why will mere glitter so far outweigh solid gold with the multitude?" he pondered. For him, Thalberg's performance of the first movement of the "Emperor" was worth all the rest of the concert together, "yet it fell dead upon the audience, while I drank it in as the mown grass does the rain. A great soul was speaking to mine, and I communed with him."[36]

CHAPTER 8

At the Matinées

Thalberg's most satisfying appearances artistically comprised a series of more than fifteen solo matinées in New York and Boston in early 1857.[1] The matinées constituted his only appearances without the standard assortment of subordinate performers (though other instrumentalists occasionally joined him for a single chamber work) and his only sustained effort at broadening his repertoire. Popular for some time in Europe for solo recitals and chamber music, afternoon concerts had only been recently introduced in the United States, most notably by Theodore Thomas and William Mason, who began a series of matinée chamber music concerts in 1855. With his series of matinées, Thalberg became the first visiting virtuoso pianist to give solo recitals in America.

One advantage of Thalberg's matinées was the change of venue to smaller halls that allowed a closer inspection of the pianist's technique, which was confirmed again and again as faultless. In Boston, where the matinées were held in the salon of Chickering & Sons, Dwight found the intimate atmosphere more congenial and believed it was "the true way to hear him; . . . one seemed to hear him for the first time, for he played as if he were at home, with only sympathetic listeners." The *Boston Post* remarked that the relaxed attitude of the pianist was evident by his "mingling among his audience as the unpretending and accomplished gentleman" between his selections.[2]

More important, in his matinées Thalberg widened his repertoire for the first time beyond his own music and the two Beethoven concertos. He performed two of Mendelssohn's *Songs without Words* ("Volkslied" and "Frühlingslied"), some Chopin mazurkas and the funeral march from the B♭ Minor Sonata, transcriptions of three Schubert songs ("Ave Maria," "Lob der Tränen," and "Ständchen"), the Hummel Septet, and several works by Beethoven: the "Moonlight" Sonata, the "Archduke" Trio, the Trio in C Minor, and a transcription of "Adelaide." He also offered transcriptions of several operatic excerpts (the quartet from *I Puritani,* the trio from *Robert de diable,* and the Miserere from *Il Trovatore*), which he performed on a reed organ manufactured by Alexandre of Paris. Ullman justified the change in repertoire by explaining that these works were written "at a time when audiences were counted by scores and not by thousands" and were not intended to "encounter the glitter of innumerable gaslights and the excitement of a modern Evening Concert." Ullman's belief that works by such composers as Beethoven, Mendelssohn, and Schubert were suited for the intimate salon and not the mammoth concert hall were common, and Dwight agreed that the matinée selections were "choicer and more varied than would serve the ends of a concert before two thousand people."[3]

Despite Thalberg's occasional uncertainty with the new repertoire, most critics were pleased with his selections and performances. Dwight claimed he had never heard the scherzo of the "Archduke" Trio (performed with Theodore Thomas and Carl Bergmann) played "with such energy and clearness, such effectiveness in all its points." He and his New York correspondent agreed that the first movement of the "Moonlight" Sonata received an unorthodox interpretation, being played, in the words of Dwight, "rather with exquisite grace and beauty than with that Beethoven-like depth and earnestness of feeling." Dwight found Thalberg's rendering of Chopin's "Marche funèbre" to be "rather hurried," while his correspondent, in a different performance, thought it "was exquisitely given, with all the breadth and grandeur in the first part, and delicacy and tenderness in the second, which it requires."[4]

Socially, Thalberg's matinées unquestionably demonstrated the extensive patronage of music by women, who at the time were widely understood to be the principal supporters of the arts. Writing two years earlier in 1855, the impresario Max Maretzek described the vital role women played: "The artistic thought of the United States is at the present moment engaged in developing itself through the female half of the population. . . . The ladies in this country are the real amateurs and patrons of our own Art. . . . Indeed, beyond the principal cities, it is the ladies alone that patronize and love the Arts. These, alone, know anything about them." Reviews of the first New York matinée testify to the preponderance of women in the audience. One stated that "a few gentlemen of strong nerves and much leisure were the solitary representatives of the sterner sex," and another claimed that "there were so few gentlemen that they might well count for nothing." The *Boston Evening Transcript* later

concurred on the allure of the matinées to women, particularly those with musical training:

> These morning *réunions* are especially attended by ladies, and amongst these there is scarcely one who is not or has not been in some measure a pianist. Necessarily a morning with Thalberg, with the certainty of hearing him play six or seven pieces, and the chance of encoring him twice or thrice—what gentleman can have the heart to refuse an *encore* from two hundred and fifty pairs of pretty and well-gloved hands— is an attraction which it would be perfectly impossible to resist.[5]

Thalberg's matinées were overwhelmingly successful with women for a practical reason as well. A respectable woman required a male escort to attend an evening event, but she could attend an afternoon concert alone.[6] Whereas groups of women sometimes traveled considerable distances to hear a performer,[7] individually they were restricted by a social barrier not always as easily overcome. A semi-autobiographical comic song by Faustina Hasse Hodges titled "The Indignant Spinster" (published 1867) gave one woman's account of this obstacle:

> They say I am free with no one to teaze,
> Where's the use of being free? I can't do as I please;
> I make up my mind to a concert to go—
> And I can't stir a peg! all for want of a Beau![8]

The assumption that more women than men would want to attend concerts and the knowledge that women could not attend alone sometimes influenced the pricing of tickets. For some of De Meyer's and Herz's concerts two tickets would "admit two ladies and a gentleman," a bargain that relieved to some extent the difficulty of finding a male companion.

Regardless of the musical advantages of the matinées and their generally sober aspirations, Ullman did not trust the public to attend them solely for musical reasons. His drawing card was to have black waiters dressed in livery serve refreshments consisting of chocolate, cake, and ice cream during an "Intermission for Lunch" (figure 8.1). The fare was probably attractive to the fashion-seeking subscriber, but, ironically, the first series of matinées in New York sold out before the delicacies were even publicized. Ullman had underestimated the public's interest in serious music and the eagerness of women audiences. The food, however, quickly became a lively topic of conversation and an easy target for satire.

When a comparable series of matinées was announced in Boston, the treats did not draw scorn, but the exclusiveness of the concerts as portrayed by the advertisement did:

> Notice. Nearly nine-tenths of the tickets for the Matinées in New York have been subscribed for by ladies belonging to the first families in the city. In view of the responsibility thus devolved upon the management, a correct address has been required

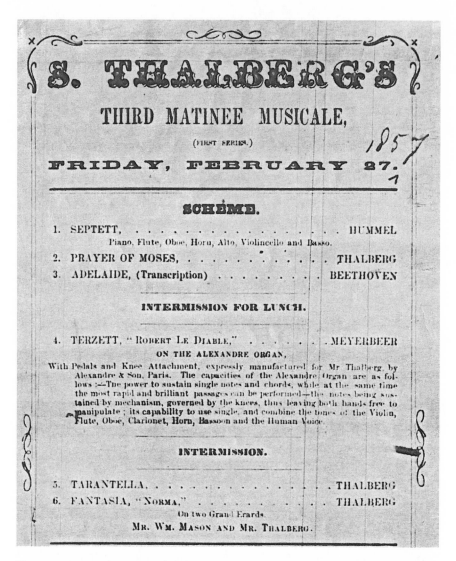

Figure 8.1. Program for Sigismund Thalberg's matinée, New York, 27 February 1857, indicating after the third piece an "Intermission for Lunch," during which refreshments were served. William Mason joined Thalberg for the latter's Fantasia on *Norma* for two pianos. (WILLIAM MASON SCRAPBOOK, MUSIC DIVISION, THE NEW YORK PUBLIC LIBRARY, ASTOR, LENOX AND TILDEN FOUNDATIONS)

from every subscriber—a determination which cannot but insure the utmost respectability of the audience, and must be appreciated by no one more than the subscribers themselves. The same regulation has been adopted for the Boston Matinées.

A similar announcement had been ignored by the New York press, but in Boston the attempt to restrict subscribers according to their social status unleashed intense opinions about the role of music in a democracy. At issue was whether music in the United

Music to Eat By

In the various jabs at the culinary offerings of Thalberg's matinées, no one surpassed the sarcastic glee of George William Curtis in his "Editor's Easy Chair" column of *Harper's*. Besides ridiculing the dainty refreshments, Curtis also mocked the pretentiousness of the matinées, specifically their "charmingly foreign" (i.e., European) character and the desire of many Americans to prove their sophistication to the world.

> It was a delightful thought of Thalberg's manager to mingle music, pound cake, . . . daylight, chocolate, and bulgy black legs in dirty white stockings. . . . One was so entirely desirous of almond cake after hearing the *Don Giovanni* fantasia, or the *Adelaide* of Beethoven. . . . It was most charmingly foreign; and the stockings added such a delicate flavor to the little cakes! Besides, the happy thought of the lunch, which was prepared in the little room opening immediately out of the hall, allowed the audience, as they bent forward to catch the zephyrs of music breathing along the keys, to hear also the rattling of cups and plates, and the cheerful voice and laugh of the African. . . . It is such a comfort to have things done well when they are done at all, and to show mankind that we know how to have morning concerts as well as any body.

In all seriousness, Curtis believed the "playing of Thalberg was never so exquisite as at the *Matinées*. It is, in truth, perfect. . . . [We] wonder whether he has not touched the utmost possibility of the piano, and ask whether, when he is gone, we have not seen and lost the most perfect pianist that ever has been or ever can be."[1]

1. *Harper's New Monthly Magazine* 14 (May 1857): 849–50. Several spoofs of the matinées appeared in *Harper's Weekly* 1 (28 February 1857): 129–30, (7 March 1857): 147, and (14 March 1857): 164. A wildly exaggerated account of them appears in Oscar Comettant's *Trois ans aux Etats-Unis,* 2d ed. (Paris: Pagnerre, 1858), 128–29 (quoted in Herz, *Travels,* 43–44). In Comettant's version, Thalberg literally opens a restaurant and women marvel at his talent "between an oyster stew, a slice of ham, and a fruit tart."

States should be reserved for the elite, as many Americans thought it was in Europe, or available to all people regardless of social or economic rank. This question touched a raw nerve in the *Boston Daily Ledger,* which railed vehemently against another example of "foreign snobbism." The paper derided the management and predicted the type of person who might be attracted to the matinées: "If you itch to be esteemed 'respectable,' and possess an 'address' that you are not desirous of concealing from the police, you will of course go to the *Matinées* of M. Thalberg; for there you will fix yourself for good in the social scale, learn what is *recherché* in these affairs, and see the *crème de la crème* of society besides." Yielding to public pressure, Ullman apologetically withdrew the restriction as gracefully as possible, explaining that its

purpose was not "to make the Matinées an exclusive entertainment." The regulation was simply a suggestion from the matinée patrons in New York "in consequence of a circumstance that occurred and rendered there this arrangement imperative."[9]

The *Daily Ledger* was incensed by the implied comparison between Boston and New York, arguing that just "because they may have 'got bit' at some one of their matinées in the emporium of murder and crime, it is not reason why they should proceed on a like supposition here in Boston." The *Ledger* gloated over Ullman's retraction and summarized its arguments against European elitism:

> Do we live in a Democratic Republic, or are we in Europe? . . . In the morning papers . . . we learned that a *very select matinée* is to come off sometime, and somewhere in Boston. We learned from this article that the company who would be permitted to listen to the matinée of Mr. "Tallbug," "Humbug," or "any other bug" [figure 8.2] must be *very select*. . . . We have had enough of *foreign snobism* . . . and wish our visitors from abroad to learn, if they are susceptible of improvement, the difference between Republicanism and their own government. . . . We are not unacquainted with the various "dodges" practised upon the "Yankees" by artists from over the waters, but this last attempt at refinement not only amuses, but convulses, the sensible portion of the American public with laughter.[10]

Although shrill in its tone, the *Ledger* correctly detected Ullman's ploy of holding up Europe as a model of sophistication and daring Americans to match it. Many Americans were sensitive about their lack of refinement, but others, whose sentiments were represented by the *Ledger,* were blatantly proud of it.

CONCERTS FOR SCHOOLCHILDREN

Months before the Boston matinée incident, Thalberg had initiated a series of free concerts for schoolchildren that should have spared him the charges of elitism, although his—or Ullman's—motive may not have been entirely altruistic. Giving free concerts to children was excellent publicity, and it created an image of an artist devoted to the furtherance of art. Ullman had been successful a few years earlier with such a gambit when managing Henriette Sontag, and Jenny Lind had done it before her. Yet Thalberg's thoroughness in carrying out the plan—at least twenty such concerts were given in ten cities—suggests a genuine sincerity. With the young audiences ranging in number from two thousand to five thousand per concert, Thalberg performed for as many as forty or fifty thousand children, and "every urchin in the street" seemed to know his name.[11]

The school concerts were heralded by published letters between Thalberg and Lowell Mason concerning the venture. Mason, who had met the pianist in 1837 during his first European trip, did little for the enterprise but add his imprimatur as America's leading music educator. Although a Philadelphia writer believed the per-

Tall Bug, a brother of the immortal Hum.

Figure 8.2. "Tall Bug, a brother of the immortal Hum." (*Yankee Notions* 6 [September 1857]: 286) (LIBRARY OF CONGRESS)

formances were a "little too scientific for the greater part of the audience," the children still registered their delight with the offerings of Thalberg and his associates. In one Boston concert, Dwight reported that they waved handkerchiefs and "hurrahed" for five minutes and "young girls loaded the artists with flowers." In New Orleans, where the violinist Vieuxtemps performed with Thalberg, a contrast was noted between the different standards of acceptable behavior for boys and for girls. Consigned to the second tier and gallery, the boys were

> uproarious, and insisted upon a repetition of everything until Vieuxtemps came out to play "The Carnival of Venice," as announced in the programme. The young rascals wouldn't have the Carnival, but shrieked from all parts of the house for "Yankee Doodle" in its stead. The great fiddler obligingly substituted the piece as requested, and gave it with all the exquisite variations for which he is so famous; and the boys were satisfied. It was altogether wonderful to hear what a quantity of whistle, shriek, and what enormous percussion of heel could be drawn from a crowd of small boys. As the girls could not indulge in the luxury of noisy applause, we could not tell what their particular preferences were, if they had any.

Thalberg's variations on "Home, Sweet Home" was a favorite selection, one the children knew well and often sang for the pianist. When they heard Thalberg's version of it at one concert, their "ruddy faces lighted up with a deeper glow, and a smile of pleasure rippled over them, and the whole house was vocal with whispered ejaculations of delight."[12]

Ullman had numerous ideas for serving up Thalberg in an endless smorgasbord of musical events. For instance, the pianist made two appearances with the Handel and Haydn Society of Boston, in which a performance of the Mozart Requiem was followed by a "sacred concert." And in the early spring of 1857, as the number of

Thalberg's Boston concerts neared twenty, he gave a series of fifty-cent concerts there and in other New England cities. When the pianist was about to make his first trek to the Midwest, Dwight remarked on the phenomenon of the Thalberg concert: "With all their names and shapes Protean—Thalberg's concerts simple, Thalberg's concerts grand, Thalberg's oratorios, festivals, children's concerts, matinées, soirées, piano recitals, &c., &c.—they are all over now. . . . They have given us a great variety of fine music, and a great deal of pleasure."[13]

OPERA AND INTRIGUE

In addition to representing Thalberg, Ullman was seeking to manage the opera at the Academy of Music in New York, newly opened in 1854. Opera management in New York was a risky undertaking, and no impresario had been financially successful at it for more than a season or two before either leaving the field or being forced to regroup. Besides its instability, the New York operatic world was filled with intrigue. A few days before Thalberg's concerts began, Ullman had been struck down in the street by a slingshot, and it was not the first time he had been assaulted in New York. Claiming he had been warned of an impending attack, Ullman suspected the assailant was a "general Man Friday" of his rival impresario Max Maretzek, who feared that Ullman and Thalberg might wrest the opera management from him. Responsible or not, Maretzek would have been right to be concerned about competition from Thalberg's approaching concerts, whose great quantity and incredible success did indeed prove disastrous for the Academy's opera season. By the middle of December, the *Herald* could state that Thalberg's troupe has the "success and the dollars," while Maretzek and his opera company had "beaten a retreat to Havana."[14]

With the conspicuous financial success he was enjoying with Thalberg, Ullman was finally able to win the bid for the lease of the Academy in early 1857, but only with the backing of the pianist.[15] Thalberg's involvement with the Academy of Music was small but not inconsequential: he supplied Ullman with much needed capital and with his name, endowing the joint venture with instant respectability and the prospect of success. Ullman soon consolidated forces in the opera house and concert hall with Maurice Strakosch, who had begun producing opera at the Academy in late January. In early March Thalberg joined with Strakosch's singers in seven concerts in New York and Brooklyn; three of the appearances (10, 12, and 19 March) included a performance of Rossini's Stabat Mater by members of the Academy's opera company and the New-York Harmonic Society. His two final New York appearances of the season were at the Academy of Music during opera intermissions, a trick to boost attendance that would be used the following season. With Thalberg's apparent commitment to the Academy of Music, most people assumed he would be on hand the following season for his operatic venture there. It appeared that Thalberg was becoming an American musical institution.

Music, Religion, and Sunday Concerts

Thalberg's two appearances with the Handel and Haydn Society of Boston were typical of several Sunday night concerts in which he participated. The morality of Sunday concerts and the repertoire appropriate for them were often hotly debated. At this time, concerts were allowable on Sunday only if they presented "sacred music," although that genre was often defined quite loosely and the requirement sometimes totally ignored. Thalberg could conveniently offer for such concerts his Fantasia on *Moses in Egypt,* based primarily on the prayer from Rossini's opera, and his Fantasia on *Les Huguenots,* which prominently used the chorale "Ein' feste Burg" as Meyerbeer did in his opera. Also deemed appropriate were Thalberg's *Andante* and *Marche funèbre.* Sunday concerts had an additional restriction of not allowing applause. At Thalberg's first appearance at a Handel and Haydn Society concert (18 January 1857), "so great was the enthusiasm of the audience that considerable exertion was required on the part of many to resist a strong temptation to overstep the conventional rule recognized for Sunday evening entertainments, and manifest their delight in manual demonstrations."

The increasingly acceptable practice of holding concerts on Sunday symbolized the separation of cultivated music from the realm of the theater and from music whose primary purpose was entertainment. Whereas the theater had been condemned by the religious community for years (as much for the extracurricular activities in the audience as what transpired on stage), music of the European concert tradition was gradually being viewed as morally edifying. In reviewing Thalberg's first concert in America, William Henry Fry in the *Tribune* had remarked that "all the pulpits, even the most puritanic, are discovering that music, pure and simple, is divine, and that the abrogation of the ten commandments is not found in the seven essential notes." A few weeks later the *Herald* concurred, believing that Jenny Lind had "roused up the enthusiasm of the religious community—a numerous, wealthy, intelligent, powerful, cultivated and refined community." Likewise, the "whole religious society" of New York had been "struck by [Thalberg] as with a shock of electricity, crowding to his concerts every night. All the clergymen of all denominations, with all the lights of the church, the brethren and sisters, who never go to the theatre—who abominate the opera—who hold up their hands in holy horror at the quarrels between the managers and the stockholders—who detest the squabbles of the tenors and the prima donnas—all these were stirred up as with the sharp end of a streak of lightning by the appearance of M. Thalberg and his wonderful performance."[1]

1. *Boston Post,* 19 January 1857; *New-York Daily Tribune,* 11 November 1856; *New York Herald,* 26 November 1856. In a lighthearted spoof of Thalberg's matinées, a fictitious "Deacon Pudge Drabflap" could not decide which he admired most about the matinées: their music or their morality. He described the events as "all respectability, hot coffee, music, and virtue. Heart, soul, mind, and sense were satisfied" (*Harper's Weekly* 2 [14 August 1858]: 515).

WITH MAURICE STRAKOSCH TO THE WEST

After more than five months in the eastern United States, Thalberg began his first of three forays into the Midwest in late April 1857 under the direction of Maurice Strakosch, now Ullman's partner at the Academy of Music. Thalberg could not have been in more capable hands. Strakosch had already given an estimated 1,755 concerts and had performed for more than 900,000 people since his arrival in 1848 in the United States.[16] Probably no one knew better the ins and outs of giving concerts across the entire country. Strakosch's experience is evident from the meticulous advance planning and nearly flawless execution of the tour. Concerts were announced in many cities three to five weeks before their occurrence, and only occasionally did concert dates have to be shifted a day or two.

Strakosch helped expand the boundaries of the musical Midwest, scheduling Thalberg in many cities he had already visited himself, as far west as Dubuque, Iowa, and Galena, Illinois, as far north as Madison and Milwaukee, Wisconsin, and in such cities as Chicago and Detroit, which had not been on the circuit during the previous decade. Maintaining the frenetic pace established by Ullman, Strakosch scheduled a concert on almost every night except Sunday and, on a few days, a matinée as well. During the eleven weeks of the tour, at least fifty-nine concerts were given in thirty cities in the Midwest and Canada. Nightly performances required Strakosch to fill in the gaps between larger cities by including smaller ones on the itinerary that performers like De Meyer and Herz had bypassed, such as Wheeling, West Virginia; Zanesville, Ohio; and Auburn, New York. Such a fast-paced itinerary was only possible with the recent network of rail lines that were quickly spreading across the country and making travel faster and more predictable. Performers now spent most days on a train en route to the next concert or, as was often the case, they traveled all night and attempted to recuperate during the day. What may have appeared to be a glamorous life at first glance was really an incessant treadmill of fatiguing travel and unrelenting performances of the identical repertoire.[17]

Not only did concerts such as Thalberg's reach a whole new level of smaller cities, but residents in the nearby communities and countryside made pilgrimages to attend performances. Although delegations from outlying areas had occasionally attended concerts of De Meyer and Herz, advertising concerts several weeks in advance instead of only a few days provided ample time for people to plan trips of considerable distance, and special efforts were often made to assist them. In some cities, seats could be reserved by mail, and in others a few reserved seats were "retained and sold on the evening of the Concert, at the door, for the convenience of those coming from a distance." Occasionally, special trains were scheduled to transport concertgoers to their home towns immediately after the concert.[18]

Strakosch employed two advance men who traveled ahead of the troupe to attend to final matters regarding the concerts, including hall arrangements and ticket sales,

although many of the details had already been taken care of by mail or telegraph. With the advance agents attending to the practical details, Strakosch traveled with Thalberg and prominently billed himself as "Director and Conductor" of the concerts, serving as piano accompanist and occasionally performing with Thalberg his Fantasia on *Norma* for two pianos. Instead of having two star performers (like De Meyer and Burke, or Herz and Sivori) who relied on local performers to round out their programs, Thalberg toured with an entire troupe of distinguished performers as in his East Coast appearances. Besides Strakosch, his troupe included the singers Teresa Parodi and Amalia Patti Strakosch and the cellist Heinrich Mollenhauer.[19] Touring with such a group of noteworthy performers, by then a common practice, provided a much higher and more consistent level of performance but greatly increased expenses. Such a troupe could be profitable only in an efficiently run tour, like Strakosch's, with performances as close together as possible.

As the opening act, Mollenhauer was frequently drowned out by latecomers. A Rochester concertgoer griped that while Mollenhauer was "performing his most exquisite part . . . the 'ushers' and 'pushers,' with a pyramid of stools on their heads, like so many Dutch women under burthens, were seating the *late strugglers,* and making a Calithumpian confusion, so that poor Mollenhauer with his beautiful master-piece, fell to the ground." Parodi offered standard arias from Italian and French operas, and Patti Strakosch delivered such ballads as "Comin' thru the Rye" and "Kathleen Mavourneen" in an unostentatious but captivating manner. The two vocalists usually closed both parts of the concert with an operatic duet, but their most popular offering was "The Star-Spangled Banner," which never failed to generate excitement. Thalberg did not vary his repertoire from his eastern concerts. Although his opera-based fantasias had been part of the standard piano repertoire for some time, a Detroit critic observed they were "new and strange to most" and were not always well received. The critic found relief in a few pieces that were "intelligible to the common ear," such as Thalberg's "delicious" performance of "Home, Sweet Home," which he believed rivaled Jenny Lind's singing of the popular tune.[20]

THE FASHIONABLE CONCERTGOER

Attendance was excellent for most concerts on the tour, and reviews frequently describe packed houses, with even standing room being filled. At one Chicago concert "hundreds were turned away," and in Rochester a newspaper claimed that the hall had never been so crowded "since the fevered excitement of Jenny Lind." The troupe's four concerts in Cincinnati averaged almost two thousand people, and a Milwaukee concert attracted more than fourteen hundred people.[21] There were a few rumblings about high ticket prices, which varied slightly depending on the size of the hall; the news that tickets to Thalberg's last few concerts in Boston went for only fifty cents did not help the attitude toward ticket prices that ranged from one

Audiences — The Fashionable

The attendance of fashionable concertgoers was frequently acknowledged in reviews with a certain amount of civic pride. Yet their distracting behavior, which made it clear they were not the least interested in the performance, was often satirized. A Chicago writer, for example, told of his assuredly imaginary friend Meonidas Muggins, who was exasperated by the sight of myriad opera glasses at a Thalberg concert "sweeping the ceiling and sweeping the gallery, and aimed perpendicularly upwards and outwards, forwards and backwards, in all possible directions" pertinaciously surveying the audience. He judged that "nine-tenths of the audience cared as little for Thalberg, and his master touch, as for the hand organ in the street, leaving a small moiety of one-tenth to be annoyed by all sorts of conversation and comments on millinery and trimmings, with a masculine sub-bass to applaud *throughout* the whole performance of each piece with 'Devilish fine,' 'Deuced good,' &c., &c." In a similar vein, a Norfolk writer, reporting on a concert there of Thalberg, captured in an elaborate satire the foibles of the fashion seeker:

> We went to the "show" Friday night—went to be seen there. Didn't care a rip for Thalberg nor his agent. . . . *We* went because we could go and because *poor* folks couldn't. Who'd be poor. What's the use. . . . Rich girls with poor but honest beaux came in. Poor girls with rich but wild beaux followed suit. Then came the *bon tons*, none of your "poor truck." . . .
>
> Mr. Skurmuggins came in with his wife and four daughters. Six all told. Nine dollars out—carriage hire not included. Rich man, but has no carriage of his own. Too bad. Next came Mr. Skirmiggins and wife, *and* daughter.—Dressed off *nice*. . . .
>
> Dick, who took Miss so— and so— and who paid his money, is now uneasy as to whether Tom over the way, and who is in company with Miss somebody—else knows that he is actually at this great show. Feels more comfortable. Recognizes each other. Smile. Intermission.
>
> John, a man in moderate circumstances goes because Tom, his rich neighbor and *nodding* friend goes, and would it pay John not to be seen by Tom? Certainly not. John's business is to be seen by Tom. What cares he for music! Nary red! . . .[1]

1. *Chicago Daily Democratic Press,* 30 May 1857; *Norfolk Day Book,* 18 January 1858.

dollar to occasionally as high as two dollars. In addition, reserved seats, which usually cost fifty cents extra, were becoming a more common feature. Their novelty is obvious from the detailed information about them contained in the advertisements.

First used extensively during Jenny Lind's tour, reserved seats were a civilized development. Previously, devoted music lovers had to arrive early to secure a prime location. A critic arriving at one of De Meyer's New York concerts more than an hour

before it began discovered that all of the good seats were already occupied. Besides wasting time, such advance seat claiming was fraught with the boredom of waiting and the additional pain of enduring unpadded seats. Once for a concert of Herz in Philadelphia, a local band was engaged to perform waltzes, polkas, and marches "to enliven the tedium . . . between the opening of the doors and the beginning of the Concert." George Templeton Strong complained after a concert of Herz, where he had waited an hour before it began at eight o'clock: "Those Tabernacle seats should be reformed—four hours use of them (7 to 11) produces a sort of necrosis of the sitting part that's unpleasant." For a Thalberg concert in Rochester, however, the newspaper was pleased to report that since the "seats are all numbered and checked, the holders of tickets will not be compelled to repair to the Hall an hour before that announced for the commencement, in order to provide themselves with seats," adding that this was an "admirable arrangement" that should be "generally adopted for concerts."[22]

While reserved seats solved some problems, they inadvertently created another. Patrons with reserved seats could now arrive late and still retain their choice spots, but only with considerable distraction to other listeners. This option was appealing to the fashionable concertgoer, who went as much to be seen as to hear the performance or attended simply because it was the rage. Such people had always been attracted to the concerts of European musicians with their higher price tags and intriguing performers. Now reserved seats made such concerts even more inviting to those who could afford the extra fee and desired to be noticed by making a grand entry. Before a Thalberg concert in Nashville, one writer tried to discourage the custom of the ceremonious arrival and urged "our fashionable people" to "strain a point . . . and try to be seated before the commencement of the concert." In Cincinnati, one critic stated matter of factly that "there will always be a large crowd of late comers especially at what is termed 'fashionable soirées.'" A letter to the editor there decried the "very vulgar practice in vogue" and the display of "*bad taste and ill breeding.*"

> If those who are in the habit of indulging themselves in this peculiar practice could only see themselves as others see them, and hear the observations their appearance provokes, they would certainly shun the position they now so readily thrust themselves into. . . . Nothing is more annoying than to be compelled to get up out of your seat in the midst of a performance to let some *come-to-be-looked-at concert-goer* pass.[23]

When the troupe returned to New York, their eleven-week campaign was hailed as "the most successful tour in the West since that of Jenny Lind." After a few appearances in the trendy watering places in late July, Strakosch returned home to New York quite ill from the strain of the tour, while Thalberg recuperated at the sea shore and in the Catskills before the new season began.[24]

CHAPTER 9

Henry Vieuxtemps and a Troubled Season ✺

Matching the unqualified success of Thalberg's first year in America would have been challenging under any circumstance, but a financial panic that coincided with the beginning of the 1857–58 season made it impossible. Fortunately, Ullman had already arranged for the Belgian violinist Henry Vieuxtemps (1820–1881) to contribute some novelty to Thalberg's second year. One of the first virtuosos to visit America, Vieuxtemps had toured here in 1843–44 at the same time as Bull and Artôt, but he had been no match for his Norwegian rival at capturing the hearts of Americans. One critic attributed Vieuxtemps's lack of success to his being "in advance of the taste." In his small audiences "very few could appreciate the grand simplicity of his style—his classic grace and strictness, his intellectual greatness and his unapproachable finish."[1]

A student of Bériot, Vieuxtemps had toured successfully in Europe and been praised by such critics as Fétis and Schumann, the latter comparing him to Paganini. He won similar recognition as a composer, a role in which he was better prepared than most virtuosos. His studies in counterpoint with Simon Sechter and in composition with Anton Reicha helped him create works more substantial than mere display pieces. In the United States, Vieuxtemps performed mostly his own music, including his Third Violin Concerto in A Minor, in addition to a few works by Paganini and several duos with Thalberg. He also humored his audiences with

variations on such popular tunes as "The Irish Washerwoman" and the obligatory "Yankee Doodle." A Toronto critic was especially taken with his "mirthful" variations on "St. Patrick's Day in the Morning" given with "wonderful power and life" and which pleased "better than all the weird Paganini music."[2]

Vieuxtemps shared with his new partner a self-effacing platform manner. In Boston he was found to be "free from all affectation and charlatanry in his demeanor" and "not unlike Thalberg in his dispassionateness and quiet ease." *Dwight's* New York correspondent ranked Vieuxtemps as the best violinist to visit America and believed he was "one of the truest of artists" because of his "utter absence of all humbug and seeking after effect." A New Orleans critic suggested that Vieuxtemps and Thalberg could not become "universally popular" in the United States because they were "undoubtedly the most correct and classic performers of the day":

> They neither roll their eyes, nor distort their faces, nor sway their bodies to and fro, nor do they indulge in other extravagant demonstrations, generally accounted acceptable to the million. They . . . have too high an opinion of art to prostitute it by resort to theatrical clap-trap. . . . They have paid the American public the compliment of regarding it as emancipated from the empire of Barnum, and as capable of forming an independent judgment of its own.[3]

Despite the financial panic that erupted in late August 1857 closing banks and making money tight, Thalberg's season began promisingly in mid-September. In three weeks he gave ten concerts in New York, Brooklyn, Philadelphia, Baltimore, and Washington, D.C., and many of the concert reports marveled at the unusually high attendance during the troubled economic conditions. One New York newspaper thought that the "public never tire of hearing" Thalberg and that he was "more popular than ever." For the first New York concert, "nearly twice as many persons desired to get into Niblo's Saloon as that pretty room will hold," and at the third concert "a great many people had to enjoy the musical treats outside, in the corridors and on the stairs."[4]

Thalberg continued to saturate audiences with his most popular works, prompting a disenchantment with his unchanging repertoire. Suggesting that Thalberg's pieces should be "laid aside for a while," a New York music journal argued that the piano literature was "too rich to justify a constant repetition of the same compositions." Yet that critic, like most others, was still fascinated by Thalberg's playing if not by his limited selection of works. *Dwight's* New York correspondent claimed that "after not having heard Thalberg for six months, the perfection of his execution stood forth unmoved by any weariness of its sameness." William Henry Fry in the *Tribune* dubbed the pianist "the evergreen Thalberg" and admitted that he "always sways his audience."[5]

Ullman had immediately made some concessions to the economic crisis: only the opening concert included an orchestra, complimentary tickets were suspended ex-

Vieuxtemps on America

When Vieuxtemps joined Thalberg in America in 1857, it was the second of three visits to the United States. He later explained that his first tour's lack of complete success was due to his visiting America too soon. He was "too classical" for the Americans, he believed, who were not yet "smitten with music-mania." He admitted that "with the exception of a few choice spirits who could appreciate my efforts, the only thing with which I could charm the Yankees and excite their enthusiasm was their national theme, 'Yankee Doodle,' with which I became popular."

Based on his first reception, Vieuxtemps hesitantly accepted Ullman's offer to join Thalberg, whom he classified as a "resuscitated celebrity." He was pleasantly surprised at the vast increase in the musical interests and discrimination of the American public: "I soon perceived that Ole Bull, Sivori, Henri Herz, Leopold Meyer, Jenny Lind, Damoreau, Alboni, etc., had been there and worked wonders. Ignorance was disappearing, instinct being revealed, and the want of harmony as well as the power of comprehension being awakened."

During his third tour of 1870–71, shortly before that of Anton Rubinstein, he discovered that "immense progress" had been made since his previous visit, and a "taste for serious music had been manifested and developed." He had no doubt that, given the "Yankees' naturally extravagant love of eccentricity," the young country would in time become "perfectly fitted to discern, understand, and assimilate great and high art."[1]

1. Henry Vieuxtemps, "Autobiographie," first published in *Guide musical*, reprinted in Maurice Kufferath, *Henri Vieuxtemps: sa vie et son oeuvre* (Brussels: J. Rozez, 1883), 13–18, trans. in *Dwight's Journal of Music* 41 (3 September 1881): 119–20.

cept for the press, and ticket prices were lowered to one dollar, with no extra charge for reserved seats. Not until the troupe's first Boston concert in the middle of October did the panic send Thalberg and his associates floundering. On the morning of the concert the Boston banks, attempting to avoid a run, suspended the payment of specie to the public, which emphasized the continuing deterioration of financial conditions. Consequently only a few hundred people attended the concert. Dwight dared not to call it the first concert of the season for he was not sure there would be a season at all. He found Thalberg's performance—"in the same cool, perfect way"—especially reassuring during the turbulent economic state. Although he had little desire to hear Thalberg's fantasias yet again, Dwight believed there was

something in such clean, bright, perfect execution of a graceful idea, though it be not a great one, which is always enjoyable; and in these troublous times, when the mind is filled with vague, indefinite, intangible intimations and suggestions of things, in the chaos of the business world, there is something really refreshing in the sight or sound of anything so sparkling, clean-cut, jubilant, and at the same time so fluid and so

graceful, as these tone-figures under the pianist's fingers. It is a comfort to meet somewhere a tone of certainty—to meet it somewhere in human endeavors, as we do in stars, and autumn leaves and shells and pebbles.

Such extravagant sentiments were offset by Dwight's disappointment that "the first classical violinist, perhaps, of the world" and "one of the greatest pianists" did not perform together more worthy music, such as a Beethoven sonata.[6]

The following two months were uncertain for Thalberg and Ullman. The troupe's schedule for New England quickly fell apart: concerts planned for Portland, Providence, and Albany as well as a second Boston concert were postponed indefinitely. Returning to New York, the troupe made only three appearances there and one in Brooklyn over the next three weeks. Brief excursions were made to Philadelphia, Baltimore, and Washington, cities that proved dependable once again, but concerts announced for Reading and Lancaster, Pennsylvania, were canceled without notice. The citizens of Reading, anticipating their first Thalberg concert, could only resort to a low opinion of the troupe—and, by extension, all musicians—at its mysterious nonappearance:

> The eager crowd who thronged to the Hall found nothing but darkness, silence and closed doors. The distinguished artists, with that indifference to their promises which characterizes musicians generally, had failed to appear in fulfillment of their engagement; and so far as we could learn, gave no reason for thus unceremoniously disappointing our citizens. It may be imagined that the comments upon this sort of treatment, by those who considered themselves wantonly trifled with, were by no means complimentary, or suggestive of a favorable response to any future calls that the Thalberg troupe may make upon their musical sympathies.[7]

The troupe returned once again to New York, where Thalberg made four measly appearances during the next six weeks (from late November to early January), all of them at the Academy of Music in conjunction with the opera. As lessee of the Academy of Music, Ullman had rotated singers between opera productions and Thalberg's concerts. As a silent partner with Ullman, Thalberg occasionally performed at the Academy during intermission to boost attendance there when it lagged.

With the season sputtering to a halt in the East, Ullman wisely decided to send Thalberg into virgin territory. But he first held an elaborate "Farewell Appearance" for the pianist on 2 January 1858 at the Academy of Music. Billed as the "Thalberg Testimonial," the event comprised four different "entertainments" beginning at 1:00: an opera, a symphonic concert, a miscellaneous performance with Thalberg and others, and a performance of Mozart's Requiem by five hundred musicians. The gala affair was so successful that it was repeated two days later with only a few changes.

Thalberg premiered a new piece written for the occasion, a fantasia on the popular song "Lilly Dale," a rather uninspired arrangement that Dwight's correspondent found "quite pretty in its way" but "unworthy both the man and the occasion."[8]

IN THE SOUTH AND MIDWEST

Immediately after the New York farewell concerts in early January 1858, Thalberg left on a southern and western tour in company with Vieuxtemps and several singers from the Academy of Music.[9] Ullman again stayed in New York to oversee the opera season, while Jacob Grau, who had served as an advance man for Strakosch and Thalberg the previous season, managed the tour. Beginning in Charlottesville, Virginia, the troupe followed the route of the tours of De Meyer and Herz, but it performed in several smaller cities, such as Lynchburg and Petersburg, Virginia, and Atlanta and Macon, Georgia. Plans to appear in Havana were canceled after an outbreak there of yellow fever. Once the troupe reached the Midwest, where Thalberg had already appeared, only the major cities certain to provide substantial audiences were included.

Thalberg made his debut in eighteen cities, where audiences were willing to part with their money even during an economic crisis for the opportunity to hear the great pianist for the first time. In Richmond, one writer found it remarkable, given the high price of admission, that the troupe had crowded houses for each of its three concerts, with the last the "fullest and most enthusiastic of all." In Augusta, "hundreds went away unable to procure seats," and in Mobile, "every seat was occupied and every nook or cranny, where a man could stand, was filled." The attendance frequently surpassed the hopes of the management. The troupe gave five concerts in Charleston instead of the three originally scheduled and in New Orleans, where "excitement increased and continued unabated," there was sufficient interest to warrant thirteen concerts rather than the four that were planned.[10]

Of course, full houses and hearty responses did not necessarily indicate complete comprehension or sincere enjoyment on behalf of the listeners. A Cleveland writer observed that one weakness of audiences was that they "invariably applaud to the echo anything that they don't understand." A Charleston critic was disappointed that Thalberg's selections were "all classical"; only in his answers to "insatiable encores" did he offer a "pleasing contrast" by favoring his audience with variations on a popular tune that could touch the heart. Even in New Orleans, where enthusiasm was intense and attendance extremely high, one writer recognized that "Home, Sweet Home," was Thalberg's "greatest triumph" because "everybody understood" it.[11]

Although modern writers may charge Thalberg with pandering to his audiences by playing his own fantasias rather than Beethoven sonatas, many of his listeners craved even simpler pieces they could more readily enjoy, especially music that had not been imported from a distant land. Similar desires had been voiced in the 1840s

with De Meyer and Herz, though somewhat tentatively. Now, after a decade of such unremitting virtuoso fare, repertoire complaints were bold and emphatic. A Cincinnati critic believed the vocal and instrumental selections at a Thalberg concert were "too foreign, too artistic, too exalted, for the musical education of the masses." A writer in Janesville, Wisconsin, mocked the "folly of those who are eternally running after 'great' names, and especially foreign 'artistes,' who bring with them the style and language of a foreign country." A direct, homespun opinion was expressed in Columbus, Georgia: "We will . . . leave to more cultivated minds the appreciation of your 'furrener' airs."[12]

Still, audiences could usually find something to relish. A critic in Wilmington, North Carolina admitted his inability to understand much of the music, but he was able to appreciate the "evident desire to please" on the part of the performers, manifested by their "courteous and respectful bearing" and their "cheerful and ready response to each *encore*." In Augusta, Thalberg and Vieuxtemps could at least astonish and delight those who "had little cultivation in music" by demonstrating a "perfect mastery" of their instruments. Others were more optimistic about the progress in musical taste and understanding. In Savannah, a critic speculated that the "*pons asinorum* seems to be fairly passed at last, and lovers of music may indulge in rational enthusiasm without being ridiculed." Or as George William Curtis wrote good humoredly in *Harper's*: "It appears that the aesthetics of the North American savage steadily improves, and that he is prepared, repressing his war-whoop for a brief season, to listen to the liquid enchantment distilled from the twinkling fingers of Thalberg upon the happy ivory of an Erard."[13]

THALBERG AS CELEBRITY

Thalberg's preparation for a career in diplomacy had made him unusually adept socially. In New Orleans he was described as a "charming man" with the "most winning personal qualities," and his obituary in London hailed him as "one of the most amiable and consequently one of the most popular of artists. He had troops of friends, and, we may say, without fear of contradiction, not a single enemy." A New York newspaper claimed he was fluent in English and had a "gifted readiness of speech, and an elegant and unimpeachable manner of expressing himself." Although the pianist was sober and decorous on stage almost to the point of being devoid of personality, Dwight reported that offstage he was "something of a wag" and prone to practical jokes. "No sooner has he turned his back upon the audience, after playing one of those wonderful fantasias, than the sedate and quiet face beams with all manner of fun, wherewith he salutes the 'few friends' in the green room."[14]

As a congenial celebrity, Thalberg was sought after as an acquaintance by such political, literary, and artistic figures as President Franklin Pierce, Henry Wadsworth Longfellow, and the young painter Frederick Church.[15] President Pierce attended

Thalberg's first Washington concert, and the following day Thalberg "paid his re-spects" in a private reception at the White House and was presented with a book commemorating Perry's expedition to Japan. A collector of autographs, Thalberg re-quested Pierce to inscribe the book, and the president's willingness to oblige was viewed as a remarkable gesture coming from a head of state to an artist.[16] In Boston, Longfellow, an avid concertgoer, attended Thalberg's first concert there and visited with him afterwards, finding him an "affable, pleasant man" who was "quietly smok-ing a cigarette with a pair of silver tongs." Longfellow discovered Thalberg's interest in acquiring autographs and promised to procure him one of George Washington, which he did quickly.[17]

Entrepreneurs were anxious to have as a spokesman a gentleman like Thalberg, who perhaps was not as virtuous as Jenny Lind, but was still above reproach. He graciously endorsed pianos and music halls as well as the services of piano tuners, singers, music teachers, and phrenologists.[18] His most surprising endorsement was for the banjo maker and teacher H. P. Jacobs, with whom he briefly studied while in New Orleans. When Jacobs and his brother gave Thalberg a banjo of their own making, the pianist was reportedly delighted with the gift since he "designs creating a sensation with it on his return to Europe," a plan that apparently never materialized.[19]

A CHICKERING IN EVERY PORT

American piano firms had already shown their eagerness to garner endorsements from the visiting European virtuosos. Herz, however, had been of no use to them as a manufacturer marketing his own pianos, and it appeared that Thalberg was firmly in the hands of Erard when he reportedly arrived with seven of their grand pianos. Seven pianos may sound excessive, but it allowed instruments to be placed in more than one city simultaneously, a scheme that must have worked well, for example, when Thalberg played on alternate nights in New York and Philadelphia. Almost immedi-ately, however, exceptions were made in his use of them, though they were clearly because of convenience rather than aesthetic choice. From the time of Thalberg's joint appearances with Gottschalk in Washington, D.C., in late December, Chick-ering pianos soon began to appear in his concerts with some regularity. Perhaps it was no coincidence that Gottschalk had begun performing on Chickerings a year earlier, or that in Boston, the home of Chickering, Thalberg played on them regularly (al-ternating with an Erard). Possibly Thalberg deferred to a recognized manufacturer, in whose own hall he presented solo matinées, and as a calculated action to win the favor of the local audience. Dwight believed Thalberg seemed "abundantly satisfied" with the Chickering and that it was "quite evident that he regards the Chickering instruments as the most formidable rivals" to the Erards.[20] Yet in New York Thalberg still played solely on his Erard.

For Thalberg's first tour of the Midwest and for most of his later concerts, Chickering sent instruments especially selected for the pianist's use to the cities on his itinerary. Advertisements and programs heralded Thalberg's use of the Chickering, but the local dealers, who oversaw the placement of the pianos in the concert hall and arranged for them to be tuned, bore the responsibility of exploiting the Thalberg connection to its fullest possibilities. In many cities, the dealers announced that the pianos to be used by Thalberg would be on display before the concert and afterwards would be sold or auctioned.

The *New York Musical World* reprinted an article that had immediately raised doubts about Thalberg's motives for performing on the Chickering. It argued that he might save thousands of dollars, but Chickering could hardly expect the public to believe he preferred their pianos when he still used the Erard in New York, "where his reputation was at stake, if anywhere." The endorsement, it believed, could "hardly be attributed to any but pecuniary motives." As Thalberg's manager, Ullman responded that the charges were "entirely untrue." He had requested that Chickering furnish pianos for Thalberg's concerts and "they kindly consented to do so. No arrangement has ever been made with reference to the expenses, and the Messrs. C. are under no obligation to furnish instruments for Mr. Thalberg's concerts."[21]

An especially heated debate over Thalberg's reasons for using the Chickering ensued in Pittsburgh between the rival music dealers John H. Mellor, a Chickering agent for more than twenty years, and Henry Kleber, who represented Erard and Steinway. While visiting Kleber's showrooms, Thalberg remarked that he never thought of playing upon any piano other than an Erard when they could be acquired for his concerts. "I hold myself entirely responsible," Kleber quoted him as saying, "for even the slightest imperfection when I play upon an Erard grand piano, but I would not like to say this of any other manufacture." Mellor countered that he possessed an endorsement of Chickering pianos by the "greatest living Pianist, M. Thalberg, *in his own hand writing,* voluntarily given to the subscriber during his visit to this city." Because foreign pianos could not withstand the American climate, he saw no point in comparing them with the Chickering. Kleber disclosed that he had the "*private* remarks of Mr. Thalberg, as made on the evenings of the concerts to his tuner, and by the latter repeated to half a dozen gentlemen of this city. They tell quite a different story."[22]

Thalberg's endorsement of the Chickering—"the instruments are the best I have seen in the United States, and will compare favorably with any I have ever known"—was cautiously ambiguous in its comparison of the Chickering with European pianos. Yet Thalberg had no hesitancy in rating it as the best American piano, especially when most American firms were concentrating on the lucrative square-piano market; the Steinway firm (founded in 1853), which was to become Chickering's biggest rival, had only begun to make grand pianos in 1856. The approval of an

American instrument by a leading European pianist was a source of pride for many Americans and a clear indication that the United States was making great strides in the arts. As one newspaper boasted: "Some years ago it was disdainfully asked abroad, 'Who plays on American pianos?' Proud are we to answer to-day, 'the best artists and connoisseurs of Europe—the great Thalberg at their head.'"[23]

Thalberg's arrangement with Chickering was a decided improvement. Instead of subjecting pianos to constant moving at considerable expense, Thalberg was assured that in each city he would find at no expense to him a brand new instrument in the very finest condition. Chickering received a prestigious endorsement for supplying pianos that still would be sold. Although Chickering had previously come to the aid of Gottschalk, not until Thalberg's American tour did it supply pianos on such an elaborate and widespread scale. Chickering's agreement with Thalberg established what was to become standard procedure for most major piano manufacturers: the seeking of an endorsement by an important concert pianist, preferably European, in exchange for providing pianos.

MUSARD CONCERTS

Upon completing his inland tour in late March 1858, Thalberg made what would be his final East Coast appearances in humbling circumstances as an assisting artist in a series of concerts with the French conductor Alfred Musard (1828–1881). The elaborate performances held at the Academy of Music were the inspiration of Ullman, who imported Musard as a remedy for the worsening opera season. A popular conductor of balls and promenade concerts, Musard specialized in dance music performed by a large orchestra and was akin to Louis Jullien, who had toured the United States with his orchestra in 1853–54.

Musard was not a natural showman like Jullien, who conducted with gloved hands and diamond-studded batons, a "vulgar humbug" according to the *Courier and Enquirer*. Musard's lack of flamboyancy was mitigated by Ullman, who rarely presented music to the public on its own merit. Boasting that the Musard Concerts would be the "most colossal and artistic entertainment that has ever been introduced in America," Ullman redecorated the Academy with "rich velvety carpets, luxurious divans . . . twenty-five monster candelabras and new and splendid chandeliers." One thousand fans were given away at every performance—ladies were "requested not to take the trouble of bringing fans with them"—and evening newspapers were sold by "young gentlemen in uniform," as was "customary in Paris and London." Ullman continued a feature he had introduced in Thalberg's matinées: "Persons wishing to take refreshments (ice creams, tea, coffee, cakes, &c.) without leaving their seats, can have them brought to them by waiters in livery, who will be stationed for that purpose in the parquet and dress circle." Two final touches were apparently novel to New York: a "new contrivance" announced the program's selection by "transparent placards on

the stage," and the beginning of the second half of the concert was signaled by the sounding of a gong.[24]

The concerts also featured stunning performances by a first-rate orchestra composed of 120 local musicians and virtuoso soloists from Paris. Musard's specialties, however, had no artistic pretensions. Many of the works he performed were light-hearted quadrilles of patchwork design often using pre-existing material. *Gotham: or the Electric Telegraph Quadrille,* for example, was a medley of popular tunes ranging from "Yankee Doodle" and "The Star-Spangled Banner" to "The Arkansas Traveller" and "Oh! Susanna." Many of the quadrilles were descriptive: *The Zouaves on the Malakoff* depicted "with startling reality" an episode from the Crimean War, and *Boeufs et moutons* imitated with instruments "the baaing of the lambs, the lowing of the cows, [and] the roaring of the bulls" as flocks and herds descend a mountain side. In *The Express Railroad Gallop,* the sounds of the conductor's whistle, the locomotive bell, "the puffing of the locomotive," and "the whiz of the cars" were produced by special machinery. The paraphernalia surrounding the concerts as well as the frivolous repertoire caused *Dwight's* New York correspondent to proclaim that "Humbug is great, and Ullman is his prophet!"[25]

The most noteworthy aspect of the concerts was the performance of more serious music under the direction of Karl Anschütz, the conductor engaged by Ullman the previous fall for the Academy of Music. Two evenings were devoted to the music of Beethoven, with Thalberg performing the first movement of the Third Piano Concerto, and Vieuxtemps the first movement of the Violin Concerto. More daring was a "Berlioz Night," given four times, that offered the most concentrated dose of Berlioz yet heard in the United States: the Overture to *Les Francs-Juges, Le carnaval romain,* the *Rákóczy March* (from *La damnation de Faust*), and Berlioz's orchestration of Weber's *Invitation to the Dance.*[26] With the assistance of the Liederkranz Society and the New-York Harmonic Society, Mozart's Requiem and Mendelssohn's *Elijah* were also performed on other evenings.

To hear a stellar array of performers, Ullman charged a rock-bottom fifty cents but still could not entice large enough crowds to turn a profit (figure 9.1). Even Thalberg's frequent role in the series—he appeared eighteen times during the first three weeks—did not seem to help. The Musard concerts ultimately failed because they were too much of a hodge-podge affair. Their sensational aspects and mostly light repertoire did not appeal to the connoisseur, whereas the Beethoven and Berlioz works intimidated the person searching for a pleasant diversion. The *Times* sarcastically praised the "entertainments," where one could "talk about the fashions without being frowned at by a surly amateur, or scowled at by an irate professor, as at the serious Philharmonic." On the other hand, the newspaper was amused with the "laborious gravity" which New York audiences listened to Musard's selections. It

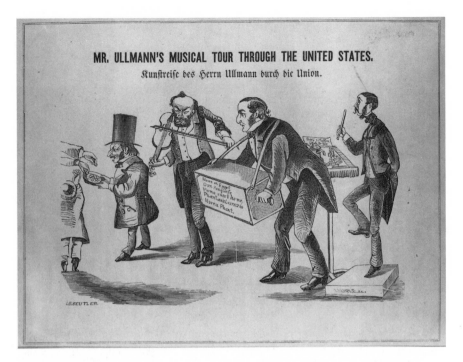

Figure 9.1. "Mr. Ullmann's Musical Tour through the United States." This caricature depicts the diminutive impresario Bernard Ullman begging for coins during the financially disastrous 1857–58 season followed by the stars of his troupe appearing as street musicians: the violinist Henry Vieuxtemps; the pianist Sigismund Thalberg as an organ grinder with the names of his most popular works on the front of his instrument (*Moses in Egypt, Don Pasquale, Home, Sweet Home, Lucrezia Borgia,* and *Norma*), suggesting that the works were so well known they were part of the musical vernacular; and the French conductor Alfred Musard with the sheet music of his *Boeufs et moutons* Quadrille in front of him. Musard's deadpan facial expression and nonchalant posture, with one hand in his pocket, emphasize his blasé stage persona. (THE HARVARD THEATRE COLLECTION, THE HOUGHTON LIBRARY)

believed that the "serious interest, the breathless expectation" evinced by American audiences would "drive a genuine French orchestra to the verge of suicide."[27]

THE FINAL TOUR AND A HASTY DEPARTURE

Beginning in early May 1858, Thalberg and company headed inland for the third and last time. Under Grau's direction again, the troupe revisited the most faithful cities of the Midwest, adding only two new ones to its itinerary—Sandusky, Ohio, and Peoria, Illinois. In the latter city, Thalberg would end his spectacular American tour inauspiciously in mid-June. In the meantime the pianist continued to glut the country with concerts, making his ninth appearance in St. Louis; his eighth in Cincinnati; his fifth in Buffalo, Louisville, and Toronto; and his fourth in Albany,

Cleveland, Detroit, Pittsburgh, and Troy. Despite lowered ticket prices in most cities, full houses were now a rarity. One critic observed that Thalberg's "star paled in the bright presence of Henry Vieuxtemps," who was making his appearance in these cities for the first time in more than a decade.[28]

The tour went smoothly if not too successfully until the troupe reached Chicago, where Grau announced that Thalberg would make only one of three scheduled appearances before returning immediately to Europe. But he was gone even before then, the only concert among more than three hundred in which he did not appear as scheduled. Grau claimed Thalberg was indisposed by a sudden illness, though no one seemed to believe him. The local critic George P. Upton remembered there was "at once a flight of rumors," including that Thalberg and Elena D'Angri, the principal vocalist on the tour, had had a "falling out" and that the pianist's wife "had arrived in New York and was anxious to see him." In a private journal he noted that Thalberg "suddenly disappeared at [the] appearance of his wife on the scene looking up D'Angri and his affairs." The impresario Max Maretzek made even greater and more explicit accusations:

> Mme. D'Angri in her many travels had learned all that is worth knowing, and, among other things, how to entangle a gentleman who had no other occupation except playing occasionally two of his own compositions on the piano, and who consequently must have felt lonesome all the rest of his time. Mme. D'Angri . . . had a young and handsome daughter . . .
>
> The mother invited Mr. Thalberg to pass his leisure hours in her parlor: and there and then they managed to cobweb Mr. Thalberg and amuse him . . .
>
> This . . . had two consequences. The first was the sudden arrival of Mrs. Thalberg . . . in Boston, which caused the sudden departure of Thalberg from New York without waiting for the fond embraces of his wife, and the second consequence was the debut of a granddaughter of Mme. D'Angri, under the name of Mlle. Thalberg, about twenty years later, as *Zerlina* in "Don Giovanni" at London.[29]

A Zaré Thalberg did make her debut at Covent Garden in 1875, and while late nineteenth-century sources indicate she was Thalberg's daughter, more recent sources claim her real name was Ethel Western and that she had been born in Derbyshire, England, in April 1858. The relationship between Thalberg, D'Angri, and her daughter will likely never be known, but Thalberg's sudden flight does not suggest innocence. The arrival of Francesca Thalberg in the United States, however, may have had nothing to do with her suspicions. Her father, the celebrated bass Luigi Lablache, had died early that year. Possibly her grief or her new freedom from caring for her father in his final illness prompted her trip to America. Or perhaps the inheritance of her father's villa and vineyard at Posillipo, near Naples, convinced her that her husband no longer needed to perform for money.

Thalberg had already amassed a hefty sum by this time, even with a financially poor second season. Unlike De Meyer, who was under his own management and had to assume the profit or loss of each concert, Thalberg received the guaranteed sum from Ullman of $10,000 a month, thus averaging about $500 per concert. By performing at approximately 320 concerts (excluding the free school concerts) while he was in the United States, Thalberg probably made more than $150,000 in two seasons, the equivalent today of about $3 million. During this time unskilled laborers received about one dollar a day, urban doctors and lawyers made about $2,000 a year, and someone making from $5,000 to $20,000 a year would have been considered rich.[30] Later, Rubinstein would receive only $200 a concert and Bülow less than $125.

Thalberg's American tour was impressive in its organization and efficiency. With his previous experience managing Herz and Sontag, Ullman was well prepared for Thalberg. His astute management, as well as that of Strakosch and Grau, brought Thalberg to at least seventy-eight cities in the United States and Canada in at least 340 concerts. Only twice—in the matinées and Musard concerts—did Ullman allow his publicity instincts to overshadow the music with the trappings of humbug. Otherwise, he supplied an imaginative array of prominent musicians to assist the pianist in his concerts.

More important than the sheer number of concerts given and cities visited, Thalberg was undoubtedly the greatest pianist yet to visit the United States. The American public responded accordingly and returned again and again to his concerts. Without a trace of empty display, Thalberg offered superbly polished performances of his own works, already well known in America. He also made a significant step toward performing the music of other composers in his concerto appearances and matinées. Unlike his predecessor Herz, Thalberg seems to have remained silent about his American sojourn, another sign of his quiet and gentlemanly manner that had kept him free from scandal and had endeared him to Americans.

Shortly after Thalberg's departure from the United States, the *New-York Musical Review and Gazette* summed up his tour:

> Thalberg . . . quite unexpectedly closed what has been a most brilliant career—completely successful, musically, giving to the talented and genial artist abundance of both fame and money. There is probably not another virtuoso, whether with instrument or voice (Liszt alone excepted), who could have excited a moiety of the enthusiasm, or gathered a fragment of the dollars, which Thalberg has excited and gathered.[31]

INTERLUDE II

The excitement that Thalberg's visit created in the American piano world would not be equaled until the appearance of Anton Rubinstein in 1872. The intervening decade of the 1860s was not totally barren of excellent touring pianists, but the Civil War was a great deterrent to European artists, who feared gunfire even more than seasickness. It is hardly a coincidence that Gottschalk, who had fled the United States during Thalberg's sojourn, belatedly achieved his great popularity among American audiences during this period when foreign virtuosos were at a minimum. Gottschalk's story will not be addressed here, for it has been told numerous times and no more eloquently than by the pianist himself, whose journal gives a poetic account of the trials of a touring artist in the midst of a brutal war.[1]

CARREÑO AND OTHER WOMEN PIANISTS

Despite the outstanding abilities of several pianists who visited the United States briefly during this interregnum, none succeeded in igniting an overwhelming enthusiasm among the American public. The most remarkable new pianist in the 1860s was Teresa Carreño (1853–1917) from Venezuela, who made her New York debut in 1862 when only eight years old. Her limited number of concerts in the United States at that time included an appearance in 1863 before Abraham Lincoln

in the White House. She soon traveled to Europe to study and returned during the 1872–73 season when still only eighteen. She appeared not as a star but as an assisting artist with the singers Giovanni Mario and Carlotta Patti and the violinist Emile Sauret. Although consistently praised, she was competing head to head with Rubinstein and had little chance of matching the acclaim lavished upon him. Based mostly in Europe and temporarily sidetracked by a vocal career, Carreño did not establish a significant presence as a pianist in the United States until the end of the century.[2]

Previously consigned to amateur status, women pianists were now entering the profession with a vengeance. European women pianists had made their way to America since the 1850s, perhaps seeking greater acceptance than possible on the continent. Several of a very high caliber toured extensively throughout the United States shortly before Rubinstein's arrival, including Alide Topp, a pupil of Hans von Bülow (in U.S. 1867–70); Anna Mehlig (1846–1928; in U.S. 1869–73), who studied briefly with Liszt, and Marie Krebs (1851–1900; in U.S. 1870–72). All three performed frequently with orchestra and gave numerous solo recitals, then still a rarity, especially for a visiting performer. Mehlig and Krebs toured primarily as soloists with Theodore Thomas and his orchestra in a demanding itinerary, performing a variety of concertos ranging from Beethoven to Liszt, as well as solo works. Mehlig, after a brief return to Europe, was also here during the 1872–73 season at the same time as Rubinstein and Carreño. Mehlig's concerto repertoire seems to have been the most extensive of the three women, with works by Mozart, Beethoven, Schumann, Henselt, and Hiller, and both concertos of Mendelssohn, Chopin, and Liszt. All three pianists held their own against the formidable challenges of the music recently composed for their instrument, and each gave at least one American premiere, demonstrating a healthy interest in the newer music.[3]

Three more significant women pianists appeared later in the decade of the 1870s: the American Julie Rivé (later Rivé-King; 1854–1937), Arabella Goddard (1836–1922), and Annette Essipoff (1851–1914). Rivé made her American debut in 1875 after studies in Europe and toured frequently with the Thomas orchestra.[4] Goddard, a pupil of Thalberg, was an important force in the London musical world partly as a result of her marriage to the tyrannical music critic J. W. Davison, or so most people thought. She made a brief appearance in the United States in 1872, principally at Patrick Gilmore's World Peace Jubilee in Boston. After visiting Australia she returned via California to New York and toured America during the 1875–76 season with Therese Tietjens in competition with Bülow. Essipoff, a pupil of Leschetizky, followed the season after Bülow in 1876–77. Neither Goddard nor Essipoff was especially well received by Americans. Goddard was said to have created little excitement simply because she was from England, a country not usually

identified as a hotbed of keyboard virtuosity.[5] As a Russian, Essipoff was more enticing, but at least one music journal believed she was not sufficiently publicized.
The *Music Trade Review,* which held she was a perfect artist, conjectured that her
small audiences resulted from her management's lack of "preparation," a necessity
for a pianist with a reputation of such recent vintage. The journal concluded that
"people go to hear a celebrated artist because they know he has pleased so many
people in Europe, and made a great reputation." An unknown performer, like Essipoff,
flaunting an immense repertoire designed to please the connoisseur, was unlikely to
attract an American audience.[6]

The technical prowess displayed by this spate of women pianists did not prevent
critics from questioning whether women could match the abilities of their male
counterparts. Rubinstein, for instance, was not enthusiastic about women performers or composers even though he had become Carreño's mentor in Europe. When
asked about Carreño in an American interview, Rubinstein replied nicely enough
that she was "very charming, very sweet, and she has talent, too." But when quizzed
about the future role of women in music, he stated with his usual frankness:
"Women have done nothing in music, absolutely nothing. It is the same in music as
it is in all the arts—they can do nothing remarkable. . . . Even when a woman has
distinguished herself in art it is by something extravagant." Bülow, on the other
hand, was supportive of his pupil Alide Topp, but he realized her gender would be
an issue with the public. He claimed that, although there were many "excellent female pianists," Topp was the best. "The *'virtuose Qualität'* which distinguishes her
makes us regard her as a male," Bülow wrote, "rather than as a female pianist. The
delicate, handsome woman has a *technique,* an energy, a fire, which enables her to
enter the lists with a Rubinstein or a Tausig."[7] In essence, he complimented her by
making her what Katharine Ellis has called an "honorary man."[8] Still, that was
progress for women artists.

The Pianist as Interpreter

The proliferation of women performers helped consolidate a pivotal change in the
repertoire of the virtuoso, the most significant development in the piano world between the visits of Thalberg and Rubinstein. Previously, an unwritten rule stated that
a pianist should perform only his own music in public. By the 1860s, however, if a
pianist offered no music of other composers he was harshly criticized and his abilities severely doubted. Gottschalk was often rebuked by Dwight and other American
critics for programming his own works, a censure he found especially ridiculous.[9]
No longer were most pianists attempting to serve the two masters of performance
and composition, often to the detriment of the latter. The typical virtuoso pianist
now interpreted works in a variety of styles by an array of composers representing

the past and present. The establishment of a standard repertoire, or "canon," of masterworks for the concert pianist, consisting primarily of works from the first half of the nineteenth century, was influenced by a number of factors, including the conservative tastes of growing middle-class audiences, the rise of the piano recital, the establishment of conservatories, and the scholarly interest in the music of the past fueled by the fledgling discipline of musicology.[10] In addition, women pianists frequently led the way in interpreting the music of other composers—specifically male composers—since women were discouraged from entering that field of creativity even more than performing and thus were by default forced to play the music of others.[11]

The concept of the interpretive pianist might have been a new one for the concert stage, but it should not be supposed that the earlier virtuosos, who had made their fame as composer-pianists, could not perform the works of others. Evidence is plentiful that they had studied and knew well the great works of their predecessors. Richard Grant White, for example, asserted that he had heard De Meyer in private "perform the compositions of Bach and Beethoven with that same rigid precision and wonderful power combined with graceful ease and sweetness which always marks his performances." Charles Salaman observed that "to be assured that Thalberg was a really great player was to hear him interpret Beethoven, which he did finely, classically, and without any attempt to embellish the work of the master."[12]

The novel idea of a virtuoso pianist performing someone else's music had begun to gather momentum in the 1840s and was espoused by notable teachers and modeled by several influential pianists. François-Joseph Fétis, a lexicographer, critic, and the director of the Brussels Conservatory, systematically explored the notion in *Méthode des méthodes de piano* (1840), written in collaboration with the pianist Ignaz Moscheles. The method book included examples of technique from the music of Bach, Scarlatti, Clementi, Mozart, Hummel, Beethoven, Chopin, and Liszt, and the authors argued that a pianist should no longer specialize in his own music, but should perform music by other composers from all periods. Similarly, the famous pianist and pedagogue Carl Czerny, in a supplement of 1847 to his piano method, included a substantial repertoire list and discussed the interpretation of music by Bach, Handel, Beethoven, and contemporary composers. This trend was reinforced, as Alan Walker observed, by newly established conservatories, including those in Leipzig (founded 1843), where Moscheles was head of the piano division, Berlin (1850), and Cologne (1852), since "their curricula were based largely on the music of the past." These repertoire lists and curricula included pieces that were first part of a "pedagogical canon" (as William Weber defines it, a body of works useful for instruction) and eventually entered a "performing canon" (a body of works chosen for public performance).[13] By far the most important examples are the Beethoven

sonatas, which were probably the driving force behind the development of the piano canon. They had been studied for decades but had been seen as more appropriate for the salon or chamber, their place of origin, and had been only recently deemed suitable for the concert hall.

Several pianists pioneered the shift in the repertoire of the virtuoso. Moscheles had already practiced what he and Fétis preached. Beginning in 1837 he had begun a series of "Classical Pianoforte Music" recitals that featured the music of Bach, Handel, Scarlatti, Beethoven, and Weber, among others, and some of the baroque pieces were even played on the harpsichord. Liszt, as the world's most famous pianist and most astonishing composer for the instrument, also had seen fit to perform the music of other composers. Liszt's example was short lived, however, for he retired from active performing in 1847, but Clara Schumann continued the transition. Although an accomplished composer herself, she achieved renown as the interpreter of other people's music, in particular the music of her husband. More significantly, her goal was not fame but the acceptance of what she considered to be the greatest music. Schumann's repertoire throughout her career illustrates the trend from the virtuoso display pieces of Herz and Thalberg that she performed during her youth in the 1830s to the loftier sonatas of Beethoven in the 1850s and beyond.[14] Rubinstein fell somewhere between the examples of Liszt and Schumann. As a composer, he consistently offered a generous supply of his own music in his concerts, but he also drew heavily on the music of composers of previous generations, providing an intentionally historical perspective of the piano repertoire.

A cadre of pianists resident in America had also been attempting to introduce a more extensive repertoire for years, though they rarely received as much attention as a visiting superstar. Richard Hoffman, William Mason, and Sebastian Bach Mills in New York; Otto Dresel and Ernst Perabo in Boston, and Carl Wolfsohn in Philadelphia (later in Chicago) were among the pianists who had neither the reputation nor the charisma of Rubinstein or Bülow but almost as much talent. Often either German-born or German-trained, they were influential in the musical education of America in a way radically different from traveling virtuosos. They established themselves in a single city rather than touring widely and usually programmed more serious repertoire than the itinerant performer, though their concerts were usually attended by a smaller group of connoisseurs. Despite the efforts of these pianists, when Rubinstein offered his programs that included music of Bach, Handel, Scarlatti, and Mozart, such antiquarian works met with little comprehension and sometimes ridicule. A piece by Mozart, for instance, was "only bearable from its exceptionally fine rendering." Another writer believed that Handel's *Harmonious Blacksmith* had "very justly . . . nearly passed into oblivion," since too much better piano music had been composed after it for the piece "ever to re-awaken any considerable popular interest."[15]

THE CHANGING ROLE OF THE PIANO

Another issue coming to the fore during this period and highlighted during Rubinstein's tour was the status of the piano itself. In the first half of the nineteenth century, the piano had become the most significant instrument in the concert hall, the chamber, and the home. Most composers were fluent on the piano, many specialized in writing for it, and some worked out their most profound musical thoughts on the instrument. By the second half of the century, that was no longer the case. The orchestra had clearly replaced the piano as the center of music making in the concert hall. As European and American resident orchestras were organized, composers refocused their efforts on works for the orchestra and many of them were either not proficient on the piano or wrote substantially less for it.

As composers were relegating the piano to a lower rank of importance, many Americans still found the abstract music of the piano to be a puzzlement; a full evening of piano music was simply too incomprehensible and monotonous. The piano had neither the extramusical associations of a text, the human touch of the voice, nor the color of the orchestra to make it accessible. The piano was fine in the home and for accompaniments, some writers suggested, but was no longer well suited as a solo instrument in the concert hall, perhaps as a result, according to one Chicago critic, of "the everlasting thrumming of thousands of neophytes, turned out as artists by boarding-schools and seminaries." Still, many critics believed that Rubinstein's sensational technique and fiery interpretation could restore the piano to its former preeminence. In an early review of Rubinstein in America, the *New York Sun* casually remarked on the "limitations and shortcomings" that make the piano "one of the most imperfect of instruments." Rubinstein, however, "compelled it to express all that is best and noblest in music." A writer for *Scribner's* who admitted that "the piano is, after all, rather an obstinate and ungrateful instrument—a little wooden, a little mechanical, even a little *tin-kettlish* on occasion," marveled that "with Rubinstein it absolutely gives up all semblance of being a machine at all and becomes a living agent, interpenetrated by and responsive to the spirit of the master."[16]

Regardless of the doubts harbored by some critics about the piano's role as a solo instrument, it had become a standard feature in middle-class homes. In 1867, an *Atlantic Monthly* article claimed that "almost every couple that sets up housekeeping on a respectable scale considers a piano only less indispensable than a kitchen range." In 1871, a contributor to *Dwight's* observed that "music is so extensively cultivated, that in nearly every house there is a piano, and a teacher employed. In passing some house in a dingy street, suggestive of nothing but poverty and want, I have often been surprised to see through the open door that the room contained a piano, or I have heard its unmistakable tones."[17] American piano manufacturers were doing a brisk business, and at least two firms—Steinway and Chickering—were pioneering

in the improvement of the instrument. By the 1870s the competition among piano manufacturers had intensified in the United States, making gentlemen's agreements like those between Chickering and Thalberg increasingly rare. Chickering now had an imposing rival in Steinway, which by the mid-1860s had surpassed the Boston firm in sales and in 1866 had opened the principal concert hall in New York. Steinway also sponsored a return visit of Leopold de Meyer in 1867–68, and in 1872 the firm celebrated the manufacture of its 25,000th grand piano. Steinway continued to set the pace in the promotion of its pianos by actively participating in the American tour of Anton Rubinstein in 1872–73, our next virtuoso.

PART FOUR

Anton Rubinstein

1872-73

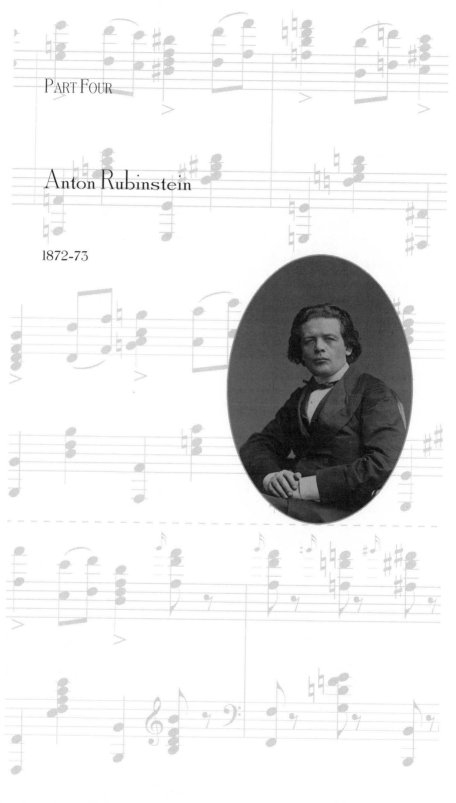

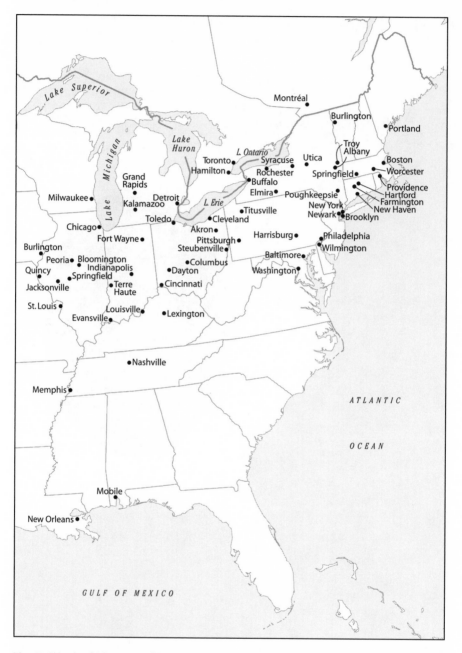

Map 5. Cities in which Anton Rubinstein performed.

CHAPTER 10

"The Shaggy Maestro"

The pianist whose American tour was by far the most spectacular was Anton Rubinstein (1829–1894). His predecessors had astonished audiences by their technical feats, but Rubinstein vividly communicated the essence of the music he performed. His enraptured listeners did not care that his performances were rarely flawless or that his historical repertoire was often beyond their comprehension. They responded to Rubinstein primarily for musical reasons; yet, their infatuation with him was equally due to his perfectly fitting the American image of the quintessential romantic virtuoso—an exotic foreigner with an abundance of technique and charisma. Furthermore, in contrast to the women who had recently preceded him, Rubinstein was publicized, as D. W. Fostle has observed, for his "rugged and virile nature."[1]

The Russian-born pianist had been a typical prodigy, demonstrating his musical talents at an early age. As a child, he studied in Moscow with Alexander Villoing, who took him to Paris in 1840, ostensibly to enroll him in the Conservatoire. Like many foreign-born child prodigies, he was refused admission, but he made an auspicious debut in the capital of virtuosos. After one concert, Liszt supposedly embraced the child, kissed him, and proclaimed him his successor.[2] Tours in England, Holland, Norway, Sweden, and Germany followed.

Between 1844 and 1846, Rubinstein and his brother Nikolay undertook a conservative grounding in theory and composition in Berlin under Siegfried Dehn, with whom Glinka had studied a decade earlier. Rubinstein was encouraged there in his

endeavors by Mendelssohn and Meyerbeer. The death of his father ended his studies, and he struggled for two years as a professional musician, too old to still be a
Wunderkind, as he put it. In 1848 he moved to St. Petersburg and soon came under
the patronage of the Grand Duchess Elena Pavlovna. For the next several years he
committed himself to composition. Another European tour, from 1854 to 1858, solidified his reputation as an extraordinary pianist and impressive composer.

Although he first made his reputation as a pianist, Rubinstein had soon become
distracted by his natural ability at composing. Unlike many of his fellow virtuosos,
he composed not only piano works but also symphonies, operas, oratorios, and chamber music. He also gained fame as a conductor and became absorbed in improving
the state of the music profession and musical education in his native Russia. Upon
returning to St. Petersburg, he established in 1859 the Russian Musical Society, dedicated to performing the works of Russian composers, and two years later founded
the St. Petersburg Conservatory, which opened in 1862, serving as its director for five
years. Because Rubinstein was so easily diverted from one arena of music to another—
unable or unwilling to devote himself to a single obsession—he never fulfilled his
potential in any one of them. The old saying was that as a pianist, he was the world's
greatest composer, and as a composer, he was the world's greatest pianist. Nevertheless, when he decided to visit America in 1872, he was widely viewed as the successor to Liszt, and when American advertisements hailed him as "the greatest living
pianist," few cared to disagree.

In the midst of the European revolutions of 1848, Rubinstein had contemplated
emigrating to the United States. When he told Dehn about his "fantastic intention,"
his teacher supposedly replied: "Heavens, are you mad! Is it possible that you can
find nothing to do in Europe? You are still but a lad, you have seen nothing of your
own country, and yet you would recklessly rush off to America, where you are likely
to meet with any kind of misfortune." As a result of Dehn's rebuff, Rubinstein later
wrote that he "at last recognized [his] folly."[3] Two and a half decades later, such a
trip to the United States was no longer a folly. With the increase in music journalism by the early 1870s, Americans were even more aware of European musical activities and were quite familiar with Rubinstein's name as a pianist, composer, and
teacher, and they eagerly awaited his arrival.

The Steinway firm is frequently credited with bringing Rubinstein to America.
His tour might not have happened without the firm's support, but Steinway did not
instigate the tour, and it was drawn into the negotiations only at a late date. Jacob
Grau, who had served as principal manager of Thalberg's last western tour, first approached Rubinstein. As a protégé of Ullman and Strakosch, Grau had learned well
the intricacies of management and during the 1860s was a relatively successful
manager of opera companies in New York and on the road. In late 1871 in Vienna,
he signed a contract for an American tour with Rubinstein, who was serving as artistic director of the Gesellschaft der Musikfreunde for the 1871–72 season. Grau

soon suffered a stroke, leaving him partially paralyzed and unable to manage the tour himself. He offered the contract to his nephew, Maurice Grau, if he could provide the security deposit required by Rubinstein.[4] Possessing little capital, Maurice approached William Steinway, whom he had never met, with the idea that the Steinway firm could receive valuable publicity in exchange for the $10,000 guarantee. Steinway readily agreed and by June 1872 the firm had deposited Rubinstein's fee in a Viennese bank.[5]

A second contract with revisions was signed, again in Vienna, on 8 June 1872 by Rubinstein and Jacob Grau, as well as by Maurice Grau and C. F. Theodor Steinway, the latter representing Steinway & Sons. In the earlier agreement Grau had reserved the right to choose the pianos of Steinway, Chickering, or another reputable American firm for Rubinstein to use in his concerts. In the final contract, in which Steinway & Sons joined as witness and as guarantor of Rubinstein's security deposit, Grau had conveniently chosen the Steinway. Rubinstein approved the choice, although he had the right to reject single pianos that did not suit him. Rubinstein was to be paid 200,000 francs for the eight-month tour, the equivalent of $40,000 or about $200 per concert; all his expenses would be paid. The money was respectable though not nearly what the pianist was worth. It was only about half as much as Thalberg had made per concert fifteen years earlier. Although Maurice Grau, writing just after the pianist's death, claimed "there was never a complaint" from Rubinstein, who had the "most lovable disposition imaginable," Maurice's brother, Robert, alleged that Rubinstein "bitterly resented" the terms of his contract, and the relationship between pianist and impresario, "while not strained, was none too friendly."[6]

The great Polish violinist Henryk Wieniawski (1835–1880) was to be Rubinstein's partner on the tour (the vocalists Louise Liebhart and Louise Ormeny would complete the troupe). The two instrumentalists knew each other well. Wieniawski had been the solo violinist to the czar since 1860 and, at Rubinstein's invitation, had served as the first professor of violin at the St. Petersburg Conservatory. However unhappy Rubinstein may have been with the financial terms of his contract, he was nevertheless paid twice as much as Wieniawski, who received only $100 a concert, an absurdly low sum for an artist of his rank—undoubtedly one of the greatest violinists of the second half of the nineteenth century. Rubinstein had heard such violinists as Vieuxtemps, Sivori, Joachim, Sarasate, and Bull, among others, and he thought Wieniawski was "by far the greatest violinist." Rubinstein recalled that Wieniawski had a "ravishing quality of tone that none of the others possessed, and he had more genius than any of them."[7]

Debut in New York

On 31 August 1872 in Liverpool, Rubinstein and Wieniawski boarded the steamship *Cuba* filled with celebrities coming to America for the new season. One of those on board, the American soprano Clara Louise Kellogg, remembered that most pas-

Rubinstein's Contract

The contract Rubinstein signed for his American tour is a twenty-three-page document in neat German script that stipulates precisely the terms of the agreement between pianist and manager. Representing an artist was obviously no longer a casual affair, but a serious business arrangement that required legal protection for both parties. The terms of the final contract are summarized below; the first two conditions were occasionally disregarded.

- Rubinstein is to play in six public concerts each week with no distinction between matinées or evening concerts.
- Rubinstein is not obliged to play more than once a day; if he plays twice on one day, he can claim the following day as a day of rest.
- Rubinstein is not obliged to accompany in these concerts, nor to play in premises that are not dedicated to artistic purposes, such as garden concerts and smoking premises.
- Rubinstein is not obliged to perform if war, revolution, or an epidemic illness occurs in the larger cities.
- Rubinstein is to receive 200,000 francs in gold ($40,000) for a season of eight months, his fee to be paid to him three times a month. (The sum of $40,000 would be worth well over $500,000 today. The gold requirement was waived by Rubinstein when he realized its impracticality.)
- Rubinstein cannot perform publicly or in private circles with or without pay without written permission from Grau.
- Rubinstein has the right to choose his repertoire for each concert and must play at least four pieces in each concert.
- Grau has chosen to use the Steinway piano in all concerts. Rubinstein has the right to reject single pianos that do not suit him, but he must perform on a Steinway.
- Grau will deposit $10,000 of U.S. bonds in a Vienna bank as a security deposit to be held in escrow.
- If either party does not fulfill its part of the contract, it is subject to a $20,000 penalty.
- Negative criticism of Rubinstein or financial disaster will not be cause to modify the contract.
- Grau and Steinway are to take out a life insurance policy on Rubinstein for ten months, effective the day he boards the ship. In the event of his death, the amount of $40,000 will be paid to his widow.

sengers were "too seasick to talk or even to listen." She "never, never saw anyone so seasick" as Rubinstein, "nor anyone so completely depressed by the fact." He "swore, faintly, that he would never cross the ocean again even to get home!" The ship arrived in New York too late on 10 September 1872 for the passengers to disembark. The next day as the crowd gathered searching for Rubinstein, Kellogg advised them gaily: "Find the queerest looking genius on the ship and you will have Rubinstein."[8]

The day after their arrival Rubinstein and Wieniawski called on William Steinway, who was delighted to record in his diary that the pianist was "much pleased both with Steinway Hall & our grand." That evening Rubinstein was serenaded by the New York Philharmonic Society, the first such reception the Philharmonic had given a visiting musical celebrity since Jenny Lind. The participants in the drama believed the tour of the Swedish singer had begun a new era in the musical life of the United States, and they predicted that the advent of Rubinstein would also launch a new, enlightened epoch in the field of piano music. More than two thousand people gathered in the street outside Rubinstein's windows in the Clarendon Hotel as 120 members of the Philharmonic led by Carl Bergmann performed Wagner's Overture to *Rienzi,* the Andante from Beethoven's Fifth Symphony, and Meyerbeer's *Fackeltanz.* The overture by Wagner, a composer championed by Bergmann, was ill-chosen. Rubinstein was often grouped with Wagner as one of the world's leading composers, but Rubinstein abhorred Wagner's music. After attending the premiere of *Tristan und Isolde* in Munich in 1865, conducted by Hans von Bülow, he thought about committing suicide, for "If that is music, what object have I in living any longer?" A few days after the serenade he supposedly told a reporter that "Wagner is a humbug, a cheat."[9]

Between the musical numbers the tumultuous crowd cried out for Rubinstein, who, after repeatedly bowing, finally addressed the crowd from his balcony: "I have no words to express my gratitude for this honor; but I assure you I am deeply sensible of your kindness, and will treasure it in my memory as one of the happiest remembrances of my life." Then "cheer after cheer rent the air." After a collation in the parlor, Rubinstein retired to his room where a select gathering awaited him. After more speeches, including one by the Philharmonic Society's president, George Templeton Strong, Rubinstein mesmerized the fortunate ones in attendance by performing several pieces.[10]

Rubinstein's American debut took place more than ten days later on 23 September 1872 in Steinway Hall on Fourteenth Street. Opened in 1866, the hall had become a prominent venue for concerts, including those of Theodore Thomas and his orchestra. The hall was packed for Rubinstein's debut, with everyone who could "tell a sonata from a sandwich" quipped the *Arcadian.* Many people were not allowed to enter and others stood on chairs throughout the performance. The *Herald* described the distinguished audience: "Artists of foreign and local celebrity fringed the hall, not only on the floor but in both galleries, and littérateurs were there by the score. . . . As for the local pianists, and we may add pianomakers, their name was Legion." When Rubinstein came on stage, the audience greeted him wildly, and he had to bow for some moments. He took his place at the piano while the applause was continuing, but the audience would not cease its hearty welcome and forced him to rise and acknowledge its greeting once again. The *World* had seldom seen an audience "so eager, so enthusiastic, and so favorably predisposed towards the artist."[11]

Despite the crowd's clamorous reception, it was probably taken aback by Rubinstein's appearance. Although his likeness had been posted in shop windows everywhere, much to the dismay of the pianist, seeing him in person could be a shock.[12] His resemblance to Beethoven was striking—Liszt had dubbed him "Van II"—although the similarity was due as much to their intense, almost scowling, demeanor as to their broad foreheads and rugged faces. Rubinstein's luxurious, unkempt locks were another source of fascination to his admirers. When he bowed low to the audience, his hair usually fell in his face, and even while playing it "constantly rebel[led] at being imprisoned behind the ears." The "shaggy *maestro*" someone called him, and several thought he was copying Liszt in his long, uncombed hair and his rapturous pose at the piano, a habit Rubinstein himself admitted he deliberately acquired. He was also compared to the biblical hero Samson. In answer to a typical nineteenth-century conundrum, Rubinstein was like Samson in that he conquered because of his hair and brought down the house with his hands.[13]

American audiences were also accustomed to performers wearing carefully tailored clothes, displaying foppish mannerisms, and graciously and frequently acknowledging the audience's presence. Rubinstein would have nothing to do with such frivolous customs that merely diverted attention from the music. As a result, some critics viewed him as an awkward artist uncomfortable with concert decorum. More significantly, Rubinstein's attitude was not readily discerned. Was he shy or simply aloof? Was he embarrassed to be in front of an audience "like a bashful school-boy," or was he contemptuous of his listeners and the whole concert-giving apparatus? As one critic wrote, "he is grave, reserved, and distant, treating his audiences with a fine disdain or a fine respect, not always easily distinguished." Nevertheless, everyone agreed on the effect of Rubinstein's manner: for other players music had seemed but an "incidental business," but when Rubinstein sat down at the piano, there was a "direct, unmistakable intimation that the music and not the man [was] to be considered."[14]

When remarking on Rubinstein's lack of affectations—ceremonially ungloving the hands, gazing languidly at the ladies—critics were usually contrasting him with Gottschalk, who had been as calculating in his stage deportment as Rubinstein was negligent. In addition, many detected a difference between their approach to art and the piano repertoire that was deeper than superficial mannerisms. A Hartford writer observed: "Gottschalk used to call out as much enthusiasm, but he could never have done it before a musical people. When we hear Rubinstein we see the difference between genuine art and that meretricious reach after popular effect. There is not the least bit of nonsense, or deference to popular ignorance or vulgar taste in Rubinstein, in his manner or in his music." Rubinstein rarely moved while playing, and *Dwight's* New York correspondent likened his "always grave" face to be "as impassible as the sphinx." He never surveyed the audience in the midst of a performance, a gimmick of many a virtuoso. Even when applauded in the middle of a group of

pieces, he did not stand or turn to his listeners, but merely bowed toward the piano as low as the keyboard would allow. The pianist fixed his eyes on the keys, occasionally closing them. The *World* jested that during Rubinstein's private performance after the Philharmonic serenade he "seemed to be in a sound sleep, and some said he snored, which was not the case, however."[15]

Rubinstein's opening selection was his own Concerto No. 4 in D Minor.[16] Rubinstein may have been oblivious to his audience, but he paid careful attention to the pickup orchestra under the direction of the Philharmonic's Carl Bergmann: "Sundry nods and signals passing from the pianist to the conductor" served to "tone down the too blatant brass" and to "send a new life thrilling through the violins." The pianist was recalled three times after the concerto and more than twenty times during the entire concert amid shouts and applause. The *World* proclaimed Rubinstein's debut a complete victory. The audience responded with "uproarious outcries in a style unprecedented in the concert-room" and did not hesitate to "throw up its hats."[17]

Rubinstein did not seem to care much for applause, however. He acted annoyed at the audience's vociferous response and never smiled, no matter how deafening the ovation. Moreover, when "relays of ushers and gardeners" tried to present him with the bouquets and wreaths that were traditionally offered to artists at the end of concerts he responded with "superb contempt" (figure 10.1). De Meyer had strategically orchestrated their presentation, but Rubinstein "disdained [them] rather ungraciously." Once he struggled with an usher who attempted to force one upon him, but the "floral tributes were left untouched to regale the nasal organs of the gentlemen of the orchestra."[18]

A few days later Rubinstein claimed in an interview that his apparent disregard for applause was a misperception. He admitted that "there is a time when an artist feels the very sounds of heaven in the rapturous applause of an appreciative audience, and when he feels like cutting his throat if the audience remains cold and unmoved." But now, at the age of forty-two, such a time had passed for him. He claimed to be "pleased with the kind reception which New York" had given him, but New Yorkers would be hard pressed to confirm it.[19]

Three more concerts followed that week, two evening concerts with orchestra and a matinée without one (a pattern followed during the next two weeks as well). In the orchestral concerts, Rubinstein offered one concerto and a selection of solo works, mostly by Beethoven, Chopin, and Schumann. His concerto repertoire included his own Second, Third, and Fourth Concertos and works by Beethoven (G major), Mozart (D minor), Schumann, and Weber (*Konzertstück*). For such an auspicious concert series the orchestra was neither large nor well rehearsed, but Bergmann was an able accompanist, a necessity with an unpredictable performer like Rubinstein. In a performance of the pianist's Third Concerto, one critic believed that "few musicians would be able to follow, or rather anticipate, the wayward imaginings of

Figure 10.1. "At Steinway Hall, 1872." This drawing by Joseph Keppler depicts some of the musical celebrities who performed in Steinway Hall in the autumn of 1872. At the piano is Rubinstein being presented with a much-despised laurel wreath. To the right are members of his company: Henryk Wieniawski, Louise Liebhart, and Louise Ormeny. On the left side are members of a concert troupe managed by Max Strakosch: Giorgio Ronconi (far left), Carlotta Patti, and Giovanni Mario. Teresa Carreño, also a member of the Strakosch troupe, appears as a bust on the right wall. In the upper left, under the word "Westward," is Theodore Thomas and his touring orchestra. (COURTESY, INTERNATIONAL PIANO ARCHIVES, UNIVERSITY OF MARYLAND, COLLEGE PARK)

a man like Rubinstein. His *tempi* are entirely arbitrary and change at the most un-expected intervals, and his impetuous spirit disregards mere conventional rules."[20]

Most of Rubinstein's opening concerts lasted from two-and-a-half to three hours. Those of the first week were even longer; the second one (25 September) dragged on for almost four hours. The hall was stifling, with the audience numbering three thousand, the temperature outside hovering around eighty-five degrees, and seven hundred gas burners inside simultaneously illuminating the hall and baking the au-dience. Yet the concert was "marked by demonstrations of delight even more unan-imous and prolonged" than those of the debut. For a performance of Schumann's *Carnaval*, still an enigmatic work for many listeners, Rubinstein received an "out-break of applause as is seldom witnessed," and even the "usually stolid" members of the orchestra were "stirred up to a certain wild and unaccustomed enthusiasm."[21]

The night of the third concert was equally hot. The windows of the hall were wide open—occasionally slamming shut—and howling dogs and extraneous noises oblit-erated the magical *pianissimos* in Rubinstein's playing. Observing the pianist's ag-

gravation with the distractions, William Steinway sent employees to investigate. They discovered a man trying to "teach an old dog new tricks" and another splitting wood. A dollar a piece managed to restore the quiet.[22] Despite the interruptions, Rubinstein was recalled four times after the Schumann Concerto.

The final concert of the week, a matinée on Saturday, was attended by an "immense audience." Even without an orchestra or concerto, the concert was a resounding success. The response to a transcription of the "Turkish March" from Beethoven's *Ruins of Athens* was so persistent that the pianist obliged with his first encore in America and with something even rarer for Rubinstein: a smile.[23]

Rarely had an artist been so immediately and unconditionally accepted by the public and critics alike, with such fervor and suspension of critical judgment. Although it never developed into the full-blown mania of Jenny Lind, after the first week of concerts the *Arcadian* was concerned that the "Rubinstein enthusiasm is slightly over-doing itself." By the third week of concerts, the *World* could report that the appreciation of Rubinstein was taking a "more sensible shape," with a "more rational and intelligent comprehension of the great artist." But in the meantime, the New York critics rushed to proclaim Rubinstein the best pianist to be heard in America. The *Times* found his tone beautiful and believed he possessed an "executive skill which no one can excel." The *Tribune* predicted that "nothing like his playing . . . probably will be heard here by the present generation unless we should some time have a visit from Liszt." The *Sun*'s critic felt he was "in the presence of the one person in all the world who is the complete master of the piano-forte, who controls most absolutely all its moods, resources, mechanism, and possibilities, and has subdued it to his own purposes."[24]

Rubinstein astonished by both his power and delicacy, a trait that De Meyer had been praised for almost thirty years before. The *Times* marveled at his "touch of inexhaustible variety."[25] Rubinstein was especially famous for his beautiful, sonorous tone, seemingly made possible by his thick fingers. Although acousticians argue that the size or shape of the finger cannot affect the tone of a piano, musicians swear otherwise.

Rubinstein appeared to pour his whole body, mind, and soul into his playing. Critics found his endurance remarkable considering the tremendous amount of energy he expended in a performance. William Foster Apthorp observed that "playing evidently fatigues him greatly . . . and we have seen him when he seemed almost completely prostrated by playing. . . . Passages that Tausig would play with the greatest ease evidently cost Rubinstein the most intense and protracted exertion."[26] Herz and Thalberg, so serene and perspirationless in performance, would have been dismayed if similar comments had been made about them.

The critics were unanimously effusive concerning Rubinstein's performances, but they disagreed on the success and significance of the opening three weeks of con-

certs in New York. Some critics perceived them attracting large audiences of attentive listeners from a wide range of people. The fame of Rubinstein and Wieniawski,
claimed the *New York Herald,* "has spread beyond the circle of ordinary concertgoers, and has already taken hold of the general public"; the interest after two weeks
of concerts "seems in no way to grow stale with enjoyment." A New York music journal was impressed by the respect that audiences gave to the serious repertoire:

> The class of music that has been given at these concerts has been of the most strictly
> classical character, and has required the closest attention and largest musical knowl-
> edge for its comprehension and appreciation; still these audiences have applauded
> every number with the wildest enthusiasm, and have displayed an acquaintance with
> the music interpreted, that was hardly to be expected in such large assemblies.

Dwight's New York correspondent, however, cautioned that "the love of art, and most
of all in music, is no mushroom growth," and contended that the large audiences
were "composed, in the main, of people not truly musical." Although attentive, most
listeners were charmed only by Rubinstein's virtuosity, matched by numerous players, and were unable to appreciate the "fine, subtle genius, the real essence of his
playing." He disagreed with those who inferred "with more charity than logic" that
the success of the Rubinstein concerts indicated that "our public has suddenly become 'musical.'" Still, there was "abundant cause for rejoicing in the fact that we are
advancing towards a purer taste and a higher standard in music, and that our
progress is plainly evident."[27]

The *New York Clipper,* more concerned about money than art, reported that "curiosity attracted good houses" to the first two concerts, but the management resorted
to "foreign papering" to fill the hall after that, and claqueurs familiar from the opera
house "were to be seen enthusiastically applauding the stars of these concerts." Repeating complaints from the 1840s, it concluded that "managerial tact and skilful
manipulation of the daily press has a great deal to do with the success of 'grand
opera' and 'concert companies' in the metropolis." The *Arcadian* agreed: if men who
cannot "tell a concerto from a cart-wheel" are ready to "fling up their hats over the
labored technical composition of a great musician . . . there is abundant evidence of
successful management."[28]

Nevertheless, Rubinstein clearly had conquered the musical world. At the end of
the first series of twelve New York concerts, the *Herald* stated that the

> representative local pianists came literally to his feet (for they occupied the first row
> of seats in the hall at each concert) to learn from him what was truly great in music
> and to catch inspiration from this modern Moses on the mountain, whose com-
> munings have been in the regions of sublimity, whose ideas have been conceived from
> genius itself, and whose influence will be lasting and deep.[29]

REPERTOIRE

In addition to a concerto, Rubinstein performed several solo works in each of his opening concerts that offered a sampling of his repertoire, at the time considered wide-ranging. His first selections included works by Beethoven ("Waldstein" and "Appassionata" Sonatas), Mendelssohn (selections from the *Songs without Words*), Chopin (G Minor Ballade, A♭ Polonaise), and Schumann (*Carnaval, Symphonic Etudes*) and at least one piece by Handel, Mozart, Schubert, and Field. Rubinstein's obviously historical repertoire was focused on composers who had been dead for a couple of decades or more (his repertoire in America appears in appendix B). Besides playing two pieces by Henselt and his own compositions, he did almost nothing to champion the cause of the contemporary composer. The only other living composer represented in his programs was Liszt, though primarily through transcriptions rather than original compositions. Rubinstein may have deferred to Liszt as a performer, but he was not sympathetic to his music. Rubinstein's repertoire accurately reflected his conservative taste in music. He would later say that he believed music to have ended with the death of Schumann and Chopin and that "nothing beautiful, great, deep, or high" was currently being composed. Rubinstein admitted he was puzzled why so little recent music appealed to him and suggested he was either "born too soon or too late."[30]

Rubinstein's advocacy of a canon of masterworks for the piano was still relatively new, and he would be variously praised and criticized for the content of his programs. Some writers were grateful for his avoidance of "selections from the namby-pamby, ear-tickling 'school' now so much in vogue" and the "clap trap trash which is usually offered by pianists."[31] Others were concerned that "portions of his performance are too severely classic for thorough comprehension by the amateur" and "that even musically cultivated minds may not be able to appreciate at once every piece he performs."[32] Rubinstein acknowledged that there were very few "good listeners who love music, and who understand it," and he grumbled that an artist always has to play to an "audience, the majority of which are utterly indifferent to music, and find his playing tedious, or do not understand it." Many listeners were surprised that he could make such serious music palatable. As one critic wrote about his selections, "none but an eminent player could make them interesting before an uneducated miscellaneous audience. He did it however."[33]

Rubinstein was often viewed as a prophet who would not only interpret the works of the masters to the musical intelligentsia but also introduce them to the musically illiterate. However concerned Rubinstein was about the instructive aspect of his tour, he had no intention of becoming a popularizer, although his charisma, in fact, made him one. He was determined to maintain the purity of his art and would do nothing to dilute it. In an interview he contended that the "popularizing and demo-

cratic tendency of music will kill that which is grand and noble in music, and the divine art . . . will pass into the hands of the organ grinder."[34]

Despite the perception that Rubinstein's repertoire was substantial and severely classic, he repeatedly included several pieces by the masters that were readily accessible: Beethoven's "Turkish March" from *The Ruins of Athens,* Mendelssohn's "Wedding March" from *A Midsummer Night's Dream,* and Liszt's transcription of Schubert's "Erlkönig." These pieces were among those he most often programmed, they invariably received the most applause, and they were influential in gaining Rubinstein his almost universal acceptance. A Chicago critic believed that these "three or four pieces of this more popular nature . . . have contributed more to the success of the Rubinstein entertainments here than any of the greater compositions which he has presented." As a Memphis newspaper put it: "To be successful in his mission of educating the popular ear, the classic must be interlarded with the popular."[35]

Not coincidentally, all three pieces were not only lighter in substance but were also transcriptions, two of them from orchestral works. The massive sound and orchestral effects that Rubinstein produced in the Beethoven and Mendelssohn marches, in particular, are what made them so appealing. Upon hearing the "Wedding March," an audience in Titusville, Pennsylvania, was "electrified at such an exhibition of power." A writer in Utica fancied it a "performance of a full orchestra wrung from a single instrument." A Philadelphia critic was not concerned when Rubinstein's concerts would no longer have an orchestra, for the pianist "can make his own orchestra from the prodigious resources which he possesses within himself."[36] The emphasis on orchestral transcriptions—a piano reduction of Beethoven's *Egmont* Overture was a favorite opening piece for Rubinstein—illustrated the difference between Rubinstein's and Thalberg's approaches to the keyboard. Thalberg had attempted to make the piano sing, emulating the lyrical quality of the human voice and producing a set of transcriptions of vocal works. Rubinstein, on the other hand, sought to make the piano rival the orchestra, whose popularity was eclipsing that of the piano in the concert hall, and appropriated its repertoire.

The Beethoven "Turkish March," which Rubinstein took at a brisk pace, particularly fascinated audiences. *Dwight's* New York correspondent complained that the piece was "utterly commonplace and cranky," and it did not allow Rubinstein to demonstrate his subtler abilities. Yet he was amazed, as was everyone else, by the decrescendo that ended the piece as the army marched away; he had never heard it "equalled, or ever approached." Audiences were always captivated by this infectious if insubstantial piece of exotica. In Memphis, some audience members had to check their programs to confirm that the delightful piece was really by Beethoven. After numerous performances of the work by the end of the season, Dwight could state that Rubinstein's "version of the Turkish March (or run), by its breathless speed and its calculated long *diminuendo,* always brings the house down."[37]

An impressive aspect of Rubinstein's sizable repertoire was his ability to perform it all "without notes," more or less. It was a rare occurrence when once in Philadelphia he was "obliged to use his notes." The practice of playing without a score—the bane of so many pianists, both amateur and professional—was still a relatively new phenomenon that helped both the performer and audience focus on the sound of the music. As George William Curtis described Rubinstein, he "sat like one rapt, playing from inspiration, not from memory." Although Rubinstein claimed not to have any memory problems until he was fifty (more than five years after his American tour), his erratic memory alternately astonished and frustrated American audiences. He generally was able to "recite," as Dwight expressed it, "with absolute certainty of memory." Nevertheless, his memory did fail him, at first only occasionally, then with considerable regularity toward the end of the season as he expanded his repertoire. Leonard Liebling's father remembered Rubinstein getting lost in his own D minor concerto in a New York appearance. Yet the pianist was undaunted: "He shook his locks, wove appropriate harmonies and sequences with his great paws, and until he finally found himself, he kept on improvising like a true lion of the piano." After a performance of the Weber *Konzertstück,* which was "marred by the omission of whole phrases," the *New York World* maintained that a "marvellous memory" should not "enter largely into concert exhibitions," particularly when, in the case of Rubinstein, one's memory was "not remarkable for accuracy of detail."[38]

BOSTON

After three weeks in New York, the Rubinstein troupe moved on to Boston. No serenade welcomed the pianist, but the leading musicians offered a reception in his behalf, a painful event due to Rubinstein's surprising timidity despite his proficiency in English. "He stood in one corner of the room, looking almost terror-stricken, as if suffering severe punishment, and wishing himself in any place but there," one person remembered. When presented to people, he tried to look pleasant but paid no attention to them. "The whole affair was like the exhibition of a lion in his cage, and smacked, uncomfortably, of the menagerie." His shyness was not limited to the party. The *Folio* reported that no one in Boston had "ever evinced such determined unwillingness to be introduced."[39]

Although socially awkward in large gatherings, Rubinstein was accessible in private and hosted an endless stream of visitors in his hotel room in most cities. Some came to sing or play for him, others to show him their compositions (one composer wanted to know if his creations were "classical"). One man boasted that he had "invented a new theory of musical composition" that would revolutionize the music of the world. Many visited him for no other reason than to obtain his autograph, a popular nineteenth-century hobby. Sometimes he obliged, other times he adamantly refused. William Mason remembered when one young woman approached him outside Stein-

way Hall to procure an autograph from Rubinstein and handed Mason a sheet of paper and pencil. When Mason relayed the young woman's request to Rubinstein in his dressing room, he quietly but resolutely threw the materials out the window.[40]

Audiences at the first two Boston concerts (14 and 15 October), with an orchestra led again by Bergmann, were smaller than expected. Bostonians had other things on their minds, including a smallpox outbreak and an epizootic disease affecting horses that suspended horse-drawn transportation in the city (and would do so in other cities that season as well). The audiences, if modest, were nonetheless demonstrative and appreciative. The Boston correspondent to the *New York World* observed that "ordinarily Boston is disposed to be cold and suspicious of anything which has received the approval of the rest of the world." Bostonians proved his point by welcoming Rubinstein only with "semi-cordiality" at first, but the pianist "quickly awoke his critical auditors to enthusiasm by his magically electrical power." According to the *Boston Post* the first movement of Rubinstein's Fourth Concerto "aroused the audience to a quite unwonted degree of enthusiasm, and shouts and applause interrupted the progress of the concerto for some minutes." Rubinstein was recalled with "uproarious plaudits" at the end of the work, but, of course, "bowed his acknowledgments very modestly and quietly." Dwight found the work to be of great interest from beginning to end with the beautiful themes of the first movement "illustrated with great wealth of fancy." The finale, though, was "a wild freak," "barbaric," and "full of diablerie," with Rubinstein appearing to be a "wonder-working gnome out of the bowels of the earth."[41]

At the second concert, Dwight believed Rubinstein's performance of the Beethoven Fourth Concerto was a "masterly performance" with a "poetic, sympathetic insight. . . . It was not an interpretation, . . . it was the music itself." His only concerns were Rubinstein's own cadenzas with their "crises of strong passionate bravura" that became "somewhat uncouth, speaking a language foreign to Beethoven." The main feature of the last evening Boston program (18 October) was the "Kreutzer" Sonata performed by Rubinstein and Wieniawski, in what Dwight termed an "exquisitely perfect rendering." Wieniawski broke a string during the finale, but astonished the audience by finishing it "as if nothing had happened" without stopping to replace it.[42]

Almost as surprising as Wieniawski's feat at the last concert was Rubinstein's acquiescence to the audience's demand for an encore, his first in Boston and only the second one he had given in the United States. The *Boston Post* believed that in his persistent refusal to grant encores, which the public so desperately craved, Rubinstein was "setting a most praiseworthy example, which we trust all musicians will be prompted to follow. The encore system, considered in the light of an unmitigated nuisance—which it is—is rapidly approaching dimensions which are as alarming as they are intolerable." The propriety of encores had been vigorously debated for some time. Was it not presumptuous of the audience to demand more of the performer

than was spelled out in the program, which served as a contract between audience and performer, between purchaser and supplier? Performers had been glad to dispense them in earlier days, for it was better to appease the audience than to lose their good-will and patronage. By the 1870s encores were invariably condemned by the press though listeners were rarely able to restrain themselves. Rubinstein obviously disdained the encore system and honored the demand sparingly and begrudgingly. On a few occasions, however, he was extremely generous. Once in New York, he gave two Chopin etudes back to back, "with scarcely a pause"; in Burlington, Iowa, he played several extra pieces; and in a Philadelphia concert, he offered Schumann's "Warum," Schubert's "Erlkönig," and Beethoven's "Turkish March," "all at one sitting."[43]

Like their New York counterparts, Boston critics praised Rubinstein effusively. Yet a few began to sound a rare but gentle warning. While highly complimentary, the *Boston Post* believed that a "close observer might be disappointed on account of the lack of clearness which was at times apparent in the heaviest passages." Dwight suggested delicately that Rubinstein was "prone to not a little of exaggeration and extravagance." Still, Dwight was as convinced as anyone of Rubinstein's abilities: "The instrument has no difficulties for him; the mechanical is absolutely mastered and need not be considered, not standing for a moment in the way of that which it is meant to serve, the expression of musical thoughts and feelings."[44]

Dwight was also ecstatic about Rubinstein's repertoire, particularly the generous supply of Schumann: the *Symphonic Etudes, Carnaval,* and *Kreisleriana,* all in one week. Moreover, he was amazed by the audience's attentiveness that never seemed to flag:

> Never in the selectest circle of a chamber concert have we perceived a more complete, absorbed attention than was given by that whole audience, not only to the grandiose and fiery A-flat Polonaise of Chopin, but quite as much to the "Moonlight Sonata," and (most remarkable of all, unparalleled in our experience of audiences) to one of the most profoundly spiritual and subtly intellectual among Beethoven's Sonatas, the last of all, op. 111. Even that most difficult, strange work, . . . for which you would hardly expect at any time more than a dozen listeners who could follow it throughout, was so presented by this masterly interpreter—or rather through this perfect "medium," as to hold the whole assembly spell-bound to the end.

Dwight realized that Rubinstein and Wieniawski had made a profound impact on the Boston musical public. Audiences had been "electrified and deeply moved," but more important, the "power of genius, personally manifested, has been realized as not before. We have had more insight into the possibilities of music and acquired a new respect for its accomplishments." He predicted that the "more *such* artists are heard, and in such music as such artists choose, the stronger is the desire to hear them."[45]

CHAPTER 11

Wieniawski

L ittle known before his arrival, Henryk Wieniawski languished at first in the shadow of his more famous colleague. His unpronounceable name (there was some concern that "bibulous amateurs" might stumble and call him "Wine and Whisky") and unartistic appearance did nothing to increase his acceptance. The violinist's first impression on an audience was that "he cannot be otherwise than clumsy," claimed a Rochester critic. Such doubts were "dispelled when he draws forth from the little instrument tones which no *artiste* has ever before caused to vibrate upon the human ear."[1] He was billed as "the only rival to the memory of Paganini," and after some hesitancy many people agreed.

Wieniawski soon developed his own following. Critics extolled Wieniawski's pure and sonorous tone, his clean and crisp bowing, and his phenomenal technique, and generally found him to surpass Vieuxtemps and Ole Bull, two of the more celebrated violinists recently touring the United States. Orchestra members vigorously joined in applauding his performances and occasionally gave him standing ovations. Audiences were often excited as much by his playing as Rubinstein's, occasionally more so. In contrast to Rubinstein's intense, almost sullen onstage demeanor, Wieniawski's genial and nonchalant personality made him more at ease with an audience than his partner. He was also more gracious in giving encores—perhaps the reason audiences applauded him so much—and more diplomatic in his refusal to perform

an unlimited number of them. Once he apologized to a St. Louis audience for retiring, and in Newark he good-humoredly pointed to his watch to indicate why he could not fulfill their request.[2]

Wieniawski's choice of instrument had as much to do with his success as did his skills as a performer. In the reception of all the pianist-violinist pairs already surveyed (De Meyer-Burke, Herz-Sivori, Thalberg-Vieuxtemps), some listeners clearly were moved more by the violin than the piano, just as some were more taken with a vocalist. Despite its ubiquitousness in the concert hall and parlor, the piano was still considered by many to be a cold, mechanical instrument, perhaps because of its inability to produce a vibrato. The hammered piano string seemed to communicate to the head, whereas the bowed violin string went straight to the heart. This was true in Terre Haute, Indiana, for example, where Wieniawski was the "favorite of the audience," not only because of his "matchless execution" but also because he played the "most popular of all instruments." The writer believed that "every heart responds to the music of the 'fiddle.'"[3]

Wieniawski's repertoire gave him a broad base of appeal as well. He could be as severely classical as Rubinstein—much to the delight of most critics—performing with distinction the Bach Chaconne, the Beethoven and Mendelssohn violin concertos, and the Beethoven Romance in F. He was more likely to offer bravura pieces by Paganini, Vieuxtemps, and Ernst, as well as some of his own works (including his Second Concerto, a *Légende,* a fantasy on *Faust,* and one on Russian airs). He also did not mind performing such sentimental pieces as "Willie, We Have Missed You" that could win over the most untrained audience member.

More often than not, Wieniawski attempted to please the general public, not the musically literate. Uneducated audiences, summed up one music journal, "preferred the trashy stuff which Wieniawski was pleased to offer for the sake of applause." His repertoire, then, was often at odds with Rubinstein's, reflecting a conflict of taste and mission that did not go unnoticed. In Brooklyn, for instance, Wieniawski charmed the audience more than Rubinstein did, since the "style of music he most delights in [is] far more in accordance with the tastes of his auditors than the more scientific school of which Rubinstein is the practical exponent." A critic in Troy appraised Wieniawski's selections to be much inferior to those of his colleague. "That's just the difference between him and Rubinstein; the latter thought the best music not too good for us, but Mr. W. was thinking how he could make the best impression," he complained. Nevertheless, he had to admit that he "applauded as loudly as any one."[4]

NEW YORK AGAIN

After concerts in Boston, Providence, Springfield, Hartford, and New Haven, the troupe returned to New York for three concerts before heading south. The *World*

suggested that, after appearing in Boston, Rubinstein was now a "soberer and a sadder man." In contrast to New Yorkers, who had tossed up their hats and gone into "paroxysms over Bach and Liszt," Bostonians had "gazed at him coldly with critical eyes, and even summed up Wieniawski like a ledger." For this new series of concerts there was no orchestra, which the *Herald* surmised was just as well, "considering the unruly character of our Teutonic instrumentalists, whom no conductor can control no more than the keeper of a menagerie with his animals when the bars are let down."[5] The absence of an orchestra gave Rubinstein an opportunity to offer several new and considerably meatier works from his repertoire: Bach's *Chromatic Fantasia and Fugue,* a group of Chopin etudes, Mendelssohn's *Variations sérieuses,* Schumann's *Studies for Pedal Piano,* and some of the pianist's own preludes and etudes.

With Wieniawski, Rubinstein played the Rondo in F Minor of Schubert and for a second time—purportedly to satisfy the public's demand—the "Kreutzer" Sonata, a work they would perform more than twenty times during the season. The *Tribune* had classified their first performance of the work a "phenomenal" one with an "exquisite" adagio, which produced "recalls seemingly interminable" according to the *Times.* The *Tribune* also praised their second rendition in its precision and their concern more for the "right expression of [Beethoven's] thought than for the display of their own technical proficiency." Still, it did not match their first presentation because of an occasional "want of true *ensemble,*" the result of "travelling and fatigue," the *Herald* critic speculated, an observation that would be made again.[6]

PHILADELPHIA

Not to be outdone by the New York Philharmonic, a group of Philadelphia musicians gathered on 26 October in the Continental Hotel waiting to serenade Rubinstein upon his arrival in their city following a New York matinée. A forty-member orchestra was ready at 10:30, but another hour passed before the pianist appeared, by which time a considerable crowd had gathered. Shouts and applause greeted him, and he dutifully listened to their performance of the *William Tell* Overture. Rubinstein then addressed the crowd with a few remarks in English. He was gratified "to meet with friends so soon after his arrival in a strange country, especially among his brother musicians. He knew very little about English, but he hoped to speak to them in a language they could better understand." More music followed—the slow movement from Beethoven's Fourth Symphony and Meyerbeer's *Fackeltanz*—then Rubinstein had a late supper in the hotel dining room. A private exhibition by him in the hotel's parlor was rumored, but he was "too much fatigued to gratify his numerous friends."[7]

After reading about Rubinstein's triumphs for the past month, Philadelphia audiences were primed to give him a frenzied reception. At the first concert (28 October) Rubinstein and Wieniawski together "excited the immense audience to such

a degree that it fairly boiled over. Shouts and thunders of applause, and the most persistent recalls, honored both the artists from the beginning to the end." The performance of Rubinstein's Concerto in D Minor was so overwhelming to a celebrated (but unidentified) local pianist that he supposedly remarked despondently: "I am going home to practice five-finger exercises, I find I don't know how to play." Wieniawski in the Mendelssohn Violin Concerto and his solo pieces created as much a stir as Rubinstein. "The audience grew almost insane over his playing, recalling him some six or eight consecutive times."[8]

Conducting the orchestra was Carl Wolfsohn, who had also led the welcome serenade. He was known primarily as a pianist and had introduced the works of Rubinstein in his recitals. Despite his limited conducting experience, both Rubinstein and Wieniawski complimented Wolfsohn on stage at the first concert. At the second concert, however, just before a performance of the Beethoven Fourth Concerto, Rubinstein reportedly warned Wolfsohn, "Be careful of your orchestra. Last night it was my music, and slips were no matter; but this is Beethoven."[9]

A Philadelphia critic observed the differences in temperament between Rubinstein and Wieniawski (and between their instruments) through their interaction with the orchestra. Rubinstein "took his seat quietly, self-absorbed, and dashed into his concerto, fairly dragging the orchestra with him, not stopping to please it or humor it, but either compelling it to obey or grandly overpowering it." Wieniawski, on the other hand, "came in, tuned his instrument carefully with the others, walked about a little among the players as if he were wishing to introduce his beautiful Stradivarius to the other violins in the orchestra, so that they might all go well together, each one lending a hand to the other." Relating this behavior to the instruments, the writer believed the piano is "necessarily an unsympathetic instrument, by reason of the magnitude of its own resources." The violin, however, is "tender, confiding," and "seems to cling to the others for support."[10]

Attendance increased for the second and third Philadelphia concerts, with several hundred standing during the latter. Three more concerts late the following week (7–9 November, after appearances in Baltimore and Washington, D.C., with little incident), however, declined in attendance because there was no orchestra and horse-drawn transportation was not available as a result of an epizootic among horses. Yet the final concert, a matinée on a clear day, produced a full house. The *Inquirer* was proud of its city's patronage of the Rubinstein concerts, which were "almost uniformly well attended," despite their "unusually high" character and "severely classical" tone.[11]

While in Philadelphia Rubinstein was given a demonstration of music's role in public education. At three different schools, students sang, were examined in theory, and performed exercises in transposition and sight singing, with Rubinstein suggesting some of the questions and tasks. The pianist could not perform for the stu-

dents because of the terms of his contract, but he congratulated them and their supervisors: "I see you are on the right way to understand music and to make good musicians, and that is what we want; I have spent a very happy morning." He planned to recommend "such a system of music to his government" upon his return to Russia.[12]

ASSISTING ARTISTS

For many listeners, the only drawback of Rubinstein's concerts was the distraction of the considerably lesser "stars" on the program. Maurice Grau clung to the common view that the public needed variety in a concert troupe and was unable to tolerate an entire evening of nothing but instrumental music. This was no doubt true for a significant number of listeners, but choosing two tired prima donnas—the soprano Louise Liebhart and the contralto Louise Ormeny—was not the answer artistically. The Boston music journal *Folio* knew of "a dozen conservatory girls who can sing with better effect." Bad enough that the public had to listen to them perform, but it meant that they robbed the two true virtuosos of opportunities to play. The function of the two singers, according to a Chicago critic, was simply to "fill up the programme and make it look symmetrical. . . . They simply serve as foils," and the effect is "very much like beer after champagne." Their ability to elicit encores at least occasionally only proved that "there are some people who don't get filled up with the piano and violin."[13]

Liebhart's current resources were slight, according to the *New-York Times,* and the *Tribune* assessed her voice as "well-worn and not very luscious." Although she rarely missed a performance, she was plagued with a cold and chronic hoarseness. She had a varied repertoire of operatic and oratorio favorites, including Handel's "Angels Ever Bright and Fair," which one critic imagined was "not altogether unsuggestive of the agonies of the unrepentant." She had gained some renown in London as a ballad singer, and her specialties of English ballads and simple German Lieder delivered with a theatrical flair made her popular with the public if not with the connoisseurs. Some critics regarded such vulgar ballads as unfit for a program containing the music of Beethoven and other exalted composers, but one from Philadelphia realized they were "needed to keep down the average of a Rubinstein programme to the average appreciation." A Milwaukee writer believed her pieces at least demonstrated "how utterly insignificant and trivial that class of compositions appears by the side of the noble creations of Beethoven, Mozart and Handel."[14]

Liebhart became notorious for her fashionable wardrobe (or *toilette,* as it was then called), which included a "gorgeous crimson velvet [dress], with oceans of thread lace." She was reportedly the "most expensively dressed woman that ever came here," and one critic lamented: Liebhart was "as usual, superbly dressed; and, as usual, sang poorly."[15] One pointed yet implausible story circulated that succinctly depicted

Liebhart's failing talent and her reliance on the diversionary tactics of histrionics and apparel. Grau had stored her supposedly twenty-eight wardrobe trunks, some of which were broken. One day while he was having them moved, Liebhart suddenly appeared and presumed he was rifling through them. "She struck a wild, ballad at-titude and exclaimed: 'Gott im Himmel, vas is das—prakin inside my kleidergestell!' 'Oh,' says Grau imperturbably, 'I was looking to see which one you had brought your voice in!'"[16]

Ormeny also had a badly worn voice and was criticized for poor intonation and a rather crude style. She could not even rely on the redeeming features of her *toilette* for she was less fashionably dressed than her co-star. Her occasional bouts of illness—she missed at least seven performances during the season—were always to the audience's benefit, for Rubinstein offered extra numbers to compensate for her absence. One newspaper even speculated that her failure to appear one evening was the result of not having enough lace to compete with Liebhart.[17] By mid-March she was no longer with the troupe.

RETURN TO NEW YORK: CHAMBER MUSIC AND THE PHILHARMONIC

One of Rubinstein's two ventures into chamber music (besides his duos with Wieni-awski) occurred during a week of New York concerts between his Philadelphia ap-pearances and the troupe's first visit to the Midwest. In three evening concerts and a matinée (12–16 November), Rubinstein and Wieniawski performed in piano trios by Beethoven (B♭), Schubert (B♭), Mendelssohn (C minor), and Rubinstein (G minor and B♭); the piano quartet and quintet (both in E♭) by Schumann; and the Hummel Septet. In addition, Wieniawski performed in string quartets by Haydn (D) and Beethoven, and in string quintets by Mozart (G minor) and Mendelssohn (B♭).

Attendance for these concerts was surprisingly good for chamber music. The *Tribune* thought the audience for the third concert was one of the best ever in New York for "this class of music," which it believed appealed to a "highly cultivated taste" and had "never been popular with the general public." The current excitement about the genre, the *Tribune* writer cynically conjectured, was due "more to the fame of the two principal performers than to an increased appreciation of the com-positions."[18]

The piano trios, in which the local cellist Frederick Bergner assisted, were the most satisfying of the performances. The *Herald* pronounced Bergner a "consummate local artist" and believed that he was one of only two resident musicians who could be "placed side by side" with Rubinstein and Wieniawski (the other was Leopold Damrosch). The *Tribune*, a little less positively, ventured that Bergner "was not un-worthy of the high company in which he found himself." In a performance of the Schubert Trio in B♭, "the tendency of the two star players to predominate unduly over

their associate was very little perceptible, and the execution in general was highly sympathetic, elegant, and carefully finished." The performances of the other works were marred by an imbalance among the parts and a lack of unity, perhaps due to inadequate rehearsals. Indeed, Watson thought the "want of sufficient rehearsals was evident" in all the works and complained that "unpremeditated chamber music" was "permissible and endurable" in private, but a public performance required more than an "accidental meeting." The disparity between the skills and personalities of the performers was a more serious charge. The critic for the *Times* concluded that Rubinstein's playing "reduces to insignificance the exertions of his associates"; he preferred fewer chamber works and more miscellaneous concerts with solo pieces, a desire he believed the public shared. Wieniawski's tendency to dominate his weaker partners made the string quartets the least successful of the works on the programs.[19]

Still, the *World* commended the series of chamber concerts, judging them more worthy than the preceding ones not only because of their more artistically challenging repertoire but also because of Rubinstein's "more conscientious work." In chamber music, he was forced to restrain his "strong individuality" and "headlong impetuosity" so evident in his solo performances, a characteristic not yet fully admitted by most critics.[20] But it was this "erratic force," to borrow the *World*'s phrase, that so many listeners admired, not the more intellectual and subdued interpretations required in his association with other musicians.

The highlight for most Rubinstein adherents that week was undoubtedly his appearance with the New York Philharmonic, which had campaigned for Rubinstein's participation in its concerts since his arrival. Perhaps its serenade to the pianist had the ulterior motive of attempting to procure his services, and soon after his opening concerts in New York, the Philharmonic Society's Board of Directors had a "long talk" with William Steinway and Maurice Grau about Rubinstein's involvement with the orchestra. The Philharmonic's success in engaging him encouraged an unusually high attendance at the concert on 16 November that included Rubinstein's Fourth Concerto, Beethoven's Seventh Symphony, and another musical *faux pas*: Wagner's *Tannhäuser* Overture. At the open rehearsal on the preceding afternoon, the pianist was "cheered to the echo." In addition to his own concerto, he performed four or five Chopin preludes, the "Erlkönig" transcription, and, for an encore, the march from the *Ruins of Athens*. At the evening concert the "audience cheered and cheered again, and for the moment the Academy [of Music] became a scene of intense excitement," according to the *Herald*. Rubinstein had performed his Fourth Concerto in his opening New York concert, and many of the society's players had probably comprised a large portion of the pickup orchestra on that occasion. Yet this time a considerably better performance was achieved with an orchestra of "trained veterans," a conductor who "reflected every phase of the composer's ideas," and a pi-

anist whose performance was a "labor of love."[21] Although assuredly a fine rendition, it would soon be surpassed with help from the rival orchestra of Theodore Thomas, straining the genial relations between Rubinstein and the Philharmonic.

The Grand Treatment

As specified in Rubinstein's contract, Steinway had the imposing task of supplying pianos for all of the pianist's more than two hundred concerts in the United States. The firm ostensibly received nothing from the agreement except a brief notice in advertisements and programs, but the approval of one of the world's leading pianists was excellent publicity and worth a considerable sum. The music firm of Blackmar & Co. in New Orleans, an agent for several makes other than Steinway, warned the public that furnishing pianos for a concert artist such as Rubinstein was an expensive means of promotion and that the cost would surely be passed on to the consumer. Steinway maintained six pianos in transit to cover Rubinstein's nightly appearances, and a Steinway employee, W. A. Haas, traveled with the troupe to supervise the transportation of the pianos and to tune and regulate them periodically. Steinway efficiently met its obligations with only a few mishaps. Once the piano to be used in Worcester was late in arriving from Hartford because of a break on the railroad. The instrument was removed from the train, carried by a team to another station, and was still being tuned while the audience arrived.[22]

In some, if not most, of his concerts, Rubinstein played a piano with an improvement called a duplex scale designed by C. F. Theodor (Theodore) Steinway and patented in the year of Rubinstein's arrival. Theodore, who had signed the contract with Rubinstein in Vienna on behalf of the firm, was the Steinway brother most actively dedicated to improving the instrument. In the duplex scale, the portion of the string that had been traditionally viewed as non-vibrating—between the tuning pin and the agraffe as well as between the hitchpin and the soundboard bridge—was made proportionate to the length of the vibrating string, so that it would vibrate at a frequency of one of the fundamental tone's partials.[23] A Philadelphia critic admired its "clear, bell-like, singing note," which was "remarkably beautiful," and reported that Rubinstein was pleased with the improvement.[24]

The Steinway piano consistently received good reviews, even in Boston, the home of the rival Chickering firm. Rubinstein performed on the finest Steinway Dwight had yet heard, and the *Boston Post* praised the "magnificent instrument," which "responded nobly to the call, and proved a faithful and capable servant to the giant who controlled its keys. Certainly never before has an American piano been put to so severe a test."[25]

For Rubinstein, the relationship with the Steinway firm was more than merely a business arrangement. William Steinway claims to have become "perhaps, his most

trusted friend," and Rubinstein looked to him for friendship and counsel. When Rubinstein received from Grau his first payment in gold—as specified by his contract to protect him from being swindled—he took the heavy bags to Steinway asking for advice, since he would be receiving twenty-three more installments during the tour. Steinway explained to him the currency system and its relation to gold and volunteered to deposit his money for him. From then on, the gold clause in the contract was waived, and Rubinstein forwarded his payment (as well as Wieniawski's) to Steinway while on the road, once with the ingenuous admonition, "Please do with it as you think best." With less than a month into the tour, he could already sign the letter "with kindest regards, many thanks, and damn many concerts."[26]

CHAPTER 12

Rubinstein's "Magnificent Faultiness"

Most reviews of Rubinstein's American concerts testify that his technique was unerring, his memory unfailing, and his interpretation ideally suited to the music of each composer. Yet there were occasional criticisms that timidly, graciously, or apologetically—seldom arrogantly—alluded to the pianist's frequent technical lapses. A critic might gently hint that Rubinstein was not always so perfect. In early January, for example, the *New-York Times* suggested that he "rarely plays so faultlessly as he did yesterday." A few weeks later in St. Louis, one critic surmised that he "does not seem to be doing the best of which he is capable."[1]

A few voices were brave enough to state baldly that Rubinstein was far from infallible and was, at times, completely atrocious. Perhaps many journalists were not familiar enough with the classical repertoire to detect Rubinstein's imperfections, and one suspects some knowledgeable writers had too much respect for his reputation as a performer and composer to be exceptionally harsh. One Philadelphia music journal, however, courageously chastised Rubinstein:

> Rubinstein's reputation as a pianist rests upon his minutes of sanity; and all his absurd mannerisms and glaring inaccuracies are extenuated on the score of his genius. . . . We do not consider that the possession of genius excuses a man, who claims to be the foremost pianist in the world, exhibiting himself, on several occasions, as a sixth-class

player. An artist who is so mentally and physically unequal, as not to be able to keep to a certain level during an hour and a half, should cease playing in public; for although the minutes of sublimity may balance the minutes of mediocrity, the impression left is one of extreme dissatisfaction.

The writer then described a performance by Rubinstein of Liszt's Fantasy on *Don Giovanni,* admittedly a fiendishly difficult work:

Rubinstein commenced it grandly and pursued it for a time in his best style, but when he came to the finale everything became chaotic. For page after page he floundered and blundered. . . . The more he advanced the more hopeless the confusion became; wrong chords in the bass, wrong chords in the treble, wrong notes everywhere, while his disheveled hair flapped against his face with a positive hirsute fury, seeming to lash him to madness. We never remember to have heard a performance so hopelessly bad.[2]

Such negative statements about Rubinstein's playing were usually voiced in retrospect—after the heat of the moment had subsided and a more objective assessment was possible. Three seasons after Rubinstein's tour, when Hans von Bülow visited America with truly an almost flawless technique, critics frequently conceded that Rubinstein had indeed missed more than a few notes. *Dwight's* New York correspondent stated the case rather boldly after hearing Bülow. He remembered hearing "Rubinstein play when he struck false notes, omitted whole bars of the music and blurred the phrase, almost distorting it beyond recognition."[3]

Rubinstein was fully aware of his failings and made no secret of them. He once apologized to an American admirer, "May the Lord forgive me for the false notes I dropped!" After his first concert in Boston, he reportedly professed his slips to Carl Zerrahn, the director of the Handel and Haydn Society:

"Mr. Zerrahn, did you hear me play last evening?"
"Yes, I did," was the answer.
"How did you like it?"
"Oh, you played wonderfully well. I never heard anything like it. You are the most remarkable player in the world."
"Ah! I am glad you liked my playing so much."
After a moment's pause, the artist said—
"Mr. Zerrahn, come and hear me tonight, and I will play for you the notes I left out last night—enough for another concert."[4]

Rubinstein's lack of total dedication to his career as a pianist was one reason he made so many mistakes. As he confided to a friend, "I am so busy composing that I don't have time for regular systematic work at the piano. If I had practiced four or five hours every day, as so many others do, I might have become a great pianist."

Rubinstein's Inaccuracies

We confess that we were greatly disappointed in his playing at some of his earlier concerts, many of his pieces being rendered in a reckless, helter-skelter, slap-dash style, which gave us the impression that his chief anxiety was to keep up the terrific pace at which he started, and to get through in the shortest possible time. In whole passages of a dozen measures the parts written for the left hand would be left out altogether; many wrong notes struck, and the entire performance to our ears an incomprehensible jumble.

The New-York Musical Gazette 7 (February 1873): 20

Sometimes he becomes almost frantic with excitement, and at such times is very liable to strike wrong notes, in fact we have never heard a really fine pianist strike wrong notes so often as he—sometimes two and three at a time.

William Foster Apthorp in *The Atlantic Monthly* 30 (December 1872): 758

Anton Rubinstein was and is the most unequal pianist (comparatively speaking) who has ever delighted or wearied an intelligent audience.... When at his best he absolutely defied criticism ... When at his worst, it was something absolutely fearful. The present writer has heard him mangle and slaughter one of Chopin's Ballades.... Tempos were altered, new *notions* introduced, dozens of false notes struck, and, in fine, the whole performance was inconceivably dreadful. This was Rubinstein at his *worst.* Those who heard him play the superb Schumann Concerto at that memorable concert in Steinway Hall will readily admit that *this* was Rubinstein at his *best.* And what a matchless performance that was! ... There was tremendous power, not mere brute force, exceeding delicacy of touch, not weakness of finger; vividly imaginative conception, not machine-like fidelity to printed notes and marks of expression.

The Music Trade Review 10 (2 August 1879): 1

Clearly, he played the piano to live, but he lived to compose, which he admitted in his interview with the *Sun* reporter: "I shall be a virtuoso only nine months longer. This is my last concert tour. After this I shall retire to private life, and devote myself entirely to composing—that is, if I don't starve. Of course, if I have nothing to eat I shall have to appear again."[5]

William Mason acknowledged Rubinstein's "unevenness," which he attributed to the "temperamental moods of a man of extreme artistic sensitiveness." Nevertheless, he remembered the pianist as a "thoroughly conscientious artist" who worked at the piano "incessantly many hours a day." Once Rubinstein told him, "I dislike nothing more than to have people say to me, as they frequently do, 'But you do not have to practise, for you are a born genius and get everything by nature.' It is provoking to listen to such stuff after having worked so hard." Steinway, in fact, delivered pianos to Rubinstein's hotel room so he could practice whenever he was in a

city for at least two days. In early March, when the pianist was compelled to expand his repertoire after giving numerous concerts in the same cities, he wrote to William Steinway requesting a piano in his room everywhere, "even if only for a day." "The piano could be of another make," he naively suggested, "I need it only for the new pieces."[6]

Rubinstein's loss of physical control was also due to his tempestuousness— Mason remarked on his "impulsive and excitable" nature—and it was this trait that ultimately helped his performances transcend their technical inadequacies. At the keyboard, he exhibited so much passion, which William Foster Apthorp believed was the "ruling element" in the pianist, that audiences were either blissfully oblivious to his flaws or willing to suspend criticism. The *Music Trade Review* suggested that Rubinstein's "magnetism," which he possessed in the "highest degree," made it impossible for his listeners "to be cold, or even dispassionate. One must feel, and feel deeply." H. E. Krehbiel believed that Rubinstein, because of his intensely fervent style, "stirred up emotional cyclones wherever he went and scattered wide the wrecks of discriminating judgment." By experiencing Rubinstein's "magnificent faultiness," as Henry C. Watson described it, American observers thoroughly understood that piano playing is more than just acrobatics: it is also poetry and communication.[7]

INTERPRETATION

If critics agreed on the powerful impact of Rubinstein's performances, they held widely divergent views on his interpretation of the masterworks he programmed. Assessing proper interpretation was a new dimension added to the role of the critic as pianists began to specialize in performing the music of other composers. When writing about a Herz or a Thalberg, the critic focused on the pianist's skill and the effects it produced, for one could hardly disparage the pianist's interpretation of his own works. The writer might remark on how the composer's performance made the music come alive as it never had before and how it illuminated the significance of the composition. With Rubinstein, and later Bülow, the music itself was the center of attention. Now the critic needed to be familiar with a broad range of piano literature and have some idea of how it should be interpreted. Of course, it is on this very point that pianists—and critics—have such a wide variety of opinions. Indeed, if they did not, the piano recital would have become obsolete or deadly dull long ago.

Rubinstein was frequently commended for his faithfulness to the composer's intentions. Dwight was among many who admired Rubinstein's "extraordinary power of identifying himself with the rarest inspirations of the great composers, and giving them clear, audible, complete expression." George Upton, of the *Chicago Daily Tribune*, doubted "whether any other pianist has so merged himself in the music and so completely devoted his gifts, both of intelligence and physique, to the correct in-

terpretation of the composer." At the end of the season, the *Boston Daily Evening Transcript* declared that there was "no doubt in the mind of the practised musician of the entire accuracy of Mr. Rubinstein's interpretations."[8] Such sweeping positive statements were common, but they were often challenged.

Rubinstein's interpretations that drew the most intriguing remarks were those of the music of Beethoven, Chopin, and Schumann, the composers most heavily represented in his programs, with the exception of himself. That Rubinstein seemed to be most in tune with Schumann was generally accepted. He shared the impetuosity of Florestan and could do full justice to the lyric qualities of Eusebius. After a performance of the Schumann Piano Concerto, the *New York Tribune* thought that Rubinstein's "sympathy with Schumann's genius seems moreover to be perfect," filling the work with "new life and splendor, and making it speak to us in tones more eloquent than it ever uttered to us before." Dwight hailed Rubinstein's performance of *Carnaval* to be perfect in conveying the work's "whole shifting, delicate phantasmagoria." Dwight also marveled at Rubinstein's interpretation of the *Symphonic Etudes* with its "sure and perfect lifting of its every thought out of the tangle of continual thorny difficulties."[9]

Reactions to Rubinstein's performances of Chopin's music were especially contradictory. The *Arcadian* believed his conception of Chopin was "too pronounced" and "opposed to all the traditions of Chopin's own playing." Because of the "excessive brilliancy and might of his delivery" which "are not easily subdued," the *New-York Times* would have preferred a "less Titanic artist" for the delicate rendering of Chopin's music. It argued that the "vigor and dash of his execution are sometimes detrimental to the effect of the vaguely-beautiful and ever-changing harmonies, and the elaborate arabesques of the Polish artist's writings." On the other hand, *Dwight's* New York correspondent was especially taken with Rubinstein's interpretation of some of the gentler pieces, including the D♭ Nocturne (Op. 27, No. 2), in which he "displayed all that exquisite delicacy and neatness of fingering, all that tender grace of expression. . . . Human fingers could not give a more positive rendering of that delicious, dreamy Nocturne." Concerning the larger works, the *Herald* believed Rubinstein grasped the polonaises "in all their grandeur." Dwight, though, was wary. Rubinstein's performances of the A♭ Polonaise and B Minor Scherzo were indeed breathtaking, but they were probably "more astonishing than wise," Dwight reflected, and he wondered "whether Art in her pure, impersonal, ideal court can ever set her seal divine" upon such effects.[10]

Rubinstein's Beethoven performances were more unanimously accepted, with his performance of the popular "Moonlight" Sonata perhaps the best received. The *Boston Post* believed it was "little short of miraculous" and "surpassed anything in the line of musical poesy which we have ever heard." It feared that neither amateurs nor professionals would "ever perform it again with any degree of confidence." The

Philadelphia Inquirer found his rendering to be the "most unassuming and yet the most perfect one we ever listened to." The *New York Herald,* on the other hand, believed that Beethoven's sonatas demand a "repose and easy flow of style foreign to the nature of the Russian pianist."[11]

Despite some consensus on Rubinstein's rapport with certain composers and works, one reels when surveying the conflicting opinions on the pianist's interpretive effectiveness. These diverse comments are partially due to the varying amounts of knowledge among critics and their different expectations, though Rubinstein's inconsistency was most likely the principal reason. Where Thalberg had been totally predictable from one performance to another, offering renditions of his own music that had probably not varied during the previous twenty years, Rubinstein's interpretations were rarely ever the same. *Dwight's* New York correspondent, for instance, contended that "we can never tell just how he is going to play, even if it is a piece which we have heard him render half a score of times." For Rubinstein, interpretation was not a purely intellectual process that could or should be precisely calculated in advance and duplicated identically in every performance. It varied according to the mood of the performer and the audience. As Rubinstein expressed it, if there were only one correct, objective interpretation of a work, then the performer might as well be a monkey.[12]

As the season wore on, critics were more likely to take exception to Rubinstein's highly individualistic and mannered performances. What at first had seemed amazingly authentic was soon viewed as willfully disobedient to the composer's intentions. Ironically, Rubinstein later complained that the "interpreters of to-day . . . delight especially in a capricious interpretation of the classic works (for which Wagner and Liszt are most to blame)—change of tempo, holds, ritardandos, stringendos, crescendos, and so on, not written by the composer." Yet he was capable of such liberties himself. In writing about a performance of the "Emperor" Concerto that he thought was "marvellous," Dwight was concerned by Rubinstein's extreme changes in dynamics, exaggerated diminuendos, and startling chords. He did not think they were "mere tricks of effect," but were "quite unconscious." Dwight regarded Rubinstein's "intensifying tendency" and "feverish exaggeration" as simply typical of the age. The writings of William Foster Apthorp for the *Atlantic Monthly* are especially instructive. Soon after Rubinstein's debut, Apthorp observed that the pianist seemed to place his audience "into direct magnetic communication with the composer," although he acknowledged that his "individuality is nevertheless immense, and all his conceptions are more or less tinged with it." More than four years later, however, Apthorp admitted that "it has become too painfully evident that Rubinstein often plays works of the great masters not as they are, but as his momentary mood impels him to feel them. He either cannot or is often too careless to merge his own fiery individuality in that of the composer."[13]

RUBINSTEIN'S MUSIC FOR PIANO

Despite his acclaim as a pianist, Rubinstein was regarded during his life to be more significant as a composer, just the reverse of the other pianist-composers who had preceded him to America. The *New York Herald,* for instance, considered Rubinstein a "greater genius as a composer than he is as an executant." Still, most critics did not bother to include any serious discussion of his solo piano works, though he consistently programmed them in his concerts, choosing instead to dissect his interpretations of the great works by the masters. Rubinstein's fondness for the early romantic piano literature reflected his own conservative musical language. Indeed, he viewed Brahms as the successor to Schumann and himself as the successor to Schubert and Chopin. The British writer William Beatty-Kingston aptly, if harshly, summarized Rubinstein's subjective interpretations and his derivative compositional style: "Rubinstein plays the music of others as though it were his own, and composes his music as though it were that of other people."[14]

The two pieces of his own that Rubinstein performed the most frequently in America, the *Mélodie in F* and the *Valse-Caprice,* illustrate his conservative style. The *Mélodie in F,* Op. 3, No. 1, the composer's most enduring work, is a character piece with a lyrical melody divided between the thumbs with simple chordal accompaniment and a tinge of chromaticism (example 12.1).[15] The work owes much to Schumann in its firm chordal foundation and unvarying rhythm and accompaniment. Chopin's influence on Rubinstein is evident in the titles of many of his works he performed in America—including a barcarolle (he frequently performed his Barcarolle No. 5), impromptu, mazurka, nocturne, scherzo, and tarantelle—if not in their musical style. The *Valse-Caprice* is a bit Chopinesque, yet without the earlier composer's harmonic sophistication (example 12.2).

Both Rubinstein works are more difficult than they sound: the *Mélodie* demands considerable skill to highlight the tune in the inner voice, and the spacing of the chords in the *Valse-Caprice* is awkward for most hands and has often been freely edited. Because of its wide leaps, the *Valse-Caprice* remained in the repertoire for several decades as a display piece. Walter Damrosch, ten years old at the time of Rubinstein's visit, remembered an impromptu performance by the pianist in his family's home that included the work:

> I stood goggle-eyed behind him, watching his hands do incredible things on the piano despite the long black hair almost completely covering his face. I remember especially his last number, his famous waltz, which ends with a constant skipping in the right hand from the middle octave to an immediate reiteration on the piano's highest notes. I was beside myself with excitement as his hand made this terrific jump over the keys, again and again hitting the high notes with the precision of a marksman hitting the target in the center with every shot.

Example 12.1. Anton Rubinstein, *Mélodie in F,* Op. 3, No. 1, mm. 1–16.

Other people remembered Rubinstein frequently missing those very same high notes. When the pianist Moriz Rosenthal heard him finally hit all the right ones, he supposedly remarked to a neighboring listener: "Poor Rubinstein! His eyesight is failing."[16]

Rubinstein seems to have been most successful in smaller pieces that could rely on his obvious lyrical gift and did not demand as much systematic development, since he was notoriously reluctant to critique and revise his music before sending it forth. Because of his reactionary tastes, he was especially effective with works in a neoclassical style. From his ten-movement, baroque-inspired *Suite,* Op. 38, he often performed the *Sarabande, Passepied, Courante,* and *Gavotte.* Dwight thought these four selections were "fresh and genial" and served as proof of Rubinstein's versatility. The sprightly *Gavotte* (example 12.3) shares with its baroque predecessor a duple meter, moderate tempo, light texture, and straightforward rhythms. The slithering chromaticism in the second measure and the quintuplet figuration at the cadences are the main clues in the opening measures that place the piece in the nineteenth century. Rubinstein often programmed the *Menuet, Sérénade, Valse,* and *Près du ruis-*

seau from a set of twelve *Miniatures.* The noble *Menuet* (example 12.4), another neo-classical piece, which Dwight found "quaintly, almost pedantically, antique," is also highly suggestive of its baroque precursor in its moderate triple meter and mostly homophonic texture. Both works possess melodic inventiveness and effective tex-tures, though to modern ears, the *Menuet* succeeds because of its adherence to the predetermined and succinct framework of its classical model, whereas the *Gavotte* soon begins to ramble through a prolix romantic development.[17]

Although several of Rubinstein's works remained in the repertoire after his death, their popularity ultimately faded. Even during his American tour, critics quickly made their own conclusions about his music based on firsthand experience. A Toronto critic surmised that Rubinstein's "chief excellence does not . . . lie in origi-nal composition" and that he was able "to give to his audience better music than his own compositions." After a full evening of Rubinstein's own piano works, the *New-York Times* concluded that "his writings for piano seem to us rather unimaginative in point of thought and labored in point of treatment."[18] There is an increasing inter-est in his music today, however, and despite a significant unevenness in the quality of his works, there are gems worth discovering.

TOUR TO THE MIDWEST

Rubinstein and his troupe made an unusually early visit to the Midwest. Such trips often waited until the spring, after the major eastern cities had reached a surfeit of concerts and when travel conditions were more favorable. Grau apparently wanted to saturate the heartland with more than one foray. As manager he accompanied the troupe while at least three advance agents traveled ahead to make arrangements.

With the development of efficient telegraph service (one newspaper boasted of "our modern system of lightning intercommunication"), an extensive railroad sys-tem, and creative marketing, concerts of touring performers were attracting more and more people from outlying areas. Many of the advertisements for Rubinstein's concerts announced that seats could be "reserved by mail or telegraph" for the con-venience of patrons in neighboring towns. Frequently special trains were run to and from nearby cities to accommodate concertgoers. To take one of many examples, in Utica, New York, the local newspaper reported that groups of concertgoers were ex-pected to travel on special trains from Boonville, Clinton, Herkimer, Ilion, Little Falls, Norwich, Richfield Springs, Rome, and Waterville.[19]

The troupe's Midwest tour was quick—just thirty-four days—but the troupe gave thirty concerts in seventeen cities from Albany to Chicago thanks to the rail-road, now the principal means of travel. The rail network had grown amazingly and hardly a town of any size was not connected to it. (The rise of railroads did mean that cities on the lower eastern seaboard, previously integral stops for performers when traveling by water, were now occasionally ignored, as they were by Rubinstein

Example 12.2. Anton Rubinstein, *Valse-Caprice,* (a) mm. 33–48; (b) mm. 118–33.

and Bülow.) The troupe usually caught a train immediately after a concert, rode most of the night, and arrived at their next concert site early the next morning. They would then check into a hotel and have the day to recuperate before the evening performance.

Occasionally, the train trip was scheduled for the morning after the concert. This was surely more desirable to the performers, who could rest more soundly in a non-moving bed, but it sometimes created headaches for the impresario because it allowed little time for delays. Several times the troupe arrived late and frazzled when the trip was left to the daylight hours. Later in the season after a concert in Burlington, Vermont, the troupe was to appear the next night in Troy, New York, where they

Example 12.2. *continued*

were scheduled to arrive at 4:40 P.M. The delayed train did not arrive until 7:30, causing the artists to straggle into the hall, "tired and supperless," Rubinstein first, followed by Wieniawski, and then Liebhart, who was detained by the necessity of "making her toilette." On other occasions the performers arrived in time, but their trunks were late, distressing the singers when their wardrobe was delayed. The most serious mishap occurred when Wieniawski's trunk was temporarily lost on the way from Akron, Ohio, to Toronto. Although Wieniawski carried his instrument with him, his concert apparel and music were in the trunk, and the violinist canceled his appearance. (Presumably, the music was essential for the accompanist, not for the soloist.) The announcement of Wieniawski's nonappearance "somewhat chilled" the enthusiasm of the audience, and one critic sarcastically wondered "how was a polite man to appear before ladies in his travelling suit?"[20]

The performers suffered most from the traveling, but audience members did not always have an easy time either, and Rubinstein's troupe was dogged with problems that hindered potential audience members making it to the concert hall. Besides the cessation of horse-drawn transportation in many eastern cities, winter weather fre-

Example 12.3. Anton Rubinstein, *Suite,* Op. 38: *Gavotte,* mm. 1–10.

quently tested the dedication of the most ardent music lovers. For concerts in Columbus, Dayton, Buffalo, and Hartford, listeners had to battle snow, bitterly cold temperatures, and piercing winds. A Hartford critic recounted the perils of trekking to a Rubinstein concert:

> Streets choked with snow. Air blue with north pole reminders. Sky turned into an immense gray refrigerator. Who could come to the concert under these circumstances and triumphantly surmount that soft white fleecy obstacle which lay piled on all the walks? None but those by whom Providence did its duty, and let them be born with a couple of horses and a servant at their disposition—the only proper way to be born into this vale of tears. These, and those others who would sacrifice their feet for the sake of their ears, and one class more, those who having purchased tickets refused to be wasteful and stay away.[21]

Small houses were often the result of the weather, but the cold did not necessitate a frosty reception for the troupe or temper the spirits of the dedicated. Sometimes the adversity increased the fervor. In Columbus, a critic reported that the hall was "about half filled; if we reckon by enthusiasm there was a house full." Sometimes the weather did not even affect attendance. At a Buffalo concert, where arrivers looked like "delegations from the Black Rock Flour Mills, or *avant couriers* of Santa Claus," there was still a "splendid house." In Detroit a "fierce blinding snow storm set in and continued with unabated fury" just hours before the concert. Despite the weather, the attendance was considerably larger than on the previous evening and the audience's enthusiasm "reached a pitch seldom if ever witnessed on any similar occasion."[22] Warnings that there would be "no postponement on account

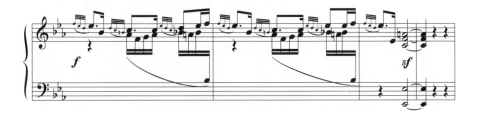

Example 12.4. Anton Rubinstein, *Miniatures: Menuet,* mm. 1–12.

of the weather" because of the tight performance schedule obviously encouraged people to brave the elements.

Another reason for occasional sparse attendance was the chronic complaint of high-priced tickets. Ticket prices for the opening concerts in New York with orchestra had been two and three dollars for reserved seats, with general admission set at $1.50 and the gallery at $1. Three dollars appears to have been a new high, but there was little discontent because the interest to hear Rubinstein was so great. Ticket prices were lower for concerts without orchestra. In the Midwest two dollars was the average price of reserved seats for the Rubinstein concerts, with the cheapest seats usually going for a dollar, occasionally less. The price had not really increased over those of Thalberg's concerts fifteen years earlier, but the protests were the same. In Chicago, a city still reeling from the great fire of the previous year, the hall was only about two-thirds full. One critic suggested that $2.50 for the top ticket price was simply too much in such "stringent times." He reminded managers that "musical intelligence and culture are not so general here as in Europe, and that they have no special public to appeal to but a mixed one, which embraces all degrees of musical intelligence, and, as a rule, possesses moderate means."[23]

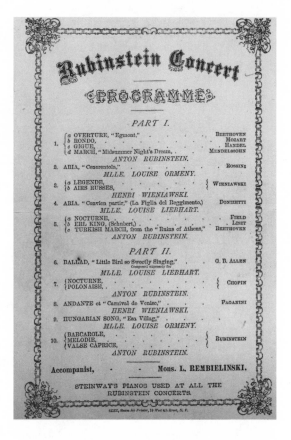

Figure 12.1. A typical Rubinstein program. With no date or location indicated, this program could be used for many of the troupe's appearances, especially in those cities that received only a single concert. The selections performed by Rubinstein were those he most frequently offered. (MUSIC DIVISION, THE NEW YORK PUBLIC LIBRARY, ASTOR, LENOX AND TILDEN FOUNDATIONS)

The more serious repertoire of the concerts may also have discouraged attendance. A Milwaukee music journal gloated that attendance in Chicago was poor due to "the average musical taste of the Chicagoans not being quite up to that sort of thing—you know." Another critic suggested that "high-priced amusements overshoot the average Terre Haute heart and pocket."[24] Ironically, Rubinstein treated the audiences on this tour to the lollipops of his repertoire: the "Erlkönig" transcription, the Mendelssohn "Wedding March," the Beethoven "Turkish March," and the *Egmont* Overture, with which he frequently opened the program. (It was rare for the star performer to appear first on a program, and many people thought it symbolized Rubinstein's lack of pretension.) A Chopin nocturne and polonaise (usually the A♭) with several of Rubinstein's own pieces were other standard offerings (figure 12.1).

In the larger cities like Cleveland, Louisville, and Detroit, where two concerts were given, Rubinstein might add Schumann's *Carnaval* or *Symphonic Etudes,* the Mendelssohn *Variations sérieuses,* a Chopin ballade or scherzo, the "Kreutzer" Sonata, and a Beethoven piano sonata. In Cincinnati and Chicago, where four and six concerts were given, respectively, his repertoire was indistinguishable from New York or Boston.

Plenty of people were apparently ready to hear such music performed by a master, however. In Detroit, the "audience listened with breathless interest" to the *Egmont* Overture and a Beethoven sonata. At the second Chicago concert, "the enthusiasm of the audience throughout the evening knew no bounds, and the house frequently rang with *bravas*." The two concerts in Cleveland were filled, and the "intense, rapt silence that prevailed showed that the auditory had come to *hear* and not to flirt. On both evenings the programmes were excessively long, and it is not the least of Rubinstein's triumph that he succeeded in chaining the closest attention until the final note was struck."[25]

The Temple of Music

At the same time that many listeners were enraptured by Rubinstein's performances, others were obviously not prepared to exert the intense concentration required to appreciate his challenging repertoire. Disruptive behavior in many concerts signaled the public's lack of interest and comprehension. Rubinstein's series of six Chicago appearances in December were especially afflicted by disturbances created by the audience in almost every concert, and on three different occasions the pianist stopped in the middle of his performance because of the commotion. George Upton, the *Tribune* critic, was embarrassed by the "many mortifying incidents" produced "as usual" by some "boors in the gallery." He lamented that "talking, hooting, whistling, slamming of doors, and heavy tramping in the gallery, while the artists were upon the stage, [had] been the rule." Upton believed it was an "inscrutable mystery" why those people, "who care nothing for music, take the trouble to go to concerts." Upton could at least report that the "boorish demonstrations were invariably hissed down by the major part of the audience."[26]

Chicago was not the only city that greeted Rubinstein with a deplorable lack of manners, including the usual spate of latecomers and early leavers. In several cities, audience members were requested to be seated on time or they would not be allowed to enter the hall until Rubinstein had finished performing his first piece, an admonition that seemed to work. In Troy, one critic predicted that "even at the resurrection there will be some Trojan with squeaking boots who will want to get up and go out before the exercises are concluded." At one Rubinstein concert there, the hall was a "babel from first to last," with ushers talking and laughing, patrons entering during the first hour of the performance (one man leaving, changing his seat at the box office, and returning to the hall), and others exiting while Rubinstein was playing, perhaps "seized with sudden pain or an overpowering desire to see their children."[27]

People tramping on hard, wooden floors was a widespread problem. In one incident in Albany, "certain donkeys with squeaking boots" created a nuisance. During an encore, "one of those unmannerly boors, who afflict all public assemblages" walked the "entire length of the gallery to the door." Rubinstein stopped and some

audience members hissed the offending party. As Rubinstein began to complete the piece, another person tramped on the opposite side of the gallery. Rubinstein stopped and "muttered audibly," "*Was meinen die dummen Menschen mit ihrem ewigen Herum-laufen? Man kann ja unmöglich spielen.*" [What do the stupid people mean by their everlasting running about? It is quite impossible to play.] He quickly exited, never to return.[28]

Rubinstein's need to halt performances (and, later, Bülow's habit of lecturing audiences on their unruly behavior) was not the result of an abrupt surge in the rowdiness of American audiences during the 1870s. De Meyer, Herz, and Thalberg had not issued such rebukes, although their audiences deserved them on occasion. It was perhaps awkward for such pianists to order respect for their own music, whose function was as much entertainment as it was art and as such could be listened to and enjoyed with a certain amount of distraction. In fact, that had been the fate of much serious music for decades, in Europe as well as in America, as has been well documented in the opera house if not so thoroughly in the concert room. One telling example is a description of a Rubinstein concert in Berlin in 1855 by the American Alexander Wheelock Thayer. He was shocked by the "talking, laughing, going out before the close, and all that sort of thing," which forced him to "leave the main floor and seek a place in the gallery," in order to hear at all.[29]

By the 1870s, Rubinstein, Bülow, and other performers aggressively demanded reverence for the great—and dead—composers like Beethoven or Chopin. Before Rubinstein appeared in Memphis, the local newspaper implored residents to "maintain the most perfect silence—a silence that should no more be obtruded upon in the concert room, lecture hall or theater than in the church." Its warning astutely summarized the trend in which performers were attempting to transform the concert hall from a sometimes disorderly place of entertainment into a sanctuary where the devotees of art could gather to contemplate their object of adoration. Music was now viewed by many performers as an art that needed to be approached quietly and reverently and, at least in the opinion of some performers, to be worshiped. The concert hall shifted from being a chaotic auditorium to a hushed temple, and performers were becoming high priests whose role was to interpret to the laity the ineffable mysteries of the great works of art. Dwight was among those who championed this sacred view of music. He experienced a profound, mystical experience, for example, upon hearing Rubinstein's interpretation of Beethoven's Op. 111:

> We know not when a piece of music has moved us so deeply. There was something holy in the tones which he brought out; sometimes they seemed to answer from another world, like a transfiguration of the theme or phrase once struck. Let us not despair now of any real inspiration from however deep a source, however complex and thick-set with difficulties in its development—of any utmost reach of any Bach's or

Audiences — The Gallery

Although many disturbances during a concert took place in the gallery, the location of the least expensive seats, it was also frequented by musicians and the most ardent music lovers. They often desired to attend as many concerts as possible and could not afford to splurge on the most expensive seats for several performances. The gallery was also attractive because the acoustics were often better there, or so many believed. A Philadelphia newspaper reported that some musicians sat in the "family circle," where "the music can be heard just as well as in any portion of the building" and because "the attendance in that part of the house is largely composed of cultivated listeners, who go with the single end in view of hearing the music." William Mason stated that Rubinstein "always sought a place in one of the galleries" when a listener at a piano recital. A Norfolk writer, whose satire on fashionable audiences has already been quoted, made a careful distinction between the knowledgeable concertgoer (sitting upstairs in the cheaper seats) and the ignorant (downstairs with the fashionable people): a singer enters "with a screeching voice. Sings a tune—song—in some unheard of language, not easily mastered by herself; the 'know nothings' down stairs applaud—the 'know somethings' up stairs grin and swallow it—saying nothing. Go on with your 'show.'"[1]

1. *Philadelphia Inquirer,* 4 November 1872, 7:1; Mason, *Memories of a Musical Life,* 228; *Norfolk Day Book,* 18 January 1858.

Beethoven's imagination and profoundest science, being communicable to any real music-lover. It strikes us, men like Rubinstein are sent into the world to show us that all this is possible.[30]

The quest for reverence in the concert hall did not begin with the managers or with the audience, although at least some of them desired it. And although performers—especially conductors like Theodore Thomas—had the most power to enforce silence, they were not the instigators either. The movement originated with the composers of the early nineteenth century, who viewed the purpose of music as edification and ennoblement instead of mere entertainment. Not long before, Mozart had been happy to accommodate both listeners who wanted pleasing, brilliant passages and connoisseurs who desired musical profundities. By contrast, Schumann, several decades later, actively crusaded against those composers and performers—above all, piano virtuosos—who catered to the general public. Music became an edifying force that required study to appreciate it and silence in the concert hall to savor it.

Rubinstein shared with Schumann and other romantic composers their high view of music, yet he was torn between an elitist and a populist stance. He believed it

was "desirable that the masses learn to know the master works of the art of music, hear them and come to hear them, bringing with them some understanding for them," but he was also convinced that "music demands . . . a consecration, a cult in a temple to which only the initiated have entrance; she requires that she be the chosen of the elect." Rubinstein admitted that he was not sure which of the "two views is the right one."[31] Such terminology fraught with theological references indicates how in an increasingly secular society, religion was being replaced by other pursuits such as music.

RETURN EAST

Returning to Boston after their midwestern tour, Rubinstein and Wieniawski joined with the local cellist Wulf Fries in four concerts to perform trios by Beethoven, Mendelssohn, and Rubinstein. Dwight was not particularly impressed with the performances. The hall was too large for chamber music, Fries was "in parts but feebly heard," and Rubinstein "seemed not beyond comparison." Dwight found the solo piano literature more enchanting and could not remember when such a "wealth" of piano music had been heard in a single week. He still admired the "intensity and individuality of [Rubinstein's] genius," the "wide range of his interpretations," and "his wonderful execution," with its "electric energy and force" and its "subtle delicacy." Nevertheless, he hoped to be relieved from the "impression of too frequent traits of wilfulness and sometimes positively wild exaggeration in the midst of so much that is beyond criticism." Although Rubinstein's Bach was *pure et simple* and several shorter pieces of Schumann were "played most exquisitely," Handel's music was "intensified and magnified" beyond its "real aim," and Dwight wondered whether Mendelssohn could have "ever dreamed of such a storm and whirlwind of passion as we witnessed . . . when he composed that noble series of '*Variations sérieuses.*'"[32]

Attendance at these concerts was unusually meager because of a smallpox epidemic, the results of a disastrous three-day fire in early November that caused an estimated $75 million in damage, bitterly cold weather, and poor scheduling (the first two concerts were on Christmas Eve and Christmas Night). After such miserable attendance, one account had the performers reply when asked if they would return to Boston: "We fear we should get out of the habit of playing in public."[33]

CHAPTER 13

Joint Venture with Theodore Thomas   ℚ

O ne of the artistic highlights of Rubinstein's tour was a series of more than forty appearances with Theodore Thomas and his orchestra. Thomas's orchestra was without question the best in the country, primarily because its players were full-time employees. Other orchestras, such as the New York Philharmonic and Boston's Harvard Musical Association, gave only a handful of concerts a year, with each concert preceded by a few rehearsals at best. Thomas kept his orchestra playing all year long, a daunting task that forced them to travel incessantly but allowed them to develop a first-rate ensemble with constant rehearsals and performances.

The joint appearances of Rubinstein and Thomas were vaunted as "The Greatest Concert Combination on Record," a rare instance in which implausible publicity claims were matched by the performances. Watson thought the combination could be "surpassed nowhere on the face of this splendid old world of ours."[1] Their first series of concerts began immediately upon the troupe's return to New York. Rubinstein and Wieniawski—at last unencumbered by their vocal cohorts—appeared with Thomas in six concerts there (and one in Brooklyn) beginning on New Year's Eve. Each performed a concerto as well as several solo works, interspersed between overtures and symphonic poems ranging from Cherubini and Beethoven to Wagner and Liszt, with a decided emphasis on the latter two composers. Rubinstein played the same concertos that he had already performed in New York, including the

Mozart D Minor, the Beethoven Fourth, Weber's *Konzertstück,* the Schumann Concerto, and his own Second and Third Concertos.

The soloists received their usual praise, and the *Times* complimented the orchestra on its "accompaniments of unimpeachable discretion." *Dwight's* New York correspondent felt it unnecessary to elaborate on the quality of the orchestra: "I need only say that it was that of Theodore Thomas!" In addition, Thomas served Rubinstein extremely well in his alertness to the pianist's impulsive interpretations, as the *Tribune* observed during a performance of the Schumann Concerto:

> Mr. Thomas caught as if by magnetism the slightest variations in the spirit, the tempo, the expression of the somewhat wayward and fitful pianist, and conveyed them so quickly and surely to his band that there seemed to be a complete sympathy between Rubinstein and each individual member of the orchestra. It is no easy matter to accompany him even moderately well; to play with him as these men did last night is a brilliant achievement.[2]

Their performance of the already beloved Schumann Concerto was a high point for many listeners. A critic for the *Music Trade Review,* who readily acknowledged Rubinstein's faults and inconsistencies, remembered more than six years later that Rubinstein's performance of this concerto was the pianist at his best. *Dwight's* New York correspondent declared that Rubinstein gave the "best rendering" he had ever heard of that "magnificent work." It quickly became clear that not only was the playing of the orchestra better than Rubinstein (and the public) had enjoyed in his concerts, but the improved accompaniment inspired him to do some of his best playing. The *New-York Musical Gazette* voiced concern about Rubinstein's "reckless, helter-skelter, slap-dash style" in evidence at his earlier appearances, but it noticed that these faults "entirely disappeared in his performance with the Thomas orchestra."[3]

WEARY TRAVELERS

In the meantime, the troupe with Liebhart and Ormeny and without Thomas had already begun the traditional long string of farewell appearances. Some artists did them for years; Rubinstein's only continued for five months. These farewell concerts included appearances in Albany, Newark, New York, and Philadelphia. In a *"matinée d'adieu"* in New York, Rubinstein performed fourteen solo works, almost all of them previously offered, with contributions from the rest of the troupe. In two farewell Philadelphia concerts (14–15 January) the troupe was well received, as one critic observed, with "Wieniawski, as usual, eliciting a greater share of applause than Rubinstein." He made such a hit that "half of his time seemed spent between the wings and the front of the stage, walking to and fro in response to the oft-repeated encores."[4]

Then on 16 January 1873 the troupe began a second and considerably longer tour to the Midwest, which lasted over two months (until 28 March) and included at least fifty-nine concerts in twenty-eight cities. Although quite a few of the cities were new to Rubinstein's itinerary, several were fast reaching a saturation point. Chicago again received six concerts, and Cincinnati was given five after its first group of four. St. Louis was virgin territory, but it received a total of six concerts in two different visits. The troupe's ten concerts in New Orleans were not particularly successful. The *Daily Picayune* suggested it would have been better to have had only four concerts because the people had "so many opportunities . . . to afford the enjoyment at their leisure."[5]

In addition to nearly satiated audiences, cold weather continued to discourage attendance or make concerts miserable. An Indianapolis newspaper reported that because of the "unpropitious" weather, "a great many of the 'floating' concert goers—those who happen in when there is nothing else that particularly attracts—were not present in the usual numbers." After an unusually frigid concert in Mobile, one of the advance agents promised that for the next concert he would "watch the thermometer there all day and pile the coal on." As a result, the next night a large audience "received the rich musical feast spread before them with absolute critical gluttony." One writer could not remember a Mobile audience having "been roused into supplementing liberal applause with universal and almost wild 'bravos!'"[6]

By early March, with more than 130 concerts behind them, members of the troupe were growing fatigued. Rumor had it that emotions were tense among the performers; Wieniawski, in particular, resented playing second fiddle to Rubinstein and receiving half the pay. The Chicago critic George Upton maintained that Wieniawski "had a bad temper, and Rubinstein had a worse one, and the old friendly relations were soon severed." In Cleveland, the usually gracious Wieniawski, who had a knack for pleasing an audience, was obviously growing jaded with the ordeal of touring:

> Wieniawski evidently knew that this was to be his last appearance before a Cleveland audience, and played in a careless, slovenly, *nonchalant* manner, glancing indifferently about the room. His tone, though broad and full, was at times anything but pleasing, his harmonic attempts very squeaky, and his whole air plainly seemed to say, "I've got to play, as I am paid for so doing; so I'll get through as soon as I can."[7]

The day before in Cincinnati, where the troupe endured another freezing concert hall that was like a "cave of winds," Rubinstein had complained in a letter to William Steinway about the ruthless schedule:

> Each day I feel unhappier and think often about breaking the contract. The tour takes no end and becomes more unbearable and more difficult for me every day. Now I even have to study and memorize new pieces because we play so often in

one and the same town that I have reached the end of my repertoire and I cannot give the public always the same—besides we are traveling daily so that I have no time to study.

Often despondent when away from home, Rubinstein also expressed concern about his family: "I have not had a letter from my wife for some time—who knows what is going on there—sickness, accidents, all kinds of thoughts of that kind go through my head when I fail to receive a letter on time—and add to that this sojourn here. You may well imagine in what rosy humor I am." Steinway recalled Rubinstein visiting him late one afternoon, probably soon after he had returned from this second western tour, and receiving a bulky letter from home, with letters and photos from his family. As tears formed in his eyes, he told Steinway: "Friend Steinway, I feel so happy that I must play for you!" Rubinstein played for him and a few friends the rest of the evening, his listeners spellbound.[8]

RUBINSTEIN ON MUSIC IN AMERICA

While the troupe was in St. Louis in mid-February, a reporter quizzed Rubinstein on the state of music in America, and the pianist, who by now had had a chance for first-hand observation, was brutally frank. Although he conceded that there were "instances of elevated musical taste and sentiment," he believed that "music, as an art, is quite unknown to the American public." Indeed, he stated that there was "no country in Europe, not even England, where music, as an art, is less generally understood and appreciated." He first attributed such a condition to the critics, some of whom had suggested that more popular music should be included in his programs. As treated by the newspapers, music appeared "not to be an art, but simply an amusement," Rubinstein observed. He insisted that "art is *not* amusement. It is, rightly appreciated and understood, instruction. It does not serve merely as a relief or relaxation from the cares and anxieties of our grosser and purely material life, and it is profanation so to regard it."[9]

Rubinstein also blamed young people's desire for wealth that prompted their commitment to more lucrative professions rather than to the "long, toilsome and painful apprenticeship which art inexorably demands of her votaries." In an even more sweeping indictment, Rubinstein predicted a grim future for music in America on the basis that the American system of government "may be unfavorable to art." Arguing illogically that music and government should be analogous, he declared that "in art there is no democracy. Music, as every other form of art, is not only Monarchism, it is Despotism."[10]

Another stumbling block to the development of musical art in the United States in Rubinstein's view was the deplorable state of musical instruction. Given Rubinstein's stature as a music educator, this accusation pierced Americans the most be-

cause they were proud of their numerous music schools. Although he had been a cordial guest at several of those institutions, he discovered that their goals were far too low to train professionals:

> You have "conservatories" of music—in name—without number, but in none of them that I have visited, or heard of, is music treated as a science, demanding long, laborious and constant study and application. There is, judging from my observation and information, a fatal lack of the vigorous and thorough instruction necessary to the master of any science, and by which the pupil is led gradually, step by step, stage by stage, to a proper comprehension and appreciation of the majesty, the beauty, the Divinity of art. Your institutions for musical instruction, naturally, if not necessarily, conform to the wishes and taste of those by whom they are supported. A parent who regards music solely as an accomplishment, a superficial knowledge of which is necessary to enable a son or daughter to make a creditable appearance in society, naturally requires or expects nothing more than that this superficial "accomplishment" shall be acquired speedily as possible. The consequence is that the patrons of these institutions—for they cannot be called students—are rarely, if ever, thoroughly grounded in music, but are hurried on to that stage where art is ignored and a fashionable accomplishment is secured. Hence you have a multitude of "players," and but few musicians.

As a foreign visitor submerged in an endless stream of concerts, Rubinstein was remarkably accurate in his assessment. Although the names of the institutions made them sound like advanced schools of music, most of them trained young people, primarily women, to be respectable amateurs, not highly trained professionals. The Cincinnati Conservatory was the only one of those he visited that would develop into a first-rate institution. The most promising musicians were still making the pilgrimage to Europe, most commonly to Germany during this period, to finish their musical education. On the steamer home, Rubinstein proposed that America needed an entire system of conservatories whose goal was the advancement of art, not the making of money. He predicted that Americans "will have no music until you can educate musicians at home."[11]

THEODORE THOMAS AGAIN

On the last leg of the troupe's western tour, Rubinstein and Wieniawski joined Theodore Thomas once more for a series of thirty-seven concerts that took place sporadically between 17 March and 1 May. Besides the obvious musical rapport the conductor had achieved with the soloists, Thomas enjoyed combining forces with them for the sake of repertoire. Thomas shared Rubinstein's reverent view of music, and he later called his concerts "sermons in tones." For several years he had introduced lighter works into his programs, particularly those in Central Park Garden, to

Rubinstein in the Music Schools

As founder of the St. Petersburg Conservatory, Rubinstein was invited to music schools across the country. Americans were eager to demonstrate their progress in music education by parading prize students before him. He was usually gracious in his comments, which were proudly reported in the press, and occasionally played for the students, although this was technically against his contract. In Boston, for example, he visited the music school of the respected pianist Carlyle Petersilea, where performances by students "elicited his hearty commendations." In a visit to the Chicago Musical College, whose president was George F. Root, the performances of students drew "warm praise from him, and then he himself played three pieces, which closed a merry, pleasant occasion." The moment was only slightly spoiled when one young lady declined to perform because she did not have her music with her, "then Rubinstein turned gravely round to one of the directors and said with frank brevity 'She is lazy.'" Rubinstein also visited the Cincinnati Conservatory of Music, which was modeled after the Stuttgart Hochschule für Musik, where its founder, Clara Baur, had studied. There he performed for the pupils and assured Miss Baur that the Cincinnati Conservatory "was the first musical institution in America, where he found scholars who rendered classical music with such marked ability and understanding."[1]

1. In addition, Rubinstein visited the St. Louis Conservatory of Music, where he and Wieniawski expressed "great satisfaction at the advancement of the pupils." For information on the Boston visit in mid-October, see *Dexter Smith's* 2 (December 1872): 276; for the Chicago visit on 6 December, see *Chicago Daily Tribune,* 7 December 1872, 5:3 (excerpted in *Church's Musical Visitor* 2 [January 1873]: 11) and *The Song Journal* 3 (February 1873): 448; for the Cincinnati visit on 14 December, see *Church's Musical Visitor* 2 (January 1873): 11; and for the St. Louis visit on 18 February, see *Missouri Republican,* 20 February 1873, 8:4.

make the serious items more tolerable to the general public, a practice he would soon suspend. Thomas later noted that because of the public's fascination with Rubinstein and Wieniawski, he could draw up programs for the first time in his life "without making allowance for ignorance or prejudice," though there were still complaints that the repertoire was "oppressively colossal and fearfully classical," as well as too "heavy" and "tedious" for many listeners.[12]

Rubinstein added to his repertoire the Mendelssohn G Minor and the Liszt E♭ Concertos. The latter work had been heard in America through performances by Topp, Mehlig, Krebs, and others, but was still little appreciated. Even though Rubinstein had a low opinion of Liszt's music, his performances of the concerto raised considerably the public's estimate of what had been considered a piece of dubious merit. The *New York Sun* believed it was a "crazy kind of work," but Rubinstein's superb performance, with "all-sufficient fire, energy, and *bravura*," made its "discor-

dant but brilliant passages seem almost coherent." The next evening in Philadelphia he played the same concerto "so magnificently," wrote one critic, "that for the time being we were compelled to admire Liszt's composition. . . . To hear him accompanied so carefully, so faithfully, so accurately as last night, through the almost painful intricacies of this Liszt work was most enjoyable." Still, for most listeners the Schumann Concerto was the crowning achievement of the Rubinstein-Thomas team. Dwight was particularly extravagant in his admiration, despite Rubinstein's occasionally quirky interpretation:

> To hear so admirable a creation as Schumann's Concerto played with such a master at the piano, and such an orchestra in perfect sympathy, was certainly a privilege. All his great powers of soul and intellect, of nerve and muscle found worthy challenge there. All his earnest absorption in the music, his intensity, his white-heat enthusiasm, his titanic strength, his exquisite delicacy of touch, his *finesses* of expression and of execution, went into the interpretation; and so did all his idiosyncracy, his bold liberties with *tempo*, his almost willful humoring of accent, his heightening of contrasts, exaggerations in respect to *pianissimo* and *fortissimo*, to such a degree that now the ear was kept painfully on the stretch to follow the receding sounds at all, and now would come a crash as if the house were falling. . . . Through all the variations of this moody reading the understanding between the pianist and the orchestra conductor was most perfect and nowhere baulked by any instrument; indeed the accompaniment seemed not less remarkable than the solo performance.[13]

Rubinstein's Fourth Concerto was performed ten times during these joint concerts—twice as many times as the Liszt or the Schumann—and it created a sensation everywhere. Applause that was "spontaneous, long, and loud" greeted the performance in Cincinnati, and in Washington, D.C., "rapturous applause" erupted at the close of each movement, followed at the end by a "hurricane of approval." Despite these accolades, Thomas once told a friend that he "disapproved of soloists relying upon their memory" and gave as an example Rubinstein forgetting this very concerto while performing with his orchestra.[14]

William Steinway claimed to have brought Rubinstein and Thomas together, and he "often rejoiced" that the musicians became "dearer to each other almost day by day." Thomas would continue to be an advocate for Rubinstein's music after the pianist's departure, leading the American premieres of his Fourth and Fifth Symphonies (in 1875 and 1881, respectively) and his opera *Nero* (1887). Similarly, Rubinstein spoke highly of Thomas and his orchestra at a dinner the evening before his departure from America:

> Never in my life, although I have given concerts in St. Petersburg, Vienna, Berlin, Paris, London and other great centers, have I found an orchestra that was as perfect as the organization Theodore Thomas has created and built up. When he accompa-

nies me with his orchestra, it is as though he could divine my thoughts, and then as though his orchestra could divine his. I know of but one orchestra that can compare with that of Theodore Thomas, and that is the orchestra of the Imperial Academy of Paris . . . but, alas, they have no Theodore Thomas to conduct them![15]

OCEAN SYMPHONY

Most of Rubinstein's predecessors in the pianist-composer tradition had focused their attention on writing music for their instrument. A compulsively prolific composer, Rubinstein seemed equally at home with the keyboard, orchestra, and stage. The decision to present Rubinstein's *Ocean Symphony* under the direction of the composer was thus an appealing one. Americans would have their first chance to view Rubinstein's talent as a conductor (he was the first triple threat to tour here: a pianist, composer, and conductor) and to hear one of his major orchestral works, which were held in higher esteem than his music for the piano.

Only a few of Rubinstein's orchestral works had been performed in America before his arrival. The Third and Fourth Piano Concertos were recently heard for the first time in 1872 and 1871, respectively; Rubinstein performed the American premiere of his Second Concerto.[16] Rubinstein's *Ocean Symphony* was undoubtedly his most famous work in the United States. Composed in 1851, it was a sprawling piece from its inception, and Rubinstein was compelled to write additional movements from time to time. In 1863, he added two supplementary movements (an adagio and a scherzo) to the original four-movement work; he composed a seventh movement in 1880. Later in life, he suggested that conductors choose only four movements from among them to perform at any one time.[17] The symphony had first been heard in the United States in 1859 at a New York concert led by Carl Bergmann and had been performed recently by the New York Philharmonic in January 1871. Theodore Thomas had frequently programmed the first two supplementary movements by themselves, and the lively scherzo had become quite popular.

Rubinstein conducted six performances of his *Ocean Symphony* in its then complete, six-movement version. Four performances were with Thomas's orchestra (in Cincinnati, New York, Brooklyn, and Philadelphia), one took place in Boston with the Harvard Musical Association, and one was with the New York Philharmonic (preceded by an open rehearsal). The performances raised new interest in the Rubinstein concerts and provided Americans the rare opportunity to hear what was then considered a masterpiece of contemporary music interpreted by the composer. (The few European composers who were lured to America in the 1870s for a concert tour, such as Franz Abt, Jacques Offenbach, and Johann Strauss, tended to specialize in lighter music.)

Rubinstein's performances with the Thomas Orchestra, with whom he was already touring, came first. In their New York performance (31 March), *Dwight's* cor-

respondent judged that the players, "inspired by the magnetism" of Rubinstein, supplied an interpretation that was "perfect and never to be forgotten." The audience was unusually responsive to the work. The *Tribune* believed it could "hardly overstate the enthusiasm of the audience. It broke out after each movement of the symphony; it was redoubled after the *scherzo*; it was quadrupled at the end, when Rubinstein was recalled again and again." In Philadelphia on 12 May, so many people were eager to hear the work with Thomas's orchestra that "great numbers were compelled to stand in the aisles or at the doors during the entire performance." Each movement was roundly applauded and Thomas's orchestra was "so well trained to obedience that [Rubinstein] seemed to mould them to every form of every idea which he conceived."[18]

Audiences could readily appreciate the work because it was firmly entrenched in the early romantic tradition. Rubinstein was adamantly opposed to the extremism of Wagner and the nationalism of his fellow Russians, who he believed relied too heavily on folk music for their inspiration, "giving evidence thereby of their own lack of invention." That his rather conservative compositions were often grouped with the "music of the future" demonstrated that his works were known more by reputation than by sound. The symphony was, as the *Tribune* described it, "clearly classical in form," "subdued in expression," with "exquisite melodies" in every movement and modulations that were "rarely extravagant." The *Herald's* comments indicate two other reasons the work was popular. First, it did not contain "one dull or uninteresting bar," and second, it had a certain familiarity because of its "reminiscences of elder composers" (especially Beethoven and Weber) that "once or twice transgress the bounds of sheer plagiarism."[19]

Thomas's New York performance of the *Ocean Symphony* jeopardized Rubinstein's scheduled appearance with the New York Philharmonic (19 April), which had been planned long before his association with Thomas. The Philharmonic had agreed to pay Grau $1,000 for the services of Rubinstein and Wieniawski with the provision that Rubinstein would not conduct the *Ocean Symphony* in New York beforehand. When Thomas edged out the Philharmonic, many of its members were outraged, including their conductor Carl Bergmann, and some were determined to withdraw from their agreement with Rubinstein. With some skillful maneuvering on the part of George Templeton Strong, the Philharmonic Society's president, and a vote by the entire membership, the orchestra decided to proceed with the concert. The anger on the part of the Philharmonic probably had more to do with the orchestra's growing resentment of Thomas and his orchestra than any ill will to Rubinstein, who, in any case, was under the authority of Grau.[20]

As a conductor Rubinstein possessed the same laudable musical qualities he had as a pianist, but he was liberated from the burden of technical slips. Conducting without a score a work of more than an hour's length, he had complete control over

the orchestra members, giving more cues than most conductors, and roused the New York Philharmonic to one of their best performances. The New York correspondent to *Dwight's* believed the performances of the Philharmonic varied "only in degrees of badness," but he admitted that under Rubinstein's direction they had never played so well and managed an "excellent rendering" of the symphony.[21]

In Boston, the original four movements of the work had recently been performed at the concerts of the Harvard Musical Association (6 February 1873), the work's debut in that city. The same group now played it under Rubinstein's direction, and even after only one rehearsal with them, he "held the orchestra in his grasp and exerted a powerful control over it." The *Transcript* reported that the customary applause after each movement was hearty and "long continued at the close." Dwight thought the lengthy work "seemed almost short" under Rubinstein's "inspiring lead" and the performance was "full of life and interest." "Hardly have we known a Boston orchestra to show such alertness, and to play with so much spirit, beginning and ending every note with such precision, so obedient to every intention of composer and conductor. He had a magnetic hold on every man." In prescient remarks, Dwight appraised the work as an "experience well worth the while," but did not perceive in it a "kindred greatness with the familiar master works."[22]

Solo Recitals

It would have been difficult to surpass the artistic delights of Rubinstein's season— a diverse repertoire, numerous concertos with the Thomas Orchestra providing splendid accompaniments, and the *Ocean Symphony* under the composer's direction. Yet Rubinstein found a way to do so, despite the reluctance of his manager to approve the scheme. The pianist's now-famous plan was to give seven farewell recitals in New York that would present an "epitome of the great piano music" from J. S. Bach to Rubinstein. The recitals were to include the "best illustration of each school of classic music," and would be "teeming with opportunities for instructive study," as the announcements boasted.[23] For Boston, three matinée recitals were scheduled, although there were easily enough works programmed for two more.

The plan was considered risky for two reasons. First, Rubinstein was to be the only performer. True, Liszt had pioneered the piano recital three decades earlier, but it was far from standard practice. The occasional solo recitals given in America usually attracted only a small number of devotees (unconcerned about the lack of variety of timbre or performers) and not the large crowds demanded by an impresario. Second, the programs were arranged historically, with one program devoted to keyboard music before Beethoven and another one containing six Beethoven sonatas. This was rather dry stuff for most people and, even worse, had a clearly educational intent. Few people could be expected to pay money to witness such an event. Grau finally relented to Rubinstein's plan and was duly rewarded. With the exception of the first

program or two, all were well attended. The largest receipts of any Rubinstein concert in America, in fact, were for one of his New York solo matinées, which took in $3,100.[24] Even Boston, which had made a poor showing for Rubinstein's first two visits there, finally rallied in the closing weeks.

Rubinstein's keyboard marathon was unprecedented in its scope and time frame: the seven recitals in New York and three in Boston took place between 10 May and 22 May. (During that period Rubinstein also appeared in two other concerts and conducted the *Ocean Symphony* twice.) Dwight believed Rubinstein's plan was "unparalleled" and praised his abilities that made it possible: "Such wonderful memory, such mental possession of the whole field of piano-forte music, such ready command of all the technical resources of the instrument, such calm audacity of enterprise and iron strength of nerve to execute it, is surely unexampled unless in the case of Liszt or Von Bülow." The *New York Herald* would later pronounce the series "the greatest work ever accomplished by a pianist on the shores of America."[25]

Each of the programs was substantial, and even though Rubinstein wasted little time between the pieces and sometimes only left his seat once during a recital, they could easily last two-and-a-half hours; the Chopin matinée in New York (19 May) lasted almost three. It was scheduled to include forty-three pieces, but Rubinstein added several more at the spur of the moment then eventually omitted several others because of the lateness of the hour. For the last Boston matinée (21 May), he performed more than what was advertised, and Dwight complained that it was "really too long." The New York recital that featured the music of Schubert, Weber, and Mendelssohn (16 May) was "too much bliss for the average concert-goer" according to the *Arcadian*. After the last concert, an all-Rubinstein one that included more than two dozen works, Henry C. Watson pleaded: "From another such a dose of Rubinstein, may the good Lord deliver us."[26]

The first matinée in New York (12 May) was devoted to the music of Bach, Handel, Scarlatti, and Mozart. Rubinstein's listeners were accustomed to a sprinkling of pieces by these composers, but a whole recital of the seemingly ancient works was imposing, and the hall was only one-third filled. Rubinstein was given credit for making such music tolerable if not completely enjoyable. The *Times* held that the "charm with which the dryest of the numbers was fraught" could only be attributed to the pianist's "exquisite delivery." No "ordinary rendering" of Bach's preludes and fugues or Handel's airs and variations could transform these works from "models for study into the things of beauty they become under Mr. Rubinstein's touch."[27]

The second New York recital (14 May) was devoted to six Beethoven sonatas, a massive undertaking perhaps even more challenging to audiences. The first four sonatas, all nicknamed ("Moonlight," "Tempest," "Waldstein," "Appassionata"), were among the most popular and not surprising choices. The last two (Opp. 109 and 111) were less well known and considerably more formidable to listeners. The American

critic W. S. B. Mathews wrote after Rubinstein's death that the pianist had "often abused" his "enormous memory" by playing a whole evening of Beethoven sonatas, a "feat not colossal for the player, but terrible for the listener." Watson thought that for a recital of six Beethoven sonatas even the "wildest enthusiast would find his stomach too weak to endure so copious a dose of the classics." Ironically, Rubinstein had earlier confided to William Mason that Bülow's performance of several Beethoven sonatas in one recital was an "extraordinary thing" and that as a musician he could not approve of it. He viewed it as a "scientific" enterprise that was "certainly not congenial to a true musical nature, which require[s] variety."[28]

The *Arcadian* praised Rubinstein's "Moonlight" Sonata, marveling at the clarity and distinctness of every note and pronouncing it the "best interpretation of it ever given in this city." Yet in one or two passages of other sonatas he "directly opposed" the directions in the score. These were especially evident, it noted, because "from this artist we have learned to expect perfection." The "Appassionata" was "everything that could be desired." The *Tribune,* which believed Rubinstein was in "close sympathy with Beethoven at almost all times," ranked his interpretation of Op. 111 as "one of the most stupendous and dazzling of all Rubinstein's successes."[29]

Interest began to build as the recitals focused on more recent music. The Chopin matinée had a "crowded hall, nine-tenths ladies"; for the following matinée featuring the music of Liszt (as well as a few pieces by Field, Henselt, and Thalberg) "hundreds of ladies thronged the stairs and lobbies at the entrance of the hall" an hour before it began, and the audience was one of the largest ever known there for a matinée.[30]

Critics again commended Rubinstein's faithful interpretation and uncanny memory exhibited during this grand series of farewell concerts, but with some notable exceptions. The *Times* thought his readings were not distinguished by "absolute accuracy of touch in very rapid passages," and although it admitted that it was "rather ungenerous to find faults with a performer who, when executing about 200 pieces from memory, departs occasionally from the text," it was clear in a couple of pieces that "Rubinstein's skill as an *improvisatore* did him good service." The *Tribune* critic believed Rubinstein confirmed that he was the best interpreter of Schumann and Chopin Americans had yet heard. Curiously, it was performances of those composers' music that also had the most technical flaws, easily detectable by the many listeners who followed with scores in hand, or attempted to do so. The *Arcadian* noticed two or three instances in the Schumann program where he "inserted bar after bar of his own until his memory supplied the missing links in the music." Another writer, more severely, suggested that some of the selections had "not met his eye for so many years that their general outlines alone were clearly remembered," resulting in "free improvisations, dashed off off-hand cartoons of the masterpieces of pianoforte literature." Although the "immense difficulties of Beethoven and Schu-

mann were gloriously surmounted," in some of the Chopin works the "hearer was continually plunged from the raptures excited by indescribable beauties, into absolute tortures produced by mechanical crudities, roughnesses and obscurities of the most aggravating kinds."[31]

Rubinstein's last two solo appearances, in Boston on 21 May and in New York the following day, were especially moving experiences, the end of an era for many listeners. For the final Boston matinée in Horticultural Hall, even women submitted to standing throughout the two-and-a-half hour performance, while hundreds were turned away at the door. Dwight observed that Rubinstein "looked somewhat exhausted," but there was "no sign of that in his performance." Grau remembered the audience tearing Rubinstein's clothes for souvenirs, women rushing to the platform to embrace him, and the "entire audience" yelling "Come back again!" Dwight remarked that "all lingered for a last look at the man whom they regarded as a benefactor and friend."[32]

The final concert in the United States, in which hundreds of people stood, was devoted to Rubinstein the composer. Like the preceding historical recitals, it was filled to the brim with works: thirty-three were scheduled to be performed, but after 10:30 Rubinstein decided to omit several of them and conclude the program with his new set of variations on "Yankee Doodle." Throughout the evening, he stood a total of three times, according to the *World,* and then "only to walk behind [the piano] and rub his hands." The large crowd and extreme heat made the room intolerable, and as the *Tribune* quipped drily, "no audience can really enjoy asphyxia for longer than two hours and a half at a time." The musical effect of the concert was disappointing. The *Tribune* shrewdly observed that although Rubinstein's works followed those of Liszt in the recital series, they were not in advance of the elder composer's music, but were guided by the "principles of the older masters." The *Times* held that Rubinstein's works for piano were in general "unimaginative" and "labored," but the evening was still memorable because of a "richness and a delicious lingering quality of tone; for a touch, now as gentle as the Summer breeze, and again as mighty as a giant; [and] for a delivery in which thought is all-pervading."[33]

Musically, the final concert was an anticlimax to a tour that had been filled with many peak experiences, although that did not dampen the audience's excitement or diminish the profound sentiment it expressed to the artist who had come to mean so much to American music lovers. Recalled half a dozen times, Rubinstein bowed with "much more evidence of emotion than he usually allow[ed] himself." Many of the women crowded to shake his hand, and the standing ovation covered by a sea of waving handkerchiefs was a haunting scene, simultaneously joyous and tearful. The *Times* regarded it as a spectacle "not soon to go out of mind," and it was "not until many minutes after he had disappeared from view that the audience dispersed."[34]

Rubinstein and "Yankee Doodle"

For his farewell recital, Rubinstein featured a new work of his: *Variations on "Yankee Doodle."* People groaned in anticipation of a work based on such a lowly tune, an outmoded gimmick that seemed more appropriate for De Meyer or Herz than the great composer Rubinstein. The *New-York Times* joked that "total annihilation of the subject by recourse to every expedient in harmony and counterpoint will earn the composer our heartiest thanks." Rubinstein dedicated the work to William Mason, who must have received the news with some trepidation. But Rubinstein told him: "They are good, I assure you, and I have taken much pleasure in writing them." The variations were certainly virtuosic if nothing else, and the *Herald* warned young women "fresh from boarding school or city *conservatoire*" not to rush out and buy them, because they were a "trifle more difficult, if possible, than Liszt's 'Don Juan' fantasie, which no one yet has succeeded in playing except Tausig, and it brought him to an early grave." *Dwight's* New York correspondent thought the work "sounded like elaborate sarcasm," but he hoped it was not intended as such. The *Times* pronounced the work "prepared in accordance with all the canons of art and ... in opposition to all the canons of taste."[1]

1. *New-York Times,* 22 May 1873, 4:7; Mason, *Memories of a Musical Life,* 236; *New York Herald,* 23 May 1873, 7:5; *Dwight's Journal of Music* 33 (14 June 1873): 40; *New-York Times,* 23 May 1873, 5:3.

The *New York Herald* stated with only slight exaggeration that the concert closed the "most remarkable concert season ever known in America." The *Herald* and other newspapers were quick to point out that Rubinstein's season was not only an artistic landmark but a financial one as well: the receipts for the entire tour had exceeded $350,000.[35] Most writers believed the extraordinary income demonstrated that Americans were growing more cultured musically. The *Herald* viewed Rubinstein's success as "significant proof of the reverence in which music is held in this country," especially since "not a taint of sensationalism" was employed during the season and because Rubinstein "never descended from his pedestal as an exponent of classical music." The *World* concurred that Rubinstein never compromised his taste. Although he was obviously unconcerned about his popularity or profitability, "never before did that self-willed thing, the public, bend its neck and lift up its voice and do honor so frankly and continuously to severity and sincerity."[36]

FAREWELL

Americans were reluctant for Rubinstein to leave. Even though critics might occasionally complain of his inaccuracies, erratic interpretations, or memory slips, his integrity and musicianship were consistently admired and he did nothing to lose

favor with the public or the musical community. In addition, he was probably the most successful of the touring pianists in securing close friendships with Americans. The night before his departure, he had dinner with a few friends, including William Steinway, Maurice Grau, Albert Steinway, and the music publisher Gustave Schirmer. Years later William Steinway remembered the pianist's charismatic personality that helped him make friends everywhere. Steinway extolled him as "one of the purest, most unselfish and honest men" he had ever known, and praised "his sterling integrity as a man, his purity of character, [and] his never-failing enthusiasm for his art." His manager, Grau, who would have seen him in the most adverse circumstances, was equally laudatory about this "great hearted man . . . whose fascinatingly sweet disposition, whose entire lack of conceit or arrogance, whose captivating personal magnetism and charm of manner made an indelible impression upon all with whom he came in contact."[37]

Rubinstein left America having developed a real affection for the country. Steinway recalled that the pianist always "bore the kindliest feelings toward the American people, and paid glowing tribute to their enthusiasm for music." On the steamer home, Rubinstein told the writer Kate Field that if it were not for his wife he "would make his home here, for, though a Russian of the Russians, he is a republican and loves liberty." Not insignificantly, Rubinstein was grateful for the proceeds of his American tour, which he used to purchase a home in Peterhof on a beautiful lake near the imperial palace, a home he called his "American-dollar villa."[38]

Despite his fondness for Americans and their country, Rubinstein never forgot the demanding life of a touring musician he experienced in the United States. In his autobiography written more than a decade later, Rubinstein recalled the tour this way: "For a time I was under the entire control of the manager. May Heaven preserve us from such slavery! Under these conditions there is no chance for art—one grows into an automaton, simply performing mechanical work; no dignity remains to the artist, he is lost. . . . It was all so tedious that I began to despise myself and my art."[39]

As the first great European pianist to visit America who primarily interpreted the music of other composers rather than his own works, Rubinstein played a strategic role in the canonization of the standard piano repertoire. Assuredly he attracted people to his concerts who had not been exposed to much music by Beethoven, Schumann, or Chopin, much less Bach, Handel, or Mozart. His impassioned performances of their works made them palatable for the first time to the general public, who flocked to his concerts because of his charisma, despite the sometimes intellectually demanding repertoire. For most listeners, his dynamic musical personality more than compensated for the occasional technical faults and highly individualistic interpretations. In addition, he communicated the immutable, as one writer observed, not because of his technique but through his "*soul,* from which emanates those spiritual

thoughts and grand inspirations, that . . . cannot be evoked by a life time of practice and study." Some writers were concerned, however, that Rubinstein was a poor role model for aspiring pianists, encouraging sloppiness in technique and anarchy in interpretation—traits that were only allowable, if, as in the case of Rubinstein, one were a genius. Yet most believed Rubinstein's visit would have a profound effect on American musical life by its demonstration of the power of art music to move and edify the public. Dwight marveled at the "deep hold which he has steadily gained upon all music-loving people by making the best works of so many master composers . . . appreciable to whole audiences. . . . Music as an Art . . . will doubtless stand in higher estimation in this country."[40]

PART FIVE

Hans von Bülow

1875-76

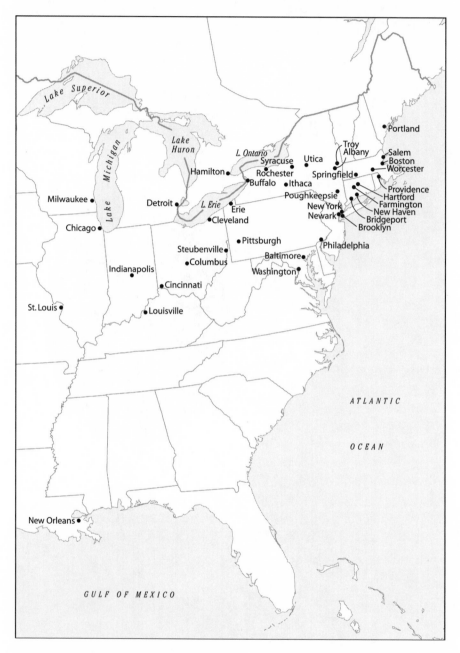

Map 6. Cities in which Hans von Bülow performed.

CHAPTER 14

Escape to the New World

Immediately after his grueling American tour, Anton Rubinstein encountered Hans von Bülow (1830–1894) in London. "Go to America," he supposedly recommended to Bülow. "I have paved the way. Previous to my visit, the American amateurs had been regaled with nothing but bravura and sensational music. The ground is now clear, and you will command success."[1] If quoted correctly, Rubinstein overstated his contribution, though he did initiate many Americans into the classical repertoire in which Bülow also specialized. Rubinstein's tour quickly took on mythic proportions, and it has consistently overshadowed the financially less successful one of Bülow just three seasons later. Bülow's undeserved reputation as a dispassionate performer, his impetuous candor that could swiftly alienate the public, and his poor emotional and physical health plagued his musically significant but troubled tour.

If Rubinstein's prediction of Bülow's guaranteed success did not quite come true, there was no ill will in his suggestion to Bülow. To be sure, Rubinstein had no intention of returning to the United States under any circumstance, and he turned down numerous sizable offers to do so. Nevertheless, he and Bülow were generally on cordial terms, much to the surprise of the public, who often assumed the two pianists were arch rivals. Each was aware of his own strengths and weaknesses as a performer, and neither seemed to mind too much sharing the title of the world's

reigning pianist. The only other pretenders to the throne were no longer active. Liszt had retired from performing in 1847 when he moved to Weimar, and Carl Tausig, who had ranked with Bülow as the greatest pupil of Liszt, had died in 1871 at the age of twenty-nine.

That America could attract such artists as Rubinstein and Bülow in their prime was surely a sign of its musical progress, or at least an indication that the nation was perceived more positively by Europeans. With some notable exceptions, many of the artists who had previously visited the United States were relatively unknown or were nearing the end of their careers. Critics frequently complained that the once first-rate European opera stars had passed their prime before they reached America. Instrumentalists did not have the same problem, for they could usually maintain their performance skills despite advancing age. Herz and Thalberg undoubtedly played as well in the United States as they had a decade or two earlier. For them, it was not a question of lost ability but of dwindling popularity and stature. Bülow, however, was assuredly not passé. His close association with Liszt and Wagner, two of the most discussed musicians of the time, had made him famous.

Wagner's music was responsible for luring Bülow into a musical career. A performance of *Rienzi* made an impression on Bülow when he was only twelve, and at seventeen he sent some compositions to Wagner, who responded with encouragement. His parents, however, resolutely opposed a career in music and insisted their son study law. Liszt's production of *Lohengrin* at Weimar in 1850 prompted Bülow to visit Wagner in Zurich. With the backing of Wagner and Liszt, a family friend, Bülow pleaded with his parents to pursue a musical career under Wagner's guidance. Despite their lack of approval, Bülow cast his lot with Wagner and worked with him in the opera company at Zurich, preparing scores and conducting. After only a few months, he had a similar brief stint in St. Gallen before deciding to study piano with Liszt.[2]

Once in Weimar under Liszt, Bülow made his teacher "unconditionally the arbiter of [his] fate" and allowed himself to be "be-Weimared," as he wrote his father. Bülow quickly became Liszt's favorite pupil and made his first concert tour as a pianist in 1853 under his teacher's sponsorship. In that year Liszt wrote of Bülow: "I do not consider him my pupil but rather my heir and successor."[3] In 1857 Bülow had the honor of giving the premiere of Liszt's single greatest work for the piano, the Sonata in B Minor. To Bülow, Liszt was not only a superb teacher but also a mentor to whom he frequently turned for advice throughout his career, and Liszt treated Bülow like a son. Their bond was made even stronger when Bülow married Liszt's daughter Cosima in 1857, and it was not broken when she left him eleven years later for Wagner.

Bülow's performing career began slowly with numerous setbacks owing to his devotion to the music of Liszt and Wagner, as well as his polemical literary activities.

In 1855 he accepted a teaching position at the Stern Conservatory in Berlin while he continued to perform and conduct. A pivotal event occurred in 1864, when Wagner arranged for Bülow to be appointed court pianist in Munich (and later royal *kapellmeister*), though in reality he was Wagner's assistant. For five strenuous years, he labored with Wagner and helped him produce two of his greatest masterpieces by conducting the premieres of *Tristan und Isolde* (1865) and *Die Meistersinger von Nürnberg* (1868). While Bülow was working steadfastly to promote the Wagnerian cause, Cosima and Wagner, who had already declared their love for each other in 1863, immediately carried on a liaison so flagrant that all of Munich knew. Cosima left Bülow for Wagner in 1868 and married the composer two years later.[4]

Bülow was humiliated to be betrayed not only by his wife but also by a man whose music he had so faithfully championed. In public, Bülow was the perfect gentleman when repeatedly quizzed about his relations with Wagner. He made it clear, however, that it was "forever impossible for [him] to ever again have any personal intercourse" with Wagner,[5] and he scrupulously rectified any misinformation about his relationship with his ex-wife and her father. His most famous letter written in America was such a correction: "Allow me most humbly to decline the honour given me this morning by the musical critic of the N[ew] Y[ork] H[erald] in calling me the son-in-law of Abbé Liszt, this honour belonging since 1870 *exclusively* to the composer of *Lohengrin*, Rich. Wagner Esq."[6] Nevertheless, Bülow maintained his loyalty to Wagner the composer: he continued to promote his music by including transcriptions from the operas on his programs, and he still considered him "the greatest musical genius that has existed since Beethoven."[7] He would not let personal injustices affect his musical goals or standards, even though his repressed anger and shame obviously tormented him and ruined his mental and physical health, which had always been fragile.

Following his separation and divorce from Cosima, Bülow spent several years in Florence, recuperating, teaching, and escaping from the Germany of Wagner. By 1872 he returned to an active career as a pianist. He had seriously considered an American tour as early as 1866, when his marriage was at a breaking point and his position in Munich seemed temporarily doomed. By the 1870s, his primary goal in such a tour was to earn enough money "not to die 'insolvent'" and to provide dowries for his three daughters by Cosima, one of whom he did not yet realize (or at least admit) was fathered by Wagner.[8]

CONTRACT NEGOTIATIONS

Armed with Rubinstein's first-hand account of his trials in the New World and apparently a copy of his original contract, Bülow was in a better bargaining position than most performers visiting America for the first time. When he began preliminary discussions with Bernard Ullman, the manager of both Herz's and Thalberg's

American tours who now had his headquarters in Paris and came recommended by Liszt, Bülow told Ullman, "a contract like the one between Grau and Rubinstein I shall never sign." Ullman firmly countered with flattery that Bülow, since he was a "man so sensible, so just, and so modest," would not be offended by Ullman's pointing out he was in no position to make such a demand when Rubinstein's receipts at the box office were greater than his.[9]

The agreement between Bülow and Ullman does not survive, but more than twenty letters from the pianist to the impresario chronicle a two-year negotiation of its terms, what Ullman called their "thirty years' war." Early in the process Bülow consulted with Liszt, his "only decision-helper in such matters," who gave his "unequivocal approval of [Ullman's] propositions"; Bülow refused, however, to let Ullman bill him as the student and son-in-law of Liszt, the latter term being no longer accurate. The contract called for Bülow to give 172 concerts over a period of eight months, performing an average of five times a week, for which he was to be paid 100,000 francs (approximately $20,000 then, more than $250,000 today).[10]

The most critical issue of the contract negotiations for both parties was not the number of concerts or the amount of compensation but Bülow's repertoire. Ullman tried to persuade Bülow to include some bravura works, but the pianist refused to waste his time learning them or lower his standards by programming them. As he told Ullman, "I do not have the time, I do not have the energy to prepare the 'firework' pieces *indispensable* for the Yankees. . . . I could not make any concession concerning the 'classical' tenor of my programs. Fantasies on motives from opera (whether from *Don Juan* or *Traviata*), transcriptions, and—in short, the whole repertoire of the period of Thalberg will find no place in my programs."[11]

As Bülow's refusal illustrates, his uncompromising attitude toward repertoire solidified the departure from the tradition of the composer-pianist of Thalberg's generation to that of the interpretive pianist focusing on a canon of masterworks. Rubinstein was an important transitional figure, but he had programmed a sizable portion of his own works. Bülow, who had only dabbled in composition, was the first of the great pianists to visit America who devoted himself entirely to the music of others. Interestingly, he did retain at least marginally the declining art of improvisation by preluding extemporaneously before a piece or joining two different selections with excerpts from them or other works.[12]

The other pivotal element in the contract bargaining was the subject of pianos. Before entering into negotiations with Ullman, Bülow had had discussions with Steinway dating back to 1866 and had made a tentative agreement with the firm for a concert tour in 1872–73, but they asked him to defer it until the following season to avoid a collision with Rubinstein.[13] Perhaps miffed at the Steinways, Ullman soon steered the negotiations toward Chickering. Rumors circulated that the Chickering, Steinway, and Weber piano companies bid up to $20,000 to acquire the exclusive

privilege of having their instruments used by Bülow in America. Ullman quickly denied that any American firm had made a financial offer. He claimed that he had approached Chickering, who had supplied pianos for Thalberg's concerts, "as old friends," wishing to receive a subsidy himself for giving them the contract for Bülow's pianos. Chickering refused this offer, but agreed to give Ullman a certain amount of the profits from the new Chickering Hall in New York that Bülow would inaugurate. According to Ullman, this agreement was subject to the approval of Bülow, who refused to decide which piano he would use until he auditioned both the Steinway and the Chickering. In the summer of 1875, a Chickering was sent to the Isle of Wight, where Bülow was busy preparing for his American concerts. After practicing on it for two months, Bülow wrote to Ullman, "I shall not be able to make so much noise on a Chickering as on a Steinway, but the tone is far more noble and distinguished, like those of Erard's."[14]

That is the story according to Ullman. Only some of it appears to be true. From Bülow's letters to Ullman it is clear that Steinway was never seriously in the running. In early January 1875, Bülow had demanded to keep his "complete independence" on the choice of pianos, which could not be decided until he had compared the Steinway and Chickering pianos. At the end of February, Bülow was already grumbling that he had sacrificed Steinway for Ullman's benefit, but he still refused Ullman's offer to share the piano maker's subvention since it would be entirely inappropriate for an artist to accept it. In late March, he again complained to Ullman that the "Chickerings *pay you* all of what *you* 'cannot' pay me in advance." Further contradictory evidence to Ullman's version of the facts appears in William Steinway's diary, where he recorded that the piano maker Albert Weber admitted offering $10,000 to have Bülow perform on his pianos.[15]

These matters involving pianos, which spawned so many rumors and denials, were of crucial importance to the music industry, whose exploitation of performers was just beginning to be institutionalized. The piano manufacturers feared that public knowledge of their subsidies to artists or their managers would negate their effectiveness. Critics were troubled about the "evil consequences of a system which so mixes up art and trade," in which musicians sold their "skill and *prestige* to makers of instruments."[16] The public, on the other hand, although pleased that Bülow did not have to play piano roulette, relying on whatever instrument happened to be available, rarely seemed concerned how the pianos magically appeared in the concert halls.

In the summer of 1875 it appeared that Bülow might not be able to fulfill the contract he had so painstakingly negotiated. During the end of the 1874–75 season, while on a tour to England, he suffered an "apoplectic stroke" that partially paralyzed the right side of his body. In late June he wrote to Cosima that his health was "completely shattered," and he feared he would be "incapable of starting for Amer-

ica." A couple of weeks later he was able to view his situation not "too tragically or pathetically" but still made arrangements for a "fatal ending," drawing up his will and giving instructions to Cosima for disbursing his possessions.[17] It was in this debilitated physical condition and cynical mental state that Bülow began the musical preparations for his American tour.

DEBUT IN BOSTON

Construction on the new Chickering Hall in New York that Bülow was to inaugurate did not begin until May 1875 and could not be finished in time for his American debut that fall. Forgoing the obeisance customarily paid first to New York, he began his concerts in Boston, where he arrived on 10 October 1875 on board the steamer *Parthia*.[18] He was met in Boston by Henry Wertheimber, an agent for Ullman who would remain by Bülow's side for the next eight months with the almost impossible assignment of keeping the pianist out of trouble. Upon arriving, Bülow inspected Boston Commons and the Music Hall where he would perform and attended a rehearsal of the Handel and Haydn Society. Most of the first week, however, he remained in seclusion at No. 23 Beacon Street, where he prepared for his series of opening concerts, reportedly practicing eight or nine hours a day.[19]

Bülow recognized his disadvantage in following Rubinstein so closely and his need to command the public's attention immediately. "I would like to drop like a bomb," he had written to Ullman, "but not making a violent noise—that will be the affair of my audience. Let me begin there where the Attila of the piano [i.e., Rubinstein] finished." He boasted to Ullman, "Rubinstein gave 8 [*recte* 7] evenings of piano at the end of his sojourn. My means will permit me to give 13." Bülow outlined a series of thirteen solo recitals similar to Rubinstein's farewell American appearances, devoting entire evenings to Bach and to Liszt, two to Chopin "and other Slavs," and three to Beethoven. Bülow later admitted he was "in a moment of illusory well-being" when he suggested the programs that Ullman wisely opposed as too academic for a debut.[20] Nevertheless, a historical perspective distinguished all of Bülow's programs, and critics deemed it necessary to point out to their readers the quasi-antiquarian nature of his concerts. He would eventually display a repertoire considerably deeper than Rubinstein's at least in regard to Beethoven, playing twice as many sonatas in addition to several other substantial works, and Liszt, offering many original pieces instead of just transcriptions (his repertoire in America appears in appendix B).

Ultimately, Bülow opted to begin his tour with a series of concerto appearances that was almost as impressive as the thirteen solo recitals originally proposed and unquestionably more appealing to the general public. In each of five concerts, he presented a group of solo pieces and two works with orchestra (Rubinstein had only performed one per concert), including Beethoven's Fourth and Fifth Concertos;

Mendelssohn's *Capriccio brillant*; concertos by his contemporaries Henselt, Raff, and Tchaikovsky; and a healthy dose of works composed or arranged by Liszt for piano and orchestra: the First Concerto in E♭, the *Hungarian Fantasy*, Schubert's *Wanderer Fantasy*, and Weber's *Polonaise brillante*. In addition, two of the concerts were repeated as matinées.

For Bülow's American debut on 18 October 1875, Boston's vast Music Hall was nearly filled, with listeners coming from as far away as Cincinnati and the leading New York newspapers sending reporters. Bülow walked crisply to the piano wearing gloves and carrying a hat—his almost inseparable onstage companion—as if coming in from a brisk stroll. He was slight and dapper, with a mustache and goatee, and yet there was a serious military air about him. After making a low, stiff bow with no expression, he sat at the keyboard, placed his hat on the piano, removed his gloves, sized up the audience, and began playing. Bülow was intense but made everything look effortless. Ordinarily he made few extraneous movements and was in a constant state of repose, "like a man that is marble from his wrists upward," as one writer hyperbolized. On the night of his debut, however, he was unusually animated:

> Herr von Bülow gives himself up not extravagantly, but frankly, to the influences of the music which he is performing, often keeping time with his head, very frequently prompting the orchestra with slight motions of his body, and sometimes conducting with his left hand while playing with his right. Sympathetic looks, thoughtful, pleasant, and even merry, flit over his face in obedience to the varied suggestions of the music, and every now and then he half turns to the audience and seems to invite them to closer confidence.[21]

Bülow's intermittent perusal of the audience was his principal idiosyncrasy. He engaged in this habit not because he enjoyed "study[ing] the local physiognomy," but as an attempt to draw his listeners toward him like close friends in a drawing room or to serve as a tour guide pointing out the finer details of a musical masterpiece. In his New York debut, for instance, he occasionally turned to the people nearest him in a "half abstracted, half explanatory manner as if he were revealing one of Beethoven's secrets in confidence."[22]

Bülow's first piece on his debut program, the "Emperor" Concerto, was warmly received. As America's foremost critic of Beethoven's music, Dwight believed the performance "in conception, execution and expression" was to a "higher degree than we have ever known before true to the whole scope and meaning of the work." The audience needed some time to adjust to a new pianist with a style considerably more restrained than Rubinstein's, but the *Post* observed that "enthusiasm gained steadily and rapidly throughout the evening." A group of Chopin pieces proved more exciting, including a nocturne and the *Berceuse,* and Bülow was forced to repeat the Op. 42 waltz. For the finale he had shrewdly chosen a showstopper: the Liszt *Fan-*

tasia on Hungarian Folk Tunes. Although more famous as a Beethoven specialist, Bülow was after all Liszt's prize student, and it was not by chance that the composition was dedicated to him (as was the *Totentanz*) and that he had given its premiere more than two decades earlier. The work as well as the performance was a *tour de force,* slightly bizarre for some listeners, but nonetheless dazzling. The audience demanded an encore, and the last portion of the work was repeated, followed by three recalls for the pianist. His debut was an "unmistakable triumph," according to the *Transcript,* which referred to the audience as the "now conquered public." The *New-York Times* was immediately willing to "assign to the newcomer the highest position to be awarded from a recollection of what has been heard in the United States within the past fifteen years." Bülow could not have been happier; after the concert he wrote Ullman: "I have a surprise for you! I am enchanted—one cannot be more— with this country. . . . What a charming public! . . . I sense that I will become as likable to them as until now I have found them likable to me. . . . I thank you cordially to have morally forced me to cross the ocean."[23]

A WORLD PREMIERE: THE TCHAIKOVSKY PIANO CONCERTO NO. 1

Bülow's debut on Monday was followed quickly by concerts on Wednesday and Friday with the opening program repeated on Saturday afternoon. The following week on 25 October, the most remarkable musical event of Bülow's entire tour took place: the world premiere of Tchaikovsky's First Piano Concerto (figure 14.1). It seems almost absurd that the first public performance of a piano concerto by one of the most promising Russian composers should take place in New England and not in St. Petersburg or Moscow.[24] Tchaikovsky had studied at the St. Petersburg Conservatory under Anton Rubinstein, who had little sympathy for the musical tastes of his pupil. Nevertheless, Rubinstein had recommended Tchaikovsky's appointment as professor to the Moscow Conservatory, which had been founded in 1866 by Rubinstein's brother, Nikolay. Tchaikovsky had written the concerto with Nikolay in mind, for his technique was as formidable as his brother's and infinitely more reliable. After hearing Tchaikovsky perform the work, however, Nikolay Rubinstein responded with a scathing tirade of the work's faults, which the composer bitterly recalled several years later:

> It transpired that my concerto was no good, that is was impossible to play, that some passages were hackneyed, awkward, and clumsy beyond redemption, that as a composition it was bad and banal, that I had pilfered this bit from here and that from there, that there were only two or three pages which would do, and that the rest would have to be either discarded or completely reworked.[25]

Rubinstein agreed to perform the concerto if it were revised according to his direction. Tchaikovsky sent it instead to Bülow, whose fellow Liszt pupil Karl Klindworth

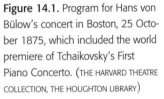

Figure 14.1. Program for Hans von Bülow's concert in Boston, 25 October 1875, which included the world premiere of Tchaikovsky's First Piano Concerto. (THE HARVARD THEATRE COLLECTION, THE HOUGHTON LIBRARY)

was a colleague at the Moscow Conservatory. Bülow had already written favorably of some of Tchaikovsky's earlier works, including the *Romeo and Juliet* Overture, a work he considered "uncommonly interesting" and commended for its "originality and luxuriant flow of melody." Upon receiving the concerto, Bülow wrote to Tchaikovsky: "The ideas are so lofty, strong, and original. The details, which although profuse, in no way obscure the work as a whole. . . . The form is so perfect, mature, and full of style—in the sense that the intention and craftsmanship are everywhere concealed."[26]

Critical reaction to what is now the world's favorite piano concerto was decidedly mixed. Its lyrical themes and colorful orchestration were immediately recognized and praised, but the sheer length of the work and the rambling first movement in particular were obstacles to appreciation. The *Boston Evening Transcript* found the "elaborate work [to be] as difficult for popular apprehension as the name of the composer," because of the "long stretches of what seems, on the first hearing at least, formless void, sprinkled only with tinklings of the piano and snatchy obbligatos from

all the various wind and string instruments in turn." Dwight judged the last movement of the "strange, wild, ultra-modern" work to be "extremely brilliant and exciting," but he wondered whether the public could "ever learn to love such music."
After the work's New York premiere a month later, the *New York Herald* complained
that the work had a "lack of inspiration" and an "entire absence of form and continued thought, which must render it distasteful to the musical mind." The *World* disagreed, finding it a "remarkable work, beautiful in melodious snatches of popular
Russian airs, constructed according to recognized musical forms, thoroughly original in thought and replete with startling effects which are never displeasing." It
speculated, however, that the work would not become popular because of its technical difficulty.[27]

The public's response was not nearly as guarded. A reporter for the *New-York
Daily Tribune,* in Boston for the premiere, thought the performance was "irresistible,
and the effect upon the audience most intense." In fact, the exhilarating last movement, despite some ensemble problems, was so enthusiastically received that it had
to be repeated. Tchaikovsky wrote to Rimsky-Korsakov after Bülow informed him of
this demand, which happened more than once: "Think what appetites these Americans have: after every performance Bülow was obliged to repeat *the entire finale!*
Such a thing could never happen here."[28]

The impressive survey of piano concertos—ten works with orchestra in two
weeks—was marred by the small pickup orchestra of about thirty-five members
hired for the concerts, a "wretched band" of "incompetent musicians." Given
Bülow's reputation as a demanding conductor, his conspicuous dissatisfaction with
the orchestra was no surprise. During the performance of the Henselt Concerto, he
"seemed to chafe under the humiliation of being associated with such a band," and
during the Liszt First Concerto he would "occasionally direct the orchestra, urging
them to accelerate their speed, or calming down a too noisy accompaniment." He
repeatedly drilled the orchestra himself during the long, unpromising rehearsals that
took place every morning. The Beethoven Fourth and the Liszt First Concertos were
"rehearsed over and over again, until one would think that the pianist never would
be satisfied." While preparing the Henselt Concerto, one of the toughest written up
to that time, he appeared to spend as much time directing comments to specific
players as he did playing the piano:

> Now the pianist sprung to his feet in his quick, nervous manner, and belabored some
> unlucky oboe, horn, cello or bassoon for a slight deviation from the inexorable rules
> laid down for the performance of this trying work. Nothing seemed to escape him in
> the orchestra. What an ordinary, or even a very good, conductor would be willing to
> pass over as a venial error, Bülow is next on his feet declaiming, gesticulating and in-
> sisting upon a repetition. There is a certain mannerism of excitement and fierce ardor

about him while sitting at the piano that must be very annoying to the leader of the orchestra. To-day I saw him jump up in the middle of a most complicated chorded run, rush to the desk of one of the cello players and make a pencil mark to emphasize a single note.

Bülow quickly became notorious in the United States for his stringent orchestral requirements and the severity with which he enforced his demands. When a rumor spread that he might conduct some orchestral concerts, a member of the New York Philharmonic suggested that a "cemetery be attached to the hall, that two coroners be in session night and day and that relays of players be provided like panels of jurors at a murder trial."[29]

Ironically, the orchestra in Boston was led by none other than Carl Bergmann, the conductor of the New York Philharmonic and, with Theodore Thomas, one of the leading conductors in America. Bergmann had also conducted the debut concerts of Rubinstein in New York. Perhaps Bergmann could do little with the musicians he was given; the *New York Herald* thought he had "wretched materials to work upon."[30] Yet it was obvious to the public that Bülow largely blamed the conductor for the shoddy performances. The Tchaikovsky Concerto, a challenging ensemble piece made even more difficult by its unfamiliarity, was responsible for rupturing the simmering relationship between Bülow and Bergmann. Bülow's decision to replace him with the young American conductor B. J. Lang to direct the Tchaikovsky premiere would have far-reaching consequences on the rest of his tour.

Lang's experience as a pianist and his connections with Liszt and Wagner made him a logical choice, even though he was not the most prominent conductor in Boston, a position that belonged to Carl Zerrahn. Lang had studied piano with Liszt in the mid-1850s and visited Wagner in 1871. In Boston, Lang was active as a pianist, giving the first Boston performances of several concertos and the American premieres of Rubinstein's Third Concerto (early in 1872 before the arrival of Rubinstein) and Saint-Saëns's Second Concerto (later in the 1875–76 season). As a conductor he founded and directed two singing societies in Boston and was the organist and assistant director under Zerrahn of the Handel and Haydn Society. Under Lang's direction, the orchestra for Bülow's concerts improved considerably. Privately, Bülow thought Lang's performance was "very decent" and a repeat performance of the Tchaikovsky was "most spirited." Publicly, he linked his arm in Lang's after his first performance and insisted on sharing the applause with him.[31] Bülow approved not only of his conducting but also of his piano playing, for he invited Lang to perform with him Chopin's Rondo for Two Pianos at one of the concerts.

Bostonians eagerly welcomed Bülow, no doubt delighting in their coup of hosting the pianist's debut. For his part, Bülow was on extremely good behavior. He "expressed much satisfaction with the religious attention and appreciation shown by

the Boston public," and he was feted with receptions and dinners by such organizations as the Papyrus Club and the Athenian Club, where he "proved hardly less entertaining socially than he has been found to be artistically." To a friend he claimed to be glad that he had begun in the "Athens of America," as Boston was frequently called, instead of "Yankeepolis" (i.e., New York). In one of his Boston concerts Bülow congratulated the audience on its favorable reception of a series of preludes and fugues by Bach, Mendelssohn, and Raff: "Ladies and gentlemen, you are Athenians; I am proud of your good opinions!" Only once did he appear to be annoyed by his listeners: while playing the "Eroica" Variations of Beethoven he was distracted by a group of ladies vigorously fanning themselves out of tempo. His praise for Boston would mellow a bit. He later commented that he found Bostonians to be "the most cultivated musical people I have met, but their views are narrow, and they are excessively pretentious."[32]

Bülow's immediate critical and popular success helped convince him that he had discovered in America a haven from his troubles. After his second Boston concert he wrote to a friend, "The New World is at least 66 2/3 percent more bearable than the Old. . . . I could count the hours spent here thus far among the happiest of my life if my health were better." Three days later to his mother: "Do not remember anywhere since Italy having felt so marvelous as now in just 14 days in this very curious, but very comfortable and truly magnificent country." Each month would confirm his initial reaction. By mid-November: "Civilization is at such a level here that I declare Europe to be more than half a century backward and still in Medieval barbarism. Marvelous country—splendid people!"[33]

AUDIENCES—SMALL BUT (USUALLY) REVERENT

From Boston, Bülow made his way to New York, performing in Worcester, Springfield, Hartford, New Haven, Farmington, and Bridgeport. The attendance at Bülow's concerts in Boston had been quite good, but orchestral concerts almost always drew a crowd. His recitals without orchestra in these other New England cities foreshadowed a major problem for Bülow and his managers: poor attendance in many of the smaller cities without a large and established musical community. In Providence, where he gave two concerts in between his appearances in Boston, he attracted only meager audiences, and there were "rows of empty benches" in New Haven.[34]

In these smaller cities, Bülow's lack of patience with discourteous audience members who did not approach great music as he did, with awe and devotion, rivaled his expectations of the professional musicians in Boston. He had no compunction in halting a performance while latecomers were seated or demanding silence by a well-aimed glare or a brief but intense interrogation. In Providence, for example, audience members were warned to be seated on time or they would be forced to wait outside until Bülow finished his opening Bach numbers. They were

also urged not to leave during the performance of a work. At the second Providence concert, the audience was warned more sternly to make "positively no disturbance whatever" during the "Moonlight" Sonata, since at the first concert Bülow had been "forced . . . to demand better silence." It would not be the last time he would have cause to reprimand his audience. The following month in Steubenville, Ohio, Bülow also addressed the audience concerning their uncouth behavior.

> While he was playing the "Spinning Song" of Wagner's, we noticed him glaring over the top of the grand piano at some men in one corner of the hall, who had their hats on. When he got through with the selection, he came to the front of the stage and said, in broken English, "Genzlemens, de ladies are in de house, pleaze take off your hats," and the hats were removed in an instant. At another time he stopped short in the midst of a piece, and putting on his eye-glasses, turned around in his seat, and sharply quizzed a party who were walking across the hall, and were making considerable noise with squeaky shoes.

Even in New York he halted an orchestral performance in midstream to wait for latecomers to be seated.[35]

Bülow, however, did not have to admonish his audiences as much as Rubinstein had. A few months later in Louisville, one writer described with some amazement the rapt concentration of the audience:

> We do not remember ever to have seen a more attentive audience than the one last night. Often it is the case at concerts and operas that we feel impelled to enter a complaint against young persons who will persist in clouding the pleasure of others by talking. Not so with Von Bülow's audience; and we here record the fact that in the two evenings we have not seen a single young lady talking with her beau during the performance. His audiences have been composed of people who love music, and finding one capable of bringing out its inmost harmony, they listened to him with wonderful attention—wonderful? yes, we may call it wonderful for an audience of eight hundred or a thousand people to sit in almost breathless silence for an hour listening to a performance, and seemingly lost to everything save the sweet power.

As the writer suggests, Bülow tended to attract more serious music lovers who attended simply because of their affection for music and not the casual concertgoer, who was occasionally drawn to only the most dynamic or celebrated performers, such as Rubinstein. Bülow sensed and often responded to the commitment of his audiences. From Hartford he boasted to a friend: "You have no idea of the popularity that I am enjoying already, and of the tremendous respect paid to me everywhere." For his concert in Springfield, Massachusetts, a group of people from Pittsfield had chartered a special train, but because of its delay, they arrived only in time

to hear the last piece on the program. When Bülow heard of their disappointment, he graciously played for them privately in his own room after the concert.[36]

Like Rubinstein, Bülow frequently invoked the language of religion when discussing music, evidencing their shared attitude toward the sacralization of that art. While addressing a Chicago audience in early February, he stated: "I worship always in the temples of the great masters." In an early interview in the United States, he expressed pleasure at the "spirit of reverence for the very names of the old masters" demonstrated by American audiences and critics. In an apparent attempt to quote the Bible, he stated that "reverence for the masters" (instead of "the fear of the Lord") "is the beginning of wisdom." This misquotation of scripture, however aptly it summarized his approach to music, offended many religious Americans in the midst of the fervent revivals of Moody and Sankey. Two similar references to scripture that became famous were preserved from master classes the following decade: "In the beginning was rhythm," and "The *Well-Tempered Clavier* is the Old Testament, the Beethoven Sonatas the New. We must believe in both."[37]

NEW YORK AND CHICKERING HALL

The new Chickering Hall in New York, though not yet "decorated," was at last ready for Bülow to inaugurate. The Chickering firm, which had been eclipsed by its formidable rival Steinway in the previous decade, hoped the hall and Bülow's tour would help it regain its former prestige as America's leading piano manufacturer (figure 14.2). The increasingly intense competition among piano makers, which led to the design of improved instruments, tours of eminent visiting artists, and construction of superior concert halls, was certainly advantageous to the public and to the general state of music.

The Chickering pianos on which Bülow performed were already receiving as much acclaim as the pianist. Critics complimented their brilliant and beautiful tone, their resonance, and, in the hands of Bülow, their capability of an amazing variety of timbres. Dwight thought the pianos "surpass[ed] anything we have ever heard anywhere in power, rich sonority, sweetness, [and] evenness of tone and action," and the *Music Trade Review* praised the instruments that served him "so faithfully, so obediently, and so lovingly."[38]

Surprisingly, Bülow seemed to enjoy his role as a representative of the Chickering firm. He earnestly declared his loyalty to Chickering in interviews and correspondence, possibly to convince the public, his friends, and perhaps himself that he had not sold out. After his first concert in Boston he had been overheard to say that the piano was "not only the finest in America, but the finest in the whole world. Who could help playing well on such an instrument?" In an interview, Bülow coined the phrase that would later be used as an advertising slogan: "On other pianos, I have to play as the piano permits; on the Chickering I play just as I wish." To his friends he

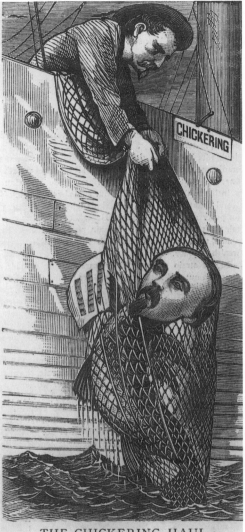

THE CHICKERING HAUL.

Figure 14.2. "The Chickering Haul." This cartoon depicts Frank Chickering netting a large fish with the head of Hans von Bülow. The caption punningly refers to the new Chickering Hall Bülow inaugurated in New York and the excellent publicity and business that Chickering was expected to receive as a result of Bülow's tour. (*The Arcadian* 4 [27 November 1875]: 1) (LIBRARY OF CONGRESS)

confided that Chickering pianos had made him into a "first-rate pianist," as he wrote his pianist friend Klindworth: "I notice the most extraordinary transformation in myself. Whereas, before, I frequently played like a pig, I now occasionally play like a god." To Eugen Spitzweg he claimed he had never played better, because he had "never [been] better supported by instruments." Even to Ullman, to whom he would most likely complain if he was dissatisfied with the instruments, he admitted: "I am more and more enamored of [Chickering's] pianos, which seem to me the best of both worlds."[39]

In New York, Bülow began on 15 November with a similar series of orchestral concerts, this time eight instead of seven, two of which were repetitions. Having fired Bergmann as his conductor, Bülow could fortunately turn to his old friend Leopold Damrosch, who had already sent a telegram to Bülow from New York congratulating him on his Boston debut.[40] The two musicians had met in Berlin in 1856, when Bülow was teaching piano at the Stern Conservatory. He and Damrosch, a violinist, had frequently performed chamber music together, and through the help of Bülow, Damrosch was invited by Liszt to become the concertmaster of the Weimar orchestra.

The orchestra for the New York concerts was considerably better than the Boston group in both size—forty-five members instead of thirty-five—and quality; the *World* thought the pickup ensemble was "surprisingly well disciplined" and one of its performances was "entirely free from the slovenliness and perfunctoriness so usual to extemporized bands." Although Damrosch was proficient and energetic, the *Herald* observed that at times there was still an "entire absence of promptitude to the conductor's baton," and Bülow was compelled to encourage the orchestra from the piano bench. Nevertheless, when the orchestra closed the first New York concert with the Overture to *Egmont,* Bülow "seated himself by the piano" on stage to listen to the orchestra and thereby show his support of Damrosch. The orchestra gradually improved for each concert, and Bülow related to Klindworth that the Tchaikovsky Concerto went "much better" in New York. "My old friend Damrosch has proven himself splendidly and conducted admirably," he wrote to his mother. "Here he has already done much good (these last four years) for musical civilization." Among other things, Damrosch had founded the Oratorio Society in 1873 at the suggestion of Rubinstein, who had visited him while in America.[41] Damrosch would also replace Bergmann the following year as conductor of the Philharmonic, but only for one disastrous season.

During Bülow's opening concerts, Chickering Hall, which had been built in just six months for the cost of $175,000, was greatly praised for its excellent acoustics. Situated uptown at the corner of Fifth Avenue and 18th Street, the fifteen-hundred-seat hall was designed without a proscenium for piano recitals and chamber music. It was slightly smaller than Steinway Hall, which was better suited for orchestral concerts. Bülow pronounced it an "extraordinarily splendid and, in the most dignified manner, all-around consecrated concert hall." A critic for *Orpheus* reinforced the sacralization theme while describing it: "Much will be gained if those who bring their gifts to sacrifice as it were on this altar, will bring those most worthy of acceptance—their best works, and not productions which have cost them, comparatively speaking, nothing."[42]

Bülow's first offering on the altar was the Beethoven Fourth Concerto, which the *World* believed had "never been interpreted in this city so intelligently, so reverently and so brilliantly." Its critic perceptively recognized that Bülow, with "less inspiration and lawless impulse" than Rubinstein, was a "musician of far more intellectual and aesthetic discipline." Perhaps to stave off too many comparisons, Bülow diplomatically assembled a new program in New York as a tribute to Rubinstein, his friend and not his rival, as Bülow put it, which added two new works to his American repertoire: Rubinstein's Third Piano Concerto and Liszt's *Fantasy on Themes from Beethoven's Ruins of Athens.* The concert included Rubinstein's Prelude and Fugue, Op. 53, No. 3, which the program indicated was dedicated to Bülow, as well as two other solo works by Rubinstein. Was it sarcasm, unfamiliarity, or fatigue, however, that

caused Bülow, in an extremely rare occurrence, to have memory slips and "many false notes" à la Rubinstein? Bülow won the most praise in the more progressive and brilliant works of Liszt and Henselt. The *Herald* could state "with all confidence that no such player of Liszt's piano compositions has appeared in America as this artist." The *Times* thought Bülow gave the Henselt Concerto the "finest piano performance listened to within the memory of the present generation."[43]

Bülow believed the New World invigorated his playing, and he consistently referred to his marvelous performances in his correspondence, where his ego is very much on display and where he rarely concedes anything but perfection in himself. After his first concert in New York he wrote his mother that it was "*tout simplement* the most *colossal* success in my career as a virtuoso. And, as my splendid manager says, the biggest triumph he has experienced in 20 years." New York audiences were indeed extremely demonstrative. After his first concert he "was summoned to the platform to acknowledge at least a dozen rounds of applause" *after* the encore.[44]

Bülow was usually recalled two or three times after each of his performances, and although he had a reputation for not dispensing encores, he now did so rather frequently and generously. If he did decline to deliver additional goods, he did so amicably. In most concerts, he would agree to repeat the piece or a portion of it that had caused such a stir. For his concert in New York on 26 November, he repeated almost the entire Weber *Polonaise brillante* arranged by Liszt, as he would later do in Philadelphia (21 December); it was a work in a more popular style with which Bülow "infused a good deal of the humor which he possesses in a large degree and knows well how and when to express," making the New York audience laugh as well as applaud. Sometimes Bülow offered a new piece as an encore, ranging from brief works by Chopin, Liszt, Schubert, and Schumann to sonata movements by Beethoven. The Scherzo from the Sonata, Op. 31, No. 3, was a favorite encore of his, which he performed with a touch of humor, and sometimes he gave the opening movement of the "Appassionata" or the "Pathétique." After being hailed tumultuously for a performance of the "Moonlight" Sonata in an early New York concert, he addressed the audience: "Ladies and gentlemen, the sonata quasi fantasia which you have just heard has a twin sister, No. 1 opus 27, and, if time allows, I will present her." And he did.[45]

CHAPTER 15

"Unfortunately ... He Also Talks"

Everything surrounding Bülow's tour was going smoothly. The public, the press, the management, and the pianist all seemed to be pleased. Then disaster struck. The morning after his New York debut, Bülow was interviewed by a reporter from the *New York Sun*. Still groggy from almost no sleep, Bülow was his forthright self with the total stranger. One of the reporter's first questions concerned the dismissal of Bergmann in Boston. No one had seemed especially troubled about it until Bülow now made known his reasons. He complained that Bergmann had not taken as much interest in the concerts as he had in drinking beer, he had missed two meetings to discuss the concerts which forced Bülow to make suggestions to the orchestra himself, and then, while Bülow was beginning his solo pieces in one of the concerts, Bergmann audibly invited the musicians to "go get some refreshments" and brought six of them back half tipsy.[1]

Even though it was not a matter of general knowledge, Bergmann had been in a period of decline after having built the New York Philharmonic into a fine orchestra. According to Howard Shanet, the modern chronicler of the Philharmonic, Bergmann "was now professionally so sloppy, spiritually so depressed, physically so decayed, and continually so drunk that only the great affection that his men bore him kept him in his post."[2] By the following spring, Bergmann would no longer be physically

able to conduct, and the Philharmonic would force him to resign. By August 1876 he would be dead.

Bergmann had emigrated like many musicians to the United States in 1849 as a result of the failed European revolutions of the previous year. He immediately became a leading musical figure in America. From 1850 to 1854 he was the conductor of the influential Germania Musical Society that toured throughout the East and Midwest. Since 1858 he had conducted the New York Philharmonic (sharing the duties with Theodore Eisfeld from 1859 to 1865). He was responsible for introducing many new works to the United States and was ironically—in light of Bülow's opinion of him—a leading advocate for the music of Liszt and Wagner. He had led the U.S. premieres of many orchestral works by Liszt, including five symphonic poems and the *Faust Symphony,* and in 1859 had conducted the American premiere of *Tannhäuser,* the first performance of a Wagner opera in the United States. Bülow was accurate about Bergmann's current ability and attitude; no one denied Bülow's public allegations, and they were much later confirmed in print by his manager.[3] Nevertheless, when he attacked the conductor's profound influence in the United States, he was insulting the entire country by condemning the man. "Bergmann is much over-estimated here," Bülow informed the *Sun* reporter, "and if I can do anything toward placing him where he belongs I shall be glad to do so."

Bülow was not satisfied with denouncing only Bergmann. He broadened his attack to include his fellow countrymen and their obsession with beer. He was amazed, for example, that reviews appeared in the newspapers the morning after his evening concerts. He thought such an occurrence was impossible in Germany, for "there our critics would be tired after the concert, and would go and eat and drink beer." He believed that beer drinking was "the great fault" with his countrymen. "They do not get drunk like the Irish people, but they drink until their blood becomes sluggish and their brains stupid."[4]

The interview created a scandal, or a "hulla*bülow*" according to *Harper's.* The *New-Yorker Musik-Zeitung* rose to Bergmann's defense in an article whose title called Bülow "A Great Artist and a Small Man." The Germans were obviously outraged, but other nationalities were suspicious. Yes, Bülow had praised American audiences—primarily at the expense of the English—but his comments were considered more flattery than truth. Above all, Americans could not understand how someone could be so unpatriotic to his country, for "no gentleman wantonly spreads his country's faults before another people." The day after the interview was published Bülow received numerous letters threatening his reputation and his life. A correspondent to a Cologne newspaper said it best: "Unfortunately, this man does not only play—he also talks."[5]

Bülow's stinging indictment of his fellow Germans was particularly damaging to his tour, because they were among the most avid supporters of musical events and

the ones most likely to attend his concerts so heavily devoted to German music. This was especially true in the Midwest, where one of his managers believed that "at least forty per cent of the music-loving community" were Germans and where the German musical societies boycotted his concerts, creating a significant financial loss. The German issue was to haunt Bülow during the entire tour. In mid-April 1876 he was still puzzled by the reaction to his statements: "I do not at all understand the entire noise—the fury of the people, that I have protested against a depraved beer lout as a conductor—or the incredible spreading and growing of this fury."[6]

In an apparent effort to support Chickering, Bülow also enjoyed taking a few jabs at Steinway in the *Sun* interview. That the Steinway family was German seemed to make them fair game. Just before his concerts in New York, Bülow had written to a friend: "The big three-week battle in New York approaches. Battle, I say—because there houses the lout Steinway, who moves whatever he can against me. . . . Well— I am not afraid—I am prepared and . . . I shall 'tame the lout,' and for the rest of his life he will think of my visit to America."[7] In the *Sun* interview Bülow claimed Rubinstein was glad to learn that he would use the Chickering, for Rubinstein thought "the Steinways were not gentlemen, and it would be unpleasant for [Bülow] to have to meet them." This slander created another uproar, for the Steinways were highly respected in the community and had apparently had a good relationship with Rubinstein.

While friends and family urged William Steinway to retaliate, he nobly resisted entering the fray. In a letter to the Steinways, Rubinstein denied having made such statements: "If perhaps I do not approve [of] everything in the Steinway pianos— the personalities I have always found of the very best kind, in every respect." He was skeptical that Bülow had made such a statement since he was a perfect gentleman. "That is the trouble in America," he wrote, "the newspapers accept and print all sorts of gossip. You should know that better than anyone else (since you have lived so long in America) and it need not surprise you." There was indeed some doubt whether the interview had been reported accurately, but Bülow never retracted any of the statements, and his public remarks about his compatriots were echoed in letters to his friends. To Karl Klindworth he had already complained from Boston: "If it were not for my beloved countrymen, who have gotten on my nerves in Paris, Petersburg, and London in turn, everything would be too heavenly." Nevertheless, Bülow at least temporarily seemed concerned about the furor he had caused. His fellow Liszt pupil William Mason confided to William Steinway that Bülow was "dreadfully excited and irritated" about the matter and promised "to say no more to newspaper reporters"[8]—a promise he would not keep.

Bülow's attack on the Germans was just one example of the frequent acerbic remarks for which he was famous. Although the public was ordinarily incensed by someone so excruciatingly honest in his opinions, they also apparently delighted in

reading the latest of his quips as long as they were aimed at someone else. Fully aware of the liability posed by his client's candor, Ullman had recommended to Bülow that he be sequestered during the entire tour and had shuddered thinking about "what tricks your tongue will play on us!" Bülow was either unwilling or unable to suppress his frankness and had warned Ullman: "I am too old to make a diplomat out of myself . . . and I shall never translate the 'You bore me' of my heart into the 'You are charming' of my lips."[9]

BÜLOW CONTRA RUBINSTEIN

Amid the turmoil created by his honest tongue, Bülow was being seduced by the physical comforts this country could provide a star performer. He described his life to his mother: "I am living it up here as I would not have thought I would ever be able to do again—housed and served like a prince . . . splendidly nourished and taken care of. . . . I have never, nowhere, for so long, felt so well, I could say, happy. . . . With horror I think back on the old rotten European world." He soon began to entertain thoughts of remaining in the New World. "Yes, truly, Europe is old and lame—there are only two young countries, Russia and America," he wrote to his mother a few weeks later from Baltimore. "If I were half as old as I am, it would draw me to the former; with my almost 46 years (excuse this lack of gallantry of a son), I belong *here,* as every hour these last eight weeks has shown me. . . . I am an entirely new man, a new artist. Every note I play, every word I say . . . ignites and succeeds."[10]

Perhaps Bülow exaggerated a bit to his mother, as any dutiful son might, but he was indeed receiving excellent notices. Everyone seemed to agree that, in the realm of technique, Bülow was undeniably the best pianist to visit the United States. Dwight thought his playing was "simply perfect. . . . He never fails; it seems impossible for him to fail." A Brooklyn critic believed that "he is as nearly faultless as it is given to mortals to attain." Accuracy, one of Bülow's hallmarks, was combined with a distinct execution of each note and passage; there was no blurring, muddling, or confusion. Herz and Thalberg had also been known for their almost flawless technique, but each of them performed his own works, carefully designed to emphasize what was natural for his own hands. Bülow, however, was grappling with the music of many different composers involving a wide variety of techniques—an infinitely more challenging task. The *Music Trade Review* even found such perfection maddening: "Oh! for a false note, such as Liszt played sometimes, and Rubinstein!"[11]

The comparisons with Rubinstein were inevitable and were frequently in Bülow's favor. Many Americans were now ready to admit that Rubinstein had in fact missed quite a few notes and had occasionally gotten lost. This was much easier to discern with the example of Bülow's unfailing technique and memory before them. William

Mason remembered Bülow once telling him, "Rubinstein can make any quantity of errors during his performance, and nobody is disturbed by it; but if I make a single mistake it will be noticed immediately by every one in the audience, and the effect will be spoiled." One key to Bülow's accuracy was his maintaining a supreme, intellectual command over his actions and never losing control, as one music journal remarked, due to passion, "mad 'inspiration,'" or "emotional insanity," as Rubinstein had done so frequently. It was Rubinstein's passion, of course, which had made his mistakes either unnoticeable or excusable. Bülow himself once said, "It is more interesting to me when Rubinstein plays incorrectly than when a thousand others play correctly."[12]

Bülow also surpassed Rubinstein on such issues as fidelity to the score and conscientious interpretation. His attention to detail was characterized by *Dwight's* New York correspondent as "absolutely—sometimes mercilessly—faithful to the composition." A Portland writer astutely observed that Bülow interpreted the composer's intention "with a faithfulness that [was] almost a religion."[13] Bülow viewed himself as an interpreter of the music, the medium through which it reached the audience. On this point he diverged most significantly from the earlier virtuosos visiting America, for whom the purpose of the music was principally to display the performer's technique. For Bülow the purpose of his technique was to offer the music as it had been composed. Even during a Rubinstein concert, the listener was always aware of the performer's presence. Many critics summed it up this way: Rubinstein interposed his own personality in the music, but with Bülow it seemed as if the composer himself—whether it was Bach, Beethoven, Chopin, or Liszt—was at the piano.

With all of Bülow's merits over Rubinstein (accuracy in execution, faultless memory, fidelity to the score), the Apollonian and noble Bülow was still often found wanting to the Dionysian and passionate Rubinstein. Bülow was frequently criticized for being too intellectual, analytical, and distant. Several years later, the *Music Trade Review*, in an extreme view, called him "a musical refrigerator." The New York correspondent to *Dwight's* pondered the end result of Bülow's interpretation: "Is his playing emotional? Are we *moved* by it? Do we shed tears? Is it ice and fire? Not in the least." Others, however, plainly disagreed. In Poughkeepsie he was judged to combine "deep emotion with high thought." A Buffalo critic did "not find, as has been charged, that he lacks warmth or sentiment, but he certainly avoids everything like an exaggeration of style, which, to some, makes his playing seem cold." William Foster Apthorp in the *Atlantic Monthly* examined this issue in some detail. He was surprised that Bülow's performances were not considered expressive, though he admitted the pianist was moderate in his use of expressive means. Yet, he never "fails to gain the *ends* of expression." The fault was in the ear of the beholder, for "some men cannot feel the presence of power unless it strikes them palpably between the

eyes and sends them reeling." Listeners might be "subdued" by performers whose goal was the "subjugation of their audience like so many artillery batteries." However, the "calling forth of violent emotions" was "not the highest province of art."

> There is a music which elevates the whole man at once, entices his whole being into a higher atmosphere; he enjoys calmly, with dignity, but intensely and largely; his pleasure is beautifully cosmic and well-ordered. Now to our mind, von Bülow has this power in a very marked degree; his power is so *powerful,* his effect upon us is so easily worked, that we only feel the result, without thinking of the force that works it.[14]

No one was more keenly aware of the differences between the two pianists than Bülow himself. In negotiations with Ullman, Bülow admitted that he did not have "the talent to grab, to stir up the masses" like Rubinstein, adding that he was "anything else but a '*Feuerwerker*' [fireworker]."[15] But once in America, he fancied that he was holding his own against his friendly rival. In mid-December he wrote his mother, again with a filial exaggeration, that "in Germany the Russian Jew was everywhere preferred before the German aristocrat, while here everywhere 'Hans' vanquishes 'Anton.'"[16]

Bülow certainly enjoyed being able to ply his mother with effusive reviews. At the end of his New York engagement, he enclosed one with these words: "Today I am writing to you only in order to mail to you one of the most marvelous criticisms ever printed about me. You *must* enjoy it if you read it carefully, as it deserves, without missing a word. Imagine the quality of a country in which journalists feel so sensitively, think so distinctly, and write with such virtuosity and originality."[17]

Shortly before Bülow's departure from New York, he and Theodore Thomas were honored at a reception given by the Lotos Club. Still in existence today, the club had been founded in 1870 by journalists who were drama, music, and art critics, and especially enjoyed hosting visiting celebrities. In response to a toast to his health, Bülow made a "neat little speech," which was summarized by the press and widely reprinted. Except for another slight dig at the Germans, who had found fault with him because he would "not worship the god Gambrinus with them to the detriment of the god Apollo," Bülow was highly flattering:

> He apologized on the ground that his fingers were his tools and not his tongue. Besides, he could not express himself without a key-board, and a "real American" key-board at that. He said he had been told that he played better in this country than he had played elsewhere, but this was easily explained by the fact that he was in sympathy with his audience and his audience was in sympathy with him. He was in danger of losing his head, he said, by reason of the treatment he was receiving, as he had already lost his heart to the American women.[18]

He did not know that this last statement would be a self-fulfilling prophecy.

BALTIMORE: A FORMER PUPIL AND ADVERTISING ANGST

From New York, Bülow went south for concerts in Baltimore, Washington, D.C., and Philadelphia. For his orchestral concerts in Baltimore he turned to the orchestra of the Peabody Institute. Not coincidentally, its conductor, Asger Hamerik of Denmark, had studied in 1862–64 at the Stern Conservatory in Berlin, where Bülow had "*un-taught* [him] piano playing to the advantage of his profession as a composer."[19] After studies in Paris with Berlioz—Hamerik claimed to have been Berlioz's only student— he was appointed the second director of Peabody's conservatory, a post he held from 1871 to 1898, when he returned to Denmark.

With Hamerik's able direction and its frequent rehearsals—four times a week for two hours—the Peabody Orchestra was quite possibly the best one that accompanied Bülow in the United States. Bülow's sponsorship by Chickering and Theodore Thomas's close association with Steinway made it virtually impossible for them to appear together. Bülow found his former pupil to be a "charming gentleman and an excellent musician (a very rare combination)." Hamerik was also praised by the poet and musician Sidney Lanier, the first chair flutist in the orchestra, who thought Hamerik was a "rare genius." Still, Lanier was amused by his "Frenchiest of French accents—tho' a Dane, he was educated in Paris." Two days before accompanying Bülow the orchestra presented its first of eight subscription concerts of the season and gave, according to Bülow, an excellent performance of his *Des Sängers Fluch* (The Minstrel's Curse), a symphonic poem in the Liszt tradition. (On 13 November the New York Philharmonic had already performed Bülow's *Julius Caesar* Overture, written in 1852 for a production of the play at the Weimar Court Theater.) The following week, at rehearsals of Beethoven's "Emperor" Concerto, the Weber *Konzert-stück,* Mendelssohn's *Capriccio brillant,* and the Henselt Concerto, Bülow could not resist interrupting Hamerik despite his admirable leadership. One observer described Bülow as "captious and fault-finding, demanding often several repetitions of a passage, yet always patient, cheerful and inspiring." The orchestra members were apparently not offended for they gave him a standing ovation.[20]

Bülow's musical success with the orchestra was offset by another eruption of his volatile artistic temperament that threatened his amiable relationship with Chickering. On the morning of his first Baltimore concert (6 December)—the very day he wrote to a friend that "compared with my playing on the ideal Chickerings in America, in Europe I have only tinkled like a suckling pig"—he committed an act of near treason to the Chickering firm. Upon arriving at the rehearsal, he warmly embraced Hamerik, but his genial disposition did not last long.

> He walked to the piano, on which hung a sign whereon was inscribed the word "Chickering." "I am not," he said with a look of scorn, "a travelling advertisement," and jerking off the sign laid the large gilt letters face downward on the stage, and cast

at it a glance of hatred as though it were a loathsome reptile. Calling out to an acquaintance in the auditorium, he said in good idiomatic English: "Mr.————, that
jackass has sent a sign-board down with the piano." He then lapsed into German, in
which the words "Lump" and "Schweinhund" were audible. After he began the rehearsal, in one of the orchestral interludes, he got up and tipped softly around, picked
up the hated sign and carried and stuck it under the tail end of the grand piano; and
then in another interval walked around there and kicked it. Thus was he appeased
with blood.[21]

This Baltimore incident sparked a renewed debate on the role of pianists as advertising agents and whether piano firms were helping or hindering themselves and
the public by sponsoring concert artists. Since most people assumed that a pianist
or his manager received a financial consideration, the public could hardly be convinced that one maker's pianos were better merely because a certain pianist used
them in a concert. More seriously, a contract with a piano firm could limit an artist's
performing opportunities. Bülow, for example, never appeared with a really fine orchestra in the United States. Unlike Rubinstein he could not join forces with
Theodore Thomas because Thomas was clearly aligned with Steinway and Bülow
had sold his soul to Chickering.

In addition, the large signs hanging from the instruments and touting the wares
of piano manufacturers detracted from the artistic purpose of the concert. The London *Concordia* held that the "name-board," however, was "but the symbol of a
tyranny" that "must be overthrown." It challenged artists that if they truly desired
"emancipation," they "must resolve not to sell their freedom." The *New-York Times*
urged the manufacturers to "abandon this pernicious and growing habit of subordi-
nating art to trade" and remove the signboard so the audience could honor an artist
"instead of a clever advertising automaton." It speculated what the next logical steps
would entail. Why not hang a sign on the pianist himself, saying "Pianists in this
style furnished only by the celebrated manufactory of Smith & Co." Then, signs
could be hung on members of the audience, saying "He listens only to Smith & Co.'s
pianos."[22]

While most writers thought the piano manufacturers were using the artists,
Theodore Steinway gives the perspective of the manufacturer. He once wrote to
William, "the damned artists consider pianomakers a cow to be milked. I wish I
could invent a piano that makes you stupid and seasick—I would donate one to
each of them."[23]

Bülow obviously had difficulty in serving the two masters of commerce and art.
He would make other public displays of his disdain for the promotional angle of his
concerts, though they—like his scuffle with the Chickering sign—probably provided more publicity than the sign alone would have. The *Arcadian* reported a few

weeks later that Bülow had "not exhibited any strongly marked signs of insanity" with the exception of using his jackknife to scrape the Chickering name off the pianos. During his New Year's Eve concert in New York, he performed on a piano that had escaped his handiwork. After his first piece, he reached in his pocket for his knife, but not finding it he walked off, and two men entered and changed the piano to a "nameless one," after which Bülow completed the concert. Bülow also probably had some hand in the "conspicuous absence" of the "usual unsightly sign hung on the piano" at a Buffalo concert. At least one critic was pleased: "What does the audience care whether Chickway or Steinring made the inanimate thing?"[24]

WASHINGTON: DIPLOMACY AND ROMANCE

Washington, D.C., could not muster an orchestra, but it boasted glittering audiences with an international representation. One might expect such audiences to be more civilized, if not more musically literate, but Bülow was forced to "publicly rebuke the noisy audience." According to one reviewer, young European diplomats were the worst offenders in the "notoriously unmannerly audiences of Washington," for coming from Europe they knew "little or nothing of the amenities and decencies of civilization."[25]

While in Washington, Bülow renewed acquaintances with Kurd von Schlözer, the head of the German embassy. One of Schlözer's previous assignments had been Rome, where he was a close friend of Liszt during the time the pianist took minor orders in the Catholic Church. Bülow described the ambassador as an "exceptionally splendid fellow," who "has done more for me than *any other person*—he has presented to me three of the noblest, most beautiful women." Bülow was especially "thunderstruck" by one of the women he met on 9 December: Romaine von Overbeck.[26] Bülow was at once profoundly and miserably in love. The day after meeting Romaine, he wrote her the first of at least two dozen, mostly pathetic letters over the next five months begging her to return his affection. She had instantly become his *idée fixe*.

His pursuit of Romaine proved to be difficult, for she came from a prominent Washington family, was married to an Austrian baron, and had two young sons. Her grandfather, Samuel F. Vinton, had long served as a congressman from Ohio, and her mother, Madeleine Vinton, had functioned as his official hostess and quickly won recognition as a celebrated socialite and expert in the etiquette peculiar to the nation's capital. Romaine's father, Daniel Goddard, died when she was young, and her mother married Rear Admiral John A. Dahlgren, a Civil War naval hero, in 1865. Romaine's wedding in 1870 to Gustav von Overbeck was attended by President and Mrs. Grant, members of the Cabinet and Congress, and the chief justice of the United States. Overbeck was involved in business ventures in the far east and occasionally participated in diplomatic missions. During Bülow's tour, he stopped off

in Washington on his way from Borneo and Hong Kong to Vienna. His resulting absence gave Bülow a sense of false hope.[27]

That the Baroness was a pianist was a significant factor in their relationship. Schlözer exalted her "talent for music to the stars" and believed she "should have become an artist."[28] Her musical leanings certainly intrigued Bülow and gave them some common ground, although he never heard her play. Her interests as a musician most likely caused her to pursue, however timidly, any kind of relationship with Bülow. In a romantic liaison, Romaine had much to forfeit, including a charming family and an important social position in the nation's capital. Bülow, on the other hand, had nothing more to lose.

Managers do not consider infatuation an admissible reason to cancel performances, and so Bülow was forced to move on to Philadelphia, lovesick or not. His first appearances there were also the last of his concerts with an orchestra. For a conductor, Bülow turned once again to Lang from Boston. Another pickup orchestra was assembled, which played accurately and expressively under Lang's meticulous direction. What he lacked in magnetism, Lang compensated for through his careful study and preparation of the orchestra. For a rehearsal of the Beethoven Fourth Piano Concerto, Lang had the orchestra meet an hour before the time scheduled for Bülow to appear. Upon arriving, Bülow listened quietly in the rear of the hall to the rehearsal already in progress. When the orchestra reached the fermata before the soloist's cadenza, Lang cut them off abruptly only to hear Bülow "shriek out behind him in his sharpest and most acrid voice: 'The wooden wind may go to h-ll [sic]!'" Bülow then rushed out of the hall and did not return until the evening performance.[29]

Bülow's faith in Lang's abilities was validated by excellent performances. Liszt's *Hungarian Fantasy,* a dependable crowd pleaser, was a highlight for Philadelphia audiences. Bülow played the finale with "such thorough *abandon* that it set the house wild, and had to be repeated, even after several of the orchestra had started to leave the stage." Bülow continued to share the credit publicly with Lang. After a performance of Beethoven's "Emperor" Concerto, Bülow grabbed both of Lang's hands and "led him impulsively to the footlights to share blushingly the honors of the occasion."[30]

BEHIND PARLOR DOORS: WOMEN AND THE PIANO

With Romaine on his mind, Bülow wrote to his mother from Philadelphia, glorifying American women, basking in their attention, and announcing his new romance. "The ladies of America replace today, with 50 percent profit, the French women of 100 years ago. . . . What I have hitherto seen of beautiful women is, compared with these gorgeous samples, stable wench or grisette. Should I continue to tell you that female admirers from New York and Boston have come to my concerts here?" He would

Bülow in Love

Excerpts from Bülow's letters to the Baroness Romaine von Overbeck

"If I don't see you again in two weeks in New York—I'll kill myself." (10 December 1875)

"Isn't it true, I was sublime last night? But if you only knew what effort this has cost me! The famous finale of the big Sonata by Beethoven, Op. 106, is child's play compared to the difficulty of finding oneself near you and not falling at your feet and crying and weeping, 'I adore you.'" (29 December 1875)

"I adore you so much that I turn not only crazy, but what is worse, dumb like a goose." (7 January 1876)

"I imagine that as a child you amused yourself by tormenting flies and butterflies, considering that you excel with virtuosity in making me suffer, me who loves you, me who adores you so— superlatively!" (12 January 1876)

"Ah—it is my fate—always to be betrayed by the people whom I love with the purest and most profound love! Oh, well—to be betrayed, even though it is perhaps very ridiculous—is nevertheless more dignified, more noble than betraying, tricking! Only I often ask myself—those who betray me, do they not have what is called a 'conscience'? . . . My word—everything I write here is absurd, foolish, feverish—but I am suffering so horribly that you forget me, abandon me, betray me! . . . And now I have to go to edify, amuse, bore this pile of imbeciles that calls itself public! Cursed slavery!" (14 February 1876)

"I must look for a woman to whom I could return a little of all the ill that you have done to me—and that you will continue to do to me through your cruelty, your indifference, your spitefulness that is all the more cruel as you know all too well that I adore you as no other person . . . has adored you—how I belong to you exclusively with all my soul, how I care not at all any more about my existence if I have to live without you!" (29 February 1876)[1]

1. Letters no. 195, Washington, D.C., 10 December 1875; no. 198, New York, 29 December 1875; no. 202, New York, 7 January 1876; no. 205, Boston, 12 January 1876; no. 216, St. Louis, 14 February 1876; no. 221, Indianapolis, 29 February 1876.

later grumble to Romaine that "so many women (alas!) come to see me after the last piece." These statements, meant to cheer a worrying mother and arouse jealousy in a potential lover, affirm that women constituted a significant portion of Bülow's audiences, and his frequent matinée performances (more than one-fifth of his appearances) catered mostly to them, as had those of Thalberg and Rubinstein. For a New York matinée in late November, the *Herald* could report that the large audience was "principally composed of ladies."[31]

The essential relationship between women and the piano had changed little between De Meyer's tour and the arrival of Bülow, although it had intensified. Pianos were readily available for the rising number of middle-class families who often sent their daughters to female seminaries, now in abundance in the 1870s, to be trained in the accomplishments. For Bülow's appearance in Steubenville, Ohio, with only two hundred people in the audience, there were "about fifty seminary girls blocked off in one corner, and if they hadn't the appearance of musical *virtuosos,* they were at least lively, impatient and full of brilliant anticipations."[32]

The repertoire, however, had shifted considerably in the past thirty years. Instead of struggling through fantasias by Herz or Thalberg, young women pianists were now more likely to try their hand at Beethoven and Chopin, works that could be less demanding technically but more challenging musically. After attending a Bülow matinée featuring the music of Chopin, an event that would always attract an "assemblage of beauty—fresh, tender, lisping beauty, between fourteen and twenty, that dreamy time of life when existence itself is a nocturne," A. C. Wheeler, the witty and perceptive critic for the *New York World,* mused at some length on the role of the piano in women's lives. Writing under his pen name Nym Crinkle, Wheeler at first seems to be writing a parody, but he develops his ideas thoroughly and systematically. In general, he believed the piano had become the "extrinsic nervous system which art has furnished to our generation for the manifestation and expression of those complex emotions and desires, and that feverish cardiac condition of our life which good taste no longer permits us to put into words or actions." This was even truer for a woman of means and high morals, who had neither the outlets of domestic chores or gossip:

> [The piano] may be looked upon as furniture by dull observers or accepted as a fashion by shallow thinkers, but it is in reality the artificial nervous system, ingeniously made of steel and silver, which civilization in its poetic justice provides for our young women. Here it is, in this parlor with closed doors, that the daughter of our day comes stealthily and pours out the torrent of her emotions through her finger-ends, directs the forces of her youth and romanticism into the obedient metal and lets it say in its own mystic way what she dare not confess or hope in articulate language. Do you not see that it is the compensation of mechanics; the conservation of a force that

we no longer permit to expend itself in conversation, in intrigue, or in the physical channels that the kitchen and the wash-tub provide? . . .

[Man] recognizes the fact that a woman must put her woman impulses into action. So, not wishing her to become a lecturer or a telegraph-operator or to play *Lady Macbeth,* he gives her the piano.

Ah, what wisdom do we discover in this. It is as if he said: My dear, if you do not change the current of your sentimentality from your brain to your muscles you will suffer with neuralgia and remorse and begin to eat hydrate of chloral before you are twenty-five. Your nerves are overtaxed; let me provide you with a patent plexus, a ganglionic grand. Save yourself and let this machine do your feeling and breathing and longing! . . .

Presently it becomes her companion, her confidant, her lover. It tells her what no one else dare utter. It responds to her passion, her playfulness, her vagaries, as nothing else can.

. . . Who would dare to talk to her as Chopin talks? Not a blush either. Ah, how well they understand each other! He reaches out his arm from the past, it encircles her, he drops his languid kisses on her cheek, he breathes his feverish aspirations into her ear.[33]

Wheeler's ideas reflected typical male attitudes of the time, accepting the highly circumscribed domain of women and viewing them as primarily emotional beings while men were more intellectual. One Chicago writer, who had yet to hear Bülow, adhered to this view, though he disagreed with Wheeler concerning Bülow's relevance to female audiences: "He does not belong to the tender-eyed melancholy, sentimental class of musicians who play to feminine hearts. He plays to men's heads. His music is the music of brains." Both writers echoed opinions held by the British clergyman and writer H. R. Haweis in his recent *Music and Morals* (1871; American ed., 1872). In a section titled "People Who Play the Piano," Haweis explained:

As a woman's life is often a life of feeling rather than of action, and if society, while it limits her sphere of action, frequently calls upon her to repress her feelings, we should not deny her the high, the recreative, the healthy outlet for emotion which music supplies. . . . A good play on the piano has not unfrequently taken the place of a good cry up stairs, and a cloud of ill temper has often been dispersed by a timely practice.[34]

Wheeler posited that the function of Bülow and other male professional pianists in women's lives was to explain in greater detail the language of Chopin and the female pianist's other "confidants." She needed to "know how he talks to other people." She looked toward the professional to "explain the occult phraseology," to reveal secrets that "lie hid in the music" and would "not divulge themselves at her

coaxing." Bülow accepted this role as he addressed his mostly female audience at the Chopin matinée: "My dears, . . . let me beg of you to disregard the piano and the player. . . . What we desire to do is to get at the heart of Chopin. If you come here to observe how it is done, you are wasting precious time. If you would ascertain what there is in it when it is done, all right!" Wheeler believed that the women pianists who had heard Bülow's masterly interpretations would "sit higher and firmer on their piano-stools."

CHAMBER MUSIC

Returning to New York on Christmas Eve, Bülow enjoyed for several days "the most beautiful of all illusions." Romaine's husband was conveniently out of the country, and she made the first of at least two trips to visit Bülow. On Christmas Day he desperately wrote Schlözer: "I am—completely deranged—all because of your devilish heavenly mediation! . . . I am resolved to commit any so-called crime in order to change the letter O[verbeck] into B[ülow]. . . . I implore you—give me an ingenious counsel—show me the least criminal way." Bülow even tried to enlist his mother in the conspiracy, hoping that she would intercede with a friend "so that the Imperial German government will prohibit the husband's return to Washington."[35]

All of Bülow's scheming to steal another man's wife after losing his own would be to no avail. He wanted love, but Romaine wanted only friendship. Although Romaine's letters to Bülow do not survive, his comments make it clear that she rarely said anything to imply she was romantically interested in him. While he poured out his heart to her, she continued to call him *monsieur.* Bülow admitted that her trip to visit him in New York was "quite innocent," but he interpreted it as a sign of hope. He consistently misconstrued her politeness as affection. Her casual admonition to "take care of himself," for example, deeply touched him.[36]

Remarkably, Bülow found time to daydream about his new love, take her to the theater (*Julius Caesar,* his favorite tragedy, in an epic production at Booth's), and continue to present new repertoire to the public. Just two days after Christmas he began a demanding series of eight concerts of chamber music (he had already given four such concerts in New York before traveling south). Chamber music required considerable rehearsal time with various local musicians, who in New York were probably recruited through the help of Leopold Damrosch. Knowing Bülow's demanding musicianship and quick temper, the *New York Herald* hoped that the musicians joining him in the concerts had life insurance.[37] Damrosch on violin was the best known of the performers, but they were all capable musicians: Edward Mollenhauer on violin (whose brother had toured with Thalberg), George Matzka on viola (who would soon fill in for Bergmann as conductor of the New York Philharmonic), and Frederick Bergner on cello, along with assorted wind players. The

repertoire ranged from violin and piano duos with Damrosch (including Beethoven's "Kreutzer" Sonata and Schubert's Rondo for Violin and Piano) to trios, quartets, and quintets by Beethoven (including the "Archduke" Trio), Mozart, Raff, Rheinberger, Rubinstein, Schumann, and Spohr, and to miscellaneous works by Chopin, Hummel, Rubinstein, and Saint-Saëns.

Chamber music, then as now, was much less popular than orchestral concerts and more favored by performers than listeners. For the chamber series immediately following the orchestral concerts there was a noticeable drop in attendance, a typical response by New York audiences according to one writer:

> A perusal of the New York papers tends to give one a high idea of the musical culture of the New York public—and you look upon every third person as a *connoisseur*. The large attendance at Mr. Thomas' concerts is adduced as evidence. But the solemn fact is, the Symphony concerts are fashionable—that is, in the sense that one sheep follows another over a wall; but when it comes to a concert of chamber music, modestly announced on its own merits, without extraneous influence, this vast army of *connoisseurs* have deserted in a body.[38]

In each concert, Bülow wisely included a significant amount of solo piano music in addition to two chamber works to attract those less interested in the chamber items, making some of the concerts quite substantial in length.

Like Rubinstein's experiences with chamber music, the performances by Bülow were blemished only by the lesser ability of his colleagues. The effectiveness of the performers was a matter of disagreement. The *Herald* thought Bülow was unequally yoked with timid players and no matter how hard he tried to recede he dominated the performances, making the works seem like a "piano solo with a skeleton accompaniment." The *Times* was more generous: it thought the "Archduke" Trio was "particularly well interpreted" and believed the Schumann quintet "went charmingly, the pianist directing or rather inspiring the other players."[39]

The fewer assisting musicians there were, the fewer distractions from Bülow's playing. Consequently, Bülow's duos with Leopold Damrosch were the most successful. Damrosch had proved to be a valuable colleague. Besides conducting the orchestral concerts in New York, he had quickly defended Bülow after his interview with the *Sun*. In a letter to the editor, he urged readers "to strike the whole report of [the] interview" from their memory and accept Bülow's statement that he was only half awake when interviewed, which should acquit him of any malice. As a violinist, Damrosch ably performed with Bülow the "Kreutzer" Sonata, a work they had played together in Europe, in a spirited and precise execution, but it apparently did not compare with that of Rubinstein and Wieniawski a few years before. Damrosch's son Walter, who would succeed his father as a prominent conductor in New York,

recalled a backstage conversation before a performance of the "Kreutzer." As the two musicians were about to go on stage, Bülow turned to Damrosch and said:

"Let us play it by heart."
"With pleasure," answered my father and laid down his music.
"No, no," said Bülow, "take it on the stage with you."
After they had taken their places on the stage Bülow ostentatiously rose, took my father's music from the stand and his own from the piano and laid them both under the piano.

According to the younger Damrosch, Bülow briefly lost his place in the last movement, and his father had to improvise until Bülow recovered.[40]

The most unusual and extravagant concert in this chamber series occurred on 27 December (with a repetition on 30 December) and featured three keyboard concertos of J. S. Bach, one each for two, three, and four keyboards, accompanied by an ensemble of ten strings. Also on the program were Bach's *Italian Concerto* and works by Handel, Haydn, Mozart, and Beethoven. The *New York Herald* called it a "strong test of the appreciation and endurance of our concert audience," not to mention the energy it would cost the performer. For the other pianists, Bülow enlisted Richard Hoffman, an English-born pianist who had emigrated to America in the mid-1840s, and two women performers: Miss Marion Brown, a former American pupil of Bülow in Florence in 1871, and Mrs. Charles B. Foote, a pupil of Hoffman. Bülow's less than complete satisfaction with the performance was made clear to the audience by his "sundry gestures" and a "hiss when anything disturb[ed] him." The *Herald* chastised his behavior and suggested that in such a situation "cordiality and encouragement should characterize his efforts in public."[41]

In fact, Bülow scolded several performers during this series of chamber concerts. His first target had been Emma Thursby, who already had an established career as a church soloist and had sung the previous season under Damrosch with the Handel and Haydn Society of Brooklyn. On a program that included works by Bach, Handel, Mozart, and Beethoven (29 November), Thursby offered as an encore a song by Franz Abt. Abt's music was extremely popular in America, particularly with German singing societies, and the composer had led a festival of those organizations in St. Louis in 1872. Bülow detested the sentimentality of Abt's music and, in another denunciation of his countrymen, he claimed that "for this rabble Franz Abt represents German music!!" Bülow was enraged that Thursby apparently proffered the song as an example of refined German music. When Bülow followed her performance, he ostentatiously wiped the cloying harmonies off the piano with his handkerchief. After the concert he confronted the singer: "Never more, I screamed at her—next time one by the Abt Franz" [i.e., Liszt].[42] The title of the Abt song? "Embarrassment."

On another occasion (5 January), Bülow followed an inept soprano, Rosa McGeachy, whom the *Music Trade Review* dubbed McScreachy in its account of the concert. Bülow "approached the piano with a somewhat Mephistophelian expression on his classical countenance" and sarcastically began his selection with the recitative from Beethoven's Ninth Symphony that sets the text, "Friends, not these tones." Although some members of the audience did not understand the cryptic rebuke, Bülow's musical gibe was met with a "burst of applause," "forcing him to rise again from his chair and perform that extremely military-looking bow of his."[43]

On the day of the last concert in the series (8 January), Bülow celebrated his forty-sixth birthday and was serenaded that morning by the Arion Society led by Damrosch. It was this German singing society's invitation to Damrosch to be their conductor that had prompted his emigration to America in 1871. New Year's Day and his birthday a week later was a time for Bülow to evaluate. He wrote to his mother on the first of January:

Last night was my 49th concert in America—I feel, thank God, much better than after the first one—and I have—*entre nous*—played like a god. In Germany one says, "The people do not sense the devil, even when grabbed at the collar." Here it is different—here I am recognized, and I hold all of them by the collar. Never would I have dreamed so loudly and so deeply of similar successes, and that I would deserve them so much.

He voiced comparable self-satisfaction in a letter to Louise von Welz: "I have never in my life been so happy, so blissful as at the border between these two years, and my New Year's Eve concert was my greatest triumph thus far. Too bad that you have not heard me—*in my American style*—my European style was, by comparison—to say respectfully—a . . .(think of 65 Tristan rehearsals) [*sic*]." Life did indeed seem to be going well for Bülow except for the continued reticence of the Baroness. He nevertheless wrote her on his birthday, "In the silence of the night, I am celebrating my birth by celebrating my rebirth, which dates from the moment I had the unfortunate good luck, the lucky misfortune . . . to meet you for the first time."[44]

The next week Bülow was in Boston again with a series of six chamber concerts, a concert each day from Monday through Saturday (10–15 January). Dwight was not happy about the scheduling, for it was difficult for anyone to make all the concerts spaced that closely together; even the "most *fanatico* of musical Athenians cannot be listening to music *all* the time," he lamented. Bülow enjoyed a more congenial partnership with the Philharmonic Club, whose members included Bernhard Listemann (the first concertmaster of the Boston Symphony Orchestra when it was founded in 1881) and his brother Fritz on violin, Emil Gramm on viola, and Adolph Hartdegen on cello. The players were probably more comfortable with the literature and their colleagues since they frequently played together, and Bülow "expressed

himself quite warmly" concerning the "conscientious and artistic co-operation" of the quartet. Dwight thought the Schumann quintet was "played admirably" and remarked on Bülow's role as an ensemble player: "It was a pleasure here, as it is always where Von Bülow takes part in a concerted piece, to see how little he seeks to interpose himself between the other artists and the audience; he is one factor in the complete whole, one tone in the chord, one voice in the polyphonic movement."[45]

Boston was not afforded the Bach concerto extravaganza, but through Bülow's connection with Tchaikovsky, the Philharmonic Club gave the American premiere of that composer's first string quartet. Although the conservative Dwight preferred the more classical Saint-Saëns's piano quintet on the same program, he thought the Tchaikovsky work was "in some respects original, decidedly unconventional, bold, wild, wayward even" with "delicate beauty in the Andante." Bülow's ability to appreciate and promote the music of other composers, such as Tchaikovsky and later Brahms, helped free him from his unhealthy relationship with Wagner and his music and brought about, as Bülow put it, his "redemption from the ultra-Wagnerian school."[46]

BÜLOW AS INTERPRETER

Bülow's first series of concerts in the major eastern cities was now completed. Some of the country's most influential critics had heard him and had made their most extensive evaluations of his playing. They unanimously praised his perfect technique, but they sometimes disagreed on the appropriateness of his interpretations, a more complicated and subjective issue.

Most critics agreed that Bülow's true métier was the music of Liszt, which may seem odd for someone often viewed as an intellectual and somewhat cold performer. Yet Bülow's perfect execution was a prerequisite for a Liszt piece to make an impact. Perhaps Rubinstein could muddle through a Beethoven sonata and still be profound, but in Liszt the notes have to be crisp, clean, and brilliant, a demand Bülow had no problem meeting. In addition, Bülow's close relationship with Liszt helped him enter into the music with greater zeal. The *Philadelphia Inquirer* observed the "fervor with which he always attacks a composition by his great master," and the *New-York Times,* reviewing a performance of the Liszt First Concerto, thought the work was in perfect accord with Bülow's "tendencies and methods" and believed that the pianist rendered it *"con amore."*[47]

Bülow as a Chopin interpreter was a much more controversial topic. The critics for the *New-York Times* and *New York Herald* consistently stated Bülow simply could not play Chopin, although they frequently praised specific elements in his performances. He lacked the soul that Chopin required and which Rubinstein had had in such abundance. The *Times* judged Bülow's performances "wanting in the dreaminess [and] the lingering sweetness" essential to Chopin's works, and the *Herald* maintained

Figure 15.1. "Echoes from Chickering Hall." Sheet music cover of a series of "Classical Pianoforte Compositions" (including works by Bach, Handel, Scarlatti, Haydn, Beethoven, and Schubert) as "interpreted and played by Dr. Hans von Bülow" with an illustration of the new Chickering Hall in New York. (MUSIC DIVISION, THE NEW YORK PUBLIC LIBRARY, ASTOR, LENOX AND TILDEN FOUNDATIONS)

that his rendition of a nocturne was "destitute of the spark of poetry." However, in most other cities, including Baltimore, Boston, and Philadelphia, Bülow was rated high for his Chopin playing, and the other critics could not understand how he could be faulted. A Baltimore writer, for example, was "surprised at the hostile criticisms of some of the New York press at his playing of Chopin. To our fancy he excels all others in this music. . . . Rubinstein played Chopin grandly; but Chopin is ethereal, capricious, morbid, not grand." In Philadelphia, one writer thought that "Chopin's music is that which gains most at his hands." Bülow was often a victim of the attitude that a single performer could not do equal justice to every composer, and he was said to be "bitter because the world refused him recognition as a 'Chopin' player."[48]

Bülow was undoubtedly the best interpreter of Bach's music that America had heard. He did not play that many different pieces, but he programmed them frequently and certainly more often than the public wanted. Even the critic for the *New-York Times* thought that "the player who renders fugues in public does still more ungrateful work than the scholar who ingeniously contrives them." Still, Bülow's performances of Bach were uniformly praised. "We have never heard anybody play a fugue more clearly and distinctly, nor can we fancy that it can be done" extolled the *Music Trade Review.* Dwight acknowledged that "never have we heard

theme and answer, and the whole interweaving of parts in a fugue so clearly individualized and made so easy for the untutored ear to follow."[49]

Despite his connections with Liszt and Wagner, Bülow was best known as a Beethoven specialist. Many American critics recognized Bülow's gift for interpreting Beethoven, and he had more authority than most as a direct student descendant of Beethoven through Czerny and Liszt. Although the *New-York Times* repeatedly considered Bülow's Beethoven interpretations to be "rather intellectual than emotional," it still had to admit that "nothing can be clearer than his exposition of the musician's thoughts, nothing more refined and beautiful in tone than his execution, nothing, in brief, more scholarly than the style characteristic of all his work." The *Philadelphia Inquirer*, however, thought the last movement of the "Appassionata" had never been heard played with "so much intensity" and "such a grand, flaming, resistless sweep of passion."[50]

The Beethoven work Bülow most offered and the one most often dissected was the "Moonlight" Sonata. Following the Czerny-Liszt tradition, Bülow played the first movement quite slowly and gently glided without pause into the Allegretto, what Bülow called an "anti-scherzo," which he took at a rather slow pace as well. He then immediately attacked the finale, playing it with great fire. Like many listeners, the *New York Herald* critic thought the rendition was "both a delight and a surprise." The *Music Trade Review* declared that the work had been "simply murdered" with the exaggerated tempos, either too slow or too fast, in all the movements. Dwight, however, thought it was a "perfect revelation" and believed he had "never heard a more exquisite or more truthful interpretation of the whole Sonata."[51]

Bülow's interpretations can be partially examined through his many editions of masterworks (figure 15.1). His edition of the Beethoven sonatas, for example, complete with fingerings and extensive notes, was highly regarded. Modern performers still consult it, although they are unlikely to agree with all of its suggestions. Editing earlier music was considerably different at the time, when editors took liberties with the text and were generous in supplying interpretive ideas.[52] Bülow later admitted that his edition of Handel's works, for example, had "too many nuances" because he was attempting to "battle" against the "lifeless hammering" then in vogue.[53]

CHAPTER 16

The Midwest and Back

Immediately after his series of chamber recitals in Boston, Bülow began his first of two forays into the Midwest, where the rigors of traveling were balanced by less severe repertoire demands. Bülow could rely on a couple of standard programs since most cities were only treated to one or two recitals (figure 16.1). Bülow typically made small changes in the programs, however, seeking variety probably for the sake of his own sanity. Only four cities on the tour received more than two concerts: New Orleans (eight), Chicago (four), Cincinnati (three), and St. Louis (three).

Outside the major eastern cities Bülow's appearances were essentially solo recitals. A single vocalist ostensibly gave him a brief respite in each half of the concert, even though he usually played her accompaniments. Rubinstein, of course, had traveled with an entire troupe who shared the burden of performing each night. At first Bülow had refused to consider appearing with another artist. He was "absolutely not manageable as an instrumental partner of a *diva*," he stated flatly to Ullman. If teamed up with, say, Christine Nilsson, he would "cut a sad figure"; "a program combined between a great female singer and me would become a monstrous absurdity." Just a few months before his tour began, however, the idea of associating with a vocalist, perhaps Therese Tietjens, who was making her American debut the same season as Bülow, sounded more appealing. "The less I shall be forced to give recitals

PROGRAMME.

A.

SATURDAY, January 22d.

PART I.

1.—J. S. BACH, (1685–1750).
    (*a*) Fantaisie chromatique et Fugue.
    (*b*) Gavotte in D Minor.

2.—L. V. BEETHOVEN (1770–1827).
    Sonata. Opus 31, No. 3, in E Flat.
        Allegro—Scherzo—Minuetto —Presto.

3.—SPOHR.
    (*a*) Romanza "La Rosa."

4.—BEETHOVEN.
    (*b*) La vita felice. Opus 88.
        Miss LIZZIE CRONYN.

PART II.

5.—F. MENDELSSOHN (1809–1847).
    (*a*) Prelude and Fugue. Opus 35, No. 1.
    (*b*) Three Songs without Words.

6.—F. CHOPIN (1810–1849).
    (*a*) Nocturne. Opus 27, No. 2, in D Flat.
    (*b*) Polish Song. (Arranged by LISZT.)
    (*c*) Berceuse. Opus 57.
    (*d*) Valse brillante. Opus 42.

7.—GOMEZ.
    (*a*) Canzonetta "Mia Piccirella." From Salvator Rosa.

8.—RUBINSTEIN.
    (*b*) Thou'rt like unto a Flower.
        Miss LIZZIE CRONYN.

9.—F. LISZT (1811–   ).
    VENEZIA e NAPOLI. Gondoliera e Tarantella.

The CHICKERING GRAND PIANOS used at all the VON BÜLOW Concerts.

Figure 16.1. These two programs of Hans von Bülow's appearances at St. James Hall, Buffalo, 22 and 25 January 1876, are typical in their scholarly apparatus (composers' dates, opus numbers), historical repertoire, and, with only two exceptions, chronological arrangement. (BUFFALO AND ERIE COUNTY PUBLIC LIBRARY, BUFFALO, NEW YORK)

PROGRAMME.

B.

TUESDAY, January 25th.

PART I.

1.—L. v. BEETHOVEN, (1770–1827.)
   Sonata, quasi fantasia. Opus 27, No. 2.
   (Moonlight Sonata.)
   Adagio—Allegretto—Presto.

2.—R. WAGNER, (1813–   .)
   (*a*) Spinning Song, from the "Flying Dutchman."
   (*b*) Grand March, from "Tannhauser."
   Arranged by LISZT.

3.—MOZART.
   (*a*) Voi che sapete, from "Nozze de Figaro."
   GORDIGIANI.
   (*b*) O Santisima Vergine Maria.
   Miss LIZZIE CRONYN.

PART II.

4.—(*a*) G. HANDEL, (1684–1759.)
   Chaconne.
   (*b*) J. S. BACH, (1685–1750.)
   Sarabande et Passepied.
   (*c*) CHR. GLUCK, (1709–1787.)
   Gavotte, from the Ballet "Don Juan."
   (*d*) MOZART, (1756–1791).
   Menuet et Gigue.

5.—F. SCHUBERT, (1787–1828.)
   (*a*) Impromptu. Op. 90, No. 2.
   (*b*) Ave Maria,
   (*c*) Valse-Caprice,   } Arranged by LISZT.

6.—BEETHOVEN.
   (*a*) La Partenza.
   (*b*) L'Amante impaziente.   From Opus 82.
   Miss LIZZIE CRONYN.

7.—F. LISZT, (1811–   .)
   (*a*) The Lake.
   (*b*) At the Brook.
   (*c*) Hungarian Rhapsody. No. 12.
   (Dedicated to JOACHIM.)

The CHICKERING PIANO FORTE used at all the VON BÜLOW Concerts.

all alone," he admitted to Ullman, "the better I shall feel." While on board ship coming to America, Bülow found the perfect foil for his concerts: Lizzie Cronyn (1852–1921), a young Canadian-American woman, just twenty-four years old, who was returning from five years of study on the continent with a promising career that already included an appearance at La Scala. She possessed a voice that, if not sensational, obviously met his high musical standards, for she would appear in more than 90 of his 139 American concerts.[1]

Demure and guileless, Cronyn was in many ways the antithesis of Bülow. Her unaffected manner on stage, so unlike the pretentious demeanor of most prima donnas, enchanted audiences. Wearing a simple dress with flowers in her hair, she made them feel as if she were a family member singing in their parlor at home. Her voice was not large, but was delicate with a "moving beauty of its own," according to the *Boston Evening Transcript*. Dwight was perhaps the most lavish in his praise: "All were charmed by the modest, unsophisticated, youthful, musically absorbed face and manner—the virginal, pure, sweet, sensitive quality of voice, so evenly developed, and so justly trained that art concealed itself—and by the fervent and yet chaste expression with which she sang."[2] The American public took her to heart as a hometown girl who could share the stage with one of the world's leading musicians.

Bülow quickly and unobtrusively assumed the role of Cronyn's accompanist, openly confirming his approval of her artistry and making their joint concerts appear like a "meeting of congenial artists playing *con amore*." Dwight wrote that Bülow played her accompaniments "with the protecting, tender appreciativeness of one pleased to show how pure a pearl he had found."[3] Bülow was held up as an example to lesser pianists who thought accompanying beneath them, and his impeccable behavior toward her during their concerts served as a much-needed antidote to his irascible reputation.

Cronyn drew most of her selections from the operatic repertoire of such early nineteenth-century composers as Bellini, Rossini, Meyerbeer, and Weber, with occasional pieces by Mozart, Mercadante, Beethoven, and Spohr. The only recent works were songs by Liszt, an aria by Gounod (the Jewel Song from *Faust*), and Rubinstein's "Thou'rt Like unto a Flower," the last usually an audience favorite. She, or perhaps Bülow, shunned the simple ballads that had been staple items on programs of other concert troupes.

Cronyn had already appeared in many of Bülow's concerts before joining him on the western tour, but it was in the heartland where she was the sole assistant to Bülow that her role was so decisive. In cities where Bülow's repertoire was considered too classical, her part in the program provided enjoyment for the general public, who frequently identified more easily with the human voice than an inanimate piano. In Rochester, for instance, one critic thought that most people could not "appreciate the high order of music which [Bülow's] *repertoire* embraces. . . . Ordinary

people pronounce it good playing without being able fully to comprehend it. With Miss Cronyn's singing the case is different. This everybody enjoys."[4]

Bülow's itinerary did not include some of the smaller cities in the Midwest that had become standard sites for concerts of touring performers (e.g., Dayton, Ohio; Lexington, Kentucky; Wheeling, West Virginia; Memphis, Tennessee). In seven weeks, he gave thirty-four concerts but in only seventeen different cities. Traveling with only one singer made his tour relatively inexpensive, and his managers could afford to neglect smaller cities where revenues were more likely to be modest. Bülow nevertheless occasionally performed six nights a week, even though his contract only specified five.

The incessant touring with sometimes daily or nightly railroad trips did not dampen Bülow's enthusiasm for the New World. In January from Cleveland, Bülow reveled in his sumptuous, if busy, existence: "How all of this fits me. How comfortable and cozy it is I can actually only express by railing at the European barbarism. . . . In the meantime, I want to enjoy the beautiful present as long as it lasts." Bülow was enthralled with American trains and the luxurious Pullman cars that had been designed in the previous decade. "This traveling is not fatiguing," he wrote his mother, "for . . . in America everything is a small century ahead. Railroad cars are like cabins, marvelously heated, beds of a perfection totally undreamed of and unthought of in Germany and surroundings." The sleeping cars are "enormous . . . like boats," containing "complete beds in which, completely undressed, one can enjoy without any disturbance the quiet of the night."[5]

In Cleveland, he exulted in his deluxe lodgings: "Imagine, for instance, my hotel room here, equipped with the softest rugs, the most elegant and solid furniture, the most splendid mattress and featherbed. . . . Cold and warm water are amply available for the bathtub as well as for the wash basin—steam heat, which one can regulate by oneself—*nota bene* the hotels are all evenly heated from top to bottom."[6]

Hotel dining rooms, where "no tobacco smoke poisons the person interested in nourishment," offered a staggering selection of "excellent food," "marvelous tea and coffee," and above all, "beneficent ice water." On a menu from the Russell House in Detroit, Bülow wrote to a friend, "You see immediately how one lives here in this country. . . . One can eat as much and as often as one wants for 4 dollars a day. Nobody invites one for a drink. One does not see beer or wine on any table—the people are satisfied at the meals with ice water" (figure 16.2). Just as his censure of Germans and their beer was a recurring motif in his public pronouncements, Bülow's fascination with Americans and their healthy addiction to water received frequent comment in his letters. Thirty years earlier, Herz had been perplexed by the "great number of water drinkers who have condemned themselves to the exclusive drinking of that much too primitive liquid in order to uphold the thesis that certain men abuse fermented liquors." Herz had discovered that temperance was a "passion in

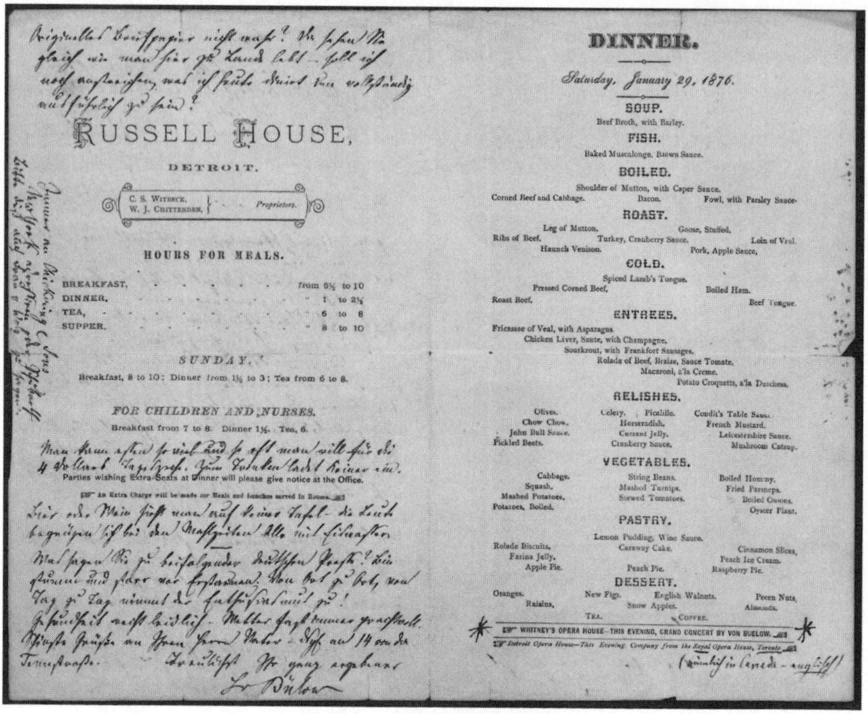

RUSSELL HOUSE,

DETROIT.

C. S. WITBECK, W. J. CHITTENDEN, Proprietors.

HOURS FOR MEALS.

BREAKFAST,	from 6½ to 10
DINNER,	" 1 to 2½
TEA,	" 6 to 8
SUPPER,	" 8 to 10

SUNDAY.

Breakfast, 8 to 10; Dinner from 1½ to 3; Tea from 6 to 8.

FOR CHILDREN AND NURSES.

Breakfast from 7 to 8. Dinner 1½. Tea, 6.

Parties wishing Extra Seats at Dinner will please give notice at the Office.

An Extra Charge will be made for Meals and Lunches served in Rooms.

DINNER.

Saturday, January 29, 1876.

SOUP.

Beef Broth, with Barley.

FISH.

Baked Muscalonge, Brown Sauce.

BOILED.

Shoulder of Mutton, with Caper Sauce.
Corned Beef and Cabbage. Bacon. Fowl, with Parsley Sauce.

ROAST.

Leg of Mutton. Goose, Stuffed.
Ribs of Beef. Turkey, Cranberry Sauce. Loin of Veal.
Haunch Venison. Pork, Apple Sauce,

COLD.

Spiced Lamb's Tongue.
Pressed Corned Beef, Boiled Ham.
Roast Beef. Beef Tongue.

ENTREES.

Fricassee of Veal, with Asparagus.
Chicken Liver, Saute, with Champagne.
Sourkrout, with Frankfort Sausages.
Rolade of Beef, Braize, Sauce Tomate.
Macaroni, a'la Creme.
Potato Croquetts, a'la Duchess.

RELISHES.

Olives. Celery. Picalille. Condit's Table Sauce.
Chow Chow. Horseradish. French Mustard.
John Bull Sauce. Currant Jelly. Leicestershire Sauce.
Pickled Beets. Cranberry Sauce. Mushroom Catsup.

VEGETABLES.

Cabbage. String Beans. Boiled Hominy.
Squash. Mashed Turnips. Fried Parsneps.
Mashed Potatoes. Stewed Tomatoes. Boiled Onions.
Potatoes, Boiled. Oyster Plant.

PASTRY.

Lemon Pudding, Wine Sauce.
Rolade Biscuits. Caraway Cake. Cinnamon Slices.
Farina Jelly. Peach Ice Cream.
Apple Pie. Peach Pie. Raspberry Pie.

DESSERT.

Oranges. New Figs. English Walnuts. Pecan Nuts.
Raisins. Snow Apples. Almonds.
TEA. COFFEE.

WHITNEY'S OPERA HOUSE—THIS EVENING, GRAND CONCERT BY VON BUELOW.

Detroit Opera House—This Evening, Company from the Royal Opera House, Toronto.

Figure 16.2. Letter from Hans von Bülow to Eugen Spitzweg, Detroit, 29 January 1876, on menu from Russell House listing its extensive selection of foods. (MUSIC DIVISION, LIBRARY OF CONGRESS)

America," and the movement had gained more momentum by the time of Bülow's arrival. In 1869 the Prohibition Party had been founded and the Women's Christian Temperance Union had been established the year before his tour. In contrast to Herz, Bülow not only admired the American ideal of temperance, he also heartily joined in their romance with water: "I live here like the president of a temperance society—not a drop of beer, wine, or coffee is being absorbed. Ice water and tea suit me extremely well by their exclusivity."[7]

Pleasurable surroundings did not eliminate the stress created by Bülow's high performance standards, and traveling all day or all night on a train did not leave much time for practice. Bülow was a disciplined person, however, and he discovered that living "*quasi* like a priest and soldier" was the "true, proper life. . . . Nevertheless, it remains slavery—the whole thing—but it belongs to the most bearable which I have thus far—enjoyed—in my life."[8]

His "two hours of evening slavery" in the concert hall were "generally not a burden but a pleasant obligation," because audiences met him "with such great sympathy and such warm respect everywhere," even if they were small in number. As Bülow

acknowledged, the attendance at his concerts was not always high, particularly in the smaller cities where solo piano recitals were still unusual. Bülow even admitted to his mother that the "times are miserable and 'business' with me is very lax." In Troy, New York, for instance, only about 250 people attended his concert, and in Indianapolis he was "welcomed by an almost beggarly array of empty benches." Business was better in other cities: around a thousand heard him in Rochester, Buffalo, and Louisville, and from a thousand to two thousand attended each of his first four concerts in Chicago. Bülow and Cronyn were particularly well received in Buffalo, a hometown concert for the singer. Bülow joined the audience in applauding Cronyn, and she was presented with baskets of flowers.[9]

Bülow did not always enjoy, however, the musicians who paid court to him and asked for advice and praise. Generally, they were "much more tiring than the concerts and the trips." In Cincinnati, Bülow described to Romaine one scene in progress: "There are two piano teachers in my room while I am writing to you. I told them that I have to answer a music publisher—they are arguing about a movement in a Beethoven sonata—they take me for an arbiter—not wishing at all, out of an excess of politeness, to tell them 'Both of you are idiots,' I agree one time with one, and then change around to the other." Yet, during an earlier stop in Ithaca, the newspaper reported that quite a few local citizens had called on him at the hotel and "found him, somewhat to their surprise, to be most agreeable socially"; despite his celebrated stature, he was not "stuck up" and "made everyone who conversed with him feel at ease."[10]

The German press appeared to be warming to Bülow, or so he thought. Bülow sent copies of favorable reviews from a German newspaper in Detroit to his mother, for whom, as the proper mother of a virtuoso, the reviews were "never beautiful enough." "The German press, which at the beginning had welcomed me with such indecent grunts, finally begins to sing psalms of praise," Bülow boasted to his mother. To a friend he also sent copies of reviews enclosed in only a brief letter because "writing is superfluous when the printed matter sounds so loud, so beautiful, so persuasive."[11]

Even with the belief that the Germans were listening more carefully to how he played and ignoring what he said, Bülow still could not resist hammering in his objections to his countrymen. At one matinée in Chicago, he began with an overly polite and obviously sarcastic speech "with a nervous and slightly agitated manner, but in intelligible English":

Ladies and Gentlemen: Permit me to say a few words. Will you allow me to take this opportunity to thank my countrymen who have given me so warm a welcome? In their solicitude for my success in the United States, they have made a certain criticism on my programmes, and I will now make a brief reply. My German fellow-countrymen

complain that I will injure my popularity by playing too much severe and classical music. They say I should produce more variety in my programmes by mixing with the highest music some that is lighter; they think that American musical culture is not equal to the best composers, and that on this account I should perform such things as "[Home,] Sweet Home," "The Last Rose of Summer," and "Yankee Doodle." Well; to this I reply, first, that I am a German artist, and that I worship always in the temples of the great masters; and, secondly, that I have found American audiences among the most cultivated and appreciative to which I have had the honor of playing in any part of the world. However, will you permit me now, just by way of prelude to the regular programme, to give you a specimen of this class of so-called "popular" music? Just by way of prelude.

He then played "a very noisy, listless, and bizarre treatment" of "The Marseillaise," "through meaningless mazes of frivolous variations." If he wanted to choose an example of music of less worth, most thought he should have chosen something from his own country, perhaps a Strauss waltz. The *Chicago Times* stated that Bülow's impromptu remarks "were brought forth by the wasps of a certain coarse and brutal portion of the German press, who have taken a vulgar and savage delight in stinging the eminent pianist ever since his arrival in this country. Von Bülow is not the only foreign artist who has had to be saved from his countrymen by his friends."[12]

Fourteen years later Bülow's acrid speech was still ringing in the ears of Bernhard Ziehn, a prominent German-born music theorist and teacher who had made his home in Chicago since 1868. When Bülow returned to Chicago in 1890, Ziehn wrote a scathing review of Bülow's Beethoven performances. Ziehn listed numerous infractions, but more than anything he was still rankling from Bülow's earlier accusations: "According to Mr. von Bülow we are only 'Dutch,' and I have not learned that he has retracted that insult. When he felt himself moved to hurl that infamy at us in McCormick's Hall on February 5, 1876, he might with some right have protested against a local criticism of his musical performances, but to abuse us was nevertheless highly unnecessary."[13]

Bülow also attacked Germans in another newspaper interview. Among other things, he blamed America's lack of knowledge and interest concerning the newly canonized masterworks of the piano repertoire on the ubiquitous German music teachers, who were often credited with spreading an appreciation for music. Bülow explained that his choice of repertoire was the result of their pernicious influence:

> I tell you the only reason why I play Beethoven, Schumann, Mendelssohn and all these, is because the gigantic ignoramus with the inevitable beer glass—the German music-teacher in America—has interpreted so many of these badly. I would rather from choice play Wagner and Liszt, for I have more sympathy with their writings . . .

but I have set myself the task to undo as far as I may the vicious work of ignorant and pretentious teachers who have given a wrong reading to the gems of the masters and locked it . . . in the minds of the Americans. . . . [I play] the Mendelssohn Spring Song too fast, eh? That is what I want; that is how it should be played, and not in the sentimental school-girl way in which it is ill treated. I heard Mendelssohn myself, and I saw him get into a passion when it was played in this slow, sentimental style. . . . [He] insisted it should be played with brilliance, but gracefully. The song . . . is a spring song, not a spleen song.[14]

Privately, Bülow also blamed America's lack of appreciation for great piano literature on the virtuosos who preceded him. "Success day before yesterday was colossal," he wrote to his mother while in Chicago.

You must not imagine that such a fever of interest for classical piano recitals is already awake in an audience still very much in its diapers. To wake up such a fever of interest—gradually—*voilà ma mission!* As you know, I am a real artist, not a public entertainer; therefore I do not make the slightest concession to bad taste. I have wisely managed to protect myself against that through my contract. If my colleagues, the great Thalberg and the, after all, more dignified Rubinstein, had done better, more systematic preparatory labor in my sense for the genuine and true, things would be in a much better condition.[15]

As often happens in Bülow's letters, particularly in those to his mother, truth is distorted by ego.

Despite his tirades issued in Chicago, Bülow was impressed with the city and the progress it had made after the fire of 1871. From there, he visited Cincinnati, another highly Germanic city. He met a compatriot there who was tired of America and was "horrified" by Bülow's "continual crescendo of enthusiasm" for the United States. Bülow agreed with his friend that there was not much charm in Cincinnati and that it awakened a "pardonable desire for a return to seasickness."[16]

Bülow was glad to escape the German Midwest and to find solace in French New Orleans. That city was not in his contract but he was told it would have "a heavenly, eternal spring-like climate, the most beautiful fruit and women—offering an abundance of pleasant impressions, which would be a necessary restorative to make [his] fatigues bearable." Bülow reported that he was "truly swimming in bliss" thanks to the warm weather, fresh strawberries, and the "patrician perfume of the South" that replaced the "German plebeian smell of the West." He particularly found pleasure in the French culture and was proud to be taken for French because of his "lively behavior" and "fluent diction."[17]

Musically, New Orleans provided an "aristocratic audience that [knew] the secret of nuances (nuances are everything—in music just as in love)," as he wrote in

a billet-doux to Romaine. "I breathed freely, seeing the plebeians of the West replaced by the patricians of the South. The sympathy has been reciprocal—I think
that my success will grow from evening to evening." Bülow's prediction did not come
to pass. His concerts were, in fact, "badly attended." Too many concerts were scheduled—eight in New Orleans when Chicago was only given four—and Bülow found
the city had "been made poor, in a certain sense desolated, as a result of the war"
and the "systematic, continuous suppression against the South."[18]

Bülow's infatuation with America peaked in early February during the middle of
his western tour when he wrote to Cosima, "I do not intend to recross the Atlantic. . . .
I have found my real fatherland here. . . . In fact, I consider myself henceforward
dead and buried as far as Europe is concerned." He was reluctant to tell his mother
the news, but thought she would accept it when she understood that his return to
Europe would be "equal to suicide." To Jessie Laussot, a trusted friend in Florence,
he was able to confide, "In this life, I will never again cross the ocean—the last quarter of my existence is dedicated to the New World, the place where, for the first
time, I can be entirely *myself*. The decision is fixed—the first steps to become an
American citizen have been taken."[19]

One of the many factors that made his decision to stay in America so appealing
was the Baroness back in Washington. He had not forgotten her, and he occupied
much time writing her. In late January, shortly after beginning the western tour, the
possibility arose that Romaine would leave the United States to join her husband in
Europe. Bülow was ready to abandon his "duty as an artist," the mission to which he
had devoted himself, and the country that he now loved in order to follow her because of "this love, this passion that every day increases in force and intensity, which
becomes an avalanche that carries away everything that resists it." Bülow would follow her to the Europe that he now abhorred or even to the Arctic![20]

RETURN EAST

Bülow's first concerts on returning to the East were to take place in Baltimore, and
he arranged to meet Romaine there for a private performance of some of his own orchestral works by the Peabody Orchestra under Hamerik. He bragged that "the
orchestra is my specialty—I write badly for the piano, but I orchestrate tolerably
well." He was furious and thoroughly disillusioned when she recanted on her promise to meet him. A few weeks later he wrote his mother about the "Washington passion, which is, unfortunately, steadily growing, and which has brought me much excitement and very little comfort."[21]

The torment of unrequited love was far from what Bülow needed as the tour advanced unmercifully and further demands were made on him. He faced another
formidable series of recitals, most of them with little or no help. For New York

he planned six evening recitals with four of them to be repeated as matinées. Philadelphia (10–15 March) and Boston (3–8 April) were allocated five concerts each. This series was as close as Bülow would come to Rubinstein's farewell series of historical recitals. In New York, Bülow devoted three evenings in one week solely to Beethoven, with each program containing enough music to be considered today at least a recital and a half. The first two Beethoven programs (20 and 22 March) each consisted of four sonatas, as well as three other major works. Bülow enclosed a copy of the program for the first Beethoven concert in a letter to his mother with the comment, "It is not exactly comfortable. But *enfin*—what value does life have without climax?"[22] The final Beethoven program (24 March) consisted of the Sonatas Op. 101 and Op. 106 ("Hammerklavier") and the *Diabelli Variations;* he performed an extra sonata (Op. 31, No. 3) for free, either out of generosity or a failure to read the program. No wonder he had to cancel the following day's matinée.

Since these appearances were not announced as farewell recitals—indeed, they were advertised as Bülow's "first series" of "classical recitals"—they did not kindle as much enthusiasm as Rubinstein's. Little did anyone know that Bülow would not appear again in the East for more than a decade. The all-Beethoven programming did nothing to encourage attendance. The *World,* for instance, doubted if New York audiences were educated enough to endure such an "exuberance of classicality." Most critics found little to discuss about the performances because, unlike Rubinstein, Bülow's interpretations, which had already been dissected at some length, were fixed. As the *World* noted, "each piece was played without the least detectable difference in time, expression, or phrasing."[23]

Three more recitals loomed the following week. As Bülow's repertoire became more varied and modern, enthusiasm increased and the final concert was packed. The first evening (27 March) was devoted to Chopin and included numerous large-scale works, some new to Bülow's American repertoire. The program consisted of the Sonata in B Minor, *Variations on a Romance of Hérold, Allegro de concert,* the C♯ Minor Scherzo, the G Minor Ballade, the A♭ Polonaise, and the *Berceuse,* with an impromptu, a nocturne, and some waltzes and mazurkas thrown in for good measure. The remaining four concerts that week included a program featuring almost twenty works by Schumann and Mendelssohn, a repetition of the Chopin recital as a matinée, a program devoted to Schubert and Liszt, and a final matinée with a miscellaneous program from Bach to Rubinstein.

By this time the rigors of the touring life were beginning to show. During one recital he made a "ridiculous exhibition of his temper and inartistic nature by stopping in the middle of a Beethoven Sonata, rushing off the stage, abusing somebody who came in and looked at the piano, and finally returning and finishing the sonata as though nothing had happened." More seriously and more surprisingly, the critic for the *Times* was astonished that during the first Beethoven recital "once or twice

the fingers slipped upon wrong notes," surely an indication of illness or fatigue. A week later "the artist looked very ill" and his playing, "usually of unimpeachable correctness, was . . . a trifle less accurate than usual." Bülow was, in fact, quite ill, visiting a physician almost twice a day and traveling directly from his bed to the concert hall. His health did not seem to concern him as much as his physician's fees ($120 for 20 visits), with which he could have bought a new suit and had money left over. Nevertheless, during this bout of illness and repertoire-laden recitals Bülow sent a futile "cry of anguish" to Ullman in order to be released from his contract.[24]

Bülow's five recitals in Boston (3–8 April) went more smoothly, and he was at least partially recovered from his immediate illness. Bülow offered his final opinion on Boston audiences: they were always "charming, a little 'methodist' but all in all not too lukewarm." Several of the pieces according to Dwight were either new or seldom heard in public: Beethoven's "Les Adieux" Sonata, Op. 81a; the Schumann Third Sonata; some smaller pieces by Mendelssohn and Schumann; and many of the larger Chopin works, including the B Minor Sonata and the *Allegro de concert*. Dwight was in awe at the "intense mental concentration" and the "muscular and nervous strain" required for such a series of concerts in which all the pieces were "rendered with a marvellous perfection." He made his most impassioned praise of Bülow:

> Five rich programmes . . . were played to well nigh absolute perfection by this wonderful artist, who holds all these things in his memory, as well as in his fingers and his brain, nor can we any longer scruple to confess that he has them all too, in the best sense of the phrase, *by heart*. For how else can we account for such an absolute fidelity of memory, such clear conceptions, sure, discriminating grasp of each composer's individuality, and of the whole intention, even into the minutest detail, of every composition? Could you set a soulless machine to do all that? If not done *con amore*, could it be done at all? This man's whole life and being are absorbed in these interpretations. Yet so true are they, and so complete, in every sense, that they impress you as entirely impersonal; you are not listening to Von Buelow, it is Beethoven, or it is Schumann, Chopin, Mendelssohn; his own individuality never obtrudes itself, never warps, nor even colors what it transmits. You wonder at the quietude, the seemingly impassive coolness of the man who sits there so intensely occupied in working miracles almost.[25]

DEFEAT

From Boston, Bülow set out on his second and last tour of New England and the Midwest, visiting a few new cities but mostly returning to the larger and more reliable ones. After the demanding concerts in New York and Boston he was physically

Audiences — The Score Followers

A significant number of pianists had always attended the concerts of the early touring pianists to hear famous pieces interpreted by the composer. In the case of Rubinstein and Bülow, pianists sought insight from master interpreters into the works of Beethoven, Mendelssohn, Liszt, Chopin, and other composers. Bülow's last series of concerts in New York, Philadelphia, and Boston, with its concentration on solo recitals and massive doses of Beethoven, made this aspect of his tour perfectly clear. The *New York World* believed that the audience at one of his Beethoven programs consisted mostly of "either professional musicians or students who look upon these recitals as a short but invaluable course of lessons in pianism, as they really are." The *American Art Journal* considered Bülow the "ablest instructor that has visited us," and observed that "his audiences listen well" because "they are there to learn," and the pianist Richard Hoffman commented on the "atmosphere of intellectual enthusiasm" that pervaded Bülow's concerts.

One obvious clue to the pedagogical role of the concerts was the number of pianists who brought scores to follow during the performances. At Bülow's Boston debut, scores were "quite frequent throughout the audience," and Bülow remarked on this practice toward the end of his tour: "While I have been giving concerts I have noticed one thing; that the people who came to hear me, came not only for the love of music, but to receive instruction in the art of music. I am a keen observer of my audiences; I see the ladies so intently watching my execution; some with the score with them, and following me, and all of them evidently intending to profit by the performance."

The critic for the *New York World,* among others, frequently mentioned the presence of students with scores, who were visible "with their music on their knees" and audible through the "rustle of leaves in the pauses." These score followers, he believed, were invariably "astonished at the fidelity and precision with which the performer executed a long and complicated work with no hint from the text." During Bülow's last Boston appearances in April, Dwight observed that "never before have we seen so many listening with the volume of [Beethoven] Sonatas in their hands." Although following scores in a live performance today may appear to be distracting to the student as well as to other listeners, Dwight thought it was "the true way to appreciate these masterly interpretations."[1]

1. *New York World,* 21 March 1876, 5:1; *American Art Journal* n.s. 1 (25 March 1876): 112; Hoffman, *Some Musical Recollections,* 147; Boston debut in *Boston Evening Transcript,* 19 October 1875, 4:4; Bülow quoted in *American Art Journal* n.s. 1 (18 March 1876): 103; *New York World,* 23 November 1875, 4:6, and 18 November 1875, 5:1; *Dwight's Journal of Music* 36 (15 April 1876): 215.

and mentally drained before even starting and found it difficult to contemplate "nerve-destroying recitals in such unholy quantity." From his second stop in Salem, he faced another five-hour train journey to Springfield, Massachusetts,

> where I again shall enjoy the not particularly encouraging pleasure of playing a classical program before a rather small audience. In this respect I stick to my principle, the insistence on which has brought me the respect of all intelligent Americans, which I do not wish to lose by unfaithfulness. Moreover, the choice of more popular material would not increase the participation of the audience, which in the provinces still stands on a rather low, half-barbarian level of musical culture.[26]

As Bülow was obviously aware, his devotion to the classics was generally blamed for the sometimes meager attendance at his appearances. After the opening splash of orchestral concerts, his recitals were quite serious and offered little or nothing that appealed to a broad audience. The detrimental effect of Bülow's repertoire did not surprise Ullman, who had urged the pianist to include more sensational pieces in his programs. He wrote to Bülow toward the end of the tour and made it clear that his own priority was money, not art:

> Bach and too much Beethoven do great harm to the receipts and (believe me) in the end also to your prestige. You have demonstrated what you can do, and it would be desirable . . . to choose less abstruse programs for the Americans next season. You will not succeed in molding them to your intellect. Without becoming trivial, perhaps you could lower yourself a little without doing violence to your artistic sensibility. . . . Renounce ideas of *mission,* you will be disappointed there. Take America for what it is: the country to make money and nothing else. Twenty more years are needed to accomplish your mission.

Ullman's opinion was correct for at least some of those who attended Bülow's concerts in the smaller cities. A reviewer from Terre Haute attending a concert in Indianapolis, for instance, was dismayed that after two hours of piano music he could not "remember the slightest semblance of a tune." In Louisville the "fugue piece" was of an "order too high for genuine appreciation by a concert audience." In Syracuse there was a "lack of sympathy by many of the audience with the programme as a whole. They could not appreciate it; it was beyond their education or understanding."[27]

The next month (10 April–9 May) of nonstop traveling and performing finally wore Bülow down completely. His obsessive perfectionism combined with his fragile health were eventually too much for his nerves. To a friend he complained of living like a "suitcase with headaches," and to his mother he confided his mental deterioration: "My head is very weak—constant half-giddinesses influence my 'famous' memory so much that I often have to rehearse for myself the most frequently

played concert program before the 'public production' in order not to have a fiasco in the evening." His formerly ecstatic appraisal of American audiences and technology plummeted in his last weeks in this country, although he admitted that the "perspective only from a concert hall does not permit real acquaintance, let alone a judgment."[28]

Bülow's early appreciation for the Chickering also declined as the pianos became "quite deteriorated through the uninterrupted transport." According to the editor of the *Music Trade Review,* on more than one occasion Bülow greatly insulted Frank Chickering and expressed disapproval with the mechanism and action of the Chickering pianos. His manager did not deny the charges but blamed them on Bülow's illness, which had made him "extremely irritable" and "hardly responsible for what he said"; in his "cooler moments" he "apologized amply" for his harsh comments. Furthermore, friends of the Chickerings claimed that many of the reports on Bülow's spiteful actions toward the piano firm were "grossly exaggerated" and were "disseminated by rival and envious" piano makers, who ironically had themselves "persistently badgered and annoyed" Bülow. As his relations with Chickering began to degenerate, Bülow effected a rapprochement with the Steinways—German or not—and in mid-March had secretly auditioned their new grand designed for the U.S. Centennial celebration and seemed "highly pleased with [the piano's] tone and action."[29]

From Buffalo on 24 April he wrote Romaine, "I am fully prepared that each concert might be the last one, and that I shall truly drop never to rise again. . . . I am afraid from one moment to the next of a new brain attack followed by some paralysis." Three days later in Cleveland, he wrote his mother that his enthusiasm for America was at its "last gasp. . . . You will spare me a description of the labors and unpleasantness of the concertizing—good music before unmusical people or empty benches in enormous halls, where it sounds confused, empty, and dry, and playing on pianos damaged by transport. *It is horrible beyond all concepts*—this kind of life."[30]

He postponed a few concerts and finally, at the urging of his manager, canceled his tour after appearances in St. Louis. In his depressed physical and emotional state, Bülow withdrew from his contract with 33 concerts remaining of 172, which required him to forfeit one-fourth of the 100,000 francs. The money as well as a sense of obligation to fulfill his commitment, despite Ullman suggesting he cancel concerts occasionally due to illness, had pushed Bülow further than he could go. As he confessed to a friend shortly before he collapsed, "You have no idea how terribly depressing, nauseating, and exhausting this slavery is, which I have entered because of vile mammon."[31]

From St. Louis, where he gave his last concert on 9 May, Bülow returned to New York on a fifty-hour train ride. "I should have believed Rubinstein, who has three times my energy," he lamented to his mother, "when he warned me to some extent three years ago." In New York he underwent medical treatment that he described

as "experimental," since his condition was "highly exceptional" and could only be designated as "nervous prostration." The *New York World* reported on the extent of Bülow's illness: "Dr. Von Bülow failed to recognize even his most intimate friends. One day when his agent entered his room the Doctor stared at him in a vacant manner and said he did not know him. When reminded who he was he seemed much moved and burst into tears. When practising, the other day, he fell to the floor in a fainting fit." While Bülow was in this dilapidated condition, his manager unbelievably announced a series of three farewell matinées beginning 30 May, but Bülow could not have had any intention of performing them. By 3 June he was on the steamer *St. Laurent* in the company of Wertheimber and his wife in search of a cure for complete exhaustion, the result, he told his friend Carl Bechstein, of "overwork in a career for which I am not really in the least suited."[32]

Aftermath

Bülow's tour of the United States serves, as does Rubinstein's, to illustrate several important developments in late-nineteenth-century American concert life. The sponsorship of his tour by a leading piano firm, for example, typifies the increasingly frequent partnership of business and art. Bülow's concerts reflect a trend toward historically oriented solo recitals and an increasingly standardized piano repertoire. In addition, Bülow's conviction that music should be edifying rather than entertaining reinforced a view rapidly gaining adherents in America.

Financially, Bülow's tour was described by the press as a complete failure, although attendance in the larger eastern cities, where Bülow focused most of his attention and energy, was generally substantial. (He performed in only thirty-seven cities, a significantly smaller number than either Rubinstein or Thalberg—fifty-nine and seventy-eight, respectively.) Ullman, in fact, willingly offered Bülow an engagement in America for the following season: 50 concerts for 40,000 francs, even better terms than the previous contract.[33] Musically, the significance of Bülow's tour was frequently acknowledged by critics, many of whom believed he was responsible for demonstrating the highest levels of performance, modeling authentic interpretations of the music of the greatest composers, and improving musical taste. *Church's Musical Visitor* of Cincinnati, for example, summarized Bülow's influence:

> It would be difficult to tell the good even this short visit of the eminent German master has accomplished in its elevating and refining effect upon the taste of our pianists and amateurs. We place great importance upon the appearance of an artist of Von Bülow's grade among us, because public players are looked up to as guides and models by those who are making music a study. They are to a great extent the teachers of advanced pupils, who are endeavoring to acquire the finishing touches of taste and style.[34]

Although Bülow and Rubinstein shared similar repertoire and attitudes toward music, their roles in America's musical life were slightly different. Rubinstein could communicate to almost any listener, whether he or she was willing to be reached or not. Bülow was concerned with providing authentic renderings faithful to the composer. He could not and did not try to reach everyone. Rubinstein, whatever aim he might have had, was a popularizer through the inclusion of several light works and his vivid communication of the emotional content of the music. On the other hand, Bülow, through his more scholarly performances, helped establish orthodox interpretations of the canonic piano repertoire for the next generation of serious performers and teachers.

Many professional musicians saw the benefit of Bülow's visit and encouraged him to stay in America, for they believed he could maintain a successful career as a performer, teacher, and conductor. Americans were particularly interested in hearing him conduct, and he had offers for the next season to conduct the concerts of the New York Philharmonic and the Harvard Musical Association in Boston.[35] Even though Bülow abandoned the idea of remaining in America, he felt at the same time estranged from Germany and had no particular desire to return there in the summer of 1876, when the first Bayreuth festival—the ultimate glorification of Wagner and his ideals—was to be the principal musical event.[36] More than once in his letters Bülow quoted a phrase from Goethe that attempted to reconcile his sense of homelessness with his dedication to his mission as a pianist: "Where I am useful, there is my country."[37]

The lasting impressions Bülow made on Americans were as firmly held as they were divergent. The *Music Trade Review* remembered Bülow's abusive personality:

Von Bülow was singularly successful—in this country—in making hosts of enemies. . . . It is difficult to comprehend how he could have been so ardently hated in so short a period of time. . . . He came, he saw, but he did not conquer, and it really speaks well for us that he did not. It is well for any artist to understand at once that conceit and arrogance are *not* passports to favor here.

Others were able to overlook his faults and focus on his talents. Henry Wertheimber, for example, who had been with Bülow throughout his tour, saw both sides of the man—the fault-finding and outspoken musician in public and the congenial gentleman in private: "I found him a great-hearted man, a noble man, easily provoked and irritated, to be sure, troubled about trifles, speaking his mind plainly and unthinkingly, and then feeling hearty sorrow for his hastiness. He fully appreciated and heartily admired America and American institutions." That the highly Germanic New York Philharmonic would consider him as a conductor proved that his outstanding musical talent transcended his personal faults.[38]

Bülow's impressions of the United States were just as disparate. Like many visiting artists, Bülow at first saw America as the mythical country that offered the ultimate solutions to all career and domestic problems. That image was a strong one, not easily erased. Only at the very end of his American tour was Bülow able to confront the realities of this country and himself. Just a few days before leaving America he wrote to his mother, "I am too old, too used up, to find roots in this New World—six years ago it would still have been possible—today it is too late. As long as possible, I desperately clung to these illusions . . . about myself and this country. . . . The whole thing was a continuous trance."[39]

POSTLUDE

∾

By the closing decades of the nineteenth century, the solo piano recital had won full acceptance. Miscellaneous concerts with a hodgepodge of performers and genres that had been common practice for decades were eliciting harsh criticisms in the 1870s. Rubinstein and to some extent Bülow helped prove that the lone soloist at the keyboard was viable artistically and financially. The public's ability to tolerate a full evening of piano music was concurrent with the orchestral concert ridding itself of vocal and instrumental solos without orchestral accompaniment. The absolute specialization in both types of concerts came from the public's greater familiarity with the repertoire and the increased view of music as edification rather than as entertainment.

During the nineteenth century, critics announced on a regular basis the end of the virtuoso era, usually meaning the end of technical display with little musical content. When virtuosos turned their attention to the newly developing canon, they lost what seemed to be their most worrisome characteristic: the focusing of attention solely on themselves when both the performance and the composition were theirs alone. The cult of the personality, which glorified the composer-performer, was not totally replaced, however, by the cult of the work, which enshrined the masterpiece. Ironically, with the establishment of a standardized and limited reper-

toire for the piano recital, there arose a need to focus on performers and their individual interpretations for the sake of variety, a necessary evil to perpetuate a seemingly immutable ritual. Today, when star soloists are the principal marketing ploy for symphony concerts, and when competitions seek to identify the next generation of celebrated performers in an efficient but artificial environment, it is impossible to believe that the virtuoso age is over.

Certainly the two decades following the American tours of Rubinstein and Bülow might be considered the golden age of piano virtuosos by some aficionados. (The concerns in the 1870s that the piano was no longer suitable for the concert hall were obviously false alarms.) Some of the legendary pianists who made their first of usually many visits to the United States before the close of the century included Leopold Godowsky (1870–1938) in 1884, Josef Hofmann (1876–1957) in 1887, Moriz Rosenthal (1862–1946) in 1888, Eugen d'Albert (1864–1932) in 1889, Vladimir de Pachmann (1848–1933) in 1890, and Ferruccio Busoni (1866–1924), Arthur Friedheim (1859–1932), and Ignacy Jan Paderewski (1860–1941) in 1891.[1] In their choice of repertoire, the new wave of late-nineteenth-century virtuosos perpetuated the canon of masterworks that had solidified by the 1870s, contributing only a few additions. The members of the new generation were more closely related to Rubinstein in their ability to excite audiences, their highly individualistic interpretations, and their penchant for offering their own dazzling arrangements and transcriptions. The more reserved, academic approach of Bülow found a small but significant following in the twentieth century.

The discrimination against American talent, an undeniably negative impact of the steady stream of visiting performers, continued despite the considerable number of well-trained American pianists seeking to establish concert careers. None gained the adulation of native audiences like their foreign counterparts, but a few achieved some success, including Julie Rivé-King, mentioned previously in Interlude II; Amy Fay (1844–1928), who performed successfully in Boston, Chicago, and New York, although she is more famous today for her *Music-Study in Germany* (1880) with its perceptive descriptions of Liszt, Tausig, and others; William H. Sherwood (1854–1911), who gave the American premiere of the Grieg Piano Concerto; the blind Edward Baxter Perry (1855–1924), who helped popularize the concept of the lecture-recital; Fannie Bloomfield Zeisler (1863–1927), who was of Polish birth but grew up in America from a young age; and Amy Beach (1867–1944), who curtailed a promising solo career to pursue composition after her marriage.[2]

The above list indicates that American women pianists were beginning to carve out a professional niche for themselves. The required but superficial piano instruction that so many young women had endured through much of the century eventually gave way to serious training of those women with talent and determination. By the turn of the century, the critic James Huneker could state with some relief that

"unless there is discovered a sharply defined aptitude, a girl is kept away from the stool and pedals. . . . The new girl is too busy to play the piano unless she has the gift; then she plays it with consuming earnestness. We listen to her, for we know that this is an age of specialization, an age when woman is coming into her own."[3]

Few innovations would occur in the practical aspects of managing touring artists until the airplane replaced the railroad as the principal means of travel, though the plush, private Pullman car of Paderewski was a far cry from the spartan coaches that Thalberg suffered. With the advent of luxurious ocean liners providing faster, safer, and more comfortable ocean voyages, the single, extended tour of America that many of the European artists braved mid-century began to be replaced by shorter but more frequent visits. Bülow, for instance, returned twice (in 1889 and 1890) for a brief tour of selected cities.[4] In the final decade of the century, Paderewski made almost annual trips to America, and was probably the first significant visiting piano virtuoso to surpass the number of American concerts given by Thalberg.

AUDIENCES

The various motives of the concertgoer have hardly changed since the time of De Meyer; the curious and fashionable will always be with us. The ability of the European virtuosos to attract the ardent music lover, the amateur pianist, and the trained professional, as well as people seeking extramusical experiences, made them highly influential in American musical life. Concert etiquette and performance conventions changed rapidly, however, and were close to being firmly established by the mid-1870s. The transformation in audience behavior from the 1840s to the 1870s has recently been the subject of considerable scholarly attention. Both Lawrence W. Levine and John F. Kasson among others have proposed the view that proper concert decorum was established in late-nineteenth-century America by the social elite, who imposed stringent standards of behavior on audiences to restrict the access of the lower classes.[5] This interpretation, the subject of much debate, focuses on the single issue of class, which does not explain all the forces at work in the concerts examined here.

The concerts of traveling virtuosos were rooted in the eighteenth-century concert tradition of music to amuse, astonish, and entertain, and were capable of subsisting within the free enterprise system and flourished without the patronage of wealthy subscribers. After all, it was the rise of public concerts in the eighteenth century that led to the extreme development of virtuosity as a highly desirable and marketable skill. The boisterous interaction of the audiences in the concerts of De Meyer and Herz was viewed as a positive sign that audiences were enjoying the music, and the outbursts of applause and stomping of feet were the direct results of the audience's involvement with the performance. Contemporary descriptions of such behavior rarely censured it or suggested that respectable audiences should refrain from it.

The radical shift in repertoire by the 1870s demanded a similar change in the participation of listeners. Fantasias on opera arias and variations on "The Last Rose of Summer" do not require the same amount of attention or exact the same type of response as a late Beethoven sonata or Mendelssohn's *Variations sérieuses*. Ralph P. Locke, in a commentary on Levine's *Highbrow/Lowbrow*, has argued persuasively that the impetus behind sacralization, most obviously manifested by silence in the concert room, was much less the result of the social elite's desire to exert their superiority but more the "musicians' and music lovers' desire for an intense aesthetic experience."[6]

Indeed, for a music lover who was a member of a lower economic class to spend one or two dollars for a single ticket to a piano concert was a sacrifice that would have encouraged a savoring of every moment of the experience. Although some disturbances came from the cheaper seats in the gallery, most of the audience members there were quiet and attentive. On the other hand, large financial resources are not required for one to be quiet, and the wealthy, who are sometimes oblivious to common courtesies, were more likely to have other motives in attending concerts than musical gratification. Once George William Curtis complained to a neighbor while leaving a concert in the 1840s: "It is a pity that such ill-mannered people should come among ladies and gentlemen." To which his neighbor replied: "Ill-mannered! . . . I assure you they are carriage company from the neighborhood of Union Square."[7]

PROS AND CONS

Echoing Schumann's gibes at virtuosos, some writers have contended that the visiting virtuosos were more harmful than beneficial. Near the end of the nineteenth century, the prominent New York critic H. E. Krehbiel wrote of this period:

> The paucity of artistic effort native to the soil made the Americans of that day peculiarly the prey of the virtuosi from abroad. They were exploited by advertising-managers of the Barnum stamp, who were quick to realize upon the eagerness to hear and know the best; the people lined the pockets of singers and pianists and violinists who contributed little or nothing to the real advancement of musical culture.

More recent writers, such as Norman Lebrecht, see the marketing of the virtuosos as the beginning of the end of classical music, when commercial goals began to supersede musical ones.[8] Others may bemoan Americans importing European concert life instead of developing their own musical traditions, or the loss of spontaneity in concert audiences.

Earlier testimony is clear, however, that at the time most Americans believed the visiting virtuosos were a beneficent phenomenon, awakening musical interest among a wide range of audiences and providing excellent models for students and aspiring professional musicians.[9] In 1876 George William Curtis appraised the

progress of music in New York during the past several decades. While he addressed all forms of music, concerts by touring pianists constitute a substantial portion of his survey. After attending a concert of Bülow, he reflected on the startling difference between Bülow and De Meyer:

> The concert throughout was the conclusive evidence of the progress of our musical taste. From De Meyer crouching and sprawling over the piano in the old Tabernacle to the perfect classic refinement and tranquil supremacy of Von Bülow in Chickering Hall the distance and the advance were prodigious. The last was as severely intent upon the best and the highest as the first was devoted to the mere pleasing and popular effect. It was the difference in manhood between a voluptuary and a devotée.[10]

Many forces were responsible for this dramatic metamorphosis, including resident performers and music teachers, fledgling symphony and choral societies, and traveling orchestras and opera troupes. Many Americans believed, however, that the virtuosos in particular were elemental in raising the public's interest in and knowledge of music. The respected critic W. S. B. Mathews, in the survey *A Hundred Years of Music in America* (1889), held that "all things considered, the great pianists must be accorded the credit of having been the most useful and successful educators of American musical taste."[11]

Not only did most Americans believe the concerts of touring artists were positive influences, they congratulated themselves for supporting the visiting musicians so generously. The reports that European performers had been well received in a city, far from proving that Americans followed, lemming-like, the latest virtuoso into the concert hall with little understanding, signaled America's appreciation of the best performers the world had to offer was equal to that of the more cultivated—or at least more condescending—Europeans. A writer in Charleston, for example, was proud that America's appreciation of Thalberg had "vindicated her claim to refinement and critical acumen to the confusion of her detractors." Thalberg's "success will be a wholesome reproof to those in Europe and at home who asserted that the taste in America was not sufficiently advanced to appreciate so refined and exquisite a performer."[12]

Such boastful and patriotic statements, reflecting the chronic need for Americans to measure up to European standards, may not be entirely honest. But it is difficult to discount the intensely emotional descriptions people gave of their personal experiences on hearing these pianists. The concerts of these virtuosos were once-in-a-lifetime experiences for many audience members, and the events remained indelibly in their memories. The meaning of what was then a rare event, which was frequently possible only by overcoming financial, geographical, climatic, or social obstacles, is difficult to appreciate when technology has made music so readily available today. Two very different writers poignantly captured the musical significance

of these concerts to nineteenth-century audiences. Dwight, a musically literate observer, exulted in Bülow's performance of the "Appassionata" Sonata:

> His rendering of the Beethoven Sonata was to our mind the most memorable among all his achievements of that week. We have heard nothing like it. It was indeed *appassionata;* and it was as full of beauty as fire; it carried you away with it, and made you feel that life is worth the while when you can sometimes live it so far within this magic, yet most real element of tones.

On the other end of the listening continuum was a rural correspondent to a Burlington, Vermont, newspaper. A simple music lover, he described an emotional and aesthetic experience similar to Dwight's upon attending New York concerts of both Thalberg and Gottschalk in 1856. After rhapsodizing at great length about the glories of those musical events, he concluded his effusive oration:[13]

> If any read this who are able to hear as much good Music throughout the year as they wish, and smile to see so many words expended on what to them is but an every day occurrence, let them remember that we who exist in the country, seldom enjoy such pleasure, and that, therefore, when it does come, we enjoy it to the greatest extent, and make it an epoch in our uneventful lives. It is something to which we can look back during all the toilsome and wearying year, with a smile and thrill of pleasure. For during those few short hours we were in truth, living—Ah, Music!

Appendix A

Itineraries

A range of dates (e.g., July 22–30) indicates only a single concert given within those dates. A superscript "m" (^{m}) designates a matinée performance, a superscript "s" (^{s}) a concert for schoolchildren. The book's companion Web site supplies more details on the concerts and provides the sources, mostly local newspapers, used to compile this list.

LEOPOLD DE MEYER

1845

Oct. 20	New York, NY
Oct. 22	New York, NY
Oct. 24	New York, NY
Oct. 28	New York, NY
Oct. 30	New York, NY
Nov. 1	New York, NY
Nov. 7	New York, NY
Nov. 10	New York, NY
Nov. 14	New York, NY
Nov. 21	Boston, MA

1846

Feb. 5	New York, NY
Feb. 12	New York, NY
Feb. 21	Philadelphia, PA
Feb. 25	Philadelphia, PA
Mar. 3	Philadelphia, PA
Mar. 10	Baltimore, MD
Mar. 13	Baltimore, MD
Mar. 17	Philadelphia, PA
Mar. 18	Baltimore, MD
Mar. 19	Washington, DC
Mar. 21	Washington, DC
Mar. 24	Richmond, VA
Mar. 30	Charleston, SC
Apr. 16	New Orleans, LA
Apr. 18	Mobile, AL
Apr. 20	New Orleans, LA
Apr. 24	New Orleans, LA
Apr. 29	Mobile, AL
May 2	Mobile, AL
May 6	New Orleans, LA
May 9	New Orleans, LA
May 13	Natchez, MS
May 15	Natchez, MS
May 20	Vicksburg, MS
May 27	St. Louis, MO
May 29	St. Louis, MO
June 1	St. Louis, MO
June 9	Louisville, KY
June 11	Louisville, KY
June 15	Cincinnati, OH
June 18	Cincinnati, OH
June 22	Cincinnati, OH
June 25	Cincinnati, OH
July 2	Pittsburgh, PA
July 6	Pittsburgh, PA
July 14	Cleveland, OH
July 20	Buffalo, NY
July 21	Niagara Falls, NY
July 22–30	Hamilton, Ontario
July 24	Toronto, Ontario
July 28	Rochester, NY
July 31	Toronto, Ontario
Aug. 5	Montréal, Québec
Aug. 7	Montréal, Québec

Aug. 15	Saratoga Springs, NY
Aug. 22	Newport, RI
Oct. 2	New York, NY
Oct. 8	New York, NY
Oct. 15	Boston, MA
Oct. 19	Boston, MA
Oct. 22	New York, NY
Oct. 30	Philadelphia, PA
Nov. 3	New York, NY
Nov. 5	Philadelphia, PA
Nov. 10	Philadelphia, PA
Nov. 13	Philadelphia, PA
Nov. 18	Baltimore, MD
Nov. 20	Baltimore, MD

1847

Feb. 3	New Orleans, LA
Feb. 6	New Orleans, LA
Feb. 14	New Orleans, LA
Feb. 23	Memphis, TN
Mar. 5	St. Louis, MO
Mar. 16	St. Louis, MO
Mar. 19	St. Louis, MO
Mar. 23	St. Louis, MO
Mar. 26	St. Louis, MO
Apr. 5	Nashville, TN
Apr. 7	Nashville, TN
Apr. 13	Louisville, KY
Apr. 21	Cincinnati, OH
Apr. 24	Cincinnati, OH
Apr. 27	Cincinnati, OH
Apr. 30	Cincinnati, OH
May 29	Philadelphia, PA

HENRI HERZ
1846

Oct. 29	New York, NY
Nov. 5	New York, NY
Nov. 10	New York, NY
Nov. 13	New York, NY
Nov. 19	Baltimore, MD
Nov. 21	Philadelphia, PA
Nov. 24	Philadelphia, PA
Nov. 27	Baltimore, MD
Nov. 30	Baltimore, MD
Dec. 4	Philadelphia, PA
Dec. 7	Wilmington, DE
Dec. 9	Philadelphia, PA
Dec. 17	Boston, MA
Dec. 18	New Bedford, MA
Dec. 19	Boston, MA

| Dec. 22 | Philadelphia, PA |
| Dec. 26 | New York, NY |

1847

Jan. 2	Boston, MA
Jan. 4	Providence, RI
Jan. 7	New York, NY
Jan. 19	Charleston, SC
Jan. 22	Charleston, SC
Jan. 25	Charleston, SC
Jan. 28	Savannah, GA
Jan. 29	Savannah, GA
Feb. 1–5	Columbus, GA
Feb. 2–6	Columbus, GA
Feb. 12	Mobile, AL
Feb. 16	Mobile, AL
Feb. 22	New Orleans, LA
Feb. 24	New Orleans, LA
Mar. 1	New Orleans, LA
Mar. 5	New Orleans, LA
Mar. 12	New Orleans, LA
Mar. 17	New Orleans, LA
Mar. 24	New Orleans, LA
Mar. 30	New Orleans, LA
Apr. 1	Mobile, AL
Apr. 5	Mobile, AL
Apr. 9	New Orleans, LA
Apr. 12	New Orleans, LA
Apr. 13–17	Donaldsonville, LA
Apr. 14–19	Baton Rouge, LA
Apr. 15–20	Baton Rouge, LA
Apr. 16–21	St. Francisville, LA
Apr. 24	Natchez, MS
Apr. 27	Natchez, MS
Apr. 29	Vicksburg, MS
May 4	Vicksburg, MS
Apr. 23– May 5	Jackson, MS
May 5–16	Memphis, TN
May 21	St. Louis, MO
May 24	St. Louis, MO
May 27	St. Louis, MO
May 28	Alton, IL
June 1	St. Louis, MO
June 3	St. Louis, MO
June 5	St. Louis, MO
June 10	Nashville, TN
June 12	Nashville, TN
June 15	Nashville, TN
June 21	Louisville, KY
June 23	Louisville, KY
June 24	Louisville, KY
June 25	Louisville, KY

June 26	Louisville, KY
June 28	Lexington, KY
June 30	Maysville, KY
July 2	Cincinnati, OH
July 6	Cincinnati, OH
July 8	Cincinnati, OH
July 10	Cincinnati, OH
July 17	Pittsburgh, PA
July 19	Pittsburgh, PA
July 24	Staten Island, NY
July 28	Saratoga Springs, NY
Aug. 2	Saratoga Springs, NY
Aug. 11	Saratoga Springs, NY
Aug. 13	Buffalo, NY
Aug. 14	Niagara Falls, NY
Aug. 17	Buffalo, NY
Aug. 18	Rochester, NY
Aug. 19	Syracuse, NY
Aug. 20	Utica, NY
Aug. 21	Utica, NY
Aug. 23–28	Newport, RI
Aug. 25	Providence, RI
Aug. 29	Fall River, MA
Aug. 30	New Bedford, MA
Sept. 1	Worcester, MA
Sept. 2	Springfield, MA
Sept. 3	Hartford, CT
Sept. 4	New Haven, CT
Sept. 9	Troy, NY
Sept. 10	Albany, NY
Sept. 14	Saratoga Springs, NY
Sept. 17	Albany, NY
Sept. 18	Troy, NY
Sept. 20	New York, NY
Sept. 28	New York, NY
Sept. 29	Philadelphia, PA
Oct. 4	Philadelphia, PA
Oct. 6	New York, NY
Oct. 11	New York, NY
Oct. 13	Brooklyn, NY
Oct. 18	Boston, MA
Oct. 19	Providence, RI
Oct. 20	Providence, RI
Oct. 21	Boston, MA
Oct. 22	New Bedford, MA
Oct. 23	Boston, MA
Oct. 25	Lowell, MA
Oct. 26	Worcester, MA
Oct. 27	Springfield, MA
Oct. 28	Hartford, CT

Oct. 29	New Haven, CT
Nov. 2	New York, NY
Nov. 4	New York, NY
Nov. 6	Boston, MA
Nov. 9	Cambridge, MA
Nov. 10	Boston, MA
Nov. 11	Portland, ME
Nov. 12	Salem, MA
Nov. 13	Boston, MA
Nov. 15	New Haven, CT
Nov. 17	Newark, NJ
Nov. 18	Brooklyn, NY
Nov. 20	Philadelphia, PA
Nov. 22	Baltimore, MD
Nov. 24	Wilmington, DE
Nov. 25	Lancaster, PA
Nov. 26	Philadelphia, PA
Nov. 27	Baltimore, MD
Nov. 30	Baltimore, MD
Dec. 8	Philadelphia, PA
Dec. 10	Washington, DC
Dec. 11	Washington, DC
Dec. 13	Richmond, VA
Dec. 14	Richmond, VA
Dec. 16	Richmond, VA
Dec. 18	Wilmington, NC
Dec. 27	Charleston, SC
Dec. 31	Charleston, SC

1848

Jan. 1	Charleston, SC
Jan. 4	Charleston, SC
Nov. 30	New York, NY
Dec. 14	New York, NY
Dec. 16	New York, NY
Dec. 21	New York, NY
Dec. 30	New York, NY

1849

Feb. 8	Boston, MA
Feb. 15	Worcester, MA
Feb. 16	Providence, RI
Feb. 17	Boston, MA
Apr. 19	Baltimore, MD
Apr. 20	Baltimore, MD
Apr. 21	Baltimore, MD
Apr. 23	Baltimore, MD
Apr. 25	Baltimore, MD
Apr. 27	Washington, DC
Apr. 28	Washington, DC
May 2	Richmond, VA
May 3	Richmond, VA
May 7	Norfolk, VA
May 8	Norfolk, VA

May 11	Richmond, VA
May 12	Richmond, VA
May 16	Charleston, SC
May 18	Charleston, SC
May 21	Charleston, SC
May 24	Savannah, GA
May 25	Savannah, GA
May 26	Savannah, GA
May 30	Augusta, GA
May 31	Augusta, GA
June 1	Augusta, GA
June 4	Columbia, SC
June 5	Columbia, SC
June 6	Columbia, SC
June 9	Charleston, SC
June 12	Charleston, SC
June 18	Columbus, GA
June 19	Columbus, GA

1850

Apr. 2	San Francisco, CA
Apr. 6	San Francisco, CA
Apr. 11	San Francisco, CA
Apr. 16	Sacramento City, CA
Apr. 18	Sacramento City, CA
Apr. 20	Sacramento City, CA
Apr. 21–26	Benicia, CA
Apr. 27	San Francisco, CA
Apr. 30	San Francisco, CA

SIGISMUND THALBERG
1856

Nov. 10	New York, NY
Nov. 11	New York, NY
Nov. 13	New York, NY
Nov. 15	New York, NY
Nov. 17	Brooklyn, NY
Nov. 18	New York, NY
Nov. 20	New York, NY
Nov. 21	New York, NY
Nov. 24	Albany, NY
Nov. 25	Troy, NY
Nov. 26	Newark, NJ
Nov. 27	New York, NY
Nov. 28	Philadelphia, PA

Nov. 29	New York, NY
Dec. 1	Brooklyn, NY
Dec. 2ˢ	New York, NY
Dec. 2	New York, NY
Dec. 3	Philadelphia, PA
Dec. 4	New York, NY
Dec. 5	Philadelphia, PA
Dec. 8	Philadelphia, PA
Dec. 9	New York, NY
Dec. 10	Philadelphia, PA
Dec. 11	New York, NY
Dec. 12	Philadelphia, PA
Dec. 13ˢ	Philadelphia, PA
Dec. 13	Philadelphia, PA
Dec. 15	Baltimore, MD
Dec. 16	Washington, DC
Dec. 17	Baltimore, MD
Dec. 18ˢ	Baltimore, MD
Dec. 19	Baltimore, MD
Dec. 20	Washington, DC
Dec. 22	Baltimore, MD
Dec. 23	Baltimore, MD
Dec. 24	Washington, DC
Dec. 26	New York, NY
Dec. 27	Philadelphia, PA
Dec. 29	Brooklyn, NY
Dec. 30	New Haven, CT
Dec. 31	Springfield, MA

1857

Jan. 1	Hartford, CT
Jan. 3	Boston, MA
Jan. 6	Providence, RI
Jan. 7	Worcester, MA
Jan. 8	Boston, MA
Jan. 9	Salem, MA
Jan. 10	Boston, MA
Jan. 12ˢ	Boston, MA
Jan. 13	Boston, MA
Jan. 14	New Bedford, MA
Jan. 15	Providence, RI
Jan. 16	Boston, MA
Jan. 17ˢ	Boston, MA
Jan. 17ᵐ	Boston, MA
Jan. 18	Boston, MA
Jan. 20ᵐ	Boston, MA
Jan. 21	Hartford, CT
Jan. 23	Albany, NY
Jan. 24	Troy, NY
Jan. 27	Albany, NY
Jan. 28	Troy, NY
Jan. 30	Philadelphia, PA
Feb. 2	Washington, DC
Feb. 3	Baltimore, MD

Feb. 4	Philadelphia, PA	Mar. 26	Boston, MA	May 11	Louisville, KY
Feb. 5[s]	Philadelphia, PA	Mar. 27[m]	Boston, MA	May 12	Lexington, KY
Feb. 5	Wilmington, DE	Mar. 27	Worcester, MA	May 13	Cincinnati, OH
Feb. 6	Lancaster, PA	Mar. 28	Boston, MA	May 14	Louisville, KY
Feb. 7	Philadelphia, PA	Mar. 29	Boston, MA	May 18	St. Louis, MO
Feb. 9	Harrisburg, PA	Mar. 30[m]	Boston, MA	May 19	St. Louis, MO
Feb. 11[s]	Philadelphia, PA	Mar. 30	Lowell, MA	May 21	St. Louis, MO
Feb. 11	Philadelphia, PA	Mar. 31	Boston, MA	May 22[m]	St. Louis, MO
Feb. 12	Washington, DC	Apr. 1	New Bedford, MA	May 22	St. Louis, MO
Feb. 13	Baltimore, MD	Apr. 2	Providence, RI	May 25	Chicago, IL
Feb. 14	Philadelphia, PA	Apr. 3[s]	Providence, RI	May 26	Chicago, IL
Feb. 16[s]	New York, NY	Apr. 3	Worcester, MA	May 27	Milwaukee, WI
Feb. 16	New York, NY	Apr. 4[m]	Boston, MA	May 28	Chicago, IL
Feb. 17	New Haven, CT	Apr. 4	Boston, MA	May 29[m]	Kenosha, WI
Feb. 18	New York, NY	Apr. 6	Lowell, MA	May 29	Milwaukee, WI
Feb. 19[s]	New York, NY	Apr. 7[s]	Boston, MA	May 30	Madison, WI
Feb. 19	Brooklyn, NY	Apr. 7	Boston, MA	June 1	Galena, IL
Feb. 20[m]	New York, NY	Apr. 8[m]	Providence, RI	June 2	Dubuque, IA
Feb. 20	New York, NY	Apr. 8	Providence, RI	June 4	Chicago, IL
Feb. 21	New York, NY	Apr. 9	Boston, MA	June 6	Detroit, MI
Feb. 24[m]	New York, NY	Apr. 10	New Bedford, MA	June 8	Detroit, MI
Feb. 24	New York, NY	Apr. 11	Boston, MA	June 9	Toledo, OH
Feb. 26[s]	New York, NY	Apr. 13	Salem, MA	June 10	Cleveland, OH
Feb. 26[m]	New York, NY	Apr. 14[m]	Boston, MA	June 12	Rochester, NY
Feb. 26	New York, NY	Apr. 15[m]	Hartford, CT	June 13	Buffalo, NY
Feb. 27[m]	New York, NY	Apr. 15	Hartford, CT	June 15[m]	Utica, NY
Feb. 27	Brooklyn, NY	Apr. 16[m]	New Haven, CT	June 15	Syracuse, NY
Feb. 28[s]	New York, NY	Apr. 16	New Haven, CT	June 16	Auburn, NY
Feb. 28	Williamsburg, NY	Apr. 17[m]	Northampton, MA	June 18	Hamilton, Ontario
Mar. 3[m]	New York, NY	Apr. 17	Springfield, MA	June 19	Toronto, Ontario
Mar. 3	New York, NY	Apr. 20[m]	Utica, NY	June 20	Kingston, Ontario
Mar. 4[m]	New York, NY	Apr. 20	Syracuse, NY	June 22	Montréal, Québec
Mar. 5[s]	Williamsburg, NY	Apr. 21	Rochester, NY	June 23	Montréal, Québec
Mar. 5[m]	New York, NY	Apr. 22	Buffalo, NY	June 25	Montréal, Québec
Mar. 5	New York, NY	Apr. 23	Toronto, Ontario	June 30	Québec, Québec
Mar. 6	Newark, NJ	Apr. 24[m]	Toronto, Ontario	July 1	Québec, Québec
Mar. 7	Brooklyn, NY	Apr. 24	Hamilton, Ontario	July 3	Burlington, VT
Mar. 10[m]	New York, NY	Apr. 25	Buffalo, NY	July 22	Cape May, NJ
Mar. 10	New York, NY	Apr. 27	Cleveland, OH	July 29	Saratoga Springs, NY
Mar. 11[s]	New York, NY	Apr. 28	Pittsburgh, PA		
Mar. 12[m]	New York, NY	Apr. 29	Pittsburgh, PA		
Mar. 12	New York, NY	Apr. 30	Wheeling, WV	Sept. 15	New York, NY
Mar. 13	New Haven, CT	May 1[s]	Wheeling, WV	Sept. 17	New York, NY
Mar. 16[m]	New York, NY	May 1	Zanesville, OH	Sept. 24	New York, NY
Mar. 16	New York, NY	May 2	Columbus, OH	Sept. 25	Philadelphia, PA
Mar. 18	Trenton, NJ	May 4	Cincinnati, OH	Sept. 26	Philadelphia, PA
Mar. 19[m]	New York, NY	May 5	Dayton, OH	Sept. 28	Baltimore, MD
Mar. 19	Brooklyn, NY	May 6	Cincinnati, OH	Sept. 29	Washington, DC
Mar. 20	New York, NY	May 7	Indianapolis, IN	Sept. 30	Baltimore, MD
Mar. 21	New York, NY	May 8	Cincinnati, OH	Oct. 2	New York, NY
Mar. 23	Hartford, CT	May 9	Louisville, KY	Oct. 3	Brooklyn, NY
Mar. 24	Boston, MA	May 11[s]	Louisville, KY	Oct. 9	New York, NY
Mar. 25[m]	Boston, MA				
Mar. 25	Providence, RI				

Date	Location	Date	Location	Date	Location
Oct. 10	New York, NY	Feb. 26ˢ	New Orleans, LA	May 21	Wheeling, WV
Oct. 14	Boston, MA	Feb. 26	New Orleans, LA	May 22	Columbus, OH
Oct. 23	New York, NY	Mar. 1ᵐ	New Orleans, LA	May 24	Cincinnati, OH
Oct. 29	Brooklyn, NY	Mar. 2ᵐ	New Orleans, LA	May 26	Cincinnati, OH
Oct. 30	New York, NY	Mar. 3	New Orleans, LA	May 27	Lexington, KY
Nov. 5	New York, NY	Mar. 5	New Orleans, LA	May 28	Louisville, KY
Nov. 11	Philadelphia, PA	Mar. 8	Natchez, MS	June 3	Nashville, TN
Nov. 13	Philadelphia, PA	Mar. 9	Natchez, MS	June 4ˢ	Nashville, TN
Nov. 16	Baltimore, MD	Mar. 12	Memphis, TN	June 4	Nashville, TN
Nov. 17	Washington, DC	Mar. 13	Memphis, TN	June 5	Nashville, TN
Nov. 18	Alexandria, VA	Mar. 17	St. Louis, MO	June 8	St. Louis, MO
Nov. 19	Baltimore, MD	Mar. 18	St. Louis, MO	June 9	St. Louis, MO
Nov. 21	Washington, DC	Mar. 20	Louisville, KY	June 10	Springfield, IL
Nov. 28	New York, NY	Mar. 22	Cincinnati, OH	June 12	Peoria, IL
Dec. 28	New York, NY	Mar. 23	Cincinnati, OH		
		Mar. 25	Pittsburgh, PA		
1858		Mar. 26	Cleveland, OH	**ANTON RUBINSTEIN**	
		Mar. 27	Buffalo, NY	**1872–73**	
Jan. 2	New York, NY	Apr. 3ᵐ	New York, NY		
Jan. 4	New York, NY	Apr. 5ᵐ	Brooklyn, NY	Sept. 23	New York, NY
Jan. 7	Charlottesville,	Apr. 12	New York, NY	Sept. 25	New York, NY
	VA	Apr. 13	New York, NY	Sept. 27	New York, NY
Jan. 8	Richmond, VA	Apr. 14	New York, NY	Sept. 28ᵐ	New York, NY
Jan. 9	Lynchburg, VA	Apr. 15	New York, NY	Sept. 30	Brooklyn, NY
Jan. 11	Lynchburg, VA	Apr. 16	New York, NY	Oct. 1	New York, NY
Jan. 12	Richmond, VA	Apr. 17	New York, NY	Oct. 3	New York, NY
Jan. 13	Petersburg, VA	Apr. 19	New York, NY	Oct. 4	New York, NY
Jan. 14	Richmond, VA	Apr. 20	New York, NY	Oct. 5ᵐ	New York, NY
Jan. 15	Norfolk, VA	Apr. 21	New York, NY	Oct. 7	New York, NY
Jan. 16	Norfolk, VA	Apr. 22ᵐ	New York, NY	Oct. 8	Brooklyn, NY
Jan. 19	Wilmington, NC	Apr. 23	New York, NY	Oct. 9ᵐ	New York, NY
Jan. 22	Charleston, SC	Apr. 24ᵐ	New York, NY	Oct. 10	Newark, NJ
Jan. 23	Columbia, SC	Apr. 25	New York, NY	Oct. 11	New York, NY
Jan. 25	Charleston, SC	Apr. 26	New York, NY	Oct. 12ᵐ	New York, NY
Jan. 26	Charleston, SC	Apr. 27	New York, NY	Oct. 14	Boston, MA
Jan. 27	Columbia, SC	Apr. 28	New York, NY	Oct. 15	Boston, MA
Jan. 28	Augusta, GA	Apr. 29ᵐ	New York, NY	Oct. 16ᵐ	Boston, MA
Jan. 29	Savannah, GA	Apr. 30	New York, NY	Oct. 17	Providence, RI
Jan. 30	Savannah, GA	May 1	New York, NY	Oct. 18	Boston, MA
Feb. 1	Charleston, SC	May 2	New York, NY	Oct. 19ᵐ	Boston, MA
Feb. 2	Charleston, SC	May 3	Albany, NY	Oct. 21	Springfield, MA
Feb. 3	Augusta, GA	May 4	Troy, NY	Oct. 22	Hartford, CT
Feb. 4	Atlanta, GA	May 5	Utica, NY	Oct. 23	New Haven, CT
Feb. 5	Macon, GA	May 6	Syracuse, NY	Oct. 24	New York, NY
Feb. 6	Columbus, GA	May 7	Rochester, NY	Oct. 25	New York, NY
Feb. 8	Montgomery, AL	May 8	Toronto, Ontario	Oct. 26ᵐ	New York, NY
Feb. 9	Montgomery, AL	May 10	Toronto, Ontario	Oct. 28	Philadelphia, PA
Feb. 11	Mobile, AL	May 11	Buffalo, NY	Oct. 29	Philadelphia, PA
Feb. 13	Mobile, AL	May 12	Hamilton,	Oct. 30	Philadelphia, PA
Feb. 15	New Orleans, LA		Ontario	Oct. 31	Baltimore, MD
Feb. 17	New Orleans, LA	May 13	Detroit, MI	Nov. 1	Baltimore, MD
Feb. 18	New Orleans, LA	May 14	Detroit, MI	Nov. 2	Baltimore, MD
Feb. 20	New Orleans, LA	May 15	Toledo, OH	Nov. 4	Washington, DC
Feb. 23ˢ	New Orleans, LA	May 17	Sandusky, OH	Nov. 5	Washington, DC
Feb. 24	New Orleans, LA	May 18	Cleveland, OH	Nov. 6	Wilmington, DE
Feb. 25ᵐ	New Orleans, LA	May 20	Pittsburgh, PA	Nov. 7	Philadelphia, PA

Date	Location	Date	Location	Date	Location
Nov. 8	Philadelphia, PA	Jan. 11	New York, NY	Mar. 21	Cincinnati, OH
Nov. 9[m]	Philadelphia, PA	Jan. 13[m]	New York, NY	Mar. 22[m]	Cincinnati, OH
Nov. 10	New York, NY	Jan. 14	Philadelphia, PA	Mar. 22	Cincinnati, OH
Nov. 11	Brooklyn, NY	Jan. 15	Philadelphia, PA	Mar. 24	Columbus, OH
Nov. 12	New York, NY	Jan. 16	Pittsburgh, PA	Mar. 25	Pittsburgh, PA
Nov. 13	New York, NY	Jan. 17	Steubenville, OH	Mar. 26	Pittsburgh, PA
Nov. 15[m]	New York, NY	Jan. 18	Pittsburgh, PA	Mar. 27	Harrisburg, PA
Nov. 15	New York, NY	Jan. 20	Indianapolis, IN	Mar. 28	Baltimore, MD
Nov. 16[m]	New York, NY	Jan. 21	Terre Haute, IN	Mar. 29	Washington, DC
Nov. 16	New York, NY	Jan. 22	St. Louis, MO	Mar. 31	New York, NY
Nov. 17	New York, NY	Jan. 23	St. Louis, MO	Apr. 1	New York, NY
Nov. 18	Albany, NY	Jan. 24	St. Louis, MO	Apr. 2[m]	New York, NY
Nov. 19	Troy, NY	Jan. 25[m]	St. Louis, MO	Apr. 2	Brooklyn, NY
Nov. 20	Utica, NY	Jan. 28	Mobile, AL	Apr. 3	New York, NY
Nov. 21	Syracuse, NY	Jan. 29	New Orleans, LA	Apr. 4	Philadelphia, PA
Nov. 22	Elmira, NY	Jan. 30	Mobile, AL	Apr. 5[m]	Philadelphia, PA
Nov. 23	Rochester, NY	Jan. 31	New Orleans, LA	Apr. 5	Philadelphia, PA
Nov. 25	Buffalo, NY	Feb. 1[m]	New Orleans, LA	Apr. 7	New Haven, CT
Nov. 27	Cleveland, OH	Feb. 2	New Orleans, LA	Apr. 8[m]	Farmington, CT
Nov. 28	Cleveland, OH	Feb. 3	New Orleans, LA	Apr. 8	Hartford, CT
Nov. 29	Columbus, OH	Feb. 5	New Orleans, LA	Apr. 9	Boston, MA
Nov. 30	Dayton, OH	Feb. 6[m]	New Orleans, LA	Apr. 10	Worcester, MA
Dec. 2	Chicago, IL	Feb. 7	New Orleans, LA	Apr. 11	Boston, MA
Dec. 3	Chicago, IL	Feb. 8[m]	New Orleans, LA	Apr. 12[m]	Boston, MA
Dec. 4	Chicago, IL	Feb. 9	New Orleans, LA	Apr. 14	Washington, DC
Dec. 5	Chicago, IL	Feb. 11	Memphis, TN	Apr. 15	Washington, DC
Dec. 6	Chicago, IL	Feb. 12	Memphis, TN	Apr. 16[m]	Washington, DC
Dec. 7[m]	Chicago, IL	Feb. 13	Nashville, TN	Apr. 16	Baltimore, MD
Dec. 9	Cincinnati, OH	Feb. 14	Nashville, TN	Apr. 17	Brooklyn, NY
Dec. 10	Cincinnati, OH	Feb. 15	Evansville, IN	Apr. 18[m]	New York, NY
Dec. 11	Louisville, KY	Feb. 17	St. Louis, MO	Apr. 18	Newark, NJ
Dec. 12	Louisville, KY	Feb. 18	St. Louis, MO	Apr. 19[m]	New York, NY
Dec. 13	Cincinnati, OH	Feb. 19	Springfield, IL	Apr. 19	New York, NY
Dec. 14[m]	Cincinnati, OH	Feb. 20	Bloomington, IL	Apr. 22	Montréal, Québec
Dec. 16	Indianapolis, IN	Feb. 21	Chicago, IL		
Dec. 17	Fort Wayne, IN	Feb. 22[m]	Chicago, IL	Apr. 23	Burlington, VT
Dec. 18	Detroit, MI	Feb. 23	Chicago, IL	Apr. 24	Troy, NY
Dec. 19	Detroit, MI	Feb. 24	Peoria, IL	Apr. 25	New York, NY
Dec. 20	Toronto, Ontario	Feb. 26	Burlington, IA	Apr. 26[m]	New York, NY
Dec. 21	Buffalo, NY	Feb. 27	Quincy, IL	Apr. 28	Albany, NY
Dec. 23	Providence, RI	Feb. 28	Jacksonville, IL	Apr. 29	Buffalo, NY
Dec. 24	Boston, MA	Mar. 3	Lexington, KY	Apr. 30	Cleveland, OH
Dec. 25	Boston, MA	Mar. 5[m]	Cincinnati, OH	May 1	Dayton, OH
Dec. 26	Hartford, CT	Mar. 6	Cleveland, OH	May 2	Akron, OH
Dec. 27	Boston, MA	Mar. 8	Titusville, PA	May 5	Toronto, Ontario
Dec. 28[m]	Boston, MA	Mar. 10	Toledo, OH	May 6	Hamilton, Ontario
Dec. 31	New York, NY	Mar. 11	Detroit, MI		
Jan. 2	Brooklyn, NY	Mar. 12	Grand Rapids, MI	May 8	Springfield, MA
Jan. 3	New York, NY			May 9	Portland, ME
Jan. 4[m]	New York, NY	Mar. 13	Kalamazoo, MI	May 10[m]	Boston, MA
Jan. 6	Albany, NY	Mar. 14	Milwaukee, WI	May 12[m]	New York, NY
Jan. 7	Poughkeepsie, NY	Mar. 15	Milwaukee, WI	May 12	Philadelphia, PA
		Mar. 17	Chicago, IL	May 13	Brooklyn, NY
Jan. 8	New York, NY	Mar. 18	Chicago, IL	May 14[m]	New York, NY
Jan. 9	New York, NY	Mar. 19[m]	Chicago, IL	May 15[m]	Boston, MA
Jan. 10	Newark, NJ	Mar. 20	Cincinnati, OH	May 16[m]	New York, NY

May 16	New York, NY
May 17m	New York, NY
May 19m	New York, NY
May 20m	New York, NY
May 21m	Boston, MA
May 21	Boston, MA
May 22	New York, NY

HANS VON BÜLOW
1875–76

Oct. 18	Boston, MA
Oct. 20	Boston, MA
Oct. 22	Boston, MA
Oct. 23m	Boston, MA
Oct. 25	Boston, MA
Oct. 26	Providence, RI
Oct. 28	Providence, RI
Oct. 29	Boston, MA
Oct. 30m	Boston, MA
Nov. 1	Worcester, MA
Nov. 3	Springfield, MA
Nov. 4	New Haven, CT
Nov. 5	Hartford, CT
Nov. 6m	Farmington, CT
Nov. 8	New Haven, CT
Nov. 9	Hartford, CT
Nov. 11	Bridgeport, CT
Nov. 15	New York, NY
Nov. 17	New York, NY
Nov. 19	New York, NY
Nov. 20m	New York, NY
Nov. 22	New York, NY
Nov. 23	Brooklyn, NY
Nov. 24	New York, NY
Nov. 26	New York, NY
Nov. 27m	New York, NY
Nov. 29	New York, NY
Dec. 1	New York, NY
Dec. 2	Brooklyn, NY
Dec. 3	New York, NY
Dec. 4m	New York, NY
Dec. 6	Baltimore, MD
Dec. 7	Washington, DC
Dec. 9	Washington, DC
Dec. 10	Baltimore, MD
Dec. 11m	Baltimore, MD
Dec. 13	Pittsburgh, PA
Dec. 14	Steubenville, OH
Dec. 15	Pittsburgh, PA

Dec. 17	Philadelphia, PA
Dec. 18m	Philadelphia, PA
Dec. 20	Newark, NJ
Dec. 21	Philadelphia, PA
Dec. 22	Philadelphia, PA
Dec. 23m	Philadelphia, PA
Dec. 27	New York, NY
Dec. 29	New York, NY
Dec. 30m	New York, NY
Dec. 31	New York, NY
Jan. 3	New York, NY
Jan. 5	New York, NY
Jan. 6	Brooklyn, NY
Jan. 7	New York, NY
Jan. 8m	New York, NY
Jan. 10	Boston, MA
Jan. 11	Boston, MA
Jan. 12	Boston, MA
Jan. 13	Boston, MA
Jan. 14	Boston, MA
Jan. 15m	Boston, MA
Jan. 17	Poughkeepsie, NY
Jan. 18	Troy, NY
Jan. 19	Albany, NY
Jan. 20	Ithaca, NY
Jan. 21	Rochester, NY
Jan. 22	Buffalo, NY
Jan. 24	Hamilton, Ontario
Jan. 25	Buffalo, NY
Jan. 26	Cleveland, OH
Jan. 28	Detroit, MI
Jan. 29	Detroit, MI
Jan. 31	Chicago, IL
Feb. 2	Chicago, IL
Feb. 3	Milwaukee, WI
Feb. 4	Chicago, IL
Feb. 5m	Chicago, IL
Feb. 7	Cincinnati, OH
Feb. 8	Cincinnati, OH
Feb. 9m	Cincinnati, OH
Feb. 10	St. Louis, MO
Feb. 11	St. Louis, MO
Feb. 12m	St. Louis, MO
Feb. 15	New Orleans, LA
Feb. 16	New Orleans, LA
Feb. 18	New Orleans, LA
Feb. 19m	New Orleans, LA
Feb. 21	New Orleans, LA
Feb. 22	New Orleans, LA

Feb. 23m	New Orleans, LA
Feb. 25m	New Orleans, LA
Feb. 28	Indianapolis, IN
Feb. 29	Indianapolis, IN
Mar. 2	Louisville, KY
Mar. 3	Louisville, KY
Mar. 6	Baltimore, MD
Mar. 7m	Baltimore, MD
Mar. 8	Washington, DC
Mar. 9m	Washington, DC
Mar. 10	Philadelphia, PA
Mar. 11m	Philadelphia, PA
Mar. 13	Philadelphia, PA
Mar. 14m	Philadelphia, PA
Mar. 15m	Philadelphia, PA
Mar. 20	New York, NY
Mar. 22	New York, NY
Mar. 23m	New York, NY
Mar. 24	New York, NY
Mar. 27	New York, NY
Mar. 29	New York, NY
Mar. 30m	New York, NY
Mar. 31	New York, NY
Apr. 1m	New York, NY
Apr. 3m	Boston, MA
Apr. 4	Boston, MA
Apr. 5	Boston, MA
Apr. 6m	Boston, MA
Apr. 7	Boston, MA
Apr. 8m	Boston, MA
Apr. 10	Portland, ME
Apr. 11	Salem, MA
Apr. 12	Springfield, MA
Apr. 13	Hartford, CT
Apr. 15m	New Haven, CT
Apr. 17	Troy, NY
Apr. 18	Albany, NY
Apr. 19	Utica, NY
Apr. 20	Syracuse, NY
Apr. 21	Rochester, NY
Apr. 22	Buffalo, NY
Apr. 24	Buffalo, NY
Apr. 25	Erie, PA
Apr. 26	Cleveland, OH
Apr. 28	Columbus, OH
May 3	Chicago, IL
May 4	Milwaukee, WI
May 5	Chicago, IL
May 6m	Chicago, IL
May 8	St. Louis, MO
May 9	St. Louis, MO

Appendix B

Rubinstein's and Bülow's Repertoire in America

Uppercase letters indicate major keys, lowercase indicate minor. Information appearing in brackets is based on editions documenting Rubinstein's historical concerts from the 1880s and on editions published by Bülow.

ANTON RUBINSTEIN'S REPERTOIRE IN AMERICA

(excluding his "Farewell Recitals")

Works for Solo Piano

Baroque

J. S. BACH

Chromatic Fantasia and Fugue
[Partita No. 1 in B♭]
  Giga
Well-Tempered Clavier (selections, including
  fugues in c, D)

HANDEL

Suite in A, [HWV 426]
  Gigue
Suite in d, [HWV 428]
  Air and Variations
Suite in E, HWV 430
  Air and Variations ("The Harmonious
    Blacksmith")

DOMENICO SCARLATTI

Cat's Fugue
Sonata

Classical

C. P. E. BACH

Rondo [=3rd movement from Sechs Clavier-
  Sonaten für Kenner und Liebhaber, Vol.
  1, No. 3 in b, H. 245]

HAYDN

Andante and Variations [in f, Hob. XVII:6]

MOZART

Rondo in a, K. 511

BEETHOVEN

Egmont Overture (transcr. Rubinstein)
Sonatas, including
  c♯ Op. 27/2 ("Moonlight")
  d   Op. 31/2 ("Tempest")
  C   Op. 53 ("Waldstein")

f　Op. 57 ("Appassionata")
c　Op. 111
Turkish March (from *The Ruins of Athens*)
　　(transcr. Rubinstein)

Romantic

FIELD

Nocturnes (selections, including E♭)

SCHUBERT

Minuet in b
Moments musicaux (selections)
Fantasy in C ("Wanderer")

WEBER

Momento capriccioso
Sonata No. 2 in A♭

MENDELSSOHN

Gondellied
Presto capriccio
Scherzo
Scherzo a capriccio
Songs without Words (selections, including a,
　　A♭, "Volkslied")
Variations sérieuses
Wedding March (from *A Midsummer Night's
　　Dream*) (transcr. Rubinstein)

CHOPIN

Ballades (selections, including g, A♭)
Berceuse
Etudes (selections, including a, c, c♯, E)
Fantaisie in f
Mazurkas (selections)
Nocturnes (selections, including D♭, c)
Polonaises (selections, including A♭)
Preludes (selections)
Scherzos (selections, including b)
Sonata in b♭
　　Marche funèbre

SCHUMANN

Carnaval, Op. 9
Phantasiestücke, Op. 12
　　Warum?
　　Des Abends
　　Traumes Wirren
Symphonic Etudes, Op. 13
Kreisleriana, Op. 16
Klavierstücke, Op. 32
　　Romanze
Studies for the Pedal Piano, Op. 56
　　(selections)
Waldscenen, Op. 82
　　Vogel als Prophet

Contemporaries of Rubinstein

LISZT

Réminiscences de *Don Juan*
Rossini transcriptions
　　La gita in gondola, La danza, La serenata
　　　　(from *Soirées musicales*)
Schubert transcriptions
　　Auf dem Wasser zu singen
　　Erlkönig
　　Soirées de Vienne: Valses-Caprices d'après
　　　　Schubert (selections)

HENSELT

Liebeslied, Op. 5/11
Si oiseau j'étais, Op. 2/6

RUBINSTEIN

Album de danses populaires des différentes
　　nations
　　Valse
Le bal
　　Contredanse (Quadrille)
　　Valse
Barcarolles (selections, including a, f, G, g)
Caprice
Etudes (selections, including C)
Impromptu
Kamenoi-Ostrow No. 7
Mélancolie
Mélodie in F
Miniatures
　　Menuet
　　Sérénade
　　Valse
　　Près du ruisseau
Nocturne
Nouvelle mélodie
Preludes and Fugues (selections, including A♭)
Romances (selections, including F)
Scherzo
Sérénade
Sérénade russe
Suite
　　Sarabande
　　Passepied
　　Courante
　　Gavotte
Tarantelle
Theme and Variations
Valse-Caprice

Works for Piano and Orchestra

J. S. BACH

Concerto for 3 Keyboards in d, BWV 1063

MOZART

Concerto in d, K. 466

BEETHOVEN

Concerto No. 4 in G
Concerto No. 5 in E♭

WEBER

Konzertstück in f

MENDELSSOHN

Concerto No. 1 in g

SCHUMANN

Concerto in a

LISZT

Concerto No. 1 in E♭

RUBINSTEIN

Concerto No. 2 in F
Concerto No. 3 in G
Concerto No. 4 in d

**Chamber Works
(for piano and strings unless otherwise
   specified)**

BEETHOVEN

Sonata for Violin and Piano, Op. 47
   ("Kreutzer")
Trio in B♭, Op. 97 ("Archduke")

HUMMEL

Septet for Winds, Strings, and Piano,
   Op. 74

SCHUBERT

Rondo for Violin and Piano, Op. 70
Trio in B♭, Op. 99

MENDELSSOHN

Trio No. 2 in c, Op. 66

SCHUMANN

Andante and Variations for 2 Pianos,
   Op. 46 (performed with Anna Mehlig)
Quartet in E♭, Op. 47
Quintet in E♭, Op. 44

RUBINSTEIN

Sonata No. 2 for Violin and Piano in a,
   Op. 19
Trio in g, Op. 15/1
Trio in B♭, Op. 52

RUBINSTEIN'S FAREWELL NEW YORK RECITALS

(all matinées except final recital)

{information in braces based on reviews}

1st Recital (12 May 1873)

J. S. BACH

Well-Tempered Clavier
   Preludes and Fugues {2 or 3}
[Partita No. 1 in B♭]
   Giga
Chromatic Fantasia and Fugue

C. P. E. BACH

Rondo [=3rd movement from Sechs Clavier-
   Sonaten für Kenner und Liebhaber, Vol.
   1, No. 3 in b, H. 245]

HANDEL

Suite in d, [HWV 428]
   Air and Variations
Suite in g, [HWV 432]
   Sarabande
   Passacaille
Suite in A, [HWV 426]
   Gigue
Suite in E, HWV 430
   Air and Variations ("The Harmonious
   Blacksmith")

HAYDN

Andante and Variations [in f, Hob. XVII:6]

DOMENICO SCARLATTI

Cat's Fugue
Sonata

MOZART

Fantasia in c, K. 475
Gigue in G, K. 574
Rondo in a, K. 511
Sonata in A, K. 331
   Rondo ("alla Turca")

2nd Recital (14 May 1873)

BEETHOVEN

Sonatas
   c♯   Op. 27/2 ("Moonlight")
   d   Op. 31/2 ("Tempest")
   C   Op. 53 ("Waldstein")
   f   Op. 57 ("Appassionata")
   E   Op. 109
   c   Op. 111
   {A♭   Op. 26, 1st movement as encore}

3rd Recital (16 May 1873)

SCHUBERT

Fantasy in C ("Wanderer")
Sonata in G, Op. 78
    Menuetto
Moments musicaux, Op. 94/1-3

WEBER

Sonata No. 2 in A♭
Momento capriccioso
Invitation to the Dance
Polacca brillante

MENDELSSOHN

Songs without Words in E, g, E♭, f♯, E♭, A♭, b, F,
    A, a, E
Scherzo a capriccio
Scherzo fantaisie
Variations sérieuses

4th Recital (17 May 1873)

SCHUMANN

Symphonic Etudes, Op. 13
Kreisleriana, Op. 16
Phantasiestücke, Op. 12
    Warum?
    Des Abends
    Traumes Wirren
Klavierstücke, Op. 32
    Romanze
Waldscenen, Op. 82
    Vogel als Prophet
Studies for the Pedal Piano, Op. 56
    a, A♭, b
Carnaval, Op. 9

5th Recital (19 May 1873)

CHOPIN

Fantaisie in f
Preludes in e, A, b, D♭, d
Mazurkas in f♯, e♭
Waltzes in E♭, a, A♭, {a}, c♯, D♭
Polonaises in A, c♯, A♭
Nocturnes in F♯, g, A♭, B, f, D♭, c
Impromptu in A♭
Berceuse
Tarantelle
Scherzo
Ballades in g, F, A♭
Etudes in A♭, f, c, c♯, E♭, c, A♭, E, a
Sonata in b♭
    Marche funèbre
{Reviews disagree on exact contents of
    program; Rubinstein probably added
    two polonaises and two waltzes, and
    omitted several etudes.}

6th Recital (20 May 1873)

FIELD

Nocturnes in E♭, A, B♭

HENSELT

Orage, Op. 2/1
Berceuse
La fontaine, Op. 6/2
Liebeslied, Op. 5/11
Si oiseau j'étais, Op. 2/6

THALBERG

Etude in a
Fantasia on *Don Giovanni*

LISZT

Réminiscences de *Don Juan*
Schubert transcriptions
    Morgenständchen
    Auf dem Wasser zu singen
    Erlkönig
    Valse {No. 6} (from *Soirées de Vienne*)
Meyerbeer transcription
    Le moine
Rossini transcriptions
    La gita in gondola, La regata veneziana, La
        serenata, La danza (from *Soirées
        musicales*)
    Cujus animam (from Stabat Mater)
Réminiscences de *Lucia di Lammermoor*
Valse impromptu in A♭
Hungarian Rhapsody in D♭

7th Recital (22 May 1873)

RUBINSTEIN

Prelude and Fugue in A♭
Preludes in E, b
Theme and Variations
Mélodies in F, B
Album des danses populaires des différentes
        nations
    Valse
    Mazurka
Barcarolles in f, G, a
Romances in F, A♭
Tarantelle
Le bal
    Valse
    Polonaise
Suite
    Sarabande
    Passepied
    Courante
    Gavotte
Sérénade russe
Album de Peterhof
    Caprice russe

Nouvelle mélodie
Impromptu
Nocturne in G♭
Scherzo
Miniatures
    Sérénade
    Près du ruisseau
Etudes in f, F, C
Nocturne in A♭
Variations on "Yankee Doodle"
{at least several and as many as eight of the
    above works omitted}

HANS VON BÜLOW'S REPERTOIRE IN AMERICA

Works for Solo Piano

Baroque

J. S. BACH

Chromatic Fantasia and Fugue
English Suite No. 5
    Sarabande
    Passepied
English Suite No. 6
    Gavotte
Italian Concerto
Prelude and Fugue for Organ in a, BWV 543
    (transcr. Liszt)

HANDEL

Chaconne in F, [HWV 485]
Suite in d, [HWV 428]
Suite in f, HWV 433
    Prelude and Fugue

DOMENICO SCARLATTI

Cat's Fugue

Classical

GLUCK

Gavotte (from *Don Juan*)

HAYDN

Rondo [=Fantasia in C, Hob. XVII:4]

MOZART

Fantasia in c, [K. 396/385f]
Minuet [in D, K. 355/576b]
Gigue in G, K. 574
Sonata in F

BEETHOVEN

Six Variations on an Original Theme in F,
    Op. 34
"Eroica" Variations, Op. 35
32 Variations on an Original Theme in c, WoO
    80
Fantasia, Op. 77
Bagatelles, Opp. 119, 126 (selections)

Diabelli Variations, Op. 120
Rondo a capriccio, Op. 129
Sonatas
    c   Op. 13 ("Pathétique")
    A♭ Op. 26
    E♭ Op. 27/1
    c♯ Op. 27/2 ("Moonlight")
    d   Op. 31/2 ("Tempest")
    E♭ Op. 31/3
    f   Op. 57 ("Appassionata")
    E♭ Op. 81a ("Les Adieux")
    A   Op. 101
    B♭ Op. 106 ("Hammerklavier")
    E   Op. 109
    A♭ Op. 110

Romantic

FIELD

Nocturne No. 4 in A

SCHUBERT

Ave Maria (transcr. Liszt)
Impromptus, Op. 90/2-3, Op. 142/2,4
Sonata in A, Op. post.

MENDELSSOHN

Songs without Words (selections, including
    nos. 3, 19, 21, 30, 34)
Capriccio in f♯, Op. 5
Sieben Charakterstücke, Op. 7
    Leicht und luftig
Caprice in E, Op. 33/2
Prelude and Fugue in e, Op. 35/1
Variations sérieuses, Op. 54
Variations in E♭, Op. 82

CHOPIN

Allegro de concert, Op. 46
Ballade in g, Op. 23
Berceuse, Op. 57
Chant polonais (transcr. Liszt)
Impromptus, Opp. 29, 36
Introduction and Variations on "Je vends des
    scapulaires" from Hérold's *Ludovic*,
    Op. 12
Mazurkas (selections, including 2 from Op. 50)
Nocturnes, Opp. 9/3, 27/2, 37/2, 48/2
Polonaises, Opp. 44, 53
Rondo for 2 Pianos, Op. 73
Scherzo in c♯, Op. 39
Sonata in b, Op. 58
Tarantelle, Op. 43
Waltzes, Opp. 34/1-3, 42

SCHUMANN

Phantasiestücke, Op. 12
    Des Abends
    Grillen

Kreisleriana, Op. 16
Blumenstück, Op. 19
Novelletten, Op. 21 (selections, including
    no. 7)
Nachtstücke, Op. 23 (selections)
Faschingsschwank aus Wien, Op. 26
Romanzen, Op. 28 (selections, including no. 2)
Sonata No. 3 in f

Contemporaries of Bülow

LISZT

Années de pèlerinage, première année, Suisse
    Au lac de Wallenstadt
    Au bord d'une source
    Eglogue
Harmonies poétiques et religieuses
    Cantique d'amour
Hungarian Rhapsody No. 12
Mazurka brillante
Polonaise in E
Rhapsodie espagnole
Soirées de Vienne: Valses-Caprices d'après
    Schubert (selections, including nos. 3,
    4, and 6)
Transcendental Etude No. 9 (Ricordanza)
Valse impromptu
Venezia e Napoli
    Gondoliera
    Tarantella
Zwei Konzertetüden (Waldesrauschen,
    Gnomenreigen)

WAGNER

Pilgrims' Chorus (from *Tannhäuser*) (transcr.
    Liszt)
Spinning Song (from *The Flying Dutchman*)
    (transcr. Liszt)

RAFF

Suite in e, Op. 72
    Prelude and Fugue

RUBINSTEIN

Le bal
    Valse
Barcarolle No. 4
Prelude and Fugue in Free Style, Op. 53/3

BRAHMS

Variations and Fugue on a Theme by Handel,
    Op. 24

Works for Piano and Orchestra

J. S. BACH

Concerto for 2 Keyboards in C, BWV 1061
Concerto for 3 Keyboards in d, BWV 1063
Concerto for 4 Keyboards in a, BWV 1065

BEETHOVEN

Concerto No. 4 in G
Concerto No. 5 in E♭

WEBER

Konzertstück in f
Polonaise brillante, Op. 72 (arr. for piano and
    orchestra by Liszt)

SCHUBERT

Wanderer Fantasy (arr. for piano and orchestra
    by Liszt)

MENDELSSOHN

Capriccio brillant, Op. 22

LISZT

Concerto No. 1 in E♭
Fantasia on Hungarian Folk Tunes
Fantasia on Themes from Beethoven's *Ruins of
    Athens*

HENSELT

Concerto in f, Op. 16

RAFF

Concerto in c, Op. 185

RUBINSTEIN

Concerto No. 3 in G

TCHAIKOVSKY

Concerto No. 1 in b♭ (world premiere)

Chamber Works
(for piano and strings unless otherwise
    specified)

MOZART

Trio in E, K. 542
Quartet in g, K. 478
Quintet in E♭ for Winds and Piano, K. 452

BEETHOVEN

Sonata for Violin and Piano, Op. 47
    ("Kreutzer")
Trio in E♭, Op. 70/2

SPOHR

Trio No. 3 in a, Op. 124
Quintet in D, Op. 130

HUMMEL

Septet for Winds, Strings, and Piano, Op. 74

SCHUBERT

Rondo for Violin and Piano, Op. 70

CHOPIN

Introduction and Polonaise for Violoncello and
    Piano, Op. 3

SCHUMANN

Quintet in E♭, Op. 44

RAFF

Trio No. 2 in G, Op. 112
Quintet in a, Op. 107

RUBINSTEIN

Sonata No. 1 in D for Violoncello and Piano,
   Op. 18
Quintet in F for Winds and Piano, Op. 55

SAINT-SAËNS

Suite for Violoncello and Piano, Op. 16
Quintet in a, Op. 14

RHEINBERGER

Quartet in E♭, Op. 38

NOTES

ABBREVIATIONS

BDET	*Boston Daily Evening Transcript*	*NYDTr*	*New-York Daily Tribune*
BET	*Boston Evening Transcript*	*NYEM*	*New York Evening Mirror*
BP	*Boston Post*	*NYEP*	*New York Evening Post*
DJM	*Dwight's Journal of Music*	*NYH*	*New York Herald*
Fm	*La France musicale*	*NYS*	*New York Sun*
MCNYE	*Morning Courier and New-York*	*NYT*	*New-York Times*
	Enquirer	*NYW*	*New York World*
MTR	*The Music Trade Review*	*PI*	*Philadelphia Inquirer*
NODP	*New Orleans Daily Picayune*	*PPL*	*Philadelphia Public Ledger*
NYDT	*New-York Daily Times*		

Page and column numbers are supplied for most newspapers from the 1870s, when many of them for the first time are longer than four pages.

Information on American premieres has been based on H. Earle Johnson, *First Performances in America to 1900* (1979). Biographical information has frequently been drawn from Stanley Sadie, ed., *The New Grove Dictionary of Music and Musicians* (1980; 2d ed., 2001) and, for many of the American musicians, from H. Wiley Hitchcock and Stanley Sadie, eds., *The New Grove Dictionary of American Music* (1986).

PRELUDE: THE NEW WORLD BECKONS

1. Richard Crawford, "Professions and Patronage II: Performing," in *The American Musical Landscape* (Berkeley: University of California Press, 1993), 73. Crawford points out in his intriguing analysis of performance trends in American history that "European dominance went unchallenged" until "Americans discovered ways to present performing styles they themselves had invented" (p. 76), such as blackface minstrelsy, a genre created at the precise moment European virtuosos were beginning to visit America

with a vengeance. Previously, native-born American musicians were more likely to be active in rural areas, devoting their energies to composing and performing sacred music.

2. Gustave Chouquet, "De l'Amérique au point de vue musical," *Fm* 8 (2 February 1845): 37–38; A. Pontécoulant, "Une révolution dans la marche des astres," *Fm* 9 (15 November 1846): 371. Translations are mine except where noted.

3. On Frances Trollope, see Carol J. Oja, "'Trollopiana': David Claypoole Johnston Counters Frances Trollope's Views on American Music," *College Music Symposium* 21 (1981): 94–102; Gungl's statements on America in *Neue Berliner Musikzeitung* 3 (28 February 1849): 70–71, trans. in *DJM* 2 (18 December 1852): 83–84. Alexander W. Thayer wrote indignantly of Gungl's accusations: "And what did he do to improve that taste? Gave full-priced concerts and filled his programmes with polkas and galops; and would seem to have avoided all great names as if he feared that Gungl would suffer by contrast" (*DJM* 1 [25 September 1852]: 196). See also Roger L. Beck and Richard K. Hansen, "Josef Gungl and his Celebrated American Tour: November 1848 to May 1849," *Studia musicologica academiae scientiarum hungaricae* 36 (1995): 55–72.

4. Fry in *The Musical World and New York Musical Times* 5 (26 March 1853): 196, quoted in *DJM* 2 (2 April 1853): 202; Louis Moreau Gottschalk, *Notes of a Pianist,* ed. Jeanne Behrend (New York: Alfred A. Knopf, 1964; reprint, New York: Da Capo Press, 1979), 52. Later in his journal Gottschalk quotes Zimmermann as saying that "America was the country of railroads but not of musicians" (p. 221).

5. Henry Raynor, *Music and Society since 1815* (London: Barrie & Jenkins, 1976), 54; Hastings in *Western Recorder* 3 (8 August 1826): 128.

6. T. B. Sivori, who traveled to America with his brother, the violinist Camillo Sivori, confirmed the terrors of an ocean voyage in a letter written to a friend upon their arrival in New York (30 July 1846): "We have just arrived in safety, after experiencing a most terrible voyage for nineteen days. We encountered three distinct hurricanes; the last, above all, most terrific, which lasted forty-eight hours, in momentary expectation of losing our lives, the loss of which, at times, appeared less terrible than death itself" (*The Musical World* 21 [7 November 1846]: 566–67).

7. The American exploits of only two of these performers, Ole Bull and Jenny Lind, have been carefully documented; see Inez Bull, *Ole Bull's Activities in the United States between 1843 and 1880* (Smithtown, N.Y.: Exposition Press, 1982); Mortimer Smith, *The Life of Ole Bull* (Princeton: Princeton University Press for the American-Scandinavian Foundation, 1943; reprint, Westport, Conn.: Greenwood Press, 1973); Einar Haugen and Camilla Cai, *Ole Bull: Norway's Romantic Musician and Cosmopolitan Patriot* (Madison: University of Wisconsin Press, 1993); W. Porter Ware and Thaddeus C. Lockard, Jr., *P. T. Barnum Presents Jenny Lind* (Baton Rouge: Louisiana State University Press, 1980). In addition, the important phenomenon of touring opera troupes, more prevalent than one might imagine, has been treated in a groundbreaking study: Katherine K. Preston, *Opera on the Road: Traveling Opera Troupes in the United States, 1825–60* (Urbana: University of Illinois Press, 1993). Preston also surveys many of the musical immigrants and visitors in "Art Music from 1800 to 1860," in *The Cambridge History of American Music,* ed. David Nicholls (Cambridge: Cambridge University Press, 1998), 186–213.

8. *NYH,* 21 October 1845.

9. Production figures in Arthur Loesser, *Men, Women and Pianos: A Social History* (New York: Simon and Schuster, 1954; reprint, New York: Dover Publications, 1990), 468–69, 492, 511–12; "Fashionable Follies," *The Western Monthly Review* 3 (February 1830): 403; Thomas Low Nichols, *Forty Years of American Life, 1821–1861* (New York: Stackpole Sons, 1937), 190.

10. See Judith Tick, *American Women Composers before 1870* (Ann Arbor: UMI Research Press, 1983), chaps. 1–4; Adrienne Fried Block, assisted by Nancy Stewart, "Women in American Music, 1800–1918," in *Women & Music: A History,* ed. Karin Pendle, 2d ed. (Bloomington: Indiana University Press, 2001), 193–223, especially 198–99; "Music as an Accomplishment," in Carol Neuls-Bates, ed., *Women in Music: An Anthology of Source Readings from the Middle Ages to the Present,* rev. ed. (Boston: Northeastern University Press, 1996), 73–79.

11. W. Nixon, *A Guide to Instruction on the Pianoforte* (Cincinnati: Josiah Drake, 1834), excerpted in *The American Musical Journal* 1 (November 1835): 283–85; *DJM* 23 (17 October 1863): 120; *Newark Daily Advertiser,* reprinted in *The World of Music* 1 (30 April 1840): 56, quoted in Mary Wallace Davidson, "Mid-Nineteenth-Century American Periodicals: A Case Study," *Notes* 54 (1997): 375. Almost forty year later, the same point is being made: "There is no social disease so wide-spread, so virulent, and so fatal in its attack, as the piano mania. Before a girl is born, nowadays, she is predestined to sit and exact dreadful screechings and wailings from some unhappy instrument, for at least ten years of her natural life. No question as to whether she possesses an ear, and no consideration for the ears of other people, is permitted to interfere with the decree" ("The Piano Mania," *MTR* 3 [18 January 1877]: 93).

12. George F. Root, *The Story of a Musical Life* (Cincinnati: The John Church Co., 1891; reprint, New York: Da Capo Press, 1970), 10.

13. *DJM* 10 (11 October 1856): 14; information on Wallace's years in the United States in Kathleen Hellyar Myers, "William Vincent Wallace: Life and Works" (Ph.D. diss., Bryn Mawr College, 1980), 49–56, 122–40, and Robert Phelan, *William Vincent Wallace: A Vagabond Composer* (Waterford, Ireland: Celtic Publications, 1994), 29–36, 48–53; Root, *Story of a Musical Life,* 16–17.

CHAPTER 1: THE LION STALKS AMERICA

1. *The Biography of Leopold de Meyer* (London: Palmer and Clayton, 1845), 3–4.

2. *The Musical World* 19 (11 July 1844): 233; *Journal de Francfort* quoted in *The Musical World* 19 (17 October 1844): 344; *L'Observateur* quoted in *The Musical World* 19 (5 December 1844): 399.

3. Quotation from *Revue et gazette musicale* 12 (26 January 1845): 30; statistics in *Revue et gazette musicale* 12 (2 March 1845): 71.

4. John Sullivan Dwight, "Musical Review: *The Biography of Leopold de Meyer,*" *The Harbinger* 2 (13 December 1845): 11.

5. *The Musical World* 20 (31 July 1845): 369, and 20 (18 September 1845): 454.

6. *NYDTr,* 20 October 1845; Scharfenberg quoted in *NYH,* 20 October 1845.

7. *NYS,* 22 October 1845; *NYH,* 21 October 1845; *The Broadway Journal* 2 (1 November 1845): 261.

8. The only pieces by other composers on De Meyer's American programs were his own arrangements of Rossini's Overture to *William Tell* and Félicien David's *Le Désert,* the latter for two pianos. With guest artists he also performed two duos for violin and piano—one on themes from *William Tell* composed by Bériot and George Osborne and one based on *La Sonnambula* by Bériot and Benedict. The *Broadway Journal* considered De Meyer's performance of the *William Tell* Overture to be "something so beautiful as to be indescribable" (2 [15 November 1845]: 291).

9. The review of De Meyer's first solo recital in Paris (14 February 1845) continued: "You cannot believe that L. de Meyer can produce such extraordinary effects with ten fingers; it is truly miraculous. The piece had to be repeated three times in the same concert; it was a success, an immense success, such as we have not seen in Paris for a long time" (*Fm* 8 [23 February 1845]: 57).

10. *Journal des débats,* 4 March 1845. On De Meyer's association with Berlioz, who orchestrated the *Marche marocaine* as well as the pianist's *Marche d'Isly,* see R. Allen Lott, "A Berlioz Premiere in America: Leopold de Meyer and the *Marche d'Isly,*" *19th-Century Music* 8 (Spring 1985): 226–30.

11. John Sullivan Dwight, "Musical Review: Leopold de Meyer," *The Harbinger* 1 (29 November 1845): 397; Richard Grant White in *MCNYE,* 30 October 1845.

12. *NYEP,* 29 October 1845; *NYDTr,* 20 October 1845. The *Musical World,* in a review of the pianist's appearance at a London Philharmonic Concert, claimed: "Perhaps Leopold de Meyer is the only pianist on record, who, after the performance of an orchestra of seventy performers, can play with such immense power as to make the audience entirely forget the colossal force of the band" (20 [12 June 1845]: 278).

13. John Sullivan Dwight, "De Meyer Again in Boston," *The Harbinger* 3 (24 October 1846): 317. Margaret Fuller made a similar analogy: De Meyer's "success is the top bubble on the champagne, and stimulates the hearer like that sparkling draught" (*NYDTr,* 2 February 1846).

14. Philip Hone, *The Diary of Philip Hone, 1828–1851,* ed. Allan Nevins (New York: Dodd, Mead, 1927; reprint, New York: Arno Press, 1970), 573; *New York Morning Telegraph,* 12 November 1846; attendance in *NYDTr,* 8 November 1845; applause in *NYEP,* 8 November 1845; ovation in *The Broadway Journal* 2 (15 November 1845): 291.

15. *MCNYE,* 7 February 1846; *Yankee Doodle* 1 (1846–47): 165.

16. Hill in Howard Shanet, *Philharmonic: A History of New York's Orchestra* (Garden City, N.Y.: Doubleday, 1975), 82; *Marche marocaine* advertisement in *NYH,* 10 November 1845; *La danse du sérail* in *MCNYE,* 15 November 1845; *The Battle of New Orleans* in *NYH,* 14 November 1845.

17. Harold C. Schonberg, *The Great Pianists,* rev. and updated ed. (New York: Simon and Schuster, 1987), 190; *Brooklyn Star* quoted in *The Albion,* 1 November 1845; Richard Hoffman, *Some Musical Recollections of Fifty Years* (New York: Charles Scribner's Sons, 1910; reprint, Detroit: Information Coordinators, 1976), 75; *NODP,* 18 April 1846; *The Musical Gazette* 1 (9 November 1846): 165. Johnson described De Meyer in some detail: "He would put on such an odd 'phiz' as he glanced to various parts of the audience, while his fingers were flying over the keys, like lightning over the telegraph wires. He would give the orchestra such a curious look, and then roll his eyes about the house again, whilst his wrists, arms, shoulders, and even his whole body, was engaged with might and main in pummeling the instrument before him. In every piece the sweat fairly poured from his face, which we took to be a part of the

performance. And then at the conclusion of each piece he *did* retire with so many smirks and smiles upon his good-humored countenance dodging as well as he could the numerous wreaths and bouquets which were thrown at him, that taking it altogether, it was with difficulty we could keep from 'roaring right out.'"

18. *Rochester Daily American,* 8 August 1846; *New-York Commercial Advertiser,* 8 November 1845.

19. *The Musical Gazette* 1 (23 November 1846): 173.

20. A New York letter quoted in *BDET,* 21 November 1845; *NYS,* 22 October 1845; Hoffman, *Some Musical Recollections,* 75.

21. William Mason, *Memories of a Musical Life* (New York: The Century Co., 1901; reprint, New York: Da Capo Press, 1970), 19–20; John Sullivan Dwight, "Musical Review: Leopold de Meyer," *The Harbinger* 1 (29 November 1845): 396–97. Mason later studied in Europe with Dreyschock, Liszt, and others, but reported that the technique of arm weight was virtually unknown: "During my whole stay abroad none of my teachers or their pupils, with many of whom I was intimately associated, seemed to know anything about the importance of the upper-arm muscles, the practical knowledge of which I had acquired through the playing of Leopold de Meyer" (p. 69).

22. John Sullivan Dwight, "Musical Review: Leopold de Meyer," *The Harbinger* 1 (29 November 1845): 396–97; New York newspaper, Henry C. Timm Scrapbook (Music Division, New York Public Library); *Charleston Courier,* 1 April 1846; *NODP,* 18 April 1846.

23. The *Musical World* of London stated that "De Meyer, with equal powers of execution to those so transcendantly possessed by Thalberg and Liszt, surpasses both in the delicacy of his touch and the purity of his tone" (20 [29 May 1845]: 259).

24. Audience enthusiasm in *BDET,* 22 November 1845; attendance in "Boston Correspondence," *NYH,* 27 November 1845; injury in *BDET,* 24 and 25 November 1845, and 30 December 1845; *The American Journal of Music, and Musical Visitor* 4 (22 January 1846): 141.

25. *NYEP,* 13 February 1846; New York newspaper, Timm Scrapbook. The *Post* (6 February 1846) claimed that for the first concert the Tabernacle was crowded with "one of the largest and most brilliant audiences we ever saw in that building." The second concert was attended by about two thousand people (*Morris's National Press: A Journal for Home* 1 [21 February 1846]: 2).

26. Leopold de Meyer, Letter to Joseph Fischhof, 7 February 1846 (Wiener Stadt- und Landesbibliothek).

27. In Philadelphia, the Musical Fund Hall, which seated almost fifteen hundred people, was "filled with the most brilliant audiences" for his first two concerts (*Philadelphia Daily Chronicle,* 28 February 1846). The third, however, attracted only five hundred people (Musical Fund Society, Memorandum Book: Musical Fund Hall, March 1, 1837–September 30, 1847, Historical Society of Pennsylvania, Philadelphia). His second concert in Baltimore attracted about fifteen hundred people to a hall that could comfortably seat only twelve hundred ("Baltimore Correspondence," *NYH,* 15 March 1846). The first of his two Washington concerts was "very crowded" with an "elegant assemblage" (*Washington Daily Union,* 19 March 1846).

28. *PPL,* 25 February 1846; applause in "Washington Correspondence," *Richmond Enquirer,* 24 March 1846; "Washington Correspondence," *NYH,* 21 March 1846.

29. In the fall of 1846, the comic magazine *Yankee Doodle* issued a mock petition to "Signor Camillo Sivori, Prince Leopold de Meyer, Baron Henry von Herz, and Every Other Most Extraordinary Artist in the World, Who May Now Be in the United States, or Intends Ever to Come into Them," which requested the visiting artists to leave such national airs as "Hail, Columbia" and "Yankee Doodle" alone. "Translate them not into Italian, sweet and plaintive though it be; and oh, render them not in German! Commit not upon them the sacrilege of putting their rough and coarse but still shapely limbs into the trowsers of fantasia or the petticoats of capriccio" (1 [24 October 1846]: 30).

30. Philadelphia newspaper quoted in *NYH,* 28 February 1846; *Baltimore Sun,* 12 March 1846.

31. *NYH,* 21 October 1845; *New Orleans Daily Delta,* 17 April 1846.

32. *Saratoga Whig,* 17 August 1846, quoted in *NYH,* 19 August 1846; *Pittsburgh Daily Commercial Journal,* 8 July 1846.

CHAPTER 2: DE MEYER IN THE SOUTH AND MIDWEST

1. Personal Erards in *Biography of Leopold de Meyer,* 17; epithet in *The Musical World* 20 (17 July 1845): 344, also quoted in *BDET,* 20 November 1845; receipt of piano in *NYH,* 12 February 1846; *PPL,* 21 February 1846.

2. The English pianist Richard Hoffman, who immigrated to the United States in 1847, stated that

during this period he generally "played upon a 'square,' as the piano manufacturers did not make a 'grand' except to order, and all foreign pianists brought their own instruments with them" (*Some Musical Recollections,* 97).

3. *Pittsburgh Daily Commercial Journal,* 2 July 1846; *Rochester Daily American,* 28 July 1846; *Saint Louis Reveille,* 7 March 1847, also quoted in *NYH,* 26 March 1847.

4. Lack of piano in *NYH,* 24 April 1846; transport of pianos in *NODP,* 4 and 11 April 1846; sale of piano in *NODP,* 30 April 1846. The piano was on display at the music store of Charles Horst, who soon announced that he had purchased the piano himself and would dispose of it by selling chances (*NODP,* 2 May 1846).

5. Piano shell anecdote in *Saint Louis Reveille,* 7 March 1847, also quoted in *NYH,* 26 March 1847; tuners in *Daily Cincinnati Commercial,* 27 April 1847, and *Saint Louis Reveille,* 19 March 1847.

6. *Mobile Register and Journal,* 16 April 1846. Reitheimer's name does not officially appear in any publicity until July 1846 in Rochester, where he signed an advertisement for De Meyer's concert as his *chargé d'affaires* (*Rochester Daily American,* 28 July 1846), a pretentious title that would be frequently ridiculed by the press.

7. *Saint Louis Reveille,* 29 May 1846.

8. *NODP,* 24 April 1846.

9. *The Autobiography of William Robyn,* edited and annotated by Ernst C. Krohn, reprinted in *Missouri Music* (New York: Da Capo Press, 1971), 270–71; *Daily Cincinnati Commercial,* 20 June 1846.

10. *NODP,* 9 May 1846; *Cincinnati Daily Enquirer,* 25 June 1846.

11. *Daily Cincinnati Commercial,* 22 June 1846; *NODP,* 18 April 1846.

12. *Nashville Daily Union,* 3 April 1847; *NODP,* 16 April 1846; *Montreal Morning Courier,* 7 August 1846.

13. *The American Review* 4 (December 1846): 647; *DJM* 4 (10 December 1853): 76; *Cincinnati Times,* 5 May 1857, quoted in *Chicago Daily Democratic Press,* 22 May 1857; Gottschalk, *Notes of a Pianist,* 239.

14. Maretzek, *Crotchets and Quavers,* 121–22; *Buffalo Commercial Advertiser* quoted in *New York Musical Pioneer* 1 (1 November 1855): 19.

15. *New-York Musical Review and Choral Advocate* 5 (17 August 1854): 288; *NODP,* 24 April 1846.

16. In Richmond "a large and brilliant audience" heard the pianist; in Mobile "an immense throng" attended one of his concerts and for another "many people were obliged to go away unable to obtain admittance"; in St. Louis a "large and fashionable assemblage" turned out; a Cincinnati concert was "full to overflowing"; his two appearances in Pittsburgh "were attended by the largest and most fashionable audiences ever drawn by any artist"; and his concert in Saratoga Springs was "crowded to suffocation" (*Richmond Enquirer,* 27 March 1846; Mobile reports in *NODP,* 3 May and 21 April 1846; *St. Louis New Era,* 28 May 1846, quoted in *NYH,* 7 June 1846; *Daily Cincinnati Commercial,* 17 June 1846; *Pittsburgh Daily Commercial Journal,* 9 July 1846; *Saratoga Whig,* 17 August 1846, quoted in *NYH,* 19 August 1846).

17. Serenade in *NYH,* 24 April 1846; first concert in *NODP,* 17 April 1846, and *New-Orleans Bee,* 17 April 1846; second concert in *New Orleans Daily Tropic,* 21 April 1846; fourth concert in *NODP,* 7 May 1846.

18. *New-Orleans Bee,* 18 April 1846; *Toronto Patriot,* 4 August 1846; William Cullen Bryant, Letter to the *Evening Post,* 24 July 1846, published in *NYEP,* 1 August 1846, reprinted in *The Letters of William Cullen Bryant, Volume II: 1836–1849,* ed. William Cullen Bryant II and Thomas G. Voss (New York: Fordham University Press, 1977), 438.

19. *Cincinnati Morning Herald,* 22 April 1847, quoted in Charles R. Wyrick, "Concert and Criticism in Cincinnati, 1840–1850" (M.M. thesis, College-Conservatory of Music, University of Cincinnati, 1965), 104; *Louisville Daily Democrat,* 10 June 1846.

Chapter 3: The Lion Tamed

1. *The Musical World* 21 (28 November 1846): 601–2, quoted in *The Musical Gazette* 1 (4 January 1847): 194; confirmation in *The Musical Gazette* 1 (4 January 1847): 196; *PPL,* 17 February 1846; *The Song Journal* 3 (January 1873): 428.

2. Burkhardt claimed he should have been paid $25 for a translation, but Reitheimer paid him only $10; he was awarded the remaining $15. A detailed summary of the case appears in *NYEM,* 12 November 1846; Burkhardt's account of his association with De Meyer is in the *New York Morning Telegraph,* 11 November 1846. De Meyer had published earlier a "Notice To My Brother Artists," which warned of

"an obscure individual," who claimed to have influence with the press and forced his services on artists (*NYH,* 14 October 1846); according to Burkhardt's account, De Meyer was referring to him. Fortunately for De Meyer, this potentially damaging episode occurred a full week after his final New York appearance and could not harm attendance at his concerts.

3. *MCNYE,* 14 February 1846. George Templeton Strong recorded in his diary on the day of De Meyer's first concert: "I took it for granted from the outrageous puffing the *Herald* has been diligently bestowing on him that he was an editor-bribing quack, but, whether he has subsidized James Gordon Bennett or not, there's no quackery in his playing" (quoted in Vera Brodsky Lawrence, *Strong on Music: The New York Music Scene in the Days of George Templeton Strong, 1836–1875, Volume 1: Resonances, 1836–1850* [New York: Oxford University Press, 1988], 312). Lawrence's three-volume edition of Strong's diary is an invaluable source of information on the New York appearances of De Meyer, Herz, and Thalberg, as well as other touring virtuosos.

4. *NYEM,* 25 May 1846, quoted in Lawrence, *Strong on Music,* 1:378.

5. Henri Herz, *My Travels in America,* trans. Henry Bertram Hill (Madison: The State Historical Society of Wisconsin for the Department of History, University of Wisconsin, 1963), 61 (originally published as *Mes voyages en Amérique* [Paris: Achille Faure, 1866]); *NYEM,* 9 October 1847.

6. Female admirers in New York newspaper, Timm Scrapbook; *New York Morning Telegraph,* 24 October 1846.

7. New York newspaper quoted in *The Musical World* 21 (28 November 1846): 603; *NYEP,* 3 October 1846. After a concert given by the violinist Camillo Sivori, the *New-York Age* (10 October 1847) reported: "We have every reason to believe that more than five hundred persons were present at Sivori's last concert who passed the doors free, paying for their admission of course, by performing the duties of *claqueurs.*"

8. Mason, *Memories of a Musical Life,* 21–22. He also described another publicity technique used for De Meyer's concerts at the Tabernacle: "De Meyer's agent, acting on the principle that 'a crowd draws a crowd,' hired a lot of carriages to make their appearance a little before the concert-hour, and to stand in front of the doors and then advance in turn, so that passers-by might receive the impression of activity on the part of the concert-goers."

9. The first citation for that meaning in the *Oxford English Dictionary* is an American source from 1841. According to John Russell Bartlett in his *Dictionary of Americanisms* (New York: Bartlett and Welford, 1848), "persons who drink at a bar, ride in an omnibus, or railroad car, travel in steamboats, or visit the theatre without charge, are called *dead heads.* These consist of the engineers, conductors, and laborers on railroads; the keepers of hotels; the editors of newspapers, &c." (p. 396).

10. *The Musical Review, and Record of Musical Science, Literature and Intelligence* 1 (27 October 1838): 243–45. The article was subtitled: "Designed as a guide to such itinerant musicians as have not sufficient talent to enable them to gain an honest living, but who have sufficient temerity and impudence to induce them to enter upon a thorough-going system of charlatanism for the sake of acquiring rapidly a fortune among our 'hospitable citizens.'"

11. Max Maretzek, *Sharps and Flats* (New York: American Musician Publishing Co., 1890; reprint, New York: Dover Publications, 1968), 38; Boston concerts in *NYDTr,* 23 January 1857. Ullman's mailing to physicians is mocked in *Harper's Weekly* 1 (28 February 1857): 129–30. A review of a Brooklyn concert by Thalberg stated that the hall "was about three-fourths filled: one-half of the audience being dead-heads, 'oyster-house critics,' and other genteel loafers of New York" (*Brooklyn Daily Eagle,* 18 November 1856).

12. *DJM* 21 (31 May 1862): 71; William Steinway, Diary, 20 February 1873; Strong diary quoted in Shanet, *Philharmonic,* 153.

13. Maretzek, *Sharps and Flats,* 38.

14. "Lyin' Pianist" in *New York Morning Telegraph,* 22 October 1846. Perabeau's first article was written for the New York German-language newspaper *Schnellpost,* trans. in *NYEP,* 28 October 1845. The article in *NYH* (10 February 1846), of which Perabeau claimed to be the "source and originator" (*NYH,* 8 May 1846), plagiarized a review of Edward Holmes's *Life of Mozart* from *Blackwood's Edinburgh Magazine* 58 (November 1845): 572–90.

15. *New York Daily Globe,* 11 October 1847; *The Musical World* 21 (28 November 1846): 601–2, quoted in *The Musical Gazette* 1 (4 January 1847): 194.

16. *MCNYE,* 7 October 1846; *The Musical Gazette* 1 (9 November 1846): 165. For the first concert the *Albion* (3 October 1846) also stated that the Tabernacle was "filled to overflowing," but the *New York*

Evening Post (3 October 1846), as a backer of Perabeau, held that De Meyer had "only an average audience," was "evidently in a bad humor, and did not appear to play as well as when we last heard him."

17. *New York Morning Telegraph,* 28 October 1846; *New York Evening Gazette,* undated clipping, Timm Scrapbook.

18. De Meyer later gave a fuller account of his endorsement of Scherr's pianos in the Philadelphia papers, in which he expressed his "unqualified preference" for Scherr's pianos and declared them the "best pianos made in the United States" (*United States Gazette,* 18 November 1846).

19. When he performed his variations on American airs at his first Boston concert, he "sat down to a Yankee instrument, the make of our townsman, Mr. Chickering" (*BDET,* 22 November 1845).

20. *United States Gazette,* 21 November 1846.

21. De Meyer in *PPL,* 26 November 1846; Conrad Meyer in *PPL,* 28 November 1846. *Yankee Doodle* (1 [19 December 1846]: 131) offered an insightful *précis* of the episode, in which a "Conrad Mire" communicates with a pianist (the magazine slipped by using Herz's name, although De Meyer is clearly the intended target). "Mire" writes telegraphically to the visiting pianist: "Foreign Genius—American Industry—Confidence in Judgment—Piano—Erard—Can't you give us a certificate?" The pianist responds with a German accent: "I know noding aboud you and not wish to." Then Mire addresses the public: "Foreign Humbug—Native Talent—Best Piano—No paid for Puffs—Indignation—Ours the best." The pianist rebuts the charges: "Sour grapes—Fawning Letters—Equivocation—Contempt—Enlightened Public—Discerning Critics—Neglect."

22. *United States Gazette,* 21 November 1846.

23. *Saint Louis Reveille,* 17 March 1847.

24. *New Orleans Daily Tropic,* 13 February 1847.

25. *Saint Louis Daily Union,* 17 March 1847; *Daily Cincinnati Commercial,* 23 April 1847.

26. *Saint Louis Reveille,* 9 March 1847.

27. *New York Morning Telegraph,* 24 October 1846; *The Albion,* 3 and 10 October 1846.

28. *The Musical World* 21 (28 November 1846): 601–2, quoted in *The Musical Gazette* 1 (4 January 1847): 195.

29. Because Herz's agent, Bernard Ullman, was the central figure in the dispute, it will be discussed in the following chapter.

30. *NYH,* 2 December 1846, 7 January, 29 January, and 5 February 1847; quotation from Serafín Ramírez, *La Habana artística: apuntes históricos* (Havana: E. M. de la Capitanía General, 1891), 477.

31. *New Orleans Daily Tropic,* 4 and 13 February 1847.

32. *Nashville Daily Union,* 7 April 1847; *Saint Louis Reveille,* 5 March 1847.

33. Second concert in *Saint Louis Reveille,* 16 and 17 March 1847; third concert in *Saint Louis Daily Union,* 20 March 1847; fifth concert in *Saint Louis Reveille,* 26 March 1847.

34. *NYH,* 7 June 1847.

35. *Fm* 10 (4 July 1847): 228. An estimate made by the *New York Herald* (quoted in *BDET,* 5 December 1845) of Ole Bull's income during his first American tour of 1843–45 gives a clue to the possible earnings of De Meyer. It calculated that the net receipts of single concerts by him ranged from $200 to $3,000 and that he averaged $400 for the entire series of 200, which would have made his total income $80,000. With his fewer than one hundred concerts, De Meyer could have made about $40,000.

36. Silver cup in *BDET,* 17 November 1846 (De Meyer's letter of thanks to the society was reprinted in *NYH,* 20 November 1846); second concert in *United States Gazette,* 29 May 1847, and *NYEM,* 4 June 1847.

37. De Meyer's promise in *Fm* 10 (18 July 1847): 242. In 1867 Dwight found De Meyer to be "still a remarkable player," but he lamented: "If he would only play good music!" *Dwight's* New York correspondent also criticized De Meyer's repertoire for an appearance with Theodore Thomas and his orchestra in which the pianist "murdered outright" a Chopin nocturne by the "insertion of flourishes and embellishments which were thoroughly meretricious" and offered encores of a "trashy character" (*DJM* 27 [9 November 1867]: 134, and 27 [21 December 1867]: 158).

CHAPTER 4: A REFINED PARISIAN PIANIST

1. "Pianists of the Past: Personal Recollections by the late Charles Salaman," *Blackwood's Edinburgh Magazine* 170 (September 1901): 310; *Le Corsaire* quoted in Schonberg, *The Great Pianists,* 191.

2. Loesser, *Men, Women and Pianos,* 350; Robert Schumann, *Gesammelte Schriften über Musik und*

Musiker, ed. Martin Kreisig, 5th ed., 2 vols. (Leipzig: Breitkopf und Härtel, 1914), 1:1, trans. in Leon Plantinga, *Schumann as Critic* (New Haven: Yale University Press, 1967; reprint, New York: Da Capo Press, 1976), 3.

3. *The Autobiography of Charles Hallé,* ed. Michael Kennedy (London: Paul Elek, 1972; reprint, New York: Da Capo Press, 1981), 30; Pamela Susskind Pettler, "Clara Schumann's Recitals, 1832–50," *19th-Century Music* 4 (Summer 1980): 70–76; Amy Fay mentions Liszt's performance of a Herz etude in 1873 (*Music-Study in Germany* [Chicago: A. C. McClurg, 1880; reprint, New York: Da Capo Press, 1979], 249). That Clara Schumann (then Clara Wieck) included no works of Herz after 1837, the year of her marriage commitment to Robert Schumann, is surely no coincidence.

4. Philadelphia newspaper quoted in *Mississippi Free Trader* (Natchez), 28 April 1847; *Charleston Courier,* 23 January 1847.

5. Herz, *Travels,* 12; Burke concert in *NYEP,* 24 October 1846; *NYDTr* quoted in *NYEP,* 24 October 1846.

6. Herz, *Travels,* 17; Lawrence, *Strong on Music,* 1:381; *The Albion,* 31 October 1846.

7. *MCNYE,* 6 November 1846. Herz has a slightly different version of the events in what he describes as his New York debut (*Travels,* 27–28). In Charleston, he made a similar speech in response to a demand for an encore, stating that "with permission of the audience he would substitute a pastoral he had that morning composed, and which in token of the gratification he had experienced from his visit to our city, he had entitled '*Le Souvenir de Charleston*'" (*Charleston Courier,* 23 January 1847).

8. *The Musical Gazette* 1 (4 January 1847): 198.

9. *Alta California* (San Francisco), 3 April 1850; *NYH,* 29 September 1847; *Courrier des Etats-Unis,* 7 November 1846; John Sullivan Dwight, "Musical Review: Sivori and Herz," *The Harbinger* 5 (30 October 1847): 327; John Sullivan Dwight, "Musical Review: Henri Herz in Boston," *The Harbinger* 4 (26 December 1846): 43.

10. John Sullivan Dwight, "Musical Review," *The Harbinger* 3 (8 August 1846): 141.

11. *Alabama Planter* (Mobile), 15 February 1847.

12. *NYDTr,* 31 October 1847; *The Albion,* 31 October 1846.

13. *NYEM,* 12 November 1846; *MCNYE,* 31 October 1846.

14. *MCNYE,* 31 October 1846.

15. *NYH,* 8 and 10 November 1846.

16. Herz and Loder rebuttals in *NYH,* 9 November 1846; *NYEM,* 11 November 1846.

17. No advertisements, programs, or reviews identify the arrangement used by Herz, but H. E. Krehbiel, who apparently heard first-hand accounts of these performances by two of its participants—William Scharfenberg and Henry C. Timm—claims it was the one made by Czerny (*The Philharmonic Society of New York* [New York: Novello, Ewer, 1892; reprinted in *Early Histories of the New York Philharmonic* (New York: Da Capo Press, 1979)], 51).

18. *NYEM,* 12 November 1846; Lawrence, *Strong on Music,* 1:386; audience response in *NYEP,* 11 November 1846, and *NYH,* 11 November 1846; premature exodus in *NYH,* 13 November 1846.

19. *NYEM,* 12 November 1846; *New York Morning Telegraph,* 12 November 1846; White in *MCNYE,* 14 November 1846. Herz was assisted by "Fifteen Professors of the Pianoforte," including such leading pianists of New York as Denis G. Etienne, Julian Fontana, W. A. King, George Loder, Hermann Saroni, William Scharfenberg, Henry C. Timm, and Hermann Wollenhaupt.

20. Performances of the *Semiramide* Overture occurred in New York (10 and 13 November 1846), Philadelphia (4 and 9 December 1846), and Baltimore (27 November 1846), with only twelve pianists performing in the last city. The Overture to *William Tell* arranged for eight pianos and sixteen pianists was performed in New York (7 January 1847), New Orleans (24 March and 9 April 1847), St. Louis (1 and 3 June 1847), Cincinnati (10 July 1847), and Mexico City (5 September 1849). Richmond (16 December 1847) heard *William Tell* performed by ten pianists on five pianos. Nashville (15 June 1847) had to settle for a performance of *Tell* on three pianos, and in Wilmington, Delaware (7 December 1846), Herz performed the Overture to *Zampa* on two pianos with two other pianists. In most of these cities, Herz had to rely on local instruments, and many of them were probably square pianos.

21. See Tick, *American Women Composers before 1870,* 44–51, for a discussion of the performance of such works in female seminaries and reproductions of several programs. Although the term "monster concert" is frequently used today to refer to performances featuring works for multiple pianos, it was not originally used to describe large *combined* forces. A long list of solo performers was all that was necessary to qualify a concert for monster status. Herz's second Boston concert, for example, was dubbed a "monstre concert" by the *Boston Daily Evening Transcript* (18 December 1846) even though it featured only four

artists, each performing individually with the support of an accompanist or orchestra. The term had become common in at least London and Paris in the 1830s and 1840s. When Liszt gave a solo recital in Paris in 1841, the *Revue et gazette musicale* remarked: "Here is an original concert: a single artist, a single instrument—the very opposite of the *concert-monstre!*" (8 [1 April 1841]: 204–5).

22. *Fm* 9 (6 December 1846): 402; Herz, *Travels,* 1.

23. Herz, *Travels,* 91.

24. Herz, "Mes souvenirs," *Fm* 15 (12 October 1851): 322.

25. Herz, *Travels,* 29–31. For information on Ullman, see Laurence Marton Lerner, "The Rise of the Impresario: Bernard Ullman and the Transformation of Musical Culture in Nineteenth Century America" (Ph.D. diss., University of Wisconsin, 1970) and R. Allen Lott, "Bernard Ullman, Nineteenth-Century American Impresario," in *A Celebration of American Music: Words and Music in Honor of H. Wiley Hitchcock,* ed. Richard Crawford, R. Allen Lott, and Carol J. Oja (Ann Arbor: University of Michigan Press, 1990), 174–91.

26. *Baltimore Sun,* 20 November 1846.

27. *Baltimore Sun,* 21 November 1846. Both De Meyer's and Ullman's communications are quoted at greater length in Schonberg, *The Great Pianists,* 195–97.

28. *New York Morning Telegraph,* 2 December 1846; *Baltimore Sun,* 21 November 1846.

29. *Baltimore Sun,* 21 November 1846.

30. Attendance figures in Musical Fund Society, Memorandum Book; advertisement in *PPL,* 4 December 1846.

31. Herz, *Travels,* 41–42. Ullman's program for the patriotic concert as recorded by Herz is reproduced in Loesser, *Men, Women and Pianos,* 486–87.

32. Attendance in *NYH,* 7 December 1846, and *PPL,* 9 December 1846; Herz, "Mes souvenirs," *Fm* 16 (25 January 1852): 33–34, trans. in *The Musical Times* 4 (10 April 1852): 364–65; last Philadelphia concert in Herz, *Travels,* 50.

33. *BDET,* 14 December 1846. This incident may be the one Herz describes in which he burns one of his hands before his first concert in the United States and a miracle salve prevents him from having to postpone his debut (*Travels,* 25–27).

34. John Sullivan Dwight, "Musical Review: Henri Herz in Boston," *The Harbinger* 4 (26 December 1846): 42–43 (includes discussion on Herz's Second Concerto); John Sullivan Dwight, "Musical Review: Sivori and Herz," *The Harbinger* 5 (30 October 1847): 327.

35. John Sullivan Dwight, "Boston Philharmonic Society," *The Harbinger* 4 (9 January 1847): 77; Herz, "Mes souvenirs," *Fm* 15 (21 December 1851): 398, trans. in *The Musical Times* 4 (3 April 1852): 348; *BDET,* 4 January 1847. Herz spins a tale about an obstinate horn player, who finally had to be dismissed because he believed as a resident in a country of liberty he had the right to perform wrong notes.

36. John Sullivan Dwight, "Musical Review: Henri Herz in Boston," *The Harbinger* 4 (26 December 1846): 42–43; *Alta California,* 3 April 1850; *NYEM,* 24 October 1846, quoted in Lawrence, *Strong on Music,* 1:377–78.

37. *NYEM,* 12 November 1846.

38. *The American Review* 6 (November 1847): 550.

39. *New-Orleans Bee,* 1 March 1847; Child in newspaper clipping, Timm Scrapbook.

40. "Letter from New-York," *Boston Courier,* 27 October 1846, reproduced in Patricia G. Holland and Milton Meltzer, eds., *The Collected Correspondence of Lydia Maria Child, 1817–1880* (Millwood, N.Y.: Kraus Microform, 1980)[microfiche]. Child was also "vexed" with De Meyer because a few laudatory phrases she had written concerning him in a private letter to Anthony Philip Heinrich had been taken out of context and published in the papers as a puff (*NYH,* 3 November 1846). She expressed to Heinrich, who had obviously shown the letter to De Meyer, her "extreme disapprobation and disgust of the prevailing system of *barter* carried on between the press and public performers. . . . I do not think the system is right and honest. Authors and performers ought to stand solely on their own merits, without any *management* to obtain puffs. . . . I want you should be aware how perfectly *hollow* and heartless all this system of mutual puffery is" (Letter 671 to Anthony Philip Heinrich, 19 October 1846, in *Collected Correspondence*).

41. *NYH,* 5 November and 26 December 1846.

42. Herz, *Travels,* 37; *New York Gazette and Times,* 8 January 1847; *NYEP,* 8 January 1847. When the pianist Maurice Strakosch later supplied a thousand extra candles, they were deemed an "inconvenience" to the audience because of the glare and the dripping wax (*The American Review* n.s. 2 [November 1848]: 546).

CHAPTER 5: WITH SIVORI AND KNOOP

1. Henri Herz, Letter to Hiram Fuller, Natchez, 22 April 1847 (Music Division, New York Public Library), summary in *NYEM,* 5 May 1847, photographic reproduction in Donald Garvelmann, Introduction to *Variations on "Non più mesta"* by Henri Herz (Bronx, N.Y.: Music Treasure Publications, 1970), 8; Herz, *Travels,* 57. Herz wrote to Fuller: "The last steamer has brought me (with no small trouble) a leave from the French government." According to records of the Conservatoire he was on an unlimited leave of absence from 1 October 1846 to 30 September 1851 (Constant Pierre, *Le conservatoire national de musique et de déclamation: documents historiques et administratifs* [Paris: Imprimerie nationale, 1900], 446).

2. See Flavio Menardi Noguera, *Camillo Sivori: La vita, i concerti, le musiche* (Genoa: Graphos, 1991).

3. *NYH,* 13 October 1846; *BDET,* 5 November 1846; John Sullivan Dwight, "Musical Review: Sivori's Last Concert in Boston," *The Harbinger* 3 (21 November 1846): 380.

4. Paganini's letter in G. I. C. de Courcy, *Paganini: The Genoese,* 2 vols. (Norman: University of Oklahoma Press, 1957; reprint, New York: Da Capo Press, 1977), 1:220; manuscript lessons in *New York Journal of Commerce,* 19 October 1846, also quoted in *BDET,* 22 October 1846; White in *MCNYE,* 20 October 1846; Sivori on Paganini in David Laurie, *The Reminiscences of a Fiddle Dealer* (Boston: Houghton Mifflin, 1925; reprint, Cape Coral, Fla.: Virtuoso Publications, 1977), 60. The dispute is well documented by newspaper clippings in the Timm Scrapbook; see also Ullman's communication in *NYH,* 9 October 1847.

5. Herz, *Travels,* 66–67.

6. *Morris's National Press: A Journal for Home* 2 (24 October 1846): 2.

7. *Charleston Courier,* 23 January 1847; *Savannah Daily Republican,* 29 January 1847; *Columbus* (Ga.) *Times,* 9 February 1847.

8. *New-Orleans Bee,* 1 March 1847. During his first season, Herz gave ten concerts in New Orleans, six in New York, four in Philadelphia, three in Baltimore, and two in Boston (excluding guest appearances). It should be noted, however, that the halls in New Orleans were generally smaller than those in the large eastern cities.

9. Herz, *Travels,* 83.

10. *New-Orleans Bee,* 24 February 1847; Herz, Letter to Frédéric Gaillardet, New Orleans, 7 March 1847, published in *Courrier des Etats-Unis,* 18 March 1847, trans. in *The Home Journal,* no. 59 (27 March 1847): 2.

11. Herz on the Soulés in *Travels,* 89; Herz on "Louisianian ladies" in Letter to Frédéric Gaillardet, 7 March 1847; Mrs. Soulé's participation in *William Tell* Overture in *NYH,* 20 May 1847; amateur status of performers in *New-Orleans Bee,* 26 March 1847; Herz on charity concert in *Travels,* 92. The *Richmond Daily Whig* (18 December 1847) later remarked that Herz's "gentlemanly bearing makes him a favorite every where."

12. *Baton Rouge Gazette,* 24 April 1847; Herz, *Travels,* 54–55.

13. *Richmond Daily Whig,* 18 December 1847; John Sullivan Dwight, "Boston Philharmonic Society," *The Harbinger* 4 (9 January 1847): 77; *Lucrezia Borgia* in *NYEM,* 18 November 1846, quoted in Lawrence, *Strong on Music,* 1:387; *I Tancredi* in *New York Morning Telegraph,* 12 November 1846. Dwight described another Herz encore as a "fantastic improvisation leading into some delicious variations" of "Home, Sweet Home" ("Musical Review: Sivori and Herz," *The Harbinger* 5 [30 October 1847]: 328).

14. Herz, *Travels,* 54, 51. Herz's initial reaction to Ullman's idea of improvising was anything but favorable: "Improvise in public! That is very dangerous. One's imagination can suddenly fail, and it is painful to reveal oneself before the world in such pretentious impotence." In Columbus, Georgia, he promised to "extemporize on any popular tune which the audience will present to him" (*Columbus Enquirer,* 19 June 1849; similar announcement in *Louisville Daily Democrat,* 26 June 1847). In San Francisco and Sacramento in 1850, he gave an "extemporaneous performance on several American, French, Italian and German popular songs" (*Alta California,* 2 April 1850; *Sacramento Transcript,* 16 April 1850).

15. *Mobile Register and Journal,* 5 and 6 April 1847; *NODP,* 9 April 1847; *Vicksburg Tri-Weekly Whig,* 4 May 1847; *Saint Louis Daily Union,* 1 June 1847; *Nashville Daily Union,* 14 June 1847. The work is reprinted in Jeffrey Kallberg, ed., *Piano Music of the Parisian Virtuosos, 1810–1860: A Ten-Volume Anthology,* vol. 4: *Henri Herz (1803–1888): Selected Works* (New York: Garland, 1993). It is possibly the same work as *The Halls of Montezuma,* a "grand fantasia," which Herz performed in Charleston for the "first time in America" (*Charleston Courier,* 25 December 1847).

16. *Mississippi Free Trader* (Natchez), 28 April 1847. Charles Hamm strongly suspects that Moore's "'Tis the Last Rose of Summer" was the first song to sell more than a million copies in the United States (*Yesterdays: Popular Song in America* [New York: W. W. Norton, 1979], 46).

17. John Sullivan Dwight, "Musical Review: Sivori and Herz," *The Harbinger* 5 (30 October 1847): 327.

18. Shortly before his death, Paganini gave Sivori a Vuillaume copy of his favorite Guarneri, which he called "my cannon." The Vuillaume had been a gift from the maker to Paganini, who asked Sivori to reimburse Vuillaume for the cost of the instrument. On his deathbed, as Sivori alternated playing the Guarneri and the Vuillaume copy, Paganini considered the latter virtually as good as the original (Menardi Noguera, *Camillo Sivori*, 56–62; Courcy, *Paganini*, 2:311–13).

19. John Sullivan Dwight, "Musical Review: Sivori and Herz," *The Harbinger* 5 (30 October 1847): 328.

20. *Vicksburg Tri-Weekly Whig*, 29 April 1847.

21. Saratoga concert in *NYH*, 18 September 1847; *Fall River Weekly News*, 2 September 1847; Herz, *Travels*, 65.

22. *NYH*, 29 September 1847.

23. *The American Review* 6 (November 1847): 549–50.

24. Strong's diary and Watson in *The Albion* (2 October 1847) quoted in Lawrence, *Strong on Music*, 1:447–48.

25. *MCNYE*, 8 October 1847; *NYEM*, 9 October 1847. In spite of White's attacks on his partner, Herz would later write that he was an "excellent musician and critic, whose writing was both clear and impartial" (*Travels*, 64).

26. *MCNYE*, 5 November 1847; John Sullivan Dwight, "Art Review: Herz, Sivori, and Knoop in Boston," *The Harbinger* 6 (13 November 1847): 11.

27. *Daily Cincinnati Commercial*, 8 July 1847; Sivori's Beethoven cycle in Ivan Mahaim, "The First Complete Beethoven Quartet Cycles, 1845–1851: Historical Notes on the London Quartett Society," trans. and ed. Evi Levin, *The Musical Quarterly* 80 (1996): 500–524.

28. Mayseder trio in John Sullivan Dwight, "Art Review: Herz, Sivori, and Knoop in Boston," *The Harbinger* 6 (13 November 1847): 11; Beethoven trio in John Sullivan Dwight, "Art Review: Music in Boston," *The Harbinger* 6 (27 November 1847): 30; Herz, *Travels*, 59.

Chapter 6: French Pianos, Italian Opera, and California Gold

1. Employment figures in *The Musical World* 19 (5 December 1844): 399; production figures in Loesser, *Men, Women and Pianos*, 386; exposition in *Fm* 7 (4 August 1844): 239–40.

2. *Pittsburgh Daily Commercial Journal*, 9 September 1847. In April 1847 Herz was expecting a new shipment from Paris of about fifty instruments (Letter to Hiram Fuller, Natchez, 22 April 1847).

3. *NYH*, 3 November 1847. Wholesale prices for Herz's pianos ranged from $250 for a pianino to $500 for a semi-grand; retail prices ranged from around $300 to $850. Wholesale prices appear in Herz's letters to L. F. Newland (an Albany music dealer), New York, 1 November and 6 December 1847 (Gratz Collection, Case 13, Box 8, Historical Society of Pennsylvania, Philadelphia).

4. *NYDTr* quoted in *BDET*, 6 November 1847; sales room in *NYH*, 14 March 1848.

5. Herz, *Travels*, 55, 13–14. Georges Cuvier (1769–1832), a French zoologist and biologist, made significant contributions to the classification of animals and was famous for his paleontological reconstructions of those that had become extinct.

6. Herz, *Travels*, 55, 36.

7. Cyril Ehrlich, *The Piano: A History*, rev. ed. (Oxford: Clarendon Press, 1990), 130; Peter Gay, *The Bourgeois Experience: Victoria to Freud*, vol. 1: *Education of the Senses* (New York: Oxford University Press, 1984), 495; Patricia Anderson, *When Passion Reigned: Sex and the Victorians* (New York: BasicBooks, 1995), 166 n.9, 10.

8. Captain Frederick Marryat, *A Diary in America, with Remarks on its Institutions*, 2 vols. (Philadelphia: Carey & Hart, 1839), 2:45. A reference to Marryat's story appears in the satirical "A Piano in Arkansas" by Thomas Bangs Thorpe, an early voice in American colloquial and frontier humor most famous today for "The Big Bear of Arkansas." The inhabitants of Hardscrabble, Arkansas, who have never seen a piano and are not sure what it is, at least know that it has legs, "for a stray volume of Capt. Maryatt's [sic] 'Diary,' was one of the most conspicuous works in the floating library of Hardscrabble. And Capt. Maryatt stated that he saw a Piano somewhere in New England, with panteletts on." In later versions, when Marryat's book had faded from public consciousness, the reference to him was changed to "some literary traveler." The story was first published in *The Spirit of the Times* (New York), 30 October 1841; it

322 NOTES TO PAGES 93–98

was reprinted in an anthology of Thorpe's works, *The Hive of "The Bee-Hunter": A Repository of Sketches* (New York: D. Appleton, 1854), 145–54, and various music journals throughout the century, including *Moore's World of Music* 1, no. 1 [1842]: 14–15, *Brainard's Musical World* 10 (January 1873): 1–2, and *American Art Journal* 60 (11 March 1893): 496–500.

9. Reception in Jules Zanger, "Foreword," in *A Diary in America* by Captain Frederick Marryat (Bloomington: Indiana University Press, 1960), 9 (this edition of Marryat's diary does not contain the concluding "remarks," where the anecdote on the piano appears); review in "The Last English Tourist in America," *The United States Magazine and Democratic Review* 6 (September 1839): 265, 255, 261, 266.

10. Xavier Eyma, *Les femmes de nouveau-monde* (Paris: Michel Lévy Frères, 1860), 136. Eyma is generally considered a trustworthy observer, but a review of his following book, *La vie dans le nouveau-monde* (Paris: Poulet-Malassis, 1862), contended that the author "loves story-telling better than disquisition, and arranges his materials rather for romantic effect than for scientific accuracy. . . . Occasionally, indeed, we meet with strange and ridiculous exaggerations" (*The North American Review* 96 [January 1863]: 257–58).

11. Perhaps not coincidentally, Philadelphia is also the site of an obvious squib late in the century that seems to discount prudery as a common motivation for the custom, since it is an American source that lampoons it: "There lives in Philadelphia a family as modest as Mrs. Grannis, for they made little petticoats for every one of the four legs of their square piano" ("Piano in Pants," *American Art Journal* 68 [27 February 1897]: 335).

12. All of White's articles in these journals may be accessed at Cornell University's *Making of America* Web site: *http://moa.cit.cornell.edu/moa*.

13. Richard Grant White, "Some Alleged Americanisms," *The Atlantic Monthly* 52 (December 1883): 801. White seems to have confused Captain Marryat's book with that of Captain Basil Hall, *Travels in North America in the Years 1827 and 1828* (1829), which appeared ten years earlier. Neither Trollope nor Hall mention piano trousers, although both make references to having seen a piano.

14. "The Piano as a Piece of 'Household Furniture,'" *Watson's Art Journal* 19 (14 June 1873): 77, reprinted in *Brainard's Musical World* 10 (July 1873): 106; Maude Haywood, "Decorations for the Piano," *The Ladies' Home Journal* 10 (January 1893): 9.

15. Havana concerts in Ramírez, *La Habana artística*, 451, 521–22; Herz, *Travels*, 98.

16. *NYEM*, 27 July, 5 and 18 August, and 25 September 1848, quoted in Lawrence, *Strong on Music*, 1:559.

17. *NYH*, 1 December 1848. The second tune is not to be confused with another minstrel song with a similar title, James Bland's "Carry Me Back to Old Virginny," written in the 1870s. Herz also published a simpler setting of several minstrel tunes, *Mélodies de Christy*, which includes "Carry Me Back to Old Virginia," "Oh! Susanna," and "Stop Dat Knocking." *La Californienne* is reprinted in Kallberg, ed., *Herz: Selected Works*, as is *Impromptu burlesques*, though the latter work appears there under the title *Fantaisie méxicaine*. It is not clear if this is a case of Herz reusing material for a different regional audience or the error of his publisher.

18. Herz, "Mes souvenirs," *Fm* 15 (26 October 1851): 337–38, free trans. in *The Musical Times* 4 (29 November 1851): 53.

19. *The United States Magazine, and Democratic Review* 24 (February 1849): 186.

20. *NYH*, 12 April 1849. The *Alabama Planter* of Mobile (7 May 1849) indicated their itinerary would include Chagres, Lima, and Valparaíso.

21. *NYH*, 17 July 1849.

22. Bernard Ullman, "Leaves from My Diary," *Musical Pioneer* 11 (March 1866): 42.

23. Reception in Mexico City in *Alabama Planter*, 30 July 1849, *NYH*, 30 July 1849, *The Message Bird* 1 (15 August 1849): 27, and Enrique de Olavarría y Ferrari, *Reseña histórica del teatro en México, 1538–1911*, 3d ed., 5 vols. (Mexico City: Editorial Porrúa, 1961), 1:485–86; reception in different city in *Alabama Planter*, 17 December 1849; success of concerts in *The Message Bird* 1 (1 June 1850): 351.

24. The hymn was soon forgotten, and several others were written before the one still used today was adopted. It was composed by Jaime Nunó, who served as piano accompanist for Thalberg's first concerts in America. See Bernardino Beltrán, *Historia del himno nacional mexicano* (Mexico City: D.A.P.P., 1939), Jesús C. Romero, *Verdadera historia del himno nacional mexicano* (Mexico City: Universidad Nacional Autónoma de México, 1961), and Esperanza Pulido, "Marcha nacional, dedicada a los mexicanos, compuesta por Henri Herz, Op. 166," *Heterofonia*, no. 88 (1985): 44–52.

25. Olavarría y Ferrari, *Teatro en México*, 1:487–88; *The Message Bird* 1 (15 November 1849): 135.

26. The only clue about the split between Herz and Ullman is Maretzek's claim that the pianist "dis-

missed [Ullman] from his service in Mexico" (Max Maretzek, *Crotchets and Quavers: or, Revelations of an Opera Manager in America* [New York: S. French, 1855; reprint, New York: Da Capo Press, 1966, and New York: Dover Publications, 1968], 307). Ullman's activities until April 1852, when he began serving as an agent for Maurice Strakosch in Havana, are unknown, and his new position then indicates a temporary setback in his managerial career (Lerner, "Bernard Ullman," 60).

27. *San Francisco Daily Pacific News,* 27 March 1850; quotation from *Sacramento City Placer Times,* 30 March 1850.

28. On music in early California, see Works Progress Administration, Northern California, San Francisco, *History of Music in San Francisco Series,* 7 vols. (San Francisco: Works Progress Administration, 1939–42; reprint, New York: AMS Press, 1972). Information on Herz appears in vol. 1: *Music of the Gold Rush Era,* 138–45; vol. 3: *Letters of Miska Hauser, 1853,* 98–101; and vol. 4: *Celebrities in El Dorado, 1850–1906,* 23–24. Herz did not return to California in 1854 as stated in 1:143 and 4:24.

29. Herz, Letter to Frédéric Gaillardet, 9 May 1850, written on board the steamer *Panama,* published in *Courrier des Etats-Unis,* 12 June 1850, reprinted in *Le moniteur universel,* 4 July 1850, trans. in *Boston Bee,* quoted in *Cist's Weekly Advertiser* (Cincinnati), 3 July 1850, and *The Message Bird,* no. 25 (1 August 1850): 407.

30. *Alta California,* 3 April 1850.

31. *Alta California,* 8 April 1850. A detailed description of the piece (or improvisation) appears in the *Sacramento Transcript,* 20 April 1850. Such a work was not an original idea. The harpist Nicholas Bochsa was famous for his *Voyage musicale,* "in which the music of every nation of the earth is represented with marvellous ability" (*NYEM,* 2 October 1847). Herz may have been inspired by the harpist, who with his wife, the singer Anna Bishop, had been in the eastern United States at the same time as Herz and had more recently vied with him for the public's favor in Mexico City. The couple visited California in 1854.

32. *Alta California,* 16 April 1850.

33. Sacramento invitation in *Sacramento Transcript,* 8 April 1850, and *San Francisco Daily Pacific News,* 5 April 1850, quoted in *Sacramento Transcript,* 18 April 1850; advertisement in *Sacramento Transcript,* 20 April 1850.

34. Stephen C. Massett, *"Drifting About," or What "Jeems Pipes of Pipesville" Saw-and-Did: An Autobiography* (New York: Carleton, 1863), 141. "Jeems Pipes" was Massett's *nom-de-plume* for his satirical newspaper articles. While visiting Paris in 1853 Massett again met Herz, who invited the singer to one of his concerts in his own hall, where "he didn't think I should see *any rats* running across the floor!" (p. 200). Some titles of Massett's routines include the "Yankee Town Meeting," "The Frenchman, the Exquisite, and the Yankee in Richard III," and "An imitation of an elderly lady and a German girl, who applied for the situations of soprano and alto singers in one of the churches in Massachusetts."

35. P. A. Fiorentino, "Henri Herz: un concert en Californie," *Le Constitutionnel,* 21 September 1851, trans. in "A Musician in California," *The Musical Times* 4 (21 February 1852): 251–53.

36. Fiorentino, "Un concert en Californie." When the *Sacramento Transcript* (30 April 1850) reported the incident, its headline was "Highly Preposterous, If Not Slightly Amusing," and it declared the person who proposed the venture had "a mind not capable of understanding the exact relation of things to each other in this world" (also quoted in *The Message Bird,* no. 25 [1 August 1850]: 410).

37. *Alta California,* 8 April 1850; ruffians in Fiorentino, "Un concert en Californie"; beauty and fashion in *San Francisco Daily Pacific News* quoted in George R. MacMinn, *The Theater of the Golden Era in California* (Caldwell, Idaho: The Caxton Printers, 1941), 368; Herz, Letter to Frédéric Gaillardet, 9 May 1850; *Sacramento Transcript,* 3 April 1850; *San Francisco Daily Pacific News,* 2 April 1850.

38. Sacramento hall in *Sacramento Transcript,* 16 April 1850, and Fiorentino, "Un concert en Californie"; Benicia incident in Herz, Letter to Frédéric Gaillardet, 9 May 1850.

39. Herz, Letter to Frédéric Gaillardet, 9 May 1850; Sacramento party in *Sacramento Transcript,* 18 April 1850; San Francisco reception in *Alta California,* 29 April 1850, with quotation from *San Francisco Daily Pacific News* quoted in MacMinn, *Theater of the Golden Era,* 369.

40. *Saroni's Musical Times* 1 (15 June 1850): 448. Saroni's imitation of Herz's speech indicates that although the pianist had assimilated many aspects of French culture, he apparently still retained his German accent.

41. Fire in Fiorentino, "Un concert en Californie"; Herz's summary of California visit in letter to Frédéric Gaillardet, 9 May 1850. Newspaper accounts of only eight concerts, in San Francisco and Sacramento, have been found. This letter contains Herz's description of a concert in Benicia.

42. Herz's intention of touring South America had been announced as early as April 1847, when he and Sivori were planning a tour there for the 1847–48 season (*Alabama Planter,* 19 April 1847). He was

particularly successful in Lima, Peru, where he gave a series of concerts beginning in mid-August 1850, including a "concierto monstruo" rivaling those of Gottschalk. His *Gran marcha nacional militar,* dedicated to the citizens of Peru, was performed on eight pianos by lady and gentleman amateurs of the city, a double orchestra, a military band, and a men's chorus. Probably the same work—for identical forces but retitled *Marcha patriótica*—was performed in Santiago and Valparaíso, Chile. He was in Chile from about November 1850 to at least February 1851, performing also in La Serena and Copiapó, and returned to Lima by June of 1851 (Rodolfo Barbacci, "Apuntes para un diccionario biográfico musical peruano," *Fénix: Revista de la Biblioteca Nacional* 6 [1949]: 463–64; Roberto Hernández, *Los primeros teatros de Valparaíso* [Valparaíso: Junta de Vecinos de Valparaíso, 1928], 189; Eugenio Pereira Salas, *Historia de la música en Chile [1850–1900]* [Santiago: Editorial del Pacífico, 1957], 112–14).

INTERLUDE I

1. Schumann on virtuosos in "Antonio Bazzini," *Neue Zeitschrift für Musik* 18 (25 May 1843): 169–70, reprinted in *Gesammelte Schriften über Musik und Musiker,* 2:134, trans. Paul Rosenfeld in *On Music and Musicians* (New York: Pantheon Books, 1946), 81; Schumann's letters quoted in Nancy B. Reich, *Clara Schumann: The Artist and the Woman,* rev. ed. (Ithaca: Cornell University Press, 2001), 113–15; *The Marriage Diaries of Robert & Clara Schumann,* ed. Gerd Nauhaus, trans. Peter Ostwald (Boston: Northeastern University Press, 1993), 127.

2. *St. Louis Intelligencer* quoted in *The Musical World and New York Musical Times* 6 (18 June 1853): 107.

3. *The Musical Gazette* 1 (23 November 1846): 173–74; *St. Louis Daily Reveille,* 27 May 1847; George William Curtis, "De Meyer in New York," *The Harbinger* 2 (21 February 1846): 173–74.

4. Elam Ives, "Music in New York," *The Harbinger* 6 (6 November 1847): 5; John Sullivan Dwight, "Music in Boston," *The Harbinger* 6 (15 January 1848): 86.

5. "Herr Smash," *The Knickerbocker* 34 (September 1849): 244–46.

6. *NYH,* 21 December 1848; on the Germania, see H. Earle Johnson, "The Germania Musical Society," *The Musical Quarterly* 39 (1953): 75–93; Thomas Ryan, *Recollections of an Old Musician* (New York: E. P. Dutton, 1899; reprint, New York: Da Capo Press, 1979), 65.

7. Austin Caswell, "Jenny Lind's Tour of America: A Discourse of Gender and Class," in *Festa Musicologica: Essays in Honor of George J. Buelow,* ed. Thomas J. Mathiesen and Benito V. Rivera (Stuyvesant, N.Y.: Pendragon Press, 1995), 319–37.

8. *DJM* 2 (16 October 1852): 13. Lind's uniquely triumphant tour especially encouraged people to enter the managerial world. In 1855 Maretzek referred to these opportunistic managers as "those musical agents who had lately so plentifully cropped out of the manure Barnum had spread upon the soil of American humanity." He claimed that while the "reputation of Jenny Lind was in the ascendant" neophyte managers "actually swarmed upon us as mosquitoes do in the months of August and September," for many desired to follow in Barnum's footsteps (*Crotchets and Quavers,* 198, 184).

9. *DJM* 1 (31 July 1852): 133. Almost five years later America was still on Marie's mind: from Dresden in February 1857 another correspondent to *Dwight's* reported that she "intimated a desire to go to the U.S. if she could feel assured of success" (10 [14 March 1857]: 189–90).

10. A biographical summary of Jaëll before his American years appears in *The Musical Times* 5 (29 May 1852): 38–39, and 5 (5 June 1852): 52.

11. *DJM* 2 (22 January 1853): 124.

12. *The Musical Times* 4 (3 January 1852): 141.

13. *The Musical World and New York Musical Times* 6 (14 May 1853): 18. Gottschalk recalled that his "first concert in New York was a success, but the receipts did not amount to half of the expenses. The second . . . was a fiasco" (*Notes of a Pianist,* 46).

14. Kenneth Gene Graber, "The Life and Works of William Mason (1829–1908)" (Ph.D. diss., University of Iowa, 1976), 53–55.

CHAPTER 7: A RIVAL OF LISZT

1. Thalberg's appearances in Rio de Janeiro and Buenos Aires (July–December 1855) in Ayres de Andrade, "Um rival de Liszt no Rio de Janeiro," *Revista brasileira de música* 1 (April–June 1962): 27–50; Rodolfo Barbacci, "Documentación para la historia de la música Argentina, 1801–1885," *Revista de estudios musicales* 1 (December 1949): 49–55; and Vicente Gesualdo, *Historia de la música en la Argentina,* 3 vols. (Buenos Aires: Editorial Beta S.R.L., 1961), 2:208–19.

2. *New-York Musical Review and Gazette* 7 (12 July 1856): 209. Bülow, however, attended a perform-ance by Thalberg in 1853 at Liszt's urging and "was very much rewarded by the real pleasure" he experi-enced hearing Thalberg's "exquisitely poetical and thoroughly finished execution" (Letter to his father, Vienna, 21 May 1853, in Marie von Bülow, ed., *The Early Correspondence of Hans von Bülow*, trans. Con-stance Bache [London: T. Fisher Unwin, 1896], 152).

3. *Journal des débats*, 3 April 1837, trans. in Alan Walker, *Franz Liszt, Volume One: The Virtuoso Years, 1811–1847* (New York: Alfred A. Knopf, 1983), 240. Walker, who sets the record straight on the draw, examines in some detail the Liszt-Thalberg rivalry (pp. 232–43).

4. Thalberg's parentage continues to confound researchers. An excellent overview of the conflicting evidence has appeared in various issues of the *Sigismund Thalberg Society Newsletter* (1990–), edited by Daniel L. Hitchcock. The evidence has also been surveyed by Dudley Newton in "Sigismund Thalberg," *The Liszt Society Journal* 16 (1991), reprinted as a supplement to the *Sigismund Thalberg Society Newsletter* 4 (1993). Count Moritz Dietrichstein, the prince's brother and a well-known patron of Beethoven, was also sometimes viewed as the pianist's father.

5. On Thalberg's career, see Daniel L. Hitchcock, "Sigismund Thalberg, 1812–1871: An Evaluation of the Famous Composer-Pianist, on the 100th Anniversary of his Death," *The Piano Quarterly*, no. 77 (Fall 1971): 12–16; Michel Béro, "Sigismond Thalberg: Aspects de la virtuosité pianistique au XIXᵉ siècle" (Mémoire de licence, Université Libre de Bruxelles, 1975); and Ian G. Hominick, "Sigismund Thalberg (1812–1871), Forgotten Piano Virtuoso: His Career and Musical Contributions" (D.M.A. diss., Ohio State University, 1991).

6. *New-York Musical Review and Gazette* 7 (4 October 1856): 305; *NYDT*, 31 October 1856.

7. *NYH*, 20 November 1856.

8. *NYDT*, 4 November 1856.

9. *New York Dispatch*, 1 March 1857, partially quoted in Vera Brodsky Lawrence, *Strong on Music: The New York Music Scene in the Days of George Templeton Strong, Volume 3: Repercussions, 1857–1862* (Chicago: University of Chicago Press, 1999), 21 n.52.

10. *DJM* 10 (24 January 1857): 132; *NYDT*, 19 February 1857; *BP*, 10 April 1857.

11. *NYH*, 12 November 1856; *Chicago Daily Democratic Press*, 22 May 1857; *DJM* 10 (10 January 1857): 118.

12. *DJM* 10 (10 January 1857): 118; *NYH*, 14 November 1856; *BET*, 24 March 1857; *Providence Daily Journal*, 8 January 1857. Thalberg's performance style is surveyed with many quotations from the European press in E. Douglas Bomberger, "The Thalberg Effect: Playing the Violin on the Piano," *The Musical Quarterly* 75 (1991): 198–208.

13. *Richmond Daily Dispatch*, 16 January 1858; *MCNYE*, 11 November 1856, reprinted in *DJM* 10 (15 November 1856): 55; Cincinnati correspondent, *DJM* 11 (30 May 1857): 70; *Weekly Review* reprinted in *DJM* 31 (20 May 1871): 27; *Springfield (Mass.) Daily Republican*, 1 January 1857.

14. *Philadelphia Evening Bulletin*, 29 November 1856, quoted in *NYH*, 1 December 1856.

15. *DJM* 10 (11 October 1856): 14; see also Fry's discussion in *NYDTr*, 11 November 1856. Dwight echoed the sentiments of François-Joseph Fétis, Thalberg's staunchest European supporter, who praised him as "an innovator in the art of piano playing," which included the use of the entire range of the in-strument, the ability to create the illusion of a full orchestra, and the combination of the "singing and bril-liant schools of piano playing." Fétis as well as others believed that Thalberg had founded a new school of piano playing ("Mm. Thalberg et Liszt," *Revue et gazette musicale* 4 [23 April 1837]: 137–42, partial trans. in Charles R. Suttoni, "Piano and Opera: A Study of the Piano Fantasies Written on Opera Themes in the Romantic Era" [Ph.D. diss., New York University, 1973], 157–59).

16. *Revue et gazette musicale* 3 (8 May 1836): 153. The significance that Thalberg placed on a singing tone was symbolized in his series of transcriptions of such vocal works as Beethoven's "Adelaide" and the quartet from Bellini's *I Puritani* (both of which he performed frequently in America) under the title *L'Art du chant appliqué au piano*. In a short preface to the series, he encouraged performers to "overcome or conceal" the piano's inability "to utter prolonged sounds similar to those of the human voice." In offering guidelines on meeting this challenge, he suggested that in "simple, tender, and graceful" pieces, one must "knead the key, manipulate it with a hand without bones and fingers of velvet" (trans. in *The Thalberg Concert Book, and Piano-Forte Album* [New York: Wardle Corbyn, 1856], 7–8).

17. *NYDT*, 11 November 1856; see Isabelle Bélance-Zank, "The 'Three-Hand' Texture: Origins and Use," *Journal of the American Liszt Society* 38 (1995): 99–121.

18. The most thorough study of Thalberg's fantasias appears in Suttoni, "Piano and Opera." Suttoni concludes that Thalberg brought a new "seriousness and a more sonorous type of lyricism" to the opera

fantasia (p. 171). A sympathetic evaluation of Thalberg's music appears in Eric Frederick Jensen, *Walls of Circumstance: Studies in Nineteenth-Century Music* (Metuchen, N.J.: Scarecrow Press, 1992), which focuses on Thalberg's Piano Sonata and Piano Trio, atypical works of a virtuoso (pp. 47–60). Schumann, who admired Thalberg's playing and was more complimentary to his music than that of most virtuosos, admitted there was a "spark of something nobler here and there" (*Neue Zeitschrift für Musik* 15 [19 October 1841]: 126, trans. in Plantinga, *Schumann as Critic,* 211).

19. *DJM* 10 (17 January 1857): 126, and 10 (11 October 1856): 14.

20. *Tarantelle* in *DJM* 10 (17 January 1857): 126, and 10 (10 January 1857): 119; *Thème original et étude* in *DJM* 10 (24 January 1857): 134.

21. Thalberg's setting of "The Last Rose of Summer" as well as all of the works mentioned in the preceding paragraph, with the exception of *Souvenirs d'Amérique,* are reprinted in Kallberg, ed., *Piano Music of the Parisian Virtuosos,* vols. 1–2: *Sigismund Thalberg (1812–1871): Selected Works.*

22. *Auburn* (N.Y.) *Daily Advertiser,* 17 June 1857; *NYEP,* 19 February 1857, quoted in Lawrence, *Strong on Music,* 3:25; *BP,* 12 January 1857; White in *MCNYE,* 28 November 1856, reprinted in *DJM* 10 (6 December 1856): 76.

23. Sigismund Thalberg, Letter to Ferdinand Hiller, 17 June 1841, in Reinhold Sietz, *Aus Ferdinand Hillers Briefwechsel (1826–1861): Beiträge zu einer Biographie Ferdinand Hillers,* Beiträge zur rheinischen Musikgeschichte, Heft 28 (Cologne: Arno Volk-Verlag, 1958), 47; Wilhelm von Lenz, *Beethoven et ses trois styles* (St. Petersburg: Bernard, 1852), 8, trans. in Suttoni, "Piano and Opera," 207. A London correspondent to *Revue et gazette musicale* ventured a similar observation about Thalberg in 1862: "Nobody in fact has been so much imitated; his manner has been parodied, exaggerated, twisted, tortured, and it may have happened more than once to all of us to curse this Thalbergian school" (trans. in *DJM* 21 [16 August 1862]: 153).

24. *DJM* 10 (17 January 1857): 125–26.

25. *NYDT,* 6 March 1857; Gottschalk and Mason in *NYDT,* 14 November 1856.

26. S. Frederick Starr, *Bamboula! The Life and Times of Louis Moreau Gottschalk* (New York: Oxford University Press, 1995), 239; Mason, *Memories of a Musical Life,* 211–13. While waiting for his concerts to begin in New York, Thalberg spent some time in West Orange, New Jersey, at the home of one of Mason's brothers. There Mason claims to have become "well acquainted with him and his method of practice. In this way he was virtually one of my best teachers, although no regular lessons were received from him" (p. 212).

27. Hoffman, *Some Musical Recollections,* 130–31; *Burlington (Vt.) Daily Free Press,* 7 February 1857.

28. Adam Badeau, "Gottschalk and Thalberg," in *The Vagabond* (New York: Rudd & Carleton, 1859), 18–19.

29. Starr, *Bamboula!,* 241.

30. *DJM* 10 (24 January 1857): 133.

31. *NYDT,* 19 February 1857; *DJM* 10 (28 March 1857): 203; complaints about the miscellaneous programs in *DJM* 10 (24 January 1857): 132, and *BET,* 25 March 1857.

32. Ullman in *NYDT,* 22 November 1856; *NYDT,* 28 November 1856.

33. From early 1834 to early 1835, Thalberg performed Beethoven's Third, Fourth, and Fifth Piano Concertos in Vienna (see the valuable chronology prepared by Daniel Hitchcock in *The Sigismund Thalberg Society Newsletter* 2 [April 1991]: 7–17). During his first season in the United States, Thalberg performed the first movement of the Beethoven Third Concerto in New York (27 and 29 November 1856), Philadelphia (27 December 1856), Boston (10 January and 31 March 1857), and Brooklyn (7 March 1857), and the first movement of the Fifth in New York (2 December 1856) and Boston (13 January and 4 April 1857).

34. *MCNYE,* 28 November 1856, reprinted in *DJM* 10 (6 December 1856): 76; *NYDTr,* 28 November 1856.

35. *MCNYE,* 28 November 1856, reprinted in *DJM* 10 (6 December 1856): 76; *NYDT,* 28 November 1856; Dwight on Fifth Concerto in *DJM* 11 (11 April 1857): 14; Dwight on Third Concerto in *DJM* 10 (17 January 1857): 126.

36. *BET,* 6 April 1857; *DJM* 10 (17 January 1857): 126; New York correspondent, *DJM* 10 (21 February 1857): 164.

CHAPTER 8: AT THE MATINÉES

1. After two private matinées in Boston (17 and 20 January 1857), Thalberg gave a series of three matinées at Dodworth's Saloon in New York beginning on 20 February, with subscriptions selling for five dol-

lars and limited to four hundred people. Two more series of two matinées each were added, as well as four single matinées and a soirée musicale in the evening. Three more matinées were given in Boston in late March.

2. *DJM* 10 (24 January 1857): 134; *BP,* 19 January 1857. Charles Salaman described a similar atmosphere at Liszt's first "recitals" in London in 1840: "After performing a piece set down in his programme, [Liszt] would leave the platform, and . . . would move about among his auditors and converse with his friends, with the gracious condescension of a prince" ("Pianists of the Past," 314).

3. Ullman in *NYDT,* 16 February 1857; *DJM* 10 (24 January 1857): 134.

4. "Archduke" and "Marche funèbre" in *DJM* 11 (4 April 1857): 7; "Moonlight" in *DJM* 10 (28 March 1857): 203; New York correspondent, *DJM* 10 (28 February 1857): 173.

5. Maretzek, *Crotchets and Quavers,* 318, 71; *NYDT,* 21 February 1857; New York correspondent, *DJM* 10 (28 February 1857): 173; *BET,* 21 March 1857. Theatrical matinées were being introduced at the same time for which women were targeted as the primary audience; see Richard Butsch, "Bowery B'hoys and Matinee Ladies: The Re-Gendering of Nineteenth-Century American Theater Audiences," *American Quarterly* 46 (1994): 374–405.

6. When Thalberg and Vieuxtemps announced a matinée in New Orleans, the *Mobile Daily Register* (17 February 1858) pleaded for one in their city, arguing that "no doubt it would pay extremely well, as there are hundreds of ladies who would like to hear these artists as often as possible, and do not wish to be under obligations to their gentlemen friends; for at the *matinées* ladies can go alone!"

7. When Thalberg performed in Charlottesville, Virginia, "several of the fair daughters of Augusta and Orange counties" were present, and for his Atlanta concert, "many of the fair ladies of Marietta, Decatur, Newman, and Lagrange" were expected (*Charlottesville Advocate,* 8 January 1858, quoted in *Lynchburg Virginian,* 13 January 1858; *Atlanta Daily Examiner,* 4 February 1858).

8. The entire song is reproduced in Tick, *American Women Composers,* 178–87.

9. Notice in *BET,* 17 March 1857; *Boston Daily Ledger,* 23 March 1857; Ullman's response in *BET,* 24 March 1857.

10. *Boston Daily Ledger,* 25 March 1857.

11. *NYDT,* 21 January 1857. He performed for twenty thousand children in six New York concerts alone (*NYDTr,* 12 March 1857).

12. Thalberg's and Mason's letters in *NYH,* 29 November 1856; *PPL,* 15 December 1856; *DJM* 10 (24 January 1857): 134; *New Orleans Daily Crescent,* 24 February 1858; "Home, Sweet Home" in *DJM* 10 (20 December 1856): 92. At the second school concert in New Orleans, one of the superintendents "requested that applause should only be given by clapping the hands" (*NODP,* 27 February 1858).

13. *DJM* 11 (18 April 1857): 22.

14. Attack on Ullman in *NYS,* 10 November 1856, and *NYH,* 9 November 1856; *NYH,* 13 December 1856.

15. Ullman's operatic activities in Lawrence, *Strong on Music,* 3:*passim;* Lerner, "Bernard Ullman"; and Maretzek, *Sharps and Flats,* 37–48.

16. *Frank Leslie's Illustrated Newspaper,* 10 January 1857. The same newspaper later hailed Strakosch as "the grandest and the most successful concert-tourist that we have ever had among us," which it attributed to his "quite remarkable . . . personal popularity," his "good faith in all his business transactions," and the "excellent entertainments he always offers," opinions that were widely held (31 October 1857).

17. For a satirical description of the plight of musicians on the road, see *Deutsche Musik-Zeitung* 2 (15 February 1858): 159–60, trans. in *New-York Musical Review and Gazette* 9 (6 March 1858): 71–72.

18. For the first Syracuse concert, the management arranged for an extra train to run from Auburn to Syracuse and to return immediately after the concert, provided one hundred tickets were sold; extra trains were also scheduled to run from Oswego and Homer (*Auburn Daily Advertiser,* 13 and 17 April 1857; *Oswego Daily Palladium,* 11 April 1857). When Thalberg returned to Syracuse, another train was run from Oswego to "accommodate persons at various points on the road who wish to attend Thalberg's Concert." The train was to return immediately after the concert; people holding concert tickets had to pay only a one-way fare (*Syracuse Daily Standard,* 15 June 1857).

One burlesque about those who traveled to concerts, which also criticized the high ticket prices and evinced a not unusual American disdain for instrumental music, concluded this way: "When we ride forty miles, at an expense of at least ten dollars, extras not included, to hear a couple of itinerant Dutchmen [Thalberg and Vieuxtemps] torture a brace of unoffending instruments into fits, until the very spirit of music howls in sympathy, if somebody will have the kindness to cave in our head with a brick-bat, we'll feel greatly obliged to him" (*Columbia* [Tenn.] *Mirror,* quoted in *DJM* 13 [26 June 1858]: 104).

19. The Italian soprano Parodi had been brought to America in 1850 by Max Maretzek, then man-

ager of the Astor Place Opera House in New York, in an attempt to compete with Jenny Lind, and soon became Strakosch's primary attraction in his frequent tours. Amalia Patti Strakosch, an older sister of the soon-to-be-famous Adelina Patti, had toured with Strakosch before marrying him in 1852. Mollenhauer had arrived in New York in 1856 to join his brothers, Friederich and Eduard, violinists who had come to the United States in 1853 as soloists in the orchestra of Louis Jullien.

20. *Rochester Daily American,* 22 April 1857; *Detroit Daily Tribune,* 9 June 1857.

21. *Chicago Daily Democratic Press,* 29 May 1857; *Rochester Daily American,* 22 April 1857; Cincinnati correspondent, *DJM* 11 (30 May 1857): 70; *Daily Milwaukee News,* 28 May 1857.

22. De Meyer concert in *The Musical Gazette* 1 (9 November 1846): 165; Herz concert in *PPL,* 26 November 1847; Strong in Lawrence, *Strong on Music,* 1:447; Thalberg concert in *Rochester Union and Advertiser,* 7 May 1858.

23. *Nashville Republican Banner,* 2 June 1858; *Cincinnati Daily Gazette,* 6 May 1857.

24. *New-York Musical Review and Gazette* 8 (11 July 1857): 210. They were announced to appear in Cape May, New Jersey; Newport, Rhode Island; Nahant, Massachusetts; Niagara Falls, Saratoga Springs, Sharon Springs, and Rockaway, New York (*NYDT,* 14 July 1857), but only the concerts in Cape May and Saratoga Springs have been documented.

CHAPTER 9: HENRY VIEUXTEMPS AND A TROUBLED SEASON

1. *Frank Leslie's Illustrated Newspaper,* 19 September 1857.

2. *Toronto Globe,* 10 May 1858. Vieuxtemps's repertoire of his own works included *Les Arpèges, Introduction and Rondo, Adagio and Tarantella,* and fantasias on *I Lombardi, Ernani,* and *Lucia di Lammermoor.* With Thalberg he performed fantasias by Bériot and Thalberg on *Les Huguenots,* by Bériot and Benedict on *La Sonnambula,* and by Vieuxtemps and Edward Wolff on *Don Giovanni.*

3. *BET,* 15 October 1857; *DJM* 11 (26 September 1857): 204; *New Orleans Daily Delta,* 20 February 1858.

4. Thalberg's popularity in *Frank Leslie's Illustrated Newspaper,* 19 September 1857; first concert in *MCNYE,* 16 September 1857, reprinted in *DJM* 11 (26 September 1857): 203; third concert in *New-York Musical Review and Gazette* 8 (3 October 1857): 307.

5. *New-York Musical Review and Gazette* 8 (19 September 1857): 291–92; *DJM* 11 (26 September 1857): 204; *NYDTr,* 17 September 1857.

6. *DJM* 12 (17 October 1857): 230–31. Only in New Orleans did Thalberg and Vieuxtemps perform works by Beethoven together, including the sonatas in D minor and F major and the first two movements of the "Kreutzer" Sonata.

7. *Reading Gazette and Democrat,* 14 November 1857.

8. *DJM* 12 (9 January 1858): 325. The program is reproduced in Lawrence, *Strong on Music,* 3:19.

9. The singers included Bertha Johannsen, who had toured the previous season with Thalberg, the recently arrived English singer Annie Kemp, and Signor Lehman with Signor E. Hasslocher as accompanist. This troupe had several cast changes en route, mostly to offer variety to the audiences at the Academy back in New York. Lehman was soon replaced in Charleston by Signor Ardavani, and in St. Louis Ardavani and Johannsen were replaced by Ernest Perring and Elisa Cairoli. In New Orleans Vieuxtemps's wife, the former Josephine Eder, replaced Hasslocher as piano accompanist. She had accompanied her husband at most, if not all, of the season's concerts, although she was rarely listed in advertisements.

10. *Richmond Daily Dispatch,* 16 January 1858; Augusta concert in *Georgia Journal and Messenger* (Macon), 3 February 1858; *Mobile Daily Register,* 13 February 1858; New Orleans correspondence, *Daily Pittsburgh Gazette,* 20 May 1858.

11. *Cleveland Daily Plain Dealer,* 27 March 1858; *Charleston Daily Courier,* 23 January 1858; *New Orleans Daily Delta,* 19 February 1858.

12. *Cincinnati Daily Gazette,* 25 May 1858; *Janesville Morning Gazette,* 12 June 1857; *Columbus (Ga.) Enquirer,* 9 February 1858.

13. *Wilmington (N.C.) Daily Journal,* 20 January 1858; *Augusta Daily Constitutionalist,* 30 January 1858; *Savannah Daily Republican,* 2 February 1858; George William Curtis, "Editor's Easy Chair," *Harper's New Monthly Magazine* 14 (January 1857): 272.

14. *NODP,* 2 March 1858; Obituary, *The Times* (London), reprinted in *DJM* 31 (17 June 1871): 43; *Frank Leslie's Illustrated Newspaper,* 25 July 1857; *DJM* 11 (1 August 1857): 142.

15. Thalberg's meeting with Church in letter from Thalberg to George William Warren, a church organist in Albany (New York, 6 March 1857 [Historical Society of Pennsylvania, Philadelphia]).

16. *Daily National Intelligencer,* 18 December 1856; Thalberg's request in *Boston Bee,* quoted in *New*

Bedford Daily Mercury, 6 January 1857. The book was probably *Narrative of the Expedition of an American Squadron to the China Seas and Japan* (1856), which was based on Perry's "original notes and journals." Thalberg supposedly stated that the volume "would henceforward be as valuable to him—(it would not be more so)—as *his own Erard."*

17. Samuel Longfellow, ed., *Life of H. W. Longfellow, with Extracts from His Journals and Correspondence,* 3 vols. (Boston: Houghton Mifflin, 1891; reprint, New York: Greenwood Press, 1969), 2:291. Longfellow wrote Thalberg two days after the concert and enclosed a "curious autograph" of Washington—a signature to a lottery ticket (Longfellow, Letter to Thalberg, Cambridge, 5 January 1857, in *The Letters of Henry Wadsworth Longfellow,* ed. Andrew Hilen, vol. 4 [Cambridge: The Belknap Press of Harvard University Press, 1972], 6).

18. Report of a phrenological exam on Thalberg in *Springfield (Mass.) Daily Republican,* 5 January 1857.

19. *New Orleans Daily Crescent,* 1 March 1858. Testimonial letters from Thalberg in *New Orleans Daily Crescent,* 1 March 1858, and *NODP,* 3 March 1858. A widely reprinted interview from the *Courrier des Etats-Unis* of New York, 13 July 1857, concerning Thalberg's newly acquired banjo skills would seem apocryphal if not for Thalberg's letter of endorsement of his banjo teacher; see *New-York Musical Review and Gazette* 8 (25 July 1857): 228; *DJM* 11 (1 August 1857): 142; *NYDT,* 1 August 1857.

20. Seven Erards in *New-York Musical Review and Gazette* 7 (18 October 1856): 321; *DJM* 10 (24 January 1857): 133.

21. "A Bargain with Thalberg," *New York Musical World* 17 (21 March 1857): 180; Ullman's response in *New York Musical World* 17 (4 April 1857): 212.

22. *Daily Pittsburgh Gazette,* 2 and 6 May 1857.

23. *Daily National Intelligencer,* 7 January 1857.

24. *MCNYE,* 13 April 1858, reprinted in *DJM* 13 (24 April 1858): 26; Ullman's advertisements in *NYT,* 3 and 12 April 1858. All these accessories were fodder for the satirists. At Burton's Theatre, where John Brougham's *The Great Tragic Revival* was playing, the program announced: "A gong will be sounded whenever a joke of sufficient magnitude is eventuated. . . . The plot of the drama, together with a pair of antique folding-doors, will be simultaneously opened by Two Waiters in Livery. . . . Should the drama not be found sufficiently absorbing, the morning and evening papers, together with Harper's Magazine or the New-York Directory, will be found admirably adapted to divert undue attention and ameliorate the rigor of intellectual fatigue" (quoted in *NYT,* 19 April 1858).

25. *DJM* 13 (8 May 1858): 45.

26. Upon Ullman's departure for Europe the previous spring, he was said to be planning an American tour for Berlioz (*DJM* 11 [11 April 1857]: 14; *New-York Musical Review and Gazette* 8 [2 May 1857]: 129). In a letter to Ullman dated 15 July 1857, Berlioz stated his intention to visit the United States the following season (reprinted in *New-York Musical Review and Gazette* 8 [22 August 1857]: 261).

27. *NYT,* 3 May and 23 April 1858.

28. *Toronto Globe,* 15 May 1858. The singers Annetta Caradori and Juliana May, the latter a native of Washington, D.C., joined Thalberg, Vieuxtemps, and the violinist's wife, who served as accompanist, on the tour. There were cast changes again: Elena D'Angri and Pedro de Abella joined the troupe in Pittsburgh to replace Caradori, who left in Wheeling, and Ernest Perring joined in Cincinnati to replace May, who left in Louisville.

29. George P. Upton, *Musical Memories: My Recollections of Celebrities of the Half Century 1850–1900* (Chicago: A. C. McClurg, 1908), 74–75; Upton, "Attractions in Chicago: 1847–1881," 1:50 (Chicago Historical Society); Maretzek, *Sharps and Flats,* 42–43.

30. Ullman's guarantee in *NYT,* 6 April 1858; Strakosch reportedly paid Thalberg $30,000 for almost sixty concerts, also about $500 per night (*New York Musical World* 17 [28 March 1857]: 197); modern equivalent based on John J. McCusker, "How Much Is That in Real Money? A Historical Price Index for Use as a Deflator of Money Values in the Economy of the United States," *Proceedings of the American Antiquarian Society* 101 (1991): 323–32; earning comparisons in Edgar W. Martin, *The Standard of Living in 1860: American Consumption Levels on the Eve of the Civil War* (Chicago: University of Chicago Press, 1942; reprint, New York: Johnson Reprint Corp., 1970), 393–94.

31. *New-York Musical Review and Gazette* 9 (24 July 1858): 226.

INTERLUDE II

1. Gottschalk, *Notes of a Pianist;* see also Starr, *Bamboula!*

2. See Marta Milinowski, *Teresa Carreño: "By the Grace of God"* (New Haven: Yale University Press, 1940; reprint, New York: Da Capo Press, 1977).

3. Topp performed Liszt's *Fantasia on Themes from Beethoven's Ruins of Athens* with the New York Philharmonic for the first time in the United States (1867), Mehlig gave the first American performance of Liszt's Second Piano Concerto with Theodore Thomas (1870), and Krebs gave the American premieres of Rubinstein's Fourth Piano Concerto with the New York Philharmonic and Liszt's *Fantasy on Hungarian Folk Tunes* and the opening movement of Brahms's First Piano Concerto with the Thomas orchestra (all in 1871).

4. See M. Leslie Petteys, "Julie Rivé-King, American Pianist" (D.M.A. diss., University of Missouri-Kansas City, 1987).

5. See Charles Reid, *The Music Monster: A Biography of James William Davison, Music Critic of* The Times *of London, 1846–78* (London: Quartet Books, 1984), 47–57. A British correspondent to the *Musical Standard* complained of Goddard's reception in New York: "She has never played better in her life than she did here, and yet was received with a frigidity that can hardly be surpassed by the thickest ice, and solely and confessedly because she came from England" (quoted in *Concordia* 2 [26 February 1876]: 134).

6. *MTR* 3 (3 December 1876): 42. The critic James Huneker thought Essipoff was "the most poetic of all women pianists" that he had heard ("The Grand Manner in Pianoforte Playing," in *Unicorns* [New York: Charles Scribner's Sons, 1917], 176).

7. "An Hour with Rubinstein," *NYS*, 27 September 1872, 2:6–7; Hans von Bülow, Letter to Steinway & Sons, quoted in *The Musical Independent* 1 (March 1869): 154. Liszt believed Topp was "quite simply a marvel." She played his Sonata in B Minor and *Mephisto Waltz* in a way which "enchanted him" (Alan Walker, *Franz Liszt, Volume Three: The Final Years, 1861–1886* [New York: Alfred A. Knopf, 1996], 71).

8. Katharine Ellis, "Female Pianists and Their Male Critics in Nineteenth-Century Paris," *Journal of the American Musicological Society* 50 (1997): 371. Ellis provides an intriguing analysis of the "gendered assumptions" that women pianists had to confront, including "their repertoire, their style of interpretation, and their physical attitude at the piano" (p. 385).

9. Gottschalk wrote of the complaint "He plays only his own music": "Of all the criticisms of which I am the object on the part of the impotent and jealous who, like thorns and barren bushes, encumber every avenue of art in America, I avow that this is the one that I am the least disposed to accept" (*Notes of a Pianist,* 173).

10. For an excellent introduction to the concept of a musical canon, see William Weber, "The History of Musical Canon," in *Rethinking Music,* ed. Nicholas Cook and Mark Everist (New York: Oxford University Press, 1999), 336–55.

11. According to Ellis, "between 1828 and 1870, no female [piano] soloist played a work of her own at the prestigious Société des Concerts; few men played anything else" ("Female Pianists and Their Male Critics," 359).

12. White in *MCNYE*, 7 February 1846; Salaman, "Pianists of the Past," 324. In addition, Herz had made tentative plans to display his knowledge of other composers' works while in America. During his first season, he advertised to take place in Philadelphia a "soirée musicale . . . chiefly devoted to classical and modern Piano Forte Music," and he also supposedly planned to give in New York a similar program "devoted to classical music of the style of Beethoven, Hummel, &c., also a lecture concert for the students of the piano forte." Neither took place, for unknown reasons, but Herz must have been familiar with the literature to have announced such a venture (*PPL*, 23 December 1846; *NYH*, 10 December 1846).

13. On *Méthode des méthodes,* see Robert Wangermée, "Fétis, François-Joseph," in *The New Grove Dictionary of Music and Musicians,* ed. Stanley Sadie, 20 vols. (London: Macmillan, 1980), 6:513, and Carolyn Denton Gresham, "Ignaz Moscheles: An Illustrious Musician in the Nineteenth Century" (Ph.D. diss., University of Rochester, 1980), 281–83; on Czerny, see Janet Ritterman, "Piano Music and the Public Concert, 1800–1850," in *The Cambridge Companion to Chopin,* ed. Jim Samson (Cambridge: Cambridge University Press, 1992), 13, and Dorothy de Val and Cyril Ehrlich, "Repertory and Canon," in *The Cambridge Companion to the Piano,* ed. David Rowland (Cambridge: Cambridge University Press, 1998), 125–26 (the latter article discusses several other keyboard tutors and anthologies and distinguishes between their didactic purposes and their attempts to establish a canon); Walker, *Liszt, Volume Three: The Final Years,* 200; Weber, "History of Musical Canon," 339–40.

14. Gresham, "Ignaz Moscheles," 40–46; on Liszt, see the "Catalogue of works which Liszt played in public, 1838–48, compiled by himself," in Walker, *Liszt, Volume One: The Virtuoso Years,* 445–48, and Michael Saffle, "Liszt's German Repertory," in *Liszt in Germany, 1840–1845: A Study in Sources, Documents, and the History of Reception* (Stuyvesant, N.Y.: Pendragon Press, 1994), 185–202; on Schumann's

early repertoire, see Pettler, "Clara Schumann's Recitals, 1832–50," 70–76, and on her influence on repertoire and recital programming, see Reich, *Clara Schumann*, 264–65.

15. *Buffalo Commercial Advertiser,* 30 April 1873, 3:2; *The Arcadian* 1 (15 May 1873): 3.

16. *Chicago Daily Tribune,* 4 December 1872, 4:4; *NYS,* 28 September 1872, 2:2; *Scribner's Monthly* 5 (November 1872): 130.

17. James Parton, "The Piano in the United States," *The Atlantic Monthly* 20 (July 1867): 82; S. M. C., "Music Lessons," *DJM* 31 (12 August 1871): 79.

CHAPTER 10: "THE SHAGGY MAESTRO"

1. D. W. Fostle, *The Steinway Saga: An American Dynasty* (New York: Scribner, 1995), 168.

2. *Anton Rubinstein: A Sketch* (New York: Charles D. Koppel, [1872]), 4; Catherine Drinker Bowen, *"Free Artist": The Story of Anton and Nicholas Rubinstein* (New York: Random House, 1939), 31. A helpful biographical summary of Rubinstein appears in Larry Sitsky, *Anton Rubinstein: An Annotated Catalog of Piano Works and Biography* (Westport, Conn.: Greenwood Press, 1998), 1–35.

3. Anton Rubinstein, *Autobiography of Anton Rubinstein, 1829–1889,* trans. Aline Delano (Boston: Little, Brown, 1890; reprint, New York: Haskell House, 1969), 36–37. In another version of the story, Dehn tells Rubinstein, "You, who are already twenty years ahead of Europe, seek the civilization which is twenty years behind us. Bah!" (*Anton Rubinstein: A Sketch,* 6).

4. Most remembered today for his management of the Metropolitan Opera in New York (with partners, 1883–84, 1891–96, and solely, 1898–1903), Maurice Grau (1849–1907) was one of the most important impresarios in late nineteenth-century America. He and his associates managed the American tours of Josef Hofmann, Eugen d'Albert, Sarah Bernhardt, Ellen Terry, and many others.

5. William Steinway, Diary, 26 January, 14 March, and 12 June 1872. Steinway's diary, which he kept from 20 April 1861 to 8 November 1896, is in the Archives Center, National Museum of American History, Smithsonian Institution. For information about and access to the diary, I am grateful to Henry Z. Steinway, Cynthia Adams Hoover, and Edwin M. Good, whose transcript of it is my source for all quotations. Copies of the diary may be consulted in the LaGuardia and Wagner Archives of LaGuardia Community College, the Metropolitan Museum of Art (New York), and the New-York Historical Society.

6. Maurice Grau, "Some Rubinstein Reminiscences," *NYH,* 25 November 1894, sec. 4, 5:3–4; Robert Grau, "Memories of Musicians: Rubinstein and Wieniawski," *The Musician* 15 (July 1910): 442. A copy of the first contract, signed by Rubinstein and Jacob Grau in Vienna on 24 October 1871, is in the Music Division of the Library of Congress. A copy of the final agreement, executed on 8 June 1872 in Vienna and signed by Rubinstein, Jacob Grau, Maurice Grau, and C. F. Theodor Steinway, is in the International Piano Archives, University of Maryland, College Park.

7. Arthur M. Abell, "Impressions of Anton Rubinstein," *Musical Courier* 99 (23 November 1929): 26.

8. Clara Louise Kellogg, *Memoirs of an American Prima Donna* (New York: G. P. Putnam's Sons, 1913; reprint, New York: Da Capo Press, 1978), 246, 248; Kellogg's advice to crowd in *NYW,* 12 September 1872, 1:6.

9. *Tristan* anecdote in Adolph Schloesser, "Anton Rubinstein (1829–1894)," *The Monthly Musical Record* 38 (1 September 1908): 199; interview in "An Hour with Rubinstein," *NYS,* 27 September 1872, 2:6–7. *Dwight's* New York correspondent believed the interview reported in the *Sun,* which made Rubinstein "give vent to a great deal of nonsense" about music, should be "taken with a grain of salt" (*DJM* 32 [5 October 1872]: 319).

10. *Watson's Art Journal* 17 (14 September 1872): 236; *NYT,* 13 September 1872, 5:5; *NYW,* 13 September 1872, 7:4; Allan Nevins and Milton Halsey Thomas, eds., *The Diary of George Templeton Strong,* 4 vols. (New York: Macmillan, 1952), 4:436. The transcription here of Rubinstein's speech is from *Watson's Art Journal;* it is slightly different in the *Times.*

11. *The Arcadian* 1 (25 September 1872): 2; *NYH,* 24 September 1872, 6:5; *NYW,* 24 September 1872, 5:1.

12. There was much discussion of Rubinstein's appearance even before he arrived in the United States. The *New-York Times* hoped that he was "not *always* afflicted with cholera morbus, as he appears to be in the portraits of him which are placed in the shop-windows. A more unhappy, pain-racked looking personage has never been on exhibition before in this City" (13 September 1872, 4:6). Grau remembers how Rubinstein was "cut . . . to the quick" by the "sight of his own portraits plastered on the walls and exhibited in the shop windows. . . . He hated to be looked upon as a curiosity or as a phenomenon" ("Some Rubinstein Reminiscences").

13. Rebellious hair in *Springfield (Mass.) Daily Republican,* 22 October 1872, 2:4; "shaggy *maestro*" in *New York Evening Mail,* 24 September 1872; Samson comparison in *Whitney's Musical Guest* 6 (June 1873): 138. Rubinstein wrote that in the 1840s he had been a "devoted imitator of Liszt, of his manners and movements, his trick of tossing back his hair, his way of holding his hands, of all the peculiar movements of his playing" (*Autobiography,* 19).

14. "School-boy" in *Whitney's Musical Guest* 6 (January 1873): 4; "disdain . . . respect" in *Independent,* 7 December 1872, quoted in *The Arcadian* 1 (19 December 1872): 3, and *DJM* 32 (28 December 1872): 357; "incidental business" in *NYW,* 24 September 1872, 5:1.

15. *Hartford Daily Courant,* 23 October 1872, 2:6; *DJM* 32 (5 October 1872): 319; *NYW,* 13 September 1872, 7:4.

16. For a detailed and highly critical survey of Rubinstein's five piano concertos, see Jeremy Norris, "The Piano Concertos of Anton Rubinstein," in *The Russian Piano Concerto, Volume I: The Nineteenth Century* (Bloomington: Indiana University Press, 1994), 21–53. Norris considers Rubinstein's Fourth Concerto "his finest contribution to the genre"; the others he finds "derivative and often poorly composed" (pp. 22, 188).

17. Rubinstein cueing Bergmann in *DJM* 32 (5 October 1872): 319; *NYW,* 24 September 1872, 5:1.

18. "Relays of ushers" in *NYW,* 24 September 1872, 5:1; disdain in *NYT,* 24 September 1872, 4:7; struggle with usher in *Orpheus* 8 (1 October 1872): 51.

19. Rubinstein, "An Hour with Rubinstein."

20. *NYH,* 2 October 1872, 7:3.

21. Second concert in *NYT,* 26 September 1872, 5:6; *Carnaval* reception in *NYS,* 28 September 1872, 2:2.

22. William Steinway, "Personal Reminiscences of Anton Rubinstein," *Freund's Musical Weekly* 8 (28 November 1894): 5, reprinted in *Music* 7 (February 1895): 394–400.

23. Attendance in *NYDTr,* 30 September 1872, 2:2; smile in *NYH,* 30 September 1872, 7:3.

24. *The Arcadian* 1 (2 October 1872): 3; *NYW,* 8 October 1872, 4:6; *NYT,* 24 September 1872, 4:7; *NYDTr,* 24 September 1872, 4:6; *NYS,* 28 September 1872, 2:2.

25. *NYT,* 24 September 1872, 4:7.

26. William Foster Apthorp, "The Season," *The Atlantic Monthly* 30 (December 1872): 757–58.

27. *NYH,* 4 October 1872, 7:5, and 8 October 1872, 8:6; *The Musical Bulletin* 6 (October 1872): 212; *DJM* 32 (19 October 1872): 321.

28. *New York Clipper,* 5 October 1872, 214:2; *The Arcadian* 1 (2 October 1872): 3.

29. *NYH,* 14 October 1872, 3:6.

30. "Nothing beautiful" in Anton Rubinstein, *A Conversation on Music,* trans. Mrs. John P. Morgan (New York: Chas. F. Tretbar, 1892; reprint, New York: Da Capo Press, 1982), 90–91; "born too soon" in Alexander McArthur [pseudonym for Lillian McArthur], "Rubinstein: The Man and the Musician," *The Century Magazine* 50 (May 1895): 28.

31. *BP,* 15 October 1872, 3:5; *Philadelphia Evening Bulletin,* 29 October 1872, 2:1.

32. *Syracuse Daily Standard,* 22 November 1872, 4:2; *Missouri Republican* (St. Louis), 16 February 1873, 10:4.

33. Rubinstein, "An Hour with Rubinstein"; *Buffalo Commercial Advertiser,* 26 November 1872, 3:1.

34. Rubinstein, "An Hour with Rubinstein."

35. *Chicago Daily Tribune,* 22 February 1873, 5:3; *Memphis Daily Appeal,* 13 February 1873, 4:5.

36. *Titusville Morning Herald,* 10 March 1873; *Utica Daily Observer,* 21 November 1872, 3:3; *PI,* 8 November 1872, 7:2.

37. New York correspondent, *DJM* 32 (19 October 1872): 321; *Memphis Daily Appeal,* 12 February 1873, 4:5; *DJM* 33 (19 April 1873): 7.

38. Philadelphia incident in *Daily Louisville Commercial,* 11 December 1872, 3:3; George William Curtis, "Editor's Easy Chair," *Harper's New Monthly Magazine* 52 (March 1876): 611; Rubinstein on memory in *Autobiography,* 17–18; *DJM* 33 (17 May 1873): 22; Leonard Liebling, "Variations," *Musical Courier* 99 (23 November 1929): 37; *NYW,* 18 November 1872, 1:3.

39. Reception in James M. Tracy, "Anton Rubinstein, As I Remember Him," *The Presto* 19 (17 April 1902): 9; *Folio* 7 (December 1872): 170. A more successful event was held in the home of Thomas Ryan, a prominent Boston musician, upon the completion of Rubinstein's Boston concerts. This time music making was the order of the evening, not socializing. The Mendelssohn Quintette Club, of whom Ryan was a member, performed Rubinstein's String Quartet in F; Wieniawski participated in a performance of a Beethoven Razumovsky Quartet and Rubinstein in the Schumann Piano Quintet. Ryan remembered

the performance of the Schumann piece more than thirty years later: "Oh, it was a joy to take part with such a man and in such a work! and how Rubinstein did spur us on by his passionate way of playing some of the great parts!" (Thomas Ryan, "Personal Recollections of Anton Rubenstein [sic] and Henri Wieniawski," *The Musical Observer* 1 [December 1907]: 25; see also *Orpheus* 8 [1 November 1872]: 70).

40. Visitors in Rubinstein, "An Hour with Rubinstein"; Mason, *Memories of a Musical Life,* 221–22.

41. *NYW,* 15 October 1872, 5:1; *BP,* 15 October 1872, 3:5; *DJM* 32 (19 October 1872): 326.

42. Concerto in *DJM* 32 (19 October 1872): 326; "Kreutzer" in *DJM* 32 (2 November 1872): 334; broken string in *BP,* 19 October 1872, 3:5. Rubinstein's own cadenzas for the Mozart D minor and the Beethoven G major were often considered questionable. *Dwight's* New York correspondent thought Rubinstein's cadenza for the Beethoven "marred and defaced that noble composition" because its style was "utterly at variance from the spirit of the work or the composer. Of course there is not the slightest objection to his executing an Indian war dance on the piano, if he chooses to do so; but, when he introduces one into the middle of a *Beethoven Concerto* it is time to remonstrate" (*DJM* 32 [25 January 1873]: 373).

43. *BP,* 15 October 1872, 3:5; New York concert in *DJM* 32 (11 January 1873): 365; Burlington concert in Ben Hur Wilson, "Grand Concert," *The Palimpsest* 17 (November 1936): 370; *PI,* 7 April 1873, 3:2.

44. *BP,* 15 October 1872, 3:5; *DJM* 32 (19 October 1872): 326.

45. *DJM* 32 (2 November 1872): 334–35.

CHAPTER 11: WIENIAWSKI

1. "Wine and Whisky" in *Utica Daily Observer,* 14 November 1872, 3:1, and *Syracuse Daily Standard,* 15 November 1872, 4:1; *Rochester Daily Union and Advertiser,* 25 November 1872, 2:5.

2. Ovations by orchestras in *NYH,* 28 September 1872, 6:6, and *Cincinnati Daily Gazette,* 21 March 1873, 8:3; *Missouri Republican* (St. Louis), 20 February 1873, 8:4; *Newark Daily Advertiser,* 19 April 1873, 2:6.

3. *Terre Haute Express,* 22 January 1873, 4:3.

4. *The Musical Independent* 4 (March 1873): 91; *Brooklyn Daily Eagle,* 12 November 1872, 7:1; *Troy Daily Times,* 25 April 1873, 3:3.

5. *NYW,* 23 October 1872, 5:1; *NYH,* 25 October 1872, 7:5.

6. *NYDTr,* 5 October 1872, 7:5; *NYT,* 5 October 1872, 5:2; *NYDTr,* 25 October 1872, 8:1; *NYH,* 25 October 1872, 7:5.

7. *PI,* 28 October 1872, 2:6.

8. *PI,* 29 October 1872, 3:4, and 30 October 1872, 3:3.

9. *PI,* 18 December 1875, 2:5.

10. *PI,* 30 October 1872, 3:3.

11. *PI,* 11 November 1872, 3:4.

12. *Philadelphia Evening Bulletin,* 9 November 1872, 6:1.

13. *Folio* 7 (December 1872): 169; *Chicago Daily Tribune,* 6 December 1872, 5:2.

14. *NYT,* 24 September 1872, 4:7; *NYDTr,* 24 September 1872, 4:6; Handel quip in *Indianapolis Sentinel,* 17 December 1872, 8:2; *Philadelphia Evening Bulletin,* 30 October 1872, 2:3; *Milwaukee Sentinel,* 15 March 1873, 8:2.

15. Velvet dress in *Indianapolis Sentinel,* 17 December 1872, 8:2; "most expensively dressed" in *The Arcadian* 1 (31 October 1872): 2; "sang poorly" in *Brainard's Musical World* 10 (April 1873): 60.

16. *The Arcadian* 1 (16 October 1872): 2, also quoted in *Dexter Smith's* 3 (January 1873): 10. The *Arcadian* ruthlessly harassed Liebhart the entire season. Once it claimed to quote from the *Peoria Review* regarding Liebhart and Ormeny: "Mlle. Liebhart didn't leave a dry eye in the wigwam when she sang 'There sno plash li kome,' ["There's no place like home"] and it was the general impression among her German auditors that she sang 'Rawbing Awdah' in English, while the English-speaking inhabitants were equally positive that 'Robin Adair' was a German ballad. Mlle. Ormeny had, and we suppose still retains, a magnificent voice for a fog-whistle. Its compass was perfectly surprising. She would shake the chandelier with a wild whoop that made every man instinctively feel for his scalp, and follow it up with a roar that would shame a bassoon" (1 [3 April 1873]: 7).

17. *Indianapolis Sentinel,* 17 December 1872, 8:2.

18. *NYDTr,* 16 November 1872, 8:2.

19. *NYH,* 16 November 1872, 7:4; *NYDTr,* 16 November 1872, 8:2; *Watson's Art Journal* 18 (23 November 1872): 43; *NYT,* 13 November 1872, 7:5.

20. *NYW,* 18 November 1872, 1:3.

21. Conversation with Philharmonic board in Steinway, Diary, 28 September 1872; Philharmonic rehearsal in *NYH,* 16 November 1872, 7:4; Philharmonic concert in *NYH,* 17 November 1872, 9:5.

22. Blackmar advertisement in *NODP,* 5 February 1873, 8:6; communication from W. A. Haas in *NODP,* 9 February 1873, 4:3; *Worcester Daily Spy,* 11 April 1873, 1:3.

23. On the Steinway firm and the duplex scale, see Cynthia Adams Hoover, "The Steinways and Their Pianos in the Nineteenth Century," *Journal of the American Musical Instrument Society* 7 (1981): 47–89, especially p. 61, and Edwin M. Good, *Giraffes, Black Dragons, and Other Pianos: A Technological History from Cristofori to the Modern Concert Grand,* 2d ed. (Stanford: Stanford University Press, 2001), *passim,* especially p. 234. Some contemporary press accounts incorrectly describe the action as functioning more like a coupler on an organ, causing a key to strike the principal note as well as the note an octave higher.

24. *Philadelphia Evening Bulletin,* 29 October 1872, 2:1. Before leaving the U.S. Rubinstein gave the customary certificate of his endorsement, which was to be used prominently in publicity: "I wish to express to you my heartfelt thanks for all the kindness and courtesy you have shown to me during my stay in the United States, but first of all for the beautiful instruments which have stood up so wonderfully during the long, difficult journey throughout the country" (Letter to William Steinway, New York, 24 May 1873; all letters from Rubinstein to the Steinways cited here are in the International Piano Archives, University of Maryland, College Park, and are quoted in translations by Theodore E. Steinway). Compared to the effusions of Berlioz, Liszt, and Wagner in their certificates given to Steinway, Rubinstein's tribute seems, as Fostle observed, "tepid and brief" (*The Steinway Saga,* 173).

25. *DJM* 32 (2 November 1872): 334; *BP,* 15 October 1872, 3:5.

26. Steinway, "Personal Reminiscences"; Rubinstein, Letter to William Steinway, Boston, 14 October 1872. Rubinstein continued his request slightly more seriously, "Should some misfortune befall me while in this country such as death or similar unpleasantnesses, please be kind enough to send the money which you hold for me to my wife."

CHAPTER 12: RUBINSTEIN'S "MAGNIFICENT FAULTINESS"

1. *NYT,* 4 January 1873, 4:7; *Missouri Republican* (St. Louis), 23 January 1873, 8:3.

2. *The Amateur* 3 (December 1872): 61.

3. *DJM* 35 (11 December 1875): 144.

4. "False notes" in Aubertine Woodward Moore, "Rubinstein's Meteoric Tour of America," *The Etude* 29 (November 1911): 732; Zerrahn conversation in Tracy, "Anton Rubinstein, As I Remember Him."

5. "Systematic work" in Abell, "Impressions of Anton Rubinstein"; Rubinstein, "An Hour with Rubinstein."

6. Mason, *Memories of a Musical Life,* 225–26; Rubinstein, Letter to William Steinway, Cincinnati, 3 March 1873.

7. Mason, *Memories of a Musical Life,* 224; William Foster Apthorp, "The Season," *The Atlantic Monthly* 30 (December 1872): 757; *MTR* 10 (2 August 1879): 1; H. E. Krehbiel, *Review of the New York Musical Season, 1888–1889* (New York: Novello, Ewer, 1889), 185; *Watson's Art Journal* 18 (5 April 1873): 271. The "emotional cyclones" stirred up by Rubinstein are colorfully portrayed by the American humorist George William Bagby (1828–1883) in "Jud Brownin's Account of Rubenstein's [*sic*] Playing," undoubtedly the most famous description of a Rubinstein performance; the piece is reprinted in *Selections from the Miscellaneous Writings of Dr. George W. Bagby,* 2 vols. (Richmond: Whittet & Shepperson, 1884–85), 1:392–98.

8. *DJM* 32 (2 November 1872): 334; *Chicago Daily Tribune,* 4 December 1872, 5:2; *BDET,* 16 May 1873, 1:7.

9. *NYDTr,* 30 September 1872, 2:2; *DJM* 32 (19 October 1872): 326–27.

10. *The Arcadian* 1 (24 April 1873): 3; *NYT,* 2 October 1872, 4:7, 1 January 1873, 1:4, and 20 May 1873, 4:7; New York correspondent, *DJM* 32 (11 January 1873): 365; *NYH,* 28 September 1872, 6:6; *DJM* 32 (11 January 1873): 367.

11. *BP,* 17 October 1872, 3:5; *PI,* 8 November 1872, 7:2; *NYH,* 28 September 1872, 6:6.

12. *DJM* 32 (25 January 1873): 373; Rubinstein, *A Conversation on Music,* 115–16. Rubinstein's pupil Josef Hofmann remembered that his teacher was "much given to whims and moods, and he often grew enthusiastic about a certain conception only to prefer a different one the next day." Once Rubinstein told him when he played a phrase the same way twice: "In fine weather you may play it as you did, but when it rains play it differently" (Josef Hofmann, *Piano Playing with Piano Questions Answered* [Philadelphia: Theodore Presser, 1920; reprint, New York: Dover Publications, 1976], 58).

13. Rubinstein, *A Conversation on Music,* 112; *DJM* 33 (19 April 1873): 7; William Foster Apthorp,

"The Season," *The Atlantic Monthly* 30 (December 1872): 758, and "Music," *The Atlantic Monthly* 39 (February 1877): 253.

14. *NYH*, 25 October 1872, 7:5; Rubinstein as successor to Schubert and Chopin in Anton Rubinstein, *Anton Rubinstein's Gedankenkorb* (Leipzig: Bartholf Senff, 1897), 145; Beatty-Kingston quoted by Philip Hale in *Anton Rubinstein: Selected Pieces for Pianoforte*, 2 vols. (New York: G. Schirmer, 1896), 1:[iv].

15. The work is reprinted along with ten other pieces of moderate difficulty in Joseph Banowetz, ed., *Anton Rubinstein: Piano Music* (Mineola, N.Y.: Dover Publications, 2001).

16. Damrosch quoted in George Martin, *The Damrosch Dynasty: America's First Family of Music* (Boston: Houghton Mifflin, 1983), 31; Rosenthal anecdote in Leonard Liebling, "Variations," *Musical Courier* 99 (23 November 1929): 37.

17. *DJM* 32 (2 November 1872): 334, and 32 (11 January 1873): 367.

18. *Toronto Globe*, 21 December 1872, 1:4; *NYT*, 23 May 1873, 5:3.

19. "Lightning intercommunication" in *Buffalo Morning Express*, 26 November 1872, 1:4; special trains in *Utica Daily Observer*, 18 November 1872, 3:4.

20. *Troy Daily Times*, 25 April 1873, 3:1; *Toronto Mail*, 6 May 1873, 4:7, and *Toronto Globe*, 6 May 1873, 1:10. Wieniawski missed only two appearances during the season, this concert in Toronto (5 May 1873) and a matinée in New York (2 April 1873). Rubinstein claimed that in Russia Wieniawski had "quite often failed to meet his appointments" because of ill health, but in America, "however ill he might be, he always contrived to find strength enough to appear on the platform," for his contract required that he forfeit 1,000 francs ($200) for every concert he missed (*Autobiography*, 116).

21. *Hartford Daily Courant*, 27 December 1872, 2:5.

22. *Daily Ohio State Journal*, 30 November 1872, 4:3; *Buffalo Commercial Advertiser*, 23 December 1872, 3:2; *Detroit Free Press*, 20 December 1872, 1:8.

23. *Chicago Daily Tribune*, 8 December 1872, 6:3—4.

24. *The Musical Echo* 1 (January 1873): 8; *Terre Haute Express*, 23 January 1873, 4:2.

25. *Detroit Free Press*, 19 December 1872, 1:4; *Chicago Daily Tribune*, 4 December 1872, 5:2; Cleveland concerts in *Brainard's Musical World* 10 (January 1873): 10.

26. *Chicago Daily Tribune*, 7 December 1872, 5:3, 8 December 1872, 5:3, and 8 December 1872, 6:4.

27. *Troy Daily Times*, 25 April 1873, 3:3.

28. *Albany Evening Journal*, 29 April 1873, 3:2—3; *The Musical Echo* 2 (June 1873): 105.

29. [Alexander Wheelock Thayer], "Diary Abroad.—No. 14," *DJM* 7 (7 April 1855): 2. See James H. Johnson, *Listening in Paris: A Cultural History* (Berkeley: University of California Press, 1995) for a survey of the transformation of the behavior of Parisian audiences from the mid-eighteenth century, when music was viewed as background noise for socializing, to the mid-nineteenth century, when they begin to listen with silence to the music's meaning.

30. *Memphis Daily Appeal*, 11 February 1873, 4:5; *DJM* 32 (2 November 1872): 335.

31. Rubinstein, *A Conversation on Music*, 110.

32. *DJM* 32 (11 January 1873): 367.

33. Arthur Elson, "Famous Pianists of Past and Present," in *The International Library of Music for Home and Studio*, ed. Charles Dennée, et al., 4 vols. (New York: The University Society, 1925), 3:11.

CHAPTER 13: JOINT VENTURE WITH THEODORE THOMAS

1. *Watson's Art Journal* 18 (18 January 1873): 139.

2. *NYT*, 1 January 1873, 1:4; *DJM* 32 (25 January 1873): 373; *NYDTr*, 4 January 1873, 5:2.

3. *MTR* 10 (2 August 1879): 1; *DJM* 32 (11 January 1873): 365; *The New-York Musical Gazette* 7 (February 1873): 20. Ezra Schabas believes that Thomas's association with Rubinstein and Wieniawski, performers who did not "sacrifice their integrity when they allow[ed] music's expressive demands to take precedence over the written page," helped his "readings become more 'human'" (*Theodore Thomas: America's Conductor and Builder of Orchestras, 1835–1905* [Urbana: University of Illinois Press, 1989], 53).

4. "Greater share of applause" in *New York Clipper*, 25 January 1873, 343:2; "walking to and fro" in *PI*, 16 January 1873, 7:1.

5. *NODP*, 8 February 1873, 8:5. Several of the cities received a visit from a major pianist for the first time: Titusville, Pennsylvania; Steubenville, Ohio; Terre Haute, Indiana; Grand Rapids and Kalamazoo, Michigan; Bloomington and Jacksonville, Illinois; and Burlington, Iowa.

6. *Indianapolis Sentinel*, 21 January 1873, 5:3; *Mobile Daily Register*, 30 January 1873, 1:4, and 31 January 1873, 1:4.

7. Upton, *Musical Memories*, 69; Cleveland concert in *Brainard's Musical World* 10 (April 1873): 60.

8. *Cincinnati Daily Gazette,* 6 March 1873, 8:1; Rubinstein, Letter to William Steinway, Cincinnati, 3 March 1873; Steinway, "Personal Reminiscences."

9. *St. Louis Times* quoted in "Rubinstein's Views about Art, Musical Taste and Culture in America," *The Song Journal* 3 (March 1873): 470; all further quotations from Rubinstein on this topic are from this source. Rubinstein later complained about interviews, which he conceded might be appropriate for politicians, but not for artists; like the mania for collecting autographs, he considered the rage for interviews with artists to be a plague in both Europe and America (*Anton Rubinstein's Gedankenkorb,* 108–9).

10. Herz had similar opinions when reflecting on his American tour: "Democracy is by no means favorable to the development of thought or the noble aspirations of art" (*Fm* 16 [25 January 1852]: 33, free trans. in *The Musical Times* 4 [10 April 1852]: 364).

11. *DJM* 33 (12 July 1873): 53. True conservatories on an advanced level were only beginning to be established shortly before Rubinstein's American visit. Oberlin Conservatory was established in 1865 and in 1867 three more conservatories were founded: the Boston Conservatory, the New England Conservatory, and the Cincinnati Conservatory. The first one to be established in the United States had been the conservatory of the Peabody Institute, founded in 1857 in Baltimore, but instruction in music did not begin until 1868.

12. Theodore Thomas, *Theodore Thomas: A Musical Autobiography,* ed. George P. Upton, 2 vols. (Chicago: A. C. McClurg, 1905; reprint, New York: Da Capo Press, 1964), 1:63; *Buffalo Courier* quoted in *The Musical Echo* 2 (June 1873): 105; *Cleveland Daily Plain Dealer,* 1 May 1873, 3:3; see also Joseph Horowitz, "'Sermons in Tones': Sacralization as a Theme in American Classical Music," *American Music* 16 (1998): 311–39.

13. *NYS,* 4 April 1873, 2:5; *PI,* 5 April 1873, 3:2; *DJM* 33 (19 April 1873): 7.

14. *Cincinnati Daily Gazette,* 21 March 1873, 8:3; *Washington Evening Star,* 15 April 1873, 1:1; Thomas quotation in John S. Van Cleve, "Concerning Musical Memory," *Music* 12 (October 1897): 642.

15. Steinway and Rubinstein quotations in Steinway, "Personal Reminiscences."

16. B. J. Lang performed the American premiere of the Third Concerto in Boston in February 1872 (with the Harvard Musical Association) and Marie Krebs premiered the Fourth Concerto in April 1871 (with the New York Philharmonic).

17. Albert Ross Parsons, "Rubinstein as Pianist and How He Composed His Ocean Symphony," *Musical Courier* 99 (23 November 1929): 39.

18. *DJM* 33 (19 April 1873): 5; *NYDTr,* 1 April 1873, 4:6, reprinted in *DJM* 33 (19 April 1873): 4; *PI,* 13 May 1873, 4:2–3.

19. Rubinstein, *A Conversation on Music,* 117; *NYDTr,* 1 April 1873, 4:6, reprinted in *DJM* 33 (19 April 1873): 4; *NYH,* 1 April 1873, 12:1.

20. Nevins and Thomas, eds., *The Diary of George Templeton Strong,* 4:473–74, 477, 479; Shanet, *Philharmonic,* 150–51. Strong recorded in his diary on the day of the vote: "I begin to perceive in the Philharmonic Society, what I suppose a shrewder person would have perceived long ago, namely, an intense jealousy of Theodore Thomas and his orchestra" (4:474). The society eventually made amends by electing Rubinstein an honorary member on 10 May; it had previously elected De Meyer, Herz, and Thalberg honorary members as well, although none of them had performed with the orchestra.

21. *DJM* 33 (3 May 1873): 15.

22. "Orchestra in his grasp" in *Orpheus* 8 (1 June 1873): 191; *BDET,* 22 May 1873, 1:4; *DJM* 33 (31 May 1873): 31.

23. The program booklet is reproduced in Ronald V. Ratcliffe, *Steinway* (San Francisco: Chronicle Books, 1989), 115–17. The programs contain numerous errors (even after being reprinted with corrections) and are annoyingly vague. Rubinstein made various deletions and additions not always readily identified by critics. A definitive list of what he performed is not possible, but see appendix B for an attempted reconstruction.

24. Robert Grau, *Forty Years Observation of Music and the Drama* (New York: Broadway Publishing Co., 1909), 291. The *New York World* (23 May 1873, 5:1) gave the receipts for each of the seven recitals, including a slightly smaller number for the most profitable one: $800, $1,200, $1,600, $1,400, $2,100, $2,600, and $3,000.

25. *DJM* 33 (17 May 1873): 22; *NYH,* 21 May 1873, 8:6.

26. *DJM* 33 (31 May 1873): 30; *The Arcadian* 1 (22 May 1873): 3; *Watson's Art Journal* 19 (24 May 1873): 43.

27. *NYT,* 13 May 1873, 4:7.

28. W. S. B. Mathews, "Antoine Rubinstein," *Music* 7 (February 1895): 387; *Watson's Art Journal* 19 (10 May 1873): 19; Mason, *Memories of a Musical Life,* 226–27.

29. *The Arcadian* 1 (22 May 1873): 3; *NYDTr,* 15 May 1873, 5:2.

30. *NYH,* 20 May 1873, 6:6, and 21 May 1873, 8:6.

31. *NYT,* 23 May 1873, 5:3, and 21 May 1873, 7:3; *NYDTr,* 19 May 1873, 5:1, and 20 May 1873, 8:3; *The Arcadian* 1 (29 May 1873): 3; A[lbert] R[oss] Parsons in *Benham's Musical Review,* quoted in *DJM* 33 (26 July 1873): 57. Rubinstein later claimed that he would "not allow myself to rely upon my own resources or ability to supply the place of some forgotten passage, because I know that there will always be many among my audiences, who, being familiar with the piece I am performing, will readily detect any alteration" (*Autobiography,* 17–18).

32. Attendance report in *BDET,* 22 May 1873, 1:4; *DJM* 33 (31 May 1873): 30–31; M. Grau, "Some Rubinstein Reminiscences." Comments about Rubinstein showing the strain of touring are relatively rare. In late April a critic in Troy was "sorry to see him so evidently worn and overtaxed last night." He believed Rubinstein should "save himself a little," since he had no successor and the "world cannot spare him" (*Troy Daily Times,* 25 April 1873, 3:3).

33. *NYW,* 23 May 1873, 4:6; *NYDTr,* 23 May 1873, 5:4; *NYT,* 23 May 1873, 5:3.

34. "Evidence of emotion" in *NYDTr,* 23 May 1873, 5:4; *NYT,* 23 May 1873, 5:3.

35. *NYH,* 23 May 1873, 7:5; *NYT,* 23 May 1873, 5:3. As manager, Maurice Grau netted $60,000 from the tour, two-thirds of which he presented to his uncle (M. Grau, "Some Rubinstein Reminiscences"). In two separate articles, Robert Grau, a brother of Maurice, gives numerous figures on receipts in various cities. The average receipts in New York were less than $1,000 per concert, while on the road the proceeds ranged from $500 to $2,200 per concert. The average receipts for concerts with the Thomas Orchestra were $2,000 ("Memories of Musicians: Rubinstein and Wieniawski"; "The Rubinstein-Wieniawski Tour of 1871 [sic]," *Musical America* 15 [4 May 1912]: 21).

36. *NYH,* 25 May 1873, 8:3; *NYW,* 23 May 1873, 5:1.

37. Steinway, "Personal Reminiscences"; M. Grau, "Some Rubinstein Reminiscences."

38. Steinway, "Personal Reminiscences"; Field conversation in *DJM* 33 (12 July 1873): 53; "American-dollar villa" in Lillian Nichia, "A Girl's Recollections of Rubinstein," *Harper's Monthly Magazine* 126 (December 1912): 47.

39. Rubinstein, *Autobiography,* 115. Steinway remembered the pianist's patiently bearing the "toils and trials" of traveling but not being able to erase the experience from his memory. "All through the remainder of his life . . . he never spoke without a shudder of the tortures he had suffered" ("Personal Reminiscences").

40. "Spiritual thoughts" in *Whitney's Musical Guest* 6 (January 1873): 4; *DJM* 33 (31 May 1873): 31.

Chapter 14: Escape to the New World

1. *Ella's Record* quoted in *The Musical Echo* 2 (August 1873): 143.

2. The best introductions in English to Bülow's student years are *The Early Correspondence of Hans von Bülow,* ed. Marie von Bülow, trans. Constance Bache (London: T. Fisher Unwin, 1896) and Alan Walker, *Franz Liszt, Volume Two: The Weimar Years, 1848–1861* (New York: Alfred A. Knopf, 1989).

3. Bülow, Letters to his father, Weimar, 25 October and 17 June 1851 (*Early Correspondence,* 93 and 82); Liszt, Letter to Anton Augusz, 12 May 1853 (quoted in Walker, *Liszt, Volume Two: The Weimar Years,* 177 n.20).

4. Bülow obviously figures prominently in the Wagner literature; see especially Geoffrey Skelton, *Richard and Cosima Wagner: Biography of a Marriage* (Boston: Houghton Mifflin, 1982). Alan Walker perceptively summarizes the complex relations between Bülow, Wagner, and Cosima, and quotes from previously unpublished letters in *Liszt, Volume Three: The Final Years,* 106–46.

5. "A Pleasant Chat with Dr. Hans Guido Von Bülow, the Great Pianist," *Chicago Times,* 6 February 1876, 4:1–2.

6. Most of Bülow's letters written in the United States and others concerning his American tour are only available in a comprehensive German edition of his writings: *Hans von Bülow: Briefe und Schriften,* ed. Marie von Bülow, 8 vols. (Leipzig: Breitkopf und Härtel, 1895–1908). Several of his American letters are translated in *Letters of Hans von Bülow,* ed. Richard Count du Moulin Eckart, trans. Hannah Waller (New York: Alfred A. Knopf, 1931; reprint, New York: Da Capo Press, 1979); a few remain unpublished altogether. Unless otherwise indicated, the letters quoted here appear in *Briefe und Schriften,*

vol. 6, as do letters to Bülow from Bernard Ullman and Tchaikovsky. I quote from them in translations suggested by Siegmund Levarie. The letter to the Editor of the *New York Herald,* New York, 28 December 1875, originally written in English, is letter no. 187 in vol. 6.

7. "Bülow on Wagner," *NYH,* 1 November 1875, 7:5.

8. 1860s tour in various letters to Carl Bechstein from 15 July through 22 November 1866 (*Letters,* 51–63); 1870s tour in letter to Cosima Wagner, Hall, 28 June 1875 (*Letters,* 264).

9. No. 170 to Bernard Ullman, London, 5 April 1875; Ullman to Bülow, quoted in Bülow, *Briefe und Schriften,* 6:280. One copy of the first Rubinstein contract with Jacob Grau of 24 October 1871 now in the Music Division of the Library of Congress contains a handwritten dedication by Bülow in French ("To the museum of antiquities of Mr. Louis Engel [signed:] Hans v. Bülow"), indicating it was at one time in Bülow's possession.

10. Ullman to Bülow, quoted in Bülow, *Briefe und Schriften,* 6:279; no. 53 to Bernard Ullman, Baden-Baden, 30 June 1873; no. 141 to Bernard Ullman, London, 2 January 1875. Bülow relates the basic terms of the contract in no. 218 to Jessie Laussot, New Orleans, 16 February 1876, and the number of concerts appears in two brief reports of his contract in *MTR* 1 (18 January 1876): 83, and 2 (3 June 1876): 33. William Steinway was shown a copy of the contract and noted that it was dated 22 June 1875 (Diary, 28 January 1876).

11. No. 92 to Bernard Ullman, Moscow, 24 March 1874; no. 141 to Bernard Ullman, London, 2 January 1875.

12. For instance, in one Boston concert "he made a kindred passage of a few measures from the Adagio of the Ninth Symphony serve as prelude to the 'Moonlight,' and very happily," according to Dwight (*DJM* 35 [13 November 1875]: 126). On another occasion he began a performance of the Beethoven Sonata, Op. 31, No. 2 ("Tempest"), with a prelude based on the opening theme of the Sonata, Op. 31, No. 3 (*NYW,* 23 March 1876, 4:5). A few people objected to the practice, but others thought it "delightful and appropriate" (*PI,* 13 March 1876, 4:5). A later writer remembered: "One keen delight in his recitals was to listen to the art with which he linked the numbers together by themes drawn from the work he had finished and the one he was about to play, one merging almost imperceptibly into the other" (Frederic S. Law, "The Piano: Brief Biographies of Pianists—Hans von Bülow," *The Musician* 10 [November 1905]: 462). On the practice of preluding, see Valerie Woodring Goertzen, "By Way of Introduction: Preluding by 18th- and Early 19th-Century Pianists," *The Journal of Musicology* 14 (1996): 299–337.

13. No. 1 to Emil Heckel, Munich, 10 June 1872. Entries from William Steinway's diary verify the firm's discussions with Bülow: "telegram from Theodore . . . Bülow next year certain" (12 June 1872); "Palmer of Jarrett & Palmer called yesterday in relation to Bülow Ullman contract" (10 September 1873).

14. Rumors in *Concordia* 1 (16 October 1875): 399, 407, and *Chicago Tribune,* 15 September 1875; Bernard Ullman, Letters to the Editor, *Concordia* 1 (23 October 1875): 422, and 1 (18 December 1875): 550–51, first letter reprinted in *MTR* 1 (18 November 1875): 15, and *DJM* 35 (13 November 1875): 125. The *Music Trade Review* (1 [3 December 1875]: 39), which was sympathetic to the piano maker's perspective, reported that Frank Chickering in a private interview stated that Ullman's letter was "substantially correct" and the firm had paid no subvention. In the same issue the journal was authorized by William Steinway to state: "The only transaction his house ever had with Dr. von Bülow or his agents was to decline an offer made them by Mr. Harry Palmer to get Bülow to use their pianos exclusively for the sum of $20,000 gold. Mr. Steinway denied that any overtures had been made by them in the matter."

15. No. 141 to Bernard Ullman, London, 2 January 1875; no. 168 to Bernard Ullman, London, 28 February 1875; no. 169 to Bernard Ullman, London, 29 March 1875; Steinway, Diary, 6 January 1876.

16. *Concordia* 1 (11 December 1875): 527. The *Pall Mall Gazette,* on the other hand, thought there was "really no great harm in the system. It is simply a question of delicacy; and, when an artist is bent on gaining money, considerations of delicacy disappear in presence of twenty thousand dollars." It assumed, however, that a pianist would not accept a second-rate piano in place of a first-rate one even for financial gain ("The Commerce of Music," reprinted in *DJM* 35 [13 November 1875]: 124–25).

17. Letters to Cosima Wagner, Hall, 28 June 1875, and Munich, 14 July 1875 (*Letters,* 264, 275); he wrote several lengthy letters to Cosima that summer apprising her of his health and the arrangements he was making for their daughters.

18. Bülow described the voyage to Ullman: "The crossing was exceptionally bad—I was seasick *coi fiocchi* as the compatriots of Verdi say. Without your *concertväterliche* solicitude to give me a cabin all to myself—I would have perhaps succumbed. It was frightful—facing me there was a cabin with four German babies crying in Saxon—imagine" (no. 179 to Bernard Ullman, Boston, 18–19 October 1875). The

multilingual character of Bülow's letters is evident here: the main text is in French with bits of Italian and German for spice.

19. *BET,* 11 October 1875, 6:1; *DJM* 35 (16 October 1875): 110.

20. No. 126 to Bernard Ullman, Liebenstein, 12 September 1874; no. 125 to Bernard Ullman, Liebenstein, 11 September 1874; no. 173 to Bernard Ullman, Munich, 9 June 1875. Bülow's substantial repertoire dates from his studies with Liszt, whose plan for him was to "make such a *répertoire . . .* as not every pianist, or indeed no pianist, can show" (Letter to his father, Weimar, 6 July 1851 [*Early Correspondence,* 86]).

21. Repose in *Salem Register,* 13 April 1876; debut in *Boston Advertiser,* 19 October 1875, quoted in *The Arcadian* 4 (23 October 1875): 4.

22. "Physiognomy" in *Detroit Evening News,* 29 January 1876, 4:2; New York debut in *NYW,* 16 November 1875, 5:1.

23. *DJM* 35 (30 October 1875): 118; *BP,* 19 October 1875, 3:4; *BET,* 19 October 1875, 4:4; *NYT,* 19 October 1875, 4:6; no. 179 to Bernard Ullman, Boston, 18–19 October 1875.

24. An equally astonishing and less well-known fact is that the premiere of Tchaikovsky's Second Piano Concerto also took place in America, on 12 November 1881 by the New York Philharmonic with the British-born Madeline Schiller as soloist and Theodore Thomas as conductor (Michael Keyton, "Madeline Schiller," *Music and Musicians* 35 [May 1987]: 29–30).

25. Tchaikovsky to Nadezhda von Meck, 2[–3] February 1878, in Galina von Meck, trans., *"To my best friend": Correspondence between Tchaikovsky and Nadezhda von Meck, 1876–1878,* ed. Edward Garden and Nigel Gotteri (Oxford: Clarendon Press, 1993), 151–52. All dates concerning Tchaikovsky's correspondence have been westernized.

26. Bülow on *Romeo and Juliet* in "Musikalisches aus Italien," *Allgemeine Zeitung,* nos. 148 and 152 (1874), reprinted in *Briefe und Schriften* (2d, expanded ed., 1911), vol. 3, part 2, p. 145, partial trans. in Modeste Tchaikovsky, *The Life and Letters of Peter Ilich Tchaikovsky,* ed. and trans. Rosa Newmarch (New York: Dodd, Mead, 1905), 157; Bülow's letter quoted in Tchaikovsky, *Life and Letters,* 167.

27. *BET,* 26 October 1875, 4:2; *DJM* 35 (13 November 1875): 126; *NYH,* 23 November 1875, 7:4; *NYW,* 23 November 1875, 5:1.

28. *NYDTr,* 2 November 1875, 5:1; Tchaikovsky, Letter to Rimsky-Korsakov, Moscow, 24 November 1875, in Tchaikovsky, *Life and Letters,* 175.

29. Orchestra in *The Musical Standard* 9 (4 December 1875): 372, and *NYH,* 21 October 1875, 10:2; Henselt performance in *NYH,* 21 October 1875, 10:2; Liszt performance in *NYT,* 24 October 1875, 7:1; Beethoven and Liszt rehearsals in *NYH,* 22 October 1875, 7:3; Henselt rehearsal in *NYH,* 20 October 1875, 7:5; Philharmonic member in *NYH,* 22 November 1875, 5:4.

30. *NYH,* 22 October 1875, 7:3.

31. "Privately" in letter to Karl Klindworth, Boston, 31 October 1875 (*Letters,* 12); "publicly" in *BET,* 26 October 1875, 4:3. One writer remembered Bülow being "extravagant in testifying his satisfaction" with Lang and reported this conversation with the pianist: "'Did you see my little scene with the conductor?' I said that I did, and asked why he was so desperately demonstrative, and why he made such a scene. 'Ah! you ask that? I expected you would,' he said. 'But why not? It did me no harm, and it may do him good. Beside, I was so grateful that the conducting was no worse, that I could not restrain myself'" (*Musical Courier* 28 [28 February 1894]: 7).

32. Satisfaction with public in *BP,* 21 October 1875, 3:5; Papyrus Club in *BET,* 30 October 1875, 8:2; Athenian Club in *BP,* 28 October 1875, 3:2; "Athens of America" in no. 181 to Jessie Laussot, Boston, 24 October 1875; address to audience in *DJM* 35 (30 October 1875): 119; "Eroica" Variations in *BP,* 21 October 1875, 3:5; Bostonians in Bülow, "A Pleasant Chat."

33. No. 180 to Eugen Spitzweg, Boston, 21 October 1875; no. 182 to his mother, Boston, 24 October 1875; no. 183 to his mother, New York, 15 November 1875.

34. *Providence Daily Journal,* 27 October 1875, 1:4, and 29 October 1875, 1:6; *New Haven Morning Journal and Courier,* 5 November 1875, 2:3.

35. *Providence Daily Journal,* 28 October 1875, 1:4; Steubenville incident in *Wheeling Daily Register,* 16 December 1875, 4:4; *NYH,* 27 November 1875, 10:2.

36. *Daily Louisville Commercial,* 4 March 1876, 4:2; letter to Eugen Spitzweg, Hartford, 7 November 1875 (all unnumbered letters to Spitzweg are in the Music Division, Library of Congress); Springfield incident in *Brainard's Musical World* 12 (December 1875): 186.

37. *Chicago Times,* 6 February 1876, 4:2–3; interview in "An Hour with Von Bülow," *NYS,* 17 November 1875, 3:1–2 (it was assumed he was adapting Psalm 111:10 or such similar passages as Proverbs

1:7, Proverbs 9:10, and Job 28:28); Pfeiffer, *Studien bei Hans von Bülow,* trans. in Zimdars, *The Piano Master Classes of Hans von Bülow,* 13, 10. Bülow formulated an even more sacrilegious credo that he supposedly told an interviewer on his return to the United States in 1889: "I believe in Bach the father, Beethoven the son, and in Brahms the holy ghost of music" ("An Interesting Talk with Von Bülow," *The Etude* 7 [May 1889]: 73).

38. *DJM* 35 (30 October 1875): 118; *MTR* 1 (18 November 1875): 16.

39. *BP,* 21 October 1875, 3:5; slogan in Bülow, "An Hour with Von Bülow"; letter to Karl Klindworth, New York, 24 November 1875 (*Letters,* 13); letter to Eugen Spitzweg, Hartford, 7 November 1875; no. 179 to Bernard Ullman, Boston, 18–19 October 1875.

40. No. 180 to Eugen Spitzweg, Boston, 21 October 1875.

41. *NYW,* 16 November 1875, 4:6; *NYH,* 20 November 1875, 10:3; Bülow's support of Damrosch in *Watson's Art Journal* 24 (20 November 1875): 44; letter to Karl Klindworth, New York, 24 November 1875 (*Letters,* 12); no. 183 to his mother, New York, 15 November 1875; Walter Damrosch recounts Rubinstein's suggestion to his father in *My Musical Life* (New York: Charles Scribner's Sons, 1930), 22–23.

42. No. 183 to his mother, New York, 15 November 1875; *Orpheus* 11 (1 December 1875): 122 (the scriptural reference here is to 1 Chronicles 21:24); a detailed description of the hall appears in *DJM* 35 (27 November 1875): 131.

43. *NYW,* 16 November 1875, 5:1; "false notes" in *NYH,* 25 November 1875, 10:1; *NYH,* 18 November 1875, 7:5; *NYT,* 18 November 1875, 4:6.

44. No. 183 to his mother, New York, 15 November 1875; *NYT,* 16 November 1875, 4:6.

45. *Polonaise brillante* in *NYW,* 27 November 1875, 5:1; encore speech in *NYH,* 23 November 1875, 7:4.

CHAPTER 15: "UNFORTUNATELY . . . HE ALSO TALKS"

1. Bülow, "An Hour with Von Bülow."

2. Shanet, *Philharmonic,* 154.

3. *NYS* quoted in "A Great Pianist's Trials," *MTR* 3 (3 January 1877): 77.

4. The *Chicago Tribune* agreed with Bülow on the subject of beer and contended that "beer as an element of music has always been its bane in Chicago." It predicted that the "German beer-drinkers" would "not make an open assault upon" Bülow, but would adopt the "underhanded German system of cliquing against him, . . . a favorite system with the average German musician," and a tactic that had been used against Theodore Thomas, who also campaigned against the combination of beer and music ("Von Bülow and Beer," *Chicago Tribune,* 21 November 1875, 4:4–5; see also "Bülow on Beer," *NYW,* 19 November 1875, 4:4–5).

5. *Harper's Weekly* 19 (4 December 1875): 979; *New-Yorker Musik-Zeitung* 18 (20 November 1875): 10; Bülow as unpatriotic in *Brainard's Musical World* 13 (January 1876): 5; New York correspondent to *Cologne Gazette* quoted in *NYDTr,* 1 April 1876, 5:3.

6. Manager in "A Great Pianist's Trials," *MTR* 3 (3 January 1877): 77; letter to Eugen Spitzweg, Hartford, 13 April 1876. Bülow's manager stated: "Bülow began with a much larger business than did Rubinstein. Before the article in the *Sun* we were making $6,000 a week with four concerts. After the article appeared we did a negative business, just about paying expenses." One Memphis writer had observed in a review of a Rubinstein concert there that the "strong tincture of the German element of our population" was "always among the best patrons and friends of music" (*Memphis Daily Appeal,* 12 February 1873, 4:5).

7. Letter to Eugen Spitzweg, Hartford, 7 November 1875. To Karl Klindworth, Bülow wrote that their mutual friend William Mason is "a nice fellow, but unfortunately, it appears, wholly in the hands of Steinway" (New York, 24 November 1875 [*Letters,* 13]). When asked why Bülow attacked the Steinways in the *Sun* interview, his manager replied: "Simply because he was in bad humor, and because they are Germans; for no other reason in the world. He bitterly regretted it, as he did the whole conversation, but he never denied having said all that was ascribed to him" ("A Great Pianist's Trials," *MTR* 3 [3 January 1877]: 77).

8. Rubinstein, Letter to Theodore Steinway, Peterhof, 21 December 1875; letter to Karl Klindworth, Boston, 31 October 1875 (*Letters,* 11); Mason in Steinway, Diary, 19 November 1875. Maurice Grau, Rubinstein's manager, saw the pianist while in Europe early the following year and reported in an interview that Rubinstein was "indignant" about Bülow's misrepresentation of his relationship with the Steinways. "He emphatically denied having ever accused the Messrs. Steinway of 'ungentlemanliness.'

He holds the Steinways in high esteem, and is greatly chagrined that such unwarrantable language should have been imputed to him" (*NYW*, 19 March 1876, 5:2–3).

9. Excerpts from Ullman's letters to Bülow, 4 and 14 September 1875, quoted in Bülow, *Briefe und Schriften*, 6:279–80; no. 175 to Bernard Ullman, Hall, 15 June 1875.

10. No. 183 to his mother, New York, 15 November 1875; no. 185 to his mother, Baltimore, 6 December 1875. He closes the second letter with a quotation from *Faust:* "If I could say to the moment/ Remain, you are so beautiful."

11. *DJM* 35 (30 October 1875): 118; *Brooklyn Daily Eagle*, 7 January 1876, 3:1; *MTR* 1 (3 December 1875): 27.

12. Mason, *Memories of a Musical Life*, 238–39; *Church's Musical Visitor*, March 1876, 150; Bülow on Rubinstein in Pfeiffer, *Studien bei Hans von Bülow*, trans. in Zimdars, *The Piano Master Classes of Hans von Bülow*, 17.

13. *DJM* 35 (11 December 1875): 143; *Portland (Maine) Daily Press*, 11 April 1876, 3:2.

14. *MTR* 10 (9 August 1879): 1; *DJM* 35 (11 December 1875): 143; *Poughkeepsie Daily News*, 19 January 1876, reprinted in *DJM* 35 (5 February 1876): 169; *Buffalo Commercial Advertiser*, 24 April 1876, 3:1; William Foster Apthorp, "Music," *The Atlantic Monthly* 37 (April 1876): 510–11.

15. No. 117 to Bernard Ullman, Salzungen, 23 July 1874. Almost a year later he reiterated to Ullman that he found himself "most incapable of doing 'sensationism' *à la* Rubinstein . . . for the purpose of playing the magician" (no. 173, Munich, 9 June 1875). Here, Bülow indulges in one of his many puns: in French—the language in which Bülow communicated with Ullman—the word for magician (*prestidigitateur*) means literally "fast fingerer."

16. No. 192 to his mother, Philadelphia, 19 December 1875.

17. No. 185 to his mother, Baltimore, 6 December 1875.

18. *NYW*, 28 November 1875, 5:4–5, partially quoted in *MTR* 1 (3 December 1875): 34.

19. No. 189 to Julius Stern, Washington, D.C., 7 December 1875.

20. Bülow on Hamerik in no. 220 to Romaine von Overbeck, Indianapolis, 28 February 1876; Sidney Lanier, Letters to his wife, Baltimore, 20 January 1875 and 2 December 1873, in *Letters of Sidney Lanier: Selections from His Correspondence, 1866–1881*, ed. Henry Wysham Lanier (New York: C. Scribner's Sons, 1899; reprint, Freeport, N.Y.: Books for Libraries Press, 1972), 109, 83; rehearsal in *Baltimore Bulletin*, 11 December 1875, reprinted in *DJM* 35 (25 December 1875): 147; ovation in *Baltimore Sun*, 7 December 1875, 2:1.

21. No. 188 to Jessie Laussot, Baltimore, 6 December 1875; rehearsal in *Baltimore Bulletin*, 11 December 1875, reprinted in *DJM* 35 (25 December 1875): 147.

22. *Concordia* 2 (15 January 1876): 41; "Piano Advertising," *NYT*, 25 December 1875, 4:4, reprinted in *MTR* 1 (3 January 1876): 63; see also "Pianists as Advertising Agents," *The Atlantic Monthly* 39 (February 1877): 229–30, reprinted in *DJM* 36 (17 February 1877): 389, and *MTR* 3 (18 April 1877): 206.

23. Theodore Steinway, Letter to William Steinway, Brunswick, Germany, 3 February 1877, quoted in Cynthia Adams Hoover, "The Great Piano War of the 1870s," in *A Celebration of American Music*, ed. Crawford, Lott, and Oja, 148.

24. *The Arcadian* 5 (8 January 1876): 4; *Buffalo Commercial Advertiser*, 24 January 1876, 3:2.

25. *The Song Journal* 6 (January 1876): 5.

26. Schlözer in no. 190 to Louise von Welz, Pittsburgh, 13 December 1875; "thunderstruck" in no. 205 to Romaine von Overbeck, Boston, 12 January 1876.

27. Articles on Romaine's mother, Madeleine Vinton Dahlgren, appear in *The Dictionary of American Biography* and *A Woman of the Century . . . Leading American Women*, ed. Frances E. Willard and Mary A. Livermore (Buffalo: Charles Wells Moulton, 1893). Mrs. Dahlgren published several books, including *Etiquette of Social Life in Washington* (1873); for its 5th edition (Philadelphia: J. B. Lippincott, 1881), Bülow set the opening text ("If Order Is Heaven's First Law") to music. Her novel *A Washington Winter* (Boston: James R. Osgood, 1883) is a thinly disguised autobiographical work about a prominent Washington hostess whose musical daughter, here a harpist rather than a pianist, is courted by a foreign diplomat. On Romaine's husband, see Rainer Pape, "Gustav Freiherr von Overbeck," *Lippische Mitteilungen aus Geschichte und Landeskunde* 28 (1959): 163–217.

28. No. 226 to Romaine von Overbeck, Albany, 19 April 1876.

29. Lang as conductor in *PI*, 18 December 1875, 2:5–6, and 22 December 1875, 8:1; rehearsal in William Foster Apthorp, "B. J. Lang," *Music* 4 (August 1893): 357–58.

30. *PI*, 18 December 1875, 2:6, and 23 December 1875, 3:2. As a young man of eighteen, the music critic James Huneker attended Bülow's Philadelphia appearances and forty years later remembered one

of them much differently, evidently with some exaggeration. In a performance of the Tchaikovsky Concerto, Lang's conducting was a "quite superfluous proceeding, as Von Bülow gave the cues from the keyboard and distinctly cursed the conductor, the band, the composition, and his own existence" ("The Grand Manner in Pianoforte Playing," 173). In his autobiography, Huneker claims that under Lang "things were soon at sixes and sevens; the solo performer was white with rage" (*Steeplejack* [New York: Charles Scribner's Sons, 1922], 247).

31. No. 192 to his mother, Philadelphia, 19 December 1875; no. 196 to Romaine von Overbeck, New York, 27 December 1875; *NYH,* 28 November 1875, 5:3. He also mentioned to his mother that "almost everywhere" there were meetings with "former pupils, male and female," from Berlin, Munich, and Florence.

32. *Wheeling Daily Register,* 16 December 1875, 4:4.

33. Nym Crinkle [pseudonym for A. C. Wheeler], "The Great Pianist," *NYW,* 5 December 1875, 6:1–2.

34. *Chicago Tribune,* 21 November 1875, 4:4–5; H. R. Haweis, *Music and Morals* (New York: Harper & Brothers, 1872), 437.

35. No. 222 to Romaine von Overbeck, New York, 18 March 1876; no. 194 to Kurd von Schlözer, New York, 24–25 December 1875; no. 219 to his mother, Louisville, 27 February 1876.

36. No. 216 to Romaine von Overbeck, St. Louis, 14 February 1876; no. 223 to Romaine von Overbeck, Boston, 3 April 1876.

37. *NYH,* 28 November 1875, 5:3.

38. *Brainard's Musical World* 13 (February 1876): 28.

39. *NYH,* 30 November 1875, 10:1; *NYT,* 30 November 1875, 4:5, and 4 December 1875, 4:6.

40. Leopold Damrosch, Letter to the Editor, *NYS,* 19 November 1875, 2:6; Walter Damrosch, *My Musical Life,* 76. Walter Damrosch later studied conducting, particularly the interpretation of Beethoven's symphonies, privately with Bülow in 1887. He was "amazed to find him throughout so companionable and so gentle in all his relations toward me. He had a heart most tender and sensitive, but life had dealt this idealist so many hard knocks that he incased his heart in a shell with which to protect it from further onslaughts" (p. 78).

41. *NYH,* 28 December 1875, 10:1.

42. "Rabble" in letter to Eugen Spitzweg, New Orleans, 19 February 1876; "Abt Franz" in no. 188 to Jessie Laussot, Baltimore, 6 December 1875. Here is another Bülow pun: by reversing Franz Abt's name, he refers to Liszt by his first name and his rank of abbot or abbé in the Roman Catholic Church. On the Thursby incident, see *Concordia* 2 (1 January 1876): 7, Richard McCandless Gipson, *The Life of Emma Thursby, 1845–1931* (New York: The New-York Historical Society, 1940; reprint, New York: Da Capo Press, 1980), 132–34, and *The Arcadian* 4 (11 December 1875): 12, which pointed out that Abt's compositions were "vastly superior" to those of Bülow.

43. *Church's Musical Visitor,* March 1876, 150; *MTR* 1 (3 February 1876): 113. The *New York World* (6 January 1876, 4:6) described McGeachy as a "brilliant but not invariably correct soprano."

44. Serenade in *NYT,* 9 January 1876, 6:7; no. 199 to his mother, New York, 1 January 1876 (the quotation is from Goethe's *Faust*); no. 200 to Louise von Welz, New York, 1 January 1876; no. 203 to Romaine von Overbeck, New York, 7–8 January 1876.

45. *DJM* 35 (5 February 1876): 174.

46. *DJM* 35 (5 February 1876): 174; Brahms in Bülow, "An Interesting Talk with Von Bülow." Bülow, who later coined the phrase "the three B's" (Bach, Beethoven, and Brahms), was grateful for the influence of Brahms and his music: "He taught me that there are many composers, many musicians, not one, and I owe him much for bringing me out of the sloughs of prejudice where the one-man worship prevails." During his 1875–76 tour, Bülow performed the first documented public performance of a solo piano work by Brahms in the United States, the *Variations and Fugue on a Theme by Handel* (Alison Deadman, "Brahms in Nineteenth-Century America," *Inter-American Music Review* 16 [Summer–Fall 1997]: 72).

47. *PI,* 13 March 1876, 4:5; *NYT,* 20 November 1875, 4:7.

48. *NYT,* 28 March 1876, 5:2; *NYH,* 18 November 1875, 7:5; *Baltimore Bulletin,* 11 December 1875, reprinted in *DJM* 35 (25 December 1875): 147; *PI,* 20 December 1875, 7:1; Bülow's bitterness reported by a friend in Alfred Veit, "Pianists and Pianism," *Music* 5 (November 1893): 6–7.

49. *NYT,* 20 November 1875, 4:7; *MTR* 1 (3 December 1875): 27–28; *DJM* 35 (30 October 1875): 119.

50. *NYT,* 30 December 1875, 4:6; *PI,* 11 March 1876, 3:1.

51. Arne Steinberg, "Liszt's Playing of the 'Moonlight' Sonata," *The Piano Quarterly,* no. 144 (Winter 1988–89): 52–57; *NYH,* 23 November 1875, 7:4; *MTR* 1 (3 December 1875): 27; *DJM* 35 (13 November 1875): 126. In his edition of the sonata in the series "Echoes from Chickering Hall" (New York: Edward Schuberth, 1876), Bülow marked the tempo for the allegretto as a dotted half note equals 56. He described the movement as "simply a lyric *'Intermezzo'* between two tragic Night-pieces," and stated that Liszt's "characterization of it as *'une fleur entre deux abîmes'* [a flower between two abysses] gives the key to the proper interpretation."

52. For a thorough discussion of Bülow's editions and his interpretations, see Hans-Joachim Hinrichsen, *Musikalische Interpretation Hans von Bülow,* Beihefte zum Archiv für Musikwissenschaft, vol. 46 (Stuttgart: Franz Steiner, 1999), which contains a complete list of Bülow's editions. See also Nicholas Cook, "The Editor and the Virtuoso, or Schenker versus Bülow," *Journal of the Royal Musical Association* 116 (1991): 78–95, and, concerning his edition of the Beethoven sonatas (with Sigmund Lebert), William S. Newman, "Liszt's Interpreting of Beethoven's Piano Sonatas," *The Musical Quarterly* 58 (1972): 185–209, esp. 203–6.

53. José Vianna da Motta, *Nachtrag zu Studien bei Hans von Bülow von Theodor Pfeiffer* (Berlin: Luckhardt, 1896), trans. in Zimdars, *The Piano Master Classes of Hans von Bülow,* 100.

CHAPTER 16: THE MIDWEST AND BACK

1. No. 117 to Bernard Ullman, Salzungen, 23 July 1874; no. 173 to Bernard Ullman, Munich, 9 June 1875. With one exception (Farmington, Conn.), Cronyn appeared in every city that Bülow did. She did not perform in his orchestral appearances or in all the chamber concerts.

2. *BET,* 11 January 1876, 1:5; *DJM* 35 (5 February 1876): 174.

3. *Orpheus* 11 (1 January 1876): 148; *DJM* 35 (5 February 1876): 174.

4. *Rochester Daily Union and Advertiser,* 22 April 1876, 2:6.

5. No. 207 to his mother, Cleveland, 26 January 1876; no. 185 to his mother, Baltimore, 6 December 1875.

6. No. 207 to his mother, Cleveland, 26 January 1876. Herz had similarly praised American hotels when he described his stay in Boston, though as a Frenchman he was less impressed with the food: "As with almost all hotels in America, the hotel where I stayed was of that high degree of comfort which astonishes and delights the European traveler. There was a lavish *table d'hote* admirably served, although not always excellently prepared (there are hardly any good cooks except in France), vast lavatory-basins in the bedrooms with hot and cold water faucets, gas lights, rugs throughout, and a great public drawing-room" (*Travels,* 13).

7. No. 207 to his mother, Cleveland, 26 January 1876; letter to Eugen Spitzweg, Detroit, 29 January 1876; Herz, *Travels,* 36; no. 183 to his mother, New York, 15 November 1875.

8. No. 210 to Louise von Welz, Chicago, 6 February 1876; no. 209 to Louise von Welz, Buffalo, 23 January 1876.

9. No. 207 to his mother, Cleveland, 26 January 1876; no. 230 to his mother, Cleveland, 27 April 1876; *Troy Daily Times,* 19 January 1876; *Indianapolis Sentinel,* 29 February 1876, 8:2; *Rochester Daily Union and Advertiser,* 22 January 1876, 2:3; *Buffalo Morning Express,* 24 January 1876, 4:4; *Daily Louisville Commercial,* 4 March 1876, 4:2; Chicago concerts in *Church's Musical Visitor,* March 1876, 146; hometown concert in *Buffalo Commercial Advertiser,* 24 January 1876, 3:2.

10. No. 215 to Romaine von Overbeck, Cincinnati, 7 February 1876; *Ithaca Daily Journal,* 21 January 1876.

11. No. 208 to his mother, Chicago, 2 February 1876; no. 210 to Louise von Welz, Chicago, 6 February 1876.

12. *Chicago Times,* 6 February 1876, 4:2–3.

13. Bernhard Ziehn, "Hans von Bülow in Chicago," *Jahrbuch der Deutsch-Amerikanischen historischen Gesellschaft von Illinois* 26–27 (1926–27): 85. A friend of Ziehn reported Bülow's reaction to Ziehn's comments in which he had greatly praised the pianist Eugen d'Albert: "When Bülow returned to Germany he met d'Albert, who asked for news from America, and Bülow said: 'You know it is perfectly immaterial what they write about me in the papers; but this has roiled me'—and he took Ziehn's criticism out of his vest pocket and gave it to d'Albert—'and do you know why I feel annoyed? because the man is perfectly right; I played very badly. When you get to Chicago do not forget to call on Ziehn and

give him my greetings and assure him of my greatest respect'" (Th. Otterstrom, "Personal Recollections of Bernhard Ziehn," *Jahrbuch der Deutsch-Amerikanischen historischen Gesellschaft von Illinois* 26–27 [1926–27]: 17).

14. Bülow, "A Pleasant Chat." The *New-York Times* (30 March 1876, 5:5) contended that Bülow played the "Spring Song" in a "rather unappreciative manner" and the *Springfield (Mass.) Daily Republican* (13 April 1876, 6:1) believed the work "would have better pleased at a slower rate." Bülow wrote that as a boy during 1844–46 he had frequently heard Mendelssohn play the piano and organ "in private circles" and had a great honor when the "master condescended, with rare patience, to offer him a lesson of several hours' duration" on the *Rondo capriccioso* and the *Capriccio brillant* (Preface to Bülow's edition of the *Rondo capriccioso,* reprinted in *Briefe und Schriften* [2d, expanded ed., 1911], vol. 3, part 2, pp. 206–9, trans. Susan Gillespie as "Felix Mendelssohn," in *Mendelssohn and His World,* ed. R. Larry Todd [Princeton: Princeton University Press, 1991], 391).

15. No. 208 to his mother, Chicago, 2 February 1876.

16. No. 218 to Jessie Laussot, New Orleans, 16 February 1876.

17. Climate in no. 209 to Louise von Welz, Buffalo, 23 January 1876; "patrician perfume" in no. 218 to Jessie Laussot, New Orleans, 16 February 1876; "lively behavior" in no. 219 to his mother, Louisville, 27 February 1876.

18. No. 217 to Romaine von Overbeck, New Orleans, 15–16 February 1876; poor attendance in no. 219 to his mother, Louisville, 27 February 1876.

19. Letter to Cosima Wagner, Chicago, 6 February 1876 (*Letters,* 275); no. 209 to Louise von Welz, Buffalo, 23 January 1876; no. 218 to Jessie Laussot, New Orleans, 16 February 1876. His agent Wertheimer remembered that "he talked seriously of becoming naturalized" and claimed he would "not be surprised should he return before many years and make his home here" ("A Great Pianist's Trials," *MTR* 3 [3 January 1877]: 77).

20. No. 206 to Romaine von Overbeck, Cleveland, 26 January 1876.

21. No. 220 to Romaine von Overbeck, Indianapolis, 28 February 1876; no. 228 to his mother, New York, 20 March 1876.

22. No. 228 to his mother, New York, 20 March 1876.

23. *NYW,* 21 March 1876, 5:1, and 24 March 1876, 5:1.

24. Temper in *The Arcadian* 5 (1 April 1876): 1; *NYT,* 21 March 1876, 5:2, and 28 March 1876, 5:2; physician's fees in no. 224 to Louise von Welz, Boston, 5 April 1876; "cry of anguish" in Bernard Ullman to Bülow, Paris, 9 April 1876, quoted in *Briefe und Schriften,* 6:369, and no. 231 to Bernard Ullman, New York, 17 May 1876.

25. Boston audiences in no. 223 to Romaine von Overbeck, Boston, 3 April 1876; *DJM* 36 (15 April 1876): 214–15.

26. No. 229 to his mother, Salem and Springfield, Massachusetts, 11–12 April 1876.

27. Bernard Ullman to Bülow, 18 April 1876, quoted in *Briefe und Schriften,* 6:370–71; *Terre Haute Evening Gazette,* 1 March 1876, 4:2; *Daily Louisville Commercial,* 3 March 1876, 4:2; *Syracuse Morning Standard,* 21 April 1876, 4:4.

28. Letter to Eugen Spitzweg, Columbus, Ohio, 28 April 1876; no. 230 to his mother, Cleveland, 27 April 1876.

29. Deterioration of pianos in letter to Eugen Spitzweg, Columbus, Ohio, 28 April 1876; *MTR* 2 (3 June 1876): 33; manager and friends of the Chickerings in *NYW,* 2 June 1876, 5:4; Steinway grand in Steinway, Diary, 21 March 1876.

30. No. 227 to Romaine von Overbeck, Buffalo, 24 April 1876; no. 230 to his mother, Cleveland, 27 April 1876.

31. Letter to Eugen Spitzweg, Columbus, Ohio, 28 April 1876.

32. No. 232 to his mother, New York, 22 May 1876; "Dr. Von Bülow's Illness," *NYW,* 2 June 1876, 5:4; letter to Carl Bechstein, New York, 1 June 1876 (*Letters,* 159). During his first concerts in Boston, he had written to William Mason that he had to "work very hard in spite of bad health and a not at all Rubinstein-like constitution." Just before his departure, Bülow inscribed an album leaf to Mason, his "dear fellow-pupil," in "remembrance of a most 'played-out' pianist" (Letter to Mason, Boston, 21 October 1875, quoted in Mason, *Memories of a Musical Life,* 239; album leaf, New York, 26 May 1876, reproduced between pp. 240–41).

33. Bernard Ullman to Bülow, Paris, 9 April 1876, quoted in *Briefe und Schriften,* 6:370. Bülow, who was quite ill at the time, was furious that Ullman had the nerve to "offer to an invalid individual put out

of combat in a current campaign an engagement for another campaign next season!" (no. 231 to Bernard Ullman, New York, 17 May 1876).

34. *Church's Musical Visitor,* March 1876, 149.

35. Philharmonic offer in *NYDTr,* 3 April 1876, 5:1, and letter to Louise von Welz, 20 March 1876, excerpt in *Briefe und Schriften,* 6:359. Dwight's letter to Bülow asking him to conduct the concerts of the Harvard Musical Association in Boston and Bülow's reply declining the offer appear in *Library of the Harvard Musical Association Bulletin,* no. 12 (October 1942). When interviewed in January 1876 about his plans following his piano tour, Bülow had replied: "I like leading; I might form an orchestra, particularly if I am able to get it together after my own ideas, intermixing nationalities as much as I can" (*MTR* 1 [18 January 1876]: 83).

36. His American colleagues B. J. Lang and Leopold Damrosch, however, would attend, and Damrosch would send back reports to the *New York Sun.* Through Lang and Cosima Wagner, Bülow also arranged for William Foster Apthorp, who had written sensitively about Bülow's playing in the *Atlantic Monthly* and would soon become one of Boston's leading critics, to write about the festival, replacing an inferior candidate. That Bülow would bother to orchestrate this for the sake of Bayreuth reflects his continued support of Wagner's music.

37. See letters to Cosima Wagner (Chicago, 6 February 1876 [*Letters,* 275]), Jessie Laussot (no. 218, New Orleans, 16 February 1876), Eugen Spitzweg (no. 258, New York, 4 April 1889 [*Briefe und Schriften,* vol. 8]), and his daughter Daniela (Boston, 16 April 1889 [*Letters,* 400]). The last two letters were written during the first of his two brief returns to the United States in 1889 and 1890.

38. *MTR* 10 (9 August 1879): 1; Wertheimer in "A Great Pianist's Trials," *MTR* 3 (3 January 1877): 77. In late March a rumor had circulated that Bülow would conduct the last Philharmonic concert of the season due to Bergmann's incapacity. One writer observed that, if true, such an invitation would "prove the christian magnanimity of the Germans, whom [Bülow] has lost no opportunity to assail since his arrival in this country" (*American Art Journal* n.s. 1 [25 March 1876]: 113). Nevertheless, Bülow was the only one of the five pianists not to be made an honorary member of the Philharmonic (see the list of honorary members in Krehbiel, *Philharmonic Society of New York,* 174).

39. No. 232 to his mother, New York, 22 May 1876.

POSTLUDE

1. Two other important European pianists, Rafael Joseffy (1853–1915) and Constantin Sternberg (1852–1924), immigrated to the United States in 1879 and 1880, respectively. On the American visits of Busoni, see Marc-André Roberge, "Ferruccio Busoni in the United States," *American Music* 13 (1995): 295–332.

2. See Margaret William McCarthy, *Amy Fay: America's Notable Woman of Music* (Warren, Mich.: Harmonie Park Press, 1995); Diana R. Hallman, "The Pianist Fannie Bloomfield Zeisler in American Music and Society" (M.M. thesis, University of Maryland, 1983); Adrienne Fried Block, *Amy Beach, Passionate Victorian: The Life and Work of an American Composer, 1867–1944* (New York: Oxford University Press, 1998).

3. James Huneker, "The Eternal Feminine," in *Overtones: A Book of Temperaments* (New York: Charles Scribner's Sons, 1904), 291–93, quoted in Neuls-Bates, ed., *Women in Music,* 182–83. See also Judith Tick, "Passed Away Is the Piano Girl: Changes in American Musical Life, 1870–1900," in *Women Making Music: The Western Art Tradition, 1150–1950,* ed. Jane Bowers and Judith Tick (Urbana: University of Illinois Press, 1986), 325–48.

4. Bülow's tour of 1889, for example, took place between March 24 and May 4, during which time he gave only about twenty concerts, including a series of four Beethoven concerts in New York featuring eighteen sonatas and seven other works. In an interview Bülow admitted that he had come "too soon before," was in bad health, and in "anything but a pleasant temper." This time he was in "splendid condition, and in good humor" and doubted that there would be "any *faux pas* to mar the pleasure of my trip" ("An Interesting Talk with Von Bülow," *The Etude* 7 [May 1889]: 73).

5. Lawrence W. Levine, *Highbrow/Lowbrow: The Emergence of Cultural Hierarchy in America* (Cambridge: Harvard University Press, 1988); John F. Kasson, "The Disciplining of Spectatorship," in *Rudeness and Civility: Manners in Nineteenth-Century Urban America* (New York: Hill and Wang, 1990), 215–56; see also Paul DiMaggio, "Cultural Entrepreneurship in Nineteenth-Century Boston," *Media, Culture and Society* 4 (1982): 33–50, 303–22.

6. Ralph P. Locke, "Music Lovers, Patrons, and the 'Sacralization' of Culture in America," *19th-Century Music* 17 (Fall 1993): 158.

7. George William Curtis, "Editor's Easy Chair," *Harper's New Monthly Magazine* 43 (July 1871): 293, also quoted in *DJM* 31 (1 July 1871): 51.

8. Krehbiel, *The Philharmonic Society of New York,* 83; Norman Lebrecht, *Who Killed Classical Music? Maestros, Managers, and Corporate Politics* (Secaucus, N.J.: Carol Publishing Group, 1998).

9. Some writers suggested, however, that Rubinstein, whose sloppiness was tolerable because he was also a genius, was not the best model for students. William Foster Apthorp, writing four years after Rubinstein's tour, believed the pianist's "influence upon young musicians has been in many cases undeniably bad." Neophyte virtuosos "premeditatedly" aped his "exaggerated passion and sentiment" and his interpretative license. One music journal remembered the "vigorous wave of musical enthusiasm which followed Rubinstein's tour through the land, to the delight of piano-tuners and the damage of piano-fortes" (William Foster Apthorp, "Music," *The Atlantic Monthly* 39 [February 1877]: 254; *Church's Musical Visitor,* March 1876, 149).

10. George William Curtis, "Editor's Easy Chair," *Harper's New Monthly Magazine* 52 (March 1876): 611–12. In 1892 Curtis reflected again on the changes in taste, with the public then infatuated with Paderewski playing Chopin instead of Thalberg performing his own fantasias. He warned, however, that the "haughty To-day must not depreciate Thalberg. He was as truly the key to the general taste of Yesterday as Paderewski is to that of To-day" ("Editor's Easy Chair," *Harper's New Monthly Magazine* 85 [July 1892]: 314).

11. W. S. B. Mathews, assoc. ed., *A Hundred Years of Music in America: An Account of Musical Effort in America* (Chicago: G. L. Howe, 1889), 112. A decade earlier the *Arcadian* had made similar claims. It believed that "those who remember the state of music in this country less than a quarter of a century ago . . . can scarcely understand how we can have made such wonderfully rapid progress," and it held that the "greatest factor in the spread of musical taste and culture is the pianoforte, for though imperfect as it may be theoretically, it is yet emphatically the home instrument" ("The Improvement in Our Musical Culture," *The Arcadian* 4 [25 December 1875]: 8).

12. *Charleston Daily Courier,* 21 January 1858.

13. *DJM* 35 (5 February 1876): 184; *Burlington (Vt.) Daily Free Press,* 7 February 1857.

Bibliography

Archival Sources

A list of extant programs for the concerts of De Meyer (9 concerts), Herz (13), and Thalberg (33) appears in Lott, "American Concert Tours." Programs for the concerts of Rubinstein and Bülow survive in abundance and are too numerous to list.

Bülow, Hans von. Letters to Eugen Spitzweg. Music Division, Library of Congress.

De Meyer, Leopold. Letter to Joseph Fischhof, New York, 7 February 1846. Wiener Stadt- und Landes-bibliothek.

Herz, Henri. Letter to Hiram Fuller, Natchez, 22 April 1847. Music Division, New York Public Library. Reproduced in Donald Garvelmann, *Variations on "Non più mesta"* by Henri Herz.

———. Letters to L. F. Newland, New York, 1 November and 6 December 1847. Historical Society of Pennsylvania, Philadelphia.

Mason, William. Scrapbook. Music Division, New York Public Library.

Musical Fund Society. Memorandum Book: Musical Fund Hall, March 1, 1837–September 30, 1847. Historical Society of Pennsylvania, Philadelphia.

Rubinstein, Anton. Contract with Jacob Grau. Vienna, 24 October 1871. Music Division, Library of Congress.

———. Contract with Jacob Grau, Maurice Grau, and Steinway and Sons. Vienna, 8 June 1872. International Piano Archives, University of Maryland, College Park.

———. Letters to William Steinway (Boston, 14 October 1872; Cincinnati, 3 March 1873; New York, 24 May 1873) and Theodore Steinway (Peterhof, 21 December 1875). International Piano Archives, University of Maryland, College Park.

Steinway, William. Diary, 20 April 1861 to 8 November 1896. Archives Center, National Museum of American History, Smithsonian Institution; copies in LaGuardia and Wagner Archives of LaGuardia Community College, the Metropolitan Museum of Art (New York), and the New-York Historical Society.

Thalberg, Sigismund. Letter to George William Warren, New York, 6 March 1857. Historical Society of Pennsylvania, Philadelphia.

Timm, Henry C. Scrapbook. Music Division, New York Public Library.

Upton, George P. "Attractions in Chicago: 1847–1881." Chicago Historical Society.

PUBLISHED SOURCES

More than fifty periodicals and three hundred newspaper titles from the nineteenth century were consulted for this study.

Abell, Arthur M. "Impressions of Anton Rubinstein." *Musical Courier* 99 (23 November 1929): 26, 39.

Anderson, Emily. *The Letters of Mozart and His Family.* 3d ed. London: Macmillan, 1985.

Anderson, Patricia. *When Passion Reigned: Sex and the Victorians.* New York: BasicBooks, 1995.

Andrade, Ayres de. "Um rival de Liszt no Rio de Janeiro." *Revista brasileira de música* 1 (April–June 1962): 27–50.

Anton Rubinstein: A Sketch. New York: Charles D. Koppel, [1872].

Apthorp, William Foster. "B. J. Lang." *Music* 4 (August 1893): 347–64.

Badeau, Adam. "Gottschalk and Thalberg." In *The Vagabond,* 15–21. New York: Rudd & Carleton, 1859.

Bagby, George W. *Selections from the Miscellaneous Writings of Dr. George W. Bagby.* 2 vols. Richmond: Whittet & Shepperson, 1884–85.

Banowetz, Joseph, ed. *Anton Rubinstein: Piano Music.* Mineola, N.Y.: Dover Publications, 2001.

Barbacci, Rodolfo. "Apuntes para un diccionario biográfico musical peruano." *Fénix: Revista de la Biblioteca Nacional* 6 (1949): 414–510.

———. "Documentación para la historia de la música Argentina, 1801–1885." *Revista de estudios musicales* 1 (December 1949): 11–63.

Bartlett, John Russell. *The Dictionary of Americanisms.* New York: Bartlett and Welford, 1848.

Beck, Roger L., and Richard K. Hansen. "Josef Gungl and his Celebrated American Tour: November 1848 to May 1849." *Studia musicologica academiae scientiarum hungaricae* 36 (1995): 55–72.

Bélance-Zank, Isabelle. "The 'Three-Hand' Texture: Origins and Use." *Journal of the American Liszt Society* 38 (1995): 99–121.

Beltrán, Bernardino. *Historia del himno nacional mexicano.* Mexico City: D.A.P.P., 1939.

Berlioz, Hector. *Correspondance générale, III, 1842–1850.* Edited by Pierre Citron. Paris: Flammarion, 1978.

———. *Hector Berlioz: A Selection from His Letters.* Edited and translated by Humphrey Searle. New York: Harcourt, Brace & World, 1966.

Béro, Michel. "Sigismond Thalberg: Aspects de la virtuosité pianistique au XIXᵉ siècle." Mémoire de licence, Université Libre de Bruxelles, 1975.

The Biography of Leopold de Meyer. London: Palmer and Clayton, 1845.

Block, Adrienne Fried. *Amy Beach, Passionate Victorian: The Life and Work of an American Composer, 1867–1944.* New York: Oxford University Press, 1998.

Block, Adrienne Fried; assisted by Nancy Stewart. "Women in American Music, 1800–1918." In *Women & Music: A History,* 2d ed., ed. Karin Pendle, 193–223. Bloomington: Indiana University Press, 2001.

Bomberger, E. Douglas. "The Thalberg Effect: Playing the Violin on the Piano." *The Musical Quarterly* 75 (1991): 198–208.

Bowen, Catherine Drinker. *"Free Artist": The Story of Anton and Nicholas Rubinstein.* New York: Random House, 1939.

Bryant, William Cullen. *The Letters of William Cullen Bryant, Volume II: 1836–1849.* Edited by William Cullen Bryant II and Thomas G. Voss. New York: Fordham University Press, 1977.

Bülow, Hans von. *The Early Correspondence of Hans von Bülow.* Edited by Marie von Bülow. Translated by Constance Bache. London: T. Fisher Unwin, 1896.

———. "Felix Mendelssohn." In *Mendelssohn and His World,* trans. Susan Gillespie, ed. R. Larry Todd, 390–94. Princeton: Princeton University Press, 1991.

———. *Hans von Bülow: Briefe und Schriften.* Edited by Marie von Bülow. 8 vols. Leipzig: Breitkopf und Härtel, 1895–1908.

———. "An Hour with Von Bülow." *New York Sun,* 17 November 1875, 3:1–2.

———. "An Interesting Talk with Von Bülow." *The Etude* 7 (May 1889): 73.

——. *Letters of Hans von Bülow*. Edited by Richard Count du Moulin Eckart. Translated by Hannah Waller. New York: Alfred A. Knopf, 1931. Reprint, New York: Da Capo Press, 1979.

——. "A Pleasant Chat with Dr. Hans Guido Von Bülow, the Great Pianist." *Chicago Times*, 6 February 1876, 4:1–2.

Bull, Inez. *Ole Bull's Activities in the United States between 1843 and 1880*. Smithtown, N.Y.: Exposition Press, 1982.

Butsch, Richard. "Bowery B'hoys and Matinee Ladies: The Re-Gendering of Nineteenth-Century American Theater Audiences." *American Quarterly* 46 (1994): 374–405.

Caswell, Austin. "Jenny Lind's Tour of America: A Discourse of Gender and Class." In *Festa Musicologica: Essays in Honor of George J. Buelow*, ed. Thomas J. Mathiesen and Benito V. Rivera, 319–37. Stuyvesant, N.Y.: Pendragon Press, 1995.

Child, Lydia Maria. *The Collected Correspondence of Lydia Maria Child, 1817–1880*. Edited by Patricia G. Holland and Milton Meltzer. Millwood, N.Y.: Kraus Microform, 1980. [microfiche]

Comettant, Oscar. *Trois ans aux Etats-Unis*. 2d ed. Paris: Pagnerre, 1858.

Cook, Nicholas. "The Editor and the Virtuoso, or Schenker versus Bülow." *Journal of the Royal Musical Association* 116 (1991): 78–95.

Courcy, G. I. C. de. *Paganini: The Genoese*. 2 vols. Norman: University of Oklahoma Press, 1957. Reprint, New York: Da Capo Press, 1977.

Crawford, Richard. *The American Musical Landscape*. Berkeley: University of California Press, 1993.

Dahlgren, Madeleine Vinton. *Etiquette of Social Life in Washington*. 5th ed. Philadelphia: J. B. Lippincott, 1881.

——. *A Washington Winter*. Boston: James R. Osgood, 1883.

Damrosch, Walter. *My Musical Life*. New York: Charles Scribner's Sons, 1930.

Davidson, Mary Wallace. "Mid-Nineteenth-Century American Periodicals: A Case Study." *Notes* 54 (1997): 371–87.

Deadman, Alison. "Brahms in Nineteenth-Century America." *Inter-American Music Review* 16 (Summer–Fall 1997): 65–84.

DiMaggio, Paul. "Cultural Entrepreneurship in Nineteenth-Century Boston." *Media, Culture and Society* 4 (1982): 33–50, 303–22.

Ehrlich, Cyril. *The Piano: A History*. Rev. ed. Oxford: Clarendon Press, 1990.

Ellis, Katharine. "Female Pianists and Their Male Critics in Nineteenth-Century Paris." *Journal of the American Musicological Society* 50 (1997): 353–85.

Elson, Arthur. "Famous Pianists of Past and Present." In *The International Library of Music for Home and Studio*, ed. Charles Dennée, et al., 3:9–12. 4 vols. New York: The University Society, 1925.

Eyma, Xavier. *Les femmes du nouveau-monde*. Paris: Michel Lévy Frères, 1860.

Fay, Amy. *Music-Study in Germany*. Chicago: A. C. McClurg, 1880. Reprint, New York: Da Capo Press, 1979.

Fiorentino, P. A. "Henri Herz: un concert en Californie." *Le Constitutionnel*, 21 September 1851; trans. in *The Musical Times* 4 (21 February 1852): 251–53.

Fostle, D. W. *The Steinway Saga: An American Dynasty*. New York: Scribner, 1995.

Garvelmann, Donald. Introduction to *Variations on "Non più mesta"* by Henri Herz. Bronx, N.Y.: Music Treasure Publications, 1970.

Gay, Peter. *The Bourgeois Experience: Victoria to Freud*, vol. 1: *Education of the Senses*. New York: Oxford University Press, 1984.

Gesualdo, Vicente. *Historia de la música en la Argentina*. 3 vols. Buenos Aires: Editorial Beta S.R.L., 1961.

Gipson, Richard McCandless. *The Life of Emma Thursby, 1845–1931*. New York: The New-York Historical Society, 1940. Reprint, New York: Da Capo Press, 1980.

Goertzen, Valerie Woodring. "By Way of Introduction: Preluding by 18th- and Early 19th-Century Pianists." *The Journal of Musicology* 14 (1996): 299–337.

Good, Edwin M. *Giraffes, Black Dragons, and Other Pianos: A Technological History from Cristofori to the Modern Concert Grand*. 2d ed. Stanford: Stanford University Press, 2001.

Gottschalk, Louis Moreau. *Notes of a Pianist*. Edited by Jeanne Behrend. New York: Alfred A. Knopf, 1964. Reprint, New York: Da Capo Press, 1979.

Graber, Kenneth Gene. "The Life and Works of William Mason (1829–1908)." Ph.D. diss., University of Iowa, 1976.

Grau, Maurice. "Some Rubinstein Reminiscences." *New York Herald,* 25 November 1894, sec. 4, 5:3–4.

Grau, Robert. *Forty Years Observation of Music and the Drama.* New York: Broadway Publishing Co., 1909.

———. "Memories of Musicians: Rubinstein and Wieniawski." *The Musician* 15 (July 1910): 442.

———. "The Rubinstein-Wieniawski Tour of 1871 [sic]." *Musical America* 15 (4 May 1912): 21.

Gresham, Carolyn Denton. "Ignaz Moscheles: An Illustrious Musician in the Nineteenth Century." Ph.D. diss., University of Rochester, 1980.

Hale, Philip. Introduction to *Anton Rubinstein: Selected Pieces for Pianoforte.* 2 vols. New York: G. Schirmer, 1896.

Hallé, Charles. *The Autobiography of Charles Hallé.* Edited by Michael Kennedy. London: Paul Elek, 1972. Reprint, New York: Da Capo Press, 1981.

Hallman, Diana R. "The Pianist Fannie Bloomfield Zeisler in American Music and Society." M.M. thesis, University of Maryland, 1983.

Hamm, Charles. *Yesterdays: Popular Song in America.* New York: W. W. Norton, 1979.

Hans von Bülow: A Biographical Sketch. His Visit to America. New York: Cushing & Bardua, 1875.

Haugen, Einar, and Camilla Cai. *Ole Bull: Norway's Romantic Musician and Cosmopolitan Patriot.* Madison: University of Wisconsin Press, 1993.

Haweis, H. R. *Music and Morals.* New York: Harper & Brothers, 1872.

Haywood, Maude. "Decorations for the Piano." *The Ladies' Home Journal* 10 (January 1893): 9.

Hernández, Roberto. *Los primeros teatros de Valparaíso.* Valparaíso: Junta de Vecinos de Valparaíso, 1928.

Herz, Henri. Letter to Frédéric Gaillardet, New Orleans, 7 March 1847. Published in *Courrier des Etats-Unis,* 18 March 1847; trans. in *The Home Journal,* no. 59 (27 March 1847): 2.

———. Letter to Frédéric Gaillardet, on board the *Panama,* 9 May 1850. Published in *Courrier des Etats-Unis,* 12 June 1850, reprinted in *Le moniteur universel,* 4 July 1850; trans. in *Boston Bee,* quoted in *Cist's Weekly Advertiser* (Cincinnati), 3 July 1850, and *The Message Bird,* no. 25 (1 August 1850): 407.

———. "Mes souvenirs de voyage en Amérique." *La France musicale* 15 (12 October 1851): 321–23, (19 October 1851): 329–31, (26 October 1851): 337–39, (9 November 1851): 353–55, (16 November 1851): 362–64, (14 December 1851): 389–91, (21 December 1851): 397–98; 16 (4 January 1852): 413–14, (25 January 1852): 33–34, (8 February 1852): 49–50, (15 February 1852): 57–58, (22 February 1852): 65–66. Abridged free trans. in *The Musical Times* 4 (29 November 1851): 53, (3 April 1852): 348–49, (10 April 1852): 364–65, (24 April 1852): 395–96; 5 (8 May 1852): 9–10.

———. *Mes voyages en Amérique.* Paris: Achille Faure, 1866. Translation by Henry Bertram Hill as *My Travels in America.* Madison: The State Historical Society of Wisconsin for the Department of History, University of Wisconsin, 1963.

Hinrichsen, Hans-Joachim. *Musikalische Interpretation Hans von Bülow.* Beihefte zum Archiv für Musikwissenschaft, vol. 46. Stuttgart: Franz Steiner, 1999.

Hitchcock, Daniel L. "Sigismund Thalberg, 1812–1871: An Evaluation of the Famous Composer-Pianist, on the 100th Anniversary of His Death." *The Piano Quarterly,* no. 77 (Fall 1971): 12–16.

Hitchcock, H. Wiley, and Stanley Sadie, eds. *The New Grove Dictionary of American Music.* 4 vols. London: Macmillan, 1986.

Hoffman, Richard. *Some Musical Recollections of Fifty Years.* New York: Charles Scribner's Sons, 1910. Reprint, Detroit: Information Coordinators, 1976.

Hofmann, Josef. *Piano Playing with Piano Questions Answered.* Philadelphia: Theodore Presser, 1920. Reprint, New York: Dover, 1976.

Hominick, Ian G. "Sigismund Thalberg (1812–1871), Forgotten Piano Virtuoso: His Career and Musical Contributions." D.M.A. diss., Ohio State University, 1991.

Hone, Philip. *The Diary of Philip Hone, 1828–1851.* Edited by Allan Nevins. New York: Dodd, Mead, 1927. Reprint, New York: Arno Press, 1970.

Hoover, Cynthia Adams. "The Great Piano War of the 1870s." In *A Celebration of American Music: Words and Music in Honor of H. Wiley Hitchcock,* ed. Richard Crawford, R. Allen Lott, and Carol J. Oja, 132–53. Ann Arbor: University of Michigan Press, 1990.

———. "The Steinways and Their Pianos in the Nineteenth Century." *Journal of the American Musical Instrument Society* 7 (1981): 47–89.

Horowitz, Joseph. "'Sermons in Tones': Sacralization as a Theme in American Classical Music." *American Music* 16 (1998): 311–39.

Huneker, James. "The Grand Manner in Pianoforte Playing." In *Unicorns,* 171–86. New York: Charles Scribner's Sons, 1917.

————. *Overtones: A Book of Temperaments*. New York: Charles Scribner's Sons, 1904.

————. *Steeplejack*. New York: Charles Scribner's Sons, 1922.

Jensen, Eric Frederick. *Walls of Circumstance: Studies in Nineteenth-Century Music*. Metuchen, N.J.: Scarecrow Press, 1992.

Johnson, H. Earle. *First Performances in America to 1900: Works with Orchestra*. Detroit: Information Co-ordinators for the College Music Society, 1979.

————. "The Germania Musical Society." *The Musical Quarterly* 39 (1953): 75–93.

Johnson, James H. *Listening in Paris: A Cultural History*. Berkeley: University of California Press, 1995.

Kallberg, Jeffrey, ed. *Piano Music of the Parisian Virtuosos, 1810–1860: A Ten-Volume Anthology*. New York: Garland, 1993.

Kasson, John F. *Rudeness and Civility: Manners in Nineteenth-Century Urban America*. New York: Hill and Wang, 1990.

Kellogg, Clara Louise. *Memoirs of an American Prima Donna*. New York: G. P. Putnam's Sons, 1913. Reprint, New York: Da Capo Press, 1978.

Keyton, Michael. "Madeline Schiller." *Music and Musicians* 35 (May 1987): 29–30.

Krehbiel, H. E. *The Philharmonic Society of New York*. New York: Novello, Ewer, 1892. Reprinted in *Early Histories of the New York Philharmonic*. New York: Da Capo Press, 1979.

————. *Review of the New York Musical Season, 1888–1889*. New York: Novello, Ewer, 1889.

Kufferath, Maurice. *Henri Vieuxtemps: sa vie et son oeuvre*. Brussels: J. Rozez, 1883.

Landrum, Carl A. "A History of Music in Quincy, Illinois," 1961. [typescript in Quincy Public Library]

Lanier, Sidney. *Letters of Sidney Lanier: Selections from His Correspondence, 1866–1881*. Edited by Henry Wysham Lanier. New York: C. Scribner's Sons, 1899. Reprint, Freeport, N.Y.: Books for Libraries Press, 1972.

Laurie, David. *The Reminiscences of a Fiddle Dealer*. Boston: Houghton Mifflin, 1925. Reprint, Cape Coral, Fla.: Virtuoso Publications, 1977.

Law, Frederic S. "The Piano: Brief Biographies of Pianists—Hans von Bülow." *The Musician* 10 (November 1905): 462.

Lawrence, Vera Brodsky. *Strong on Music: The New York Music Scene in the Days of George Templeton Strong, 1836–1875, Volume 1: Resonances, 1836–1850*. New York: Oxford University Press, 1988.

————. *Strong on Music: The New York Music Scene in the Days of George Templeton Strong, Volume 2: Reverberations, 1850–1856*. Chicago: University of Chicago Press, 1995.

————. *Strong on Music: The New York Music Scene in the Days of George Templeton Strong, Volume 3: Repercussions, 1857–1862*. Chicago: University of Chicago Press, 1999.

Lebrecht, Norman. *Who Killed Classical Music? Maestros, Managers, and Corporate Politics*. Secaucus, N.J.: Carol Publishing Group, 1998.

Lenz, Wilhelm von. *Beethoven et ses trois styles*. St. Petersburg: Bernard, 1852.

Lerner, Laurence Marton. "The Rise of the Impresario: Bernard Ullman and the Transformation of Musical Culture in Nineteenth Century America." Ph.D. diss., University of Wisconsin, 1970.

Levarie, Siegmund. "Hans von Bülow in America." *Institute for Studies in American Music Newsletter* 11 (November 1981): 8–10.

Levine, Lawrence W. *Highbrow/Lowbrow: The Emergence of Cultural Hierarchy in America*. Cambridge: Harvard University Press, 1988.

Liszt, Franz. *Letters of Franz Liszt*. Edited by Marie Lipsius. Translated by Constance Bache. 2 vols. London: H. Grevel, 1894.

Locke, Ralph P. "Music Lovers, Patrons, and the 'Sacralization' of Culture in America." *19th-Century Music* 17 (Fall 1993): 149–73.

Loesser, Arthur. *Men, Women and Pianos: A Social History*. New York: Simon and Schuster, 1954. Reprint, New York: Dover Publications, 1990.

Longfellow, Henry Wadsworth. *The Letters of Henry Wadsworth Longfellow*. Edited by Andrew Hilen. 6 vols. Cambridge: The Belknap Press of Harvard University Press, 1967–82.

Longfellow, Samuel, ed. *Life of Henry Wadsworth Longfellow, with Extracts from His Journals and Correspondence*. 3 vols. Boston: Houghton, Mifflin, 1891. Reprint, New York: Greenwood Press, 1969.

Lott, R. Allen. "The American Concert Tours of Leopold de Meyer, Henri Herz, and Sigismond Thalberg." Ph.D. diss., City University of New York, 1986.

————. "A Berlioz Premiere in America: Leopold de Meyer and the *Marche d'Isly*." *19th-Century Music* 8 (Spring 1985): 226–30.

————. "Bernard Ullman, Nineteenth-Century American Impresario." In *A Celebration of American*

Music: Words and Music in Honor of H. Wiley Hitchcock, ed. Richard Crawford, R. Allen Lott, and Carol J. Oja, 174–91. Ann Arbor: University of Michigan Press, 1990.

———. "Chickering, Steinway, and Three Nineteenth-Century European Piano Virtuosos." *Journal of the American Musical Instrument Society* 21 (1995): 65–85.

———. "'A Continuous Trance': Hans von Bülow's Tour of America." *The Journal of Musicology* 12 (1994): 529–49.

McArthur, Alexander [pseudonym for Lillian McArthur]. "Rubinstein: The Man and the Musician." *The Century Magazine* 50 (May 1895): 28–32.

McCarthy, Margaret William. *Amy Fay: America's Notable Woman of Music.* Warren, Mich.: Harmonie Park Press, 1995.

McCusker, John J. "How Much Is That in Real Money? A Historical Price Index for Use as a Deflator of Money Values in the Economy of the United States." *Proceedings of the American Antiquarian Society* 101 (1991): 297–373.

MacMinn, George R. *The Theater of the Golden Era in California.* Caldwell, Idaho: The Caxton Printers, 1941.

Mahaim, Ivan. "The First Complete Beethoven Quartet Cycles, 1845–1851: Historical Notes on the London Quartett Society." Translated and edited by Evi Levin. *The Musical Quarterly* 80 (1996): 500–524.

Maretzek, Max. *Crotchets and Quavers: or, Revelations of an Opera Manager in America.* New York: S. French, 1855. Reprint, New York: Da Capo Press, 1966, and New York: Dover Publications, 1968.

———. *Sharps and Flats.* New York: American Musician Publishing Co., 1890. Reprint, New York: Dover Publications, 1968.

Marryat, Captain Frederick. *A Diary in America, with Remarks on its Institutions.* 2 vols. Philadelphia: Carey & Hart, 1839.

———. *A Diary in America.* Edited with a foreword by Jules Zanger. Bloomington: Indiana University Press, 1960.

Martin, Edgar W. *The Standard of Living in 1860: American Consumption Levels on the Eve of the Civil War.* Chicago: University of Chicago Press, 1942. Reprint, New York: Johnson Reprint Corporation, 1970.

Martin, George. *The Damrosch Dynasty: America's First Family of Music.* Boston: Houghton Mifflin, 1983.

Marzo, Eduardo. "Touring the States with Strakosch's Stars in '73." *Musical America* 27 (2 February 1918): 9, 11.

Mason, William. *Memories of a Musical Life.* New York: The Century Co., 1901. Reprint, New York: Da Capo Press, 1970.

Massett, Stephen C. *"Drifting About," or What "Jeems Pipes of Pipesville" Saw-and-Did: An Autobiography.* New York: Carleton, 1863.

Mathews, W. S. B. "Antoine Rubinstein." *Music* 7 (February 1895): 384–89.

Mathews, W. S. B., assoc. ed. *A Hundred Years of Music in America: An Account of Musical Effort in America.* Chicago: G. L. Howe, 1889.

Meck, Galina von, trans. *"To my best friend": Correspondence between Tchaikovsky and Nadezhda von Meck, 1876–1878.* Edited by Edward Garden and Nigel Gotteri. Oxford: Clarendon Press, 1993.

Menardi Noguera, Flavio. *Camillo Sivori: La vita, i concerti, le musiche.* Genoa: Graphos, 1991.

Milinowski, Marta. *Teresa Carreño: "By the Grace of God."* New Haven: Yale University Press, 1940. Reprint, New York: Da Capo Press, 1977.

Moore, Aubertine Woodward. "Rubinstein's Meteoric Tour of America." *The Etude* 29 (November 1911): 731–32.

Myers, Kathleen Hellyar. "William Vincent Wallace: Life and Works." Ph.D. diss., Bryn Mawr College, 1980.

Neuls-Bates, Carol, ed. *Women in Music: An Anthology of Source Readings from the Middle Ages to the Present.* Rev. ed. Boston: Northeastern University Press, 1996.

Nevins, Allan, and Milton Halsey Thomas, eds. *The Diary of George Templeton Strong.* 4 vols. New York: Macmillan, 1952.

Newman, William S. "Liszt's Interpreting of Beethoven's Piano Sonatas." *The Musical Quarterly* 58 (1972): 185–209.

Newton, Dudley. "Sigismund Thalberg." *The Liszt Society Journal* 16 (1991). Reprinted as a supplement to the *Sigismund Thalberg Society Newsletter* 4 (1993).

Nichia, Lillian. "A Girl's Recollections of Rubinstein." *Harper's Monthly Magazine* 126 (December 1912): 39–47.

Nichols, Thomas Low. *Forty Years of American Life, 1821–1861*. New York: Stackpole Sons, 1937.

Norris, Jeremy. "The Piano Concertos of Anton Rubinstein." In *The Russian Piano Concerto, Volume I: The Nineteenth Century,* 21–53. Bloomington: Indiana University Press, 1994.

Oja, Carol J. "'Trollopiana': David Claypoole Johnston Counters Frances Trollope's Views on American Music." *College Music Symposium* 21 (1981): 94–102.

Olavarría y Ferrari, Enrique de. *Reseña histórica del teatro en México, 1538–1911*. 3d ed. 5 vols. Mexico City: Editorial Porrúa, 1961.

Otterstrom, Th. "Personal Recollections of Bernhard Ziehn." *Jahrbuch der Deutsch-Amerikanischen historischen Gesellschaft von Illinois* 26–27 (1926–27): 17–25.

Pape, Rainer. "Gustav Freiherr von Overbeck." *Lippische Mitteilungen aus Geschichte und Landeskunde* 28 (1959): 163–217.

Parsons, Albert Ross. "Rubinstein as Pianist and How He Composed His Ocean Symphony." *Musical Courier* 99 (23 November 1929): 39.

Parton, James. "The Piano in the United States." *The Atlantic Monthly* 20 (July 1867): 82–98.

Pereira Salas, Eugenio. *Historia de la música en Chile (1850–1900)*. Santiago: Editorial del Pacífico, 1957.

Petteys, M. Leslie. "Julie Rivé-King, American Pianist." D.M.A. diss., University of Missouri-Kansas City, 1987.

Pettler, Pamela Susskind. "Clara Schumann's Recitals, 1832–50." *19th-Century Music* 4 (Summer 1980): 70–76.

Phelan, Robert. *William Vincent Wallace: A Vagabond Composer*. Waterford, Ireland: Celtic Publications, 1994.

Pierre, Constant. *Le conservatoire national de musique et de déclamation: documents historiques et administratifs*. Paris: Imprimerie nationale, 1900.

Plantinga, Leon. *Schumann as Critic*. New Haven: Yale University Press, 1967. Reprint, New York: Da Capo Press, 1976.

Preston, Katherine K. "Art Music from 1800 to 1860." In *The Cambridge History of American Music*, ed. David Nicholls, 186–213. Cambridge: Cambridge University Press, 1998.

———. *Opera on the Road: Traveling Opera Troupes in the United States, 1825–60*. Urbana: University of Illinois Press, 1993.

Pulido, Esperanza. "Marcha nacional, dedicada a los mexicanos, compuesta por Henri Herz, Op. 166." *Heterofonia,* no. 88 (1985): 44–52.

Ramírez, Serafín. *La Habana artística: apuntes históricos*. Havana: E. M. de la Capitanía General, 1891.

Ratcliffe, Ronald V. *Steinway*. San Francisco: Chronicle Books, 1989.

Raynor, Henry. *Music and Society since 1815*. London: Barrie & Jenkins, 1976.

Regal, Francis E. "Anecdotes of von Bülow." *Music* 5 (April 1894): 681–87.

Reich, Nancy B. *Clara Schumann: The Artist and the Woman*. Rev. ed. Ithaca: Cornell University Press, 2001.

Reid, Charles. *The Music Monster: A Biography of James William Davison, Music Critic of* The Times *of London, 1846–78*. London: Quartet Books, 1984.

Ritterman, Janet. "Piano Music and the Public Concert, 1800–1850." In *The Cambridge Companion to Chopin*, ed. Jim Samson, 11–31. Cambridge: Cambridge University Press, 1992.

Roberge, Marc-André. "Ferruccio Busoni in the United States." *American Music* 13 (1995): 295–332.

Robyn, William. *The Autobiography of William Robyn*. Edited and annotated by Ernst C. Krohn. Reprinted in *Missouri Music*. New York: Da Capo Press, 1971.

Romero, Jesús C. *Verdadera historia del himno nacional mexicano*. Mexico City: Universidad Nacional Autónoma de México, 1961.

Root, George F. *The Story of a Musical Life*. Cincinnati: The John Church Co., 1891. Reprint, New York: Da Capo Press, 1970.

Rubinstein, Anton. *Anton Rubinstein's Gedankenkorb*. Leipzig: Bartholf Senff, 1897.

———. *Autobiography of Anton Rubinstein, 1829–1889*. Translated by Aline Delano. Boston: Little, Brown, 1890. Reprint, New York: Haskell House, 1969.

———. *A Conversation on Music*. Translated by Mrs. John P. Morgan. New York: Chas. F. Tretbar, 1892. Reprint, New York: Da Capo Press, 1982.

———. "An Hour with Rubinstein." *New York Sun,* 27 September 1872, 2:6–7.

Ryan, Thomas. "Personal Recollections of Anton Rubenstein [*sic*] and Henri Wieniawski." *The Musical Observer* 1 (December 1907): 25.

————. *Recollections of an Old Musician*. New York: E. P. Dutton, 1899. Reprint, New York: Da Capo Press, 1979.

Sadie, Stanley, ed. *The New Grove Dictionary of Music and Musicians*. 20 vols. London: Macmillan, 1980.

Sadie, Stanley, ed., and John Tyrrell, executive ed. *The New Grove Dictionary of Music and Musicians*. 2d ed. 29 vols. London: Macmillan, 2001.

Saffle, Michael. *Liszt in Germany, 1840–1845: A Study in Sources, Documents, and the History of Reception*. Stuyvesant, N.Y.: Pendragon Press, 1994.

Salaman, Charles. "Pianists of the Past: Personal Recollections by the late Charles Salaman." *Blackwood's Edinburgh Magazine* 170 (September 1901): 307–30.

Schabas, Ezra. *Theodore Thomas: America's Conductor and Builder of Orchestras, 1835–1905*. Urbana: University of Illinois Press, 1989.

Schloesser, Adolph. "Anton Rubinstein (1829–1894)." *The Monthly Musical Record* 38 (1 September 1908): 198–99.

Schonberg, Harold C. *The Great Pianists*. Rev. and updated ed. New York: Simon and Schuster, 1987.

Schumann, Robert. *Gesammelte Schriften über Musik und Musiker*. Edited by Martin Kreisig. 5th ed. 2 vols. Leipzig: Breitkopf und Härtel, 1914.

————. *On Music and Musicians*. Translated by Paul Rosenfeld. Edited by Konrad Wolff. New York: Pantheon Books, 1946.

Schumann, Robert, and Clara Schumann. *The Marriage Diaries of Robert & Clara Schumann*. Edited by Gerd Nauhaus. Translated by Peter Ostwald. Boston: Northeastern University Press, 1993.

Shanet, Howard. *Philharmonic: A History of New York's Orchestra*. Garden City, N.Y.: Doubleday, 1975.

Sietz, Reinhold. *Aus Ferdinand Hillers Briefwechsel (1826–1861): Beiträge zu einer Biographie Ferdinand Hillers*. Beiträge zur rheinischen Musikgeschichte, Heft 28. Cologne: Arno Volk-Verlag, 1958.

Sitsky, Larry. *Anton Rubinstein: An Annotated Catalog of Piano Works and Biography*. Westport, Conn.: Greenwood Press, 1998.

Skelton, Geoffrey. *Richard and Cosima Wagner: Biography of a Marriage*. Boston: Houghton Mifflin, 1982.

Smith, Mortimer. *The Life of Ole Bull*. Princeton: Princeton University Press for the American-Scandinavian Foundation, 1943. Reprint, Westport, Conn.: Greenwood Press, 1973.

Starr, S. Frederick. *Bamboula! The Life and Times of Louis Moreau Gottschalk*. New York: Oxford University Press, 1995.

Steinberg, Arne. "Liszt's Playing of the 'Moonlight' Sonata." *The Piano Quarterly*, no. 144 (Winter 1988–89): 52–57.

Steinway, William. "Personal Reminiscences of Anton Rubinstein." *Freund's Musical Weekly* 8 (28 November 1894): 5. Reprinted in *Music* 7 (February 1895): 394–400.

Suttoni, Charles R. "Piano and Opera: A Study of the Piano Fantasies Written on Opera Themes in the Romantic Era." Ph.D. diss., New York University, 1973.

Tchaikovsky, Modeste. *The Life and Letters of Peter Ilich Tchaikovsky*. Edited and translated by Rosa Newmarch. New York: Dodd, Mead, 1905.

Thalberg, Sigismund. Introduction to *L'Art du chant appliqué au piano*. Translated by Wardle Corbyn in *The Thalberg Concert Book, and Piano-Forte Album*. New York: Wardle Corbyn, 1856.

Thomas, Theodore. *Theodore Thomas: A Musical Autobiography*. Edited by George P. Upton. 2 vols. Chicago: A. C. McClurg, 1905. Reprint, New York: Da Capo Press, 1964.

Thorpe, T. B. "A Piano in Arkansas." In *The Hive of "The Bee-Hunter": A Repository of Sketches*, 145–54. New York: D. Appleton, 1854.

Tick, Judith. *American Women Composers before 1870*. Ann Arbor: UMI Research Press, 1983.

————. "Passed Away Is the Piano Girl: Changes in American Musical Life, 1870–1900." In *Women Making Music: The Western Art Tradition, 1150–1950*, ed. Jane Bowers and Judith Tick, 325–48. Urbana: University of Illinois Press, 1986.

Tracy, James M. "Anton Rubinstein, As I Remember Him." *The Presto* 19 (17 April 1902): 9.

Ullman, Bernard. "Leaves from My Diary." *Musical Pioneer* 11 (March 1866): 41–43.

Upton, George P. *Musical Memories: My Recollections of Celebrities of the Half Century 1850–1900*. Chicago: A. C. McClurg, 1908.

Val, Dorothy de, and Cyril Ehrlich. "Repertory and Canon." In *The Cambridge Companion to the Piano*, ed. David Rowland, 117–34. Cambridge: Cambridge University Press, 1998.

Van Cleve, John S. "Concerning Musical Memory." *Music* 12 (October 1897): 636–44.

Veit, Alfred. "Pianists and Pianism." *Music* 5 (November 1893): 1–20.

Walker, Alan. *Franz Liszt, Volume One: The Virtuoso Years, 1811–1847*. New York: Alfred A. Knopf, 1983.

————. *Franz Liszt, Volume Two: The Weimar Years, 1848–1861*. New York: Alfred A. Knopf, 1989.

————. *Franz Liszt, Volume Three: The Final Years, 1861–1886*. New York: Alfred A. Knopf, 1996.

Wangermée, Robert. "Fétis, François-Joseph." In *The New Grove Dictionary of Music and Musicians,* ed. Stanley Sadie, 6:511–14. 20 vols. London: Macmillan, 1980.

Ware, W. Porter, and Thaddeus C. Lockard, Jr. *P. T. Barnum Presents Jenny Lind.* Baton Rouge: Louisiana State University Press, 1980.

Weber, William. "The History of Musical Canon." In *Rethinking Music,* ed. Nicholas Cook and Mark Everist, 336–55. New York: Oxford University Press, 1999.

White, Richard Grant. "Some Alleged Americanisms." *The Atlantic Monthly* 52 (December 1883): 792–805.

Willard, Frances E., and Mary A. Livermore, eds. *A Woman of the Century . . . Leading American Women.* Buffalo: Charles Wells Moulton, 1893.

Wilson, Ben Hur. "Grand Concert." *The Palimpsest* 17 (November 1936): 361–72.

Works Progress Administration, Northern California, San Francisco. *History of Music in San Francisco Series.* 7 vols. San Francisco: Works Progress Administration, 1939–42. Reprint, New York: AMS Press, 1972.

Wyrick, Charles R. "Concert and Criticism in Cincinnati, 1840–1850." M.M. thesis, College-Conservatory of Music, University of Cincinnati, 1965.

Ziehn, Bernhard. "Hans von Bülow in Chicago." *Jahrbuch der Deutsch-Amerikanischen historischen Gesellschaft von Illinois* 26–27 (1926–27): 77–86.

Zimdars, Richard Louis. *The Piano Master Classes of Hans von Bülow: Two Participants' Accounts.* Bloomington: Indiana University Press, 1993.

Index